MAJOR & MR
Concise Illustrated
Battlefield Guide to

THE WESTERN FRONT
– SOUTH

First Battle of The Marne • St Mihiel Salient: The Formation • The Aisne • The Somme • Chemin des Dames • Cambrai • The Kaiser's Offensive • Second Battle of The Marne (the Ourcq, Château Thierry, Belleau Wood) • Champagne • St Mihiel Salient: The Recapture • Meuse-Argonne • Breaking the Hindenburg Line

A Companion Volume to
The Western Front – North

Valmai & Tonie Holt

France provided the playing field for all the devastating games of war described in this book.
She paid dearly for her liberty.

'L'Armistice du 11 novembre 1918 fit taire les canons. La Paix ne permit même pas aux habitants de revenir, car la contrée était morte. Plus que morte: anéantie, brûlée, fricassée, devenue une planète sans arbre, sinistrement peuplée de squelettes ou de cadavres desséchées en uniformes bleu horizon ou vert de gris... de matériels rouillés, démolis, d'armes brisées, d'ossements d'animaux de bât, gisant en tout sens un fouillis inextricable, farcie de dangereuses munitions non explosées.'
(Col L. Rodier (President of the ANSBV))

'The Armistice of 11 November quietened the guns. But the Peace did not permit the inhabitants to come back, for the countryside was dead. More than dead: annihilated, burnt, 'fricasséd', become a treeless planet, sinisterly peopled by skeletons or dried up corpses in horizon blue or grey-green uniforms... demolished or rusty materiel, broken weapons, bones of pack animals, lying inextricably tangled up in all directions, stuffed with dangerous non-exploded ammunition.'
These uninhabitable areas were declared Zones Rouges.

Pen & Sword
MILITARY

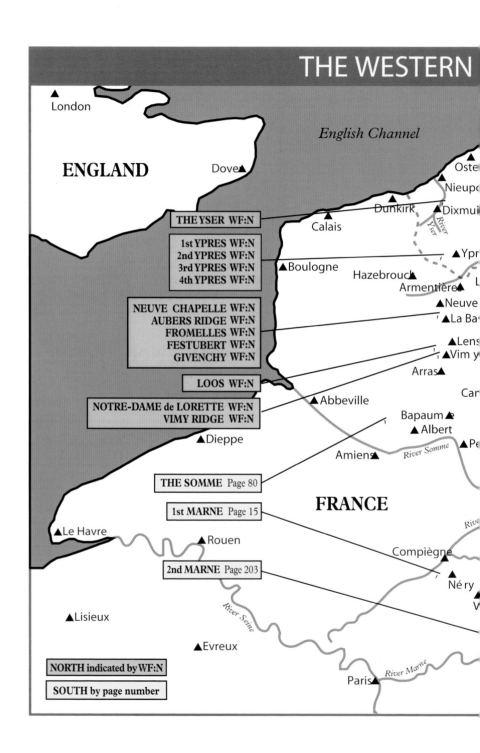

THE WESTERN

London ▲

English Channel

ENGLAND

Dover ▲

Oste ▲

Nieupo

Dunkirk ▲

▲ Dixmui

THE YSER WF:N

Calais ▲

River Yser

1st YPRES WF:N
2nd YPRES WF:N
3rd YPRES WF:N
4th YPRES WF:N

▲ Boulogne

Hazebrouck ▲

▲ Ypr

Armentières ▲   L

NEUVE CHAPELLE WF:N
AUBERS RIDGE WF:N
FROMELLES WF:N
FESTUBERT WF:N
GIVENCHY WF:N

▲ Neuve

▲ La Ba

▲ Lens

▲ Vim y

Arras ▲

LOOS WF:N

NOTRE-DAME de LORETTE WF:N
VIMY RIDGE WF:N

▲ Abbeville

Car

Bapaum ▲

▲ Albert

▲ Dieppe

▲ Pe

Amiens ▲   *River Somme*

THE SOMME Page 80

FRANCE

1st MARNE Page 15

Riv

▲ Le Havre

▲ Rouen

Compiègne ▲

2nd MARNE Page 203

Né ry ▲

V

▲ Lisieux

River Seine

▲ Evreux

River Marne

NORTH indicated by WF:N

SOUTH by page number

Paris ▲

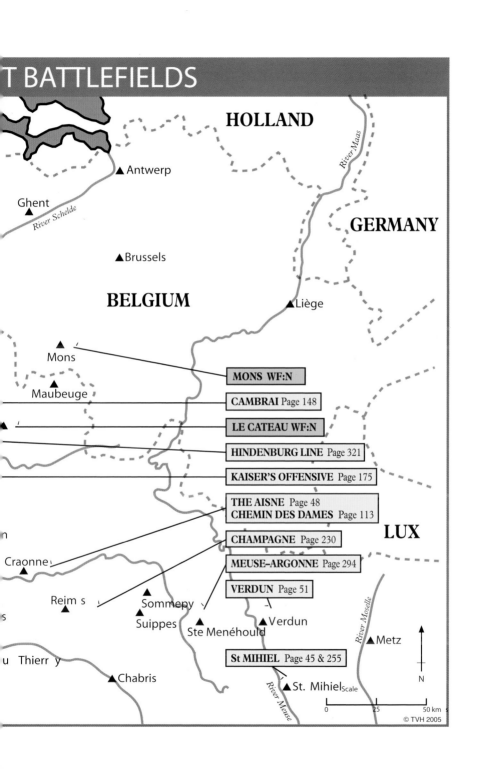

T BATTLEFIELDS

HOLLAND

River Maas

▲Antwerp

Ghent
▲

River Schelde

GERMANY

▲Brussels

BELGIUM

▲Liège

▲
Mons

▲
Maubeuge

| MONS WF:N |
| CAMBRAI Page 148 |
| LE CATEAU WF:N |
| HINDENBURG LINE Page 321 |
| KAISER'S OFFENSIVE Page 175 |
| THE AISNE Page 48 CHEMIN DES DAMES Page 113 |
| CHAMPAGNE Page 230 |
| MEUSE–ARGONNE Page 294 |
| VERDUN Page 51 |
| St MIHIEL Page 45 & 255 |

LUX

Craonne
▲

Reim s
▲

▲
Sommepy

▲
Suippes ▲
Ste Menéhould

▲Verdun

River Moselle

▲Metz

u Thierr y

▲Chabris

River Meuse

▲ St. Mihiel

N

Scale

0   25   50 km

© TVH 2005

By the same authors:

Battlefield Guide Books

Holts' Battlefield Guidebooks: Normandy-Overlord/Market-Garden/Somme/Ypres, 1982-1988

Visitor's Guide to the Normandy Landing Beaches, 1989, 1990

Battlefields of the First World War: A Traveller's Guide, 1993, 1995, 1998, 1999

Major & Mrs Holt's Concise Battlefield Guide to the Ypres Salient, 1994, 1995, 1996

Major & Mrs Holt's Battlefield Guide to the Somme + Battle Map, 1996, 1998, 1999, 2000, 2003, 2007, 2008

Major & Mrs Holt's Battlefield Guide to Gallipoli + Battle Map, 2000

Major & Mrs Holt's Battlefield Guide to MARKET-GARDEN (Arnhem) + Battle Map, 2001, 2004

Major & Mrs Holt's Battlefield Guide to Normandy D-Day Landing Beaches + Battle Map, 1999, 2000, 2002, 2004, 2006, 2008, 2009

Major & Mrs Holt's Definitive Battlefield Guide to the Normandy D-Day Landing Beaches, 2011

Major & Mrs Holt's Concise, Illustrated Battlefield Guide to the Western Front – North, 2004, 2007

Major & Mrs Holt's Concise, Illustrated Battlefield Guide to the Western Front – South, 2005

Major & Mrs Holt's Pocket Battlefield Guide to Ypres and Passchendaele, 2006, 2008, 2010

Major & Mrs Holt's Pocket Battlefield Guide to The Somme 1916/1918, 2006, 2008

Major & Mrs Holt's Pocket Battlefield Guide to D-Day Normandy Landing Beaches, 2009

Biography

Violets From Oversea: 25 Poets of the First World War 1996, reprinted as **Poets of the Great War,** 1999, 201

My Boy Jack?: The Search for Kipling's Only Son, 1998, revised and reprinted 2001, 2007, 2008, 2009

In Search of the Better 'Ole: The Life, Works and Collectables of Bruce Bairnsfather, 1985, revised and reprinted, 2001

Picture Postcard Artists: Landscapes, Animals and Characters, 1984

Military History

Till the Boys Come Home: the Picture Postcards of th First World War, 1977

I'll Be Seeing You: the Picture Postcards of World War 1987

Germany Awake! The Rise of National Socialism, illustrated by Contemporary Postcards, 1986

General

Picture Postcards of the Golden Age: A Collector's Guide, 1971, 1978

The Best of Fragments from France by Capt Bruce Bairnsfather (Editors), 1978, 1983, 1998, revised editi with authors' royalties to 'Help for Heroes', 2009

Stanley Gibbons Postcard Catalogue: 1980, 1981, 198 1984, 1985, 1987

Battlefield Maps

Major & Mrs Holt's Battle Maps: The Somme/The Yp Salient/Normandy/Gallipoli/Market-Garden (Arnhem 1986-2011

First published in Great Britain in 2005, this edition 2011, by
Pen & Sword Military
an imprint of Pen & Sword Books Limited 47 Church Street,
Barnsley, South Yorkshire, S70 2AS

Text copyright © Tonie and Valmai Holt, 2005, 2011
Except where otherwise credited, all illustrations remain the copyright of
Tonie and Valmai Holt. The moral rights of the authors have been asserted.
ISBN 1 84415 239 1

The right of Tonie and Valmai Holt to be identified as Authors of this Work has been
asserted by them in accordance with the Copyright, Designs and Patents Act 1988.

A CIP catalogue record for this book is available from the British Library.

*All rights reserved. No part of this book may be reproduced or transmitted in any form or by any
means, electronic or mechanical including photocopying, recording or by any information
storage and retrieval system, without permission from the Publisher in writing.*

Typeset in 9pt Palatino by Pen & Sword Books Limited
Printed in China through Printworks Int.Ltd

For a complete list of Pen & Sword titles please contact
Pen & Sword Books Ltd, 47 Church St, Barnsley, S Yorkshire, S70 2AS, England
email: enquiries@pen-and-sword.co.uk - website: www.pen-and-sword.co.uk

CONTENTS

LIST OF MAPS

Legend for Maps

● Bunkers
◑ Demarcation Stones
◔ Memorials
● Museums

▲ Place names
○ Sites of Special Interest
● War Cemeteries

ABOUT THE AUTHORS

Respected military authors Tonie and Valmai Holt are generally acknowledged as the founders of the modern battlefield tour and have established a sound reputation for the depth of their research. Their *Major & Mrs Holt's Battlefield Guides* series comprises without doubt the leading guide books describing the most visited battlefields of the First World War and Second World War. They have a unique combination of male and female viewpoints and can draw upon over a quarter of a century's military and travel knowledge and experience gained in personally conducting thousands of people around the areas they have written about.

Valmai Holt took a BA(Hons) in French and Spanish and taught History. Tonie Holt took a BSc(Eng) and is a graduate of the Royal Military Academy, Sandhurst and of the Army Staff College at Camberley. They are both Fellows of the Royal Society of Arts and Science and have made frequent appearances on the lecture circuit, radio and television.

In December 2003 the Holts sponsored and unveiled a memorial to Capt Bruce Bairnsfather (the subject of their biography *In Search of the Better 'Ole*) at St Yvon near 'Plugstreet Wood'.

In 2007 an updated edition of their biography of John Kipling, *My Boy Jack?*, was published to coincide with the ITV drama, *My Boy Jack*, starring Daniel Radcliffe and they acted as consultants for the IWM Exhibition of the same name.

In 2008 they celebrated their Golden Wedding Anniversary.

In 2009, the 50th Anniversary year of the death of the cartoonist Bruce Bairnsfather, they updated their 1978 published collection of 140 of his most enduring cartoons, *The Best of Fragments from France*, and this, together with tribute cartoons donated by some of the world's leading cartoonists for a Charity Auction for 'Help for Heroes', raised some £7,000.00. All authors' royalties from the sale of the book also go to the Charity.

For more information and news
VISIT THEIR WEBSITE:
www.guide-books.co.uk

The authors at the Soissons Memorial.

INTRODUCTION

'All wars end; even this war will some day
end, and the ruins will be
rebuilt and the field full of death
will grow food,
and all this frontier of trouble
will be forgotten.
When the trenches are filled in, and the
plough has gone over them,
the ground will not long keep
the look of war.
One summer with its flowers will cover
most of the ruins that man
can make and then these places,
from which the driving back of the
enemy began, will be hard indeed to
trace, even with maps.'

John Masefield in *The Old Front Line or
The Beginning of the Battle of the Somme.* 1917

'Pile the bodies high at
Austerlitz and Waterloo.
Shovel them under and let me work.
I am the grass: I cover all.
And pile them high at Gettysburg
And pile them high at Ypres and Verdun.
Shovel them under and let me work.
Two years, ten years,
and passengers ask the conductor:
What place is this?
Where are we now?
I am the grass.
Let me work.'

Carl Sandburg. American poet 1878-1967.

'As the War years recede, visits to the battlefields are becoming not
less rare, but are increasing.'

Lt Col Graham Seton Hutchison, DSO, MC in *Pilgrimage*, his 1935 battlefields guide.

This book, which covers the battlefields of the Western Front from the Somme to the
Marne, is the continuation of our *Major & Mrs Holt's Battlefield Guide to the Western Front –
North*, which covers the battlefields from The Yser, through Ypres, Mons, Le Cateau, Aubers
Ridge, Fromelles, Festubert, Neuve Chapelle and Loos, Notre-Dame de Lorette and Vimy
Ridge. Together the two volumes, the culmination of over thirty years of visiting,
researching and interviewing in the area, cover not only the well-known sites of the
Western Front but others that have only recently been 'rediscovered' and made safe to visit.
In particular groups of dedicated and enthusiastic local historians have formed associations
of knowledgeable amateurs to explore and to clear craters, tunnels and trenchlines. They
are restoring monuments, creating paths and erecting informative sign boards in many sites
that lay 'dormant' for some eighty or so years in the areas of the St Mihiel Salient, in the
Meuse-Argonne, in the Champagne and along the Chemin des Dames. The result is a
range of superbly interesting sites, hitherto little-known to visitors from the UK and North
America, that will astonish the first-time visitor and are well worth the extra mileage (easy
enough on France's excellent motorway network).

The Butte de Vauquois in the Meuse-Argonne, the Kaiser Tunnel on the Haute
Chevauchée, the German Hospital, the Trenches and Fortifications in the Bois Brûlé and the
Tranchées des Bavarois in the St Mihiel Salient, the sculptured grottoes of the Ferme de
Confrécourt – these, and many more such relatively newly-opened vestiges, are redolent of
the sacrifices and bitter struggles of '14-'18. There the memory lingers strongly in great
craters, huge underground chambers, sophisticated tunnels, well-preserved lengths of
Decauville narrow gauge railway lines and soldiers' chiselled graffiti.

In the American sectors of the Meuse-Argonne, the St Mihiel Salient and on the Marne from Fismes to Château Thierry much work has been done in locating neglected and long-lost private memorials to soldiers who came 4,000 miles to die for Liberty and La France. These areas too yield stories of heroism, of tragedy, of humour and dogged persistence – the varied tapestry that is the story of *The War that will end War* as H.G. Wells so mistakenly prophesied in 1914.

The itineraries, many of which take you off the beaten tourist track, cover some outstandingly beautiful areas of France – glorious woodland and sweeping vistas, vine-covered hillsides and quaint villages. In them some examples of powerful military architecture are visited, like Paul Landowski extraordinary *'Fantomes'* at the Butte de Chalmont, Paul Cret's dignified American Monuments and Eric Kennington's acclaimed 'Soissons Trinity'. There are many brilliant jewel-coloured and imaginative memorial SGWs. Then there are the delights of French cuisine and some great hotel along the way. We intend the travelling to be a pleasurable as well as an informative and emotional experience, a treat for all the senses.

Our aim in writing these books is to help to perpetuate the memory of the special breed of men and women who suffered on our behalf for the freedoms we enjoy today. It has been a labour of love and a passionate interest over many years. We have travelled thousands of miles during which we have formed friendships with some extraordinary people who have generously shared their knowledge and experience with us. We hope that our efforts will add to your understanding of the period and further your interest in it.

Tonie and Valmai Holt, Woodnesborough, January 200

UPDATE INFORMATION FOR THIS 2011 EDITION

The impending 100th Anniversaries of the 'Great War' have spurred on many projects in all the Departments in the Western Front-South area. Existing sites, monuments and museums have been greatly improved, new ones have been been initiated. See the following websites:

French Ministry of Defence: www.cheminsdememoire.gouv.fr
Assoc International des Sites et Musées de la Guerre **1914-1918:** www.memoiregrandeguerre.org
Conseil General de la Meuse: www.cg55.fr
Verdun: www.en.verdun-tourisme.com
ANSM (qv): www.lesaillantdesaintmihiel.fr
Virtual Memorial Roll, Chemin des Dames. Project to list the 46,000+ combattants of the battles:
  www.memoiredeshommes.sga.defense.gouv.fr
Trip Wire: superb on-line WW1 magazine. www.worldwar1.com/tripwire/ For information and to subscribe
  Contact: Mike Hanlon, Editor and experienced guide: greatwar@earthlink.net

SOME IMPORTANT CHANGES/ADDITIONS TO THE 2005 EDITION ARE LISTED BELOW.

41. Musée de la Grande Guerre, Meaux. Adjoining the American Memorial (Map 1/29, which has been completely renovated) inaugurated on 11 November 2011 by Pres Sarkozy, this important museum, costing Euros 28,000,000, is based on the private ction of Jean-Pierre Verney. Concentrating on the First Battle of the Marne it des over 50,000 objects and documents, uniforms, weapons, ephemera, dioramas nd uses the latest technology. It contains a 115-seat auditorium, boutique and café. :.museedelagrandeguerre.eu

73. Memorial to Henry N. Gunther, thought to be the last member of the AEF e in combat in WW1. Gunther, of Coy A, 313th Inf, was killed one minute before the hours Armistice of 11 November 1918. The Memorial, unveiled in 2011, is on a p above Chaumont-devant-Damvillers, which is 1.5 miles north east of Flabas e. GPS 49.31535 5.42833.

86. Tommy Statue. This has been moved to the grounds of the new Ibis Hotel on)929 from Albert. Tel: + (0)3 22 75 52 52. E-mail: h6234@accor.com

119. Musée Franco-Américaine, Blérancourt. Museum now scheduled for reopening late 2014. Gardens always open.

Memorial to Henry N. Gunther, last Doughboy killed in action - on 11.11.1918 at Chaumont-devant-Damvillers.

Page 137. Caverne des Dragons. A programme of ongoing improvements, interesting events and exhibitions in what has now become 'The Museum of the Chemin des Dames'. Of note is the powerfully emotional memorial in the grounds to the many Senegalese Fusiliers who lost their lives in the April 1917 offensive – nine stark, elongated black figures entitled Constellation de la Douleur'. Sculptor Christian Lapie designed them without arms or face to be 'deliberately disquieting'.

Another helpful **Contact**: Authorised guide and researcher Cyrille Delahaye. E-mail: cd.tourisme@voila.fr He reports another fascinating **Quarry**, with amazing American (from Feb '18) and German graffiti at **La Ferme de Froidmont** at Braye en Laonnois. Much vandalised in the 1980s and '90s it was protected by being declared a *Monument Historique* in 1994 and on 15 June 2008 a memorial to the 26th 'Yankee' Division was inaugurated in the presence of American and French military and dignitaries. **GPS 49.44303 3.60342. Contact**: Gilles Chauvin. Tel: + (0)3 23 23 09 13

f the striking figures of the alese Fusiliers' Memorial, ne des Dragons.

Pages 145-147. Chemin des Dames/N2. Major roadworks have completely altered the junction the Chemin des Dames and the N2 to Soissons which is now a roundabout and the large Calvary has been moved. To visit the ux Group of Memorials it is necessary to take the small road parallel to the widened N2, continue to the roundabout and take nd exit signed Moulin de Laffaux over the N2. Note that the splendid old **Monument to the Crapouillots** was struck by ning in June 2007 and it is being moved and repaired for the *Centenaire*. The **Monument to the Fusiliers Marins** has been ed to the left of the road in a better position. **Fruty Quarry** is now on the edge of the new N2, but is difficult to spot.

193. Australian Corps Memorial, le Hamel. The Memorial, which was crumbling, had to be rebuilt (at a cost of Aust$7.9 million) using Laurentian Green granite cladding. It was rededicated on 8 November 2008.

Croix Rouge 167th ama) Inf Regt Memorial e by James Butler, RA.

Page 207. Memorial *Lavoir* to Lt William Muir Russell, 95th Aero Sqn. By turning left, not right, at the junction with the D368 and continuing some 3 miles to Courville, the imposing Memorial is reached. Russell, a friend of Quentin Roosevelt (qv), was shot down flying his Spad from nearby Courville airfield on 11 August 1918. The money for the *Lavoir* was willed to the village by 25 year old Russell's dying father in 1920. On 12 September 2010 the beautifully renovated Memorial was rededicated in the presence of Russell's four great-nieces. GPS 49.26813 3.69656. See the informative site www.courvillepatrimoine.fr

The William Muir Russell Memorial Lavoir, Courville.

Page 216. Statue to 167th (Alabama) Inf Regt. On returning to **Fère-en-Tardenois**, by turning left on the D967 and thence the D3 and continuing some 5 miles you will arrive at a beautiful 3 metre high Statue of a Doughboy tenderly carrying his dead comrade. It is at Croix Rouge Farm and commemorates the taking of the farm on 26/27 July 1918 by the regiment after bitter fighting. Sculpted by James Butler, MBE, RA (who also sculpted the fine

Green Howard's statue at **Crépon**) it was displayed at London's Royal Academy before being unveiled here on 12 November 201 **GPS 49.1317 3.52189**. See www.croixrougefarm.org/history-battle

Pages 226/228. Rock of the Marne. The 38th Regt's heroic stand against Ludendorff's offensive took place at Mézy which is be reached by crossing the river here and taking the N3 eastbound to Crézancy (a 30 minute round trip). The 3rd Division wei responsible for this entire stretch of the front and held the river bank as far as Mézy. In Crézancy turn north towards Mézy and sto short of the railway bridge at **GPS 49.06700 3.50466**. The high ground straight ahead, which is on the other side of the river, wa occupied by the Germans. Before dawn on the 15th July the enemy crossed the river heading directly this way and by midday ha forced back the 30th Infantry who were on the left of this road. Establishing positions along the railway line, the Germans on th right pushed past the 38th who hung on to the river bank ahead and the area from here to about 2,000 yards east. Thus the 38th an their Commander Col McAlexander were under fire from three sides. Though almost everywhere else along this part of the front th

Germans made progress, the 38th held on, sticking out like a sore thumb. By the end of the day a German withdrawal was beginning and the whole of the 3rd Division front once more secure. There are nascent plans to erect a memorial to the 'Rock of the Marne' episode.

Page 229. MAFA Building, Château Thierry. The crumbling interior was demolished in 2009, leaving the original façade behind which there is now a daycare centre and Tourist Office as well as the renovated Museum. Quentin Roosevelt's nephew Richard attended the inauguration.

Page 235. Plaque to French Colonial Forces, Reims. This is on Ave Gouraud and shows a picture of the original fine bronze statue.

Plaque to French Colonial Forces, Reims.

Page 237. Suippes Interpretation Centre: Marne 14-18. This imaginative museum, opened in 2009, uses modern technology to draw the visitor emotionally into many aspects of the 14-18 war in the area. Ruelle Bayard (by the Mairie)
Contact: Tel: + (0)3 26 68 24 09. E-mail: contact@marne14-18.fr Website: www.marne14-18.fr

Page 255: St Mihiel Salient. The ANSM continues wonderful renovation work in the Salient, notably on the trenches in the Bo Brulé (p281/2) Bavarian Lion (page 285) and other German sites, for which President Norbert Kugel was awarded the Médaille de l'Europe de l'Etat de Bavière.
Contact – see page 348.

Page 317. Sgt York Memorials and Trail. Much valuable research and hard work has been put in (often aided by US Eagle Scouts) by instigators Doug Mastriano and Kory O'Keefe. On 4 October 2008 two Memorials were unveiled at the site of York's action: one tells his story, the other commemorates 17 US soldiers involved in the battle of 8 October 1918. The start point for the Trail is signed in the main street.
Contact: Doug Mastriano, SYDE (Sgt York Discovery Expedition). E-mail: hooah4yeshua@msn.com Website: www.sgtyorkdiscovery.com

Page 319. The Lost Battalion. A new Memorial and Information Panel were unveiled at Charlevaux at **GPS 49.25090 4.90675** near Binarville on 7 October 2008 by Maj-Gen William Terpeluk, last CO of the 77th Regional Readiness Command. Interest has been renewed in the epic story by the 2002 US TV A&E Channel film The Lost Battalion starring Ricky Schroeder.

2008 Unveiling of Memorials to the Lost Battalion, Charlevaux, showing release of symbolic pigeons.

Page 344. Lil Pfluke is no longer with the ABMC. She has now founded **American War Memorials Overseas Inc**, a non-prof organisation whose mission is to document, raise awareness of and care for, private American gravesites and memorials where th US Government has no responsibility, liaising with local, national and international organisations.
Contact: Lil Pfluke. 6 rue du Commandant de Larienty 92210, St Cloud. Tel: (0)6 1173 1332 E-mail: info@uswarmemorials.o Website: www.uswarmemorials.org

Page 353. The Hotel Mercure at Chamouille is now the renovated **Hôtel du Golf de l'Ailette**. Tel: + (0)3 23 24 84 85. E-ma hotelrestaurant@ailette.fr. Across the Lac d'Ailette is a **Center Parks** activity holiday complex with accommodation in attractiv cottages. Tel: 0891 700 800. Website: www.centerparcs.fr

PICTURE ACKNOWLEDGEMENTS

Rainbow Division Memorial by James Butler, RA, honoring the Alabama 167t Infantry Regiment, courtesy of the Croix Rouge Farm Memoria Foundation
US Army for new Lost Battalion Memorial unveiling
Mike Hanlon for Memorial to Henry N. Gunther
Doug Mastriano for new Sgt York Memorial unveiling

Unveiling of Sgt York Memorial, 2008. Present: Left to right, Lt-Col Mastriano, Col Gerald York (grandson), George York (son), Deborah York (grand-daughter), Mayor of Châtel Chéhéry, Kory O'Keefe.

ABBREVIATIONS

Abbreviations and acronyms used for military units are listed below. Many of these are printed in full at intervals throughout the text to aid clarity. Others are explained where they occur.

Am	American		GHQ	General Head Quarters
ANSBV	*Association Nationale du Souvenir de la Bataille de Verdun*		Gnr	Gunner
			Inf	Infantry
			Kia	Killed in action
ANSM	*Association Nationale le Saillant de St Mihiel*		KORL	King's Own Royal Lancs
			KOYLI	King's Own Yorkshire Light Infantry
ASH	Argyll & Sutherland Highlanders		KRRC	King's Royal Rifle Corps
Attd	Attached		MAFA	*Maison d'Amitié Franco-Américain*
Aust	Australian			
Bav	Bavarian		Mia	Missing in action
BCA	*Battaillon de Chasseurs Alpins*		MC	Military Cross
			Mem	Memorial
BCP	*Battaillon de Chasseurs à Pied*		M-G	Machine-Gun
			MiD	Mentioned in Despatches
BEF	British Expeditionary Force		MM	Military Medal
			MoH	Medal of Honour
Bn	Battalion		Mon	Monument
CAP	*Chasseurs à Pied*		NZ	New Zealand
Cem	Cemetery		OP	Observation Point
CdeG	*Croix de Guerre*		ORBAT	Order of Battle
CGS/H	*Conseil Général de la Somme/Historial*		POW's	Prince of Wales's/Prisoners of War
C-in-C	Commander-in-Chief		Pte	Private
CO	Commanding Officer		RI	*Régiment d'Infanterie*
Col	*Colonial*		Russ	Russian
CWGC	Commonwealth War Graves Commission		RWF	Royal Welsh Fusiliers
			SGW	Stained Glass Window
Dem	Demarcation		SLI	Somerset Light Infantry
Div	Division		SMLE	Short muzzle Lee Enfield
DSC	Distinguished Service Cross		Sp	Special
			T/	Temporary
Eng	Engineers		TA	Territorial
Ext	Extension		VC	Victoria Cross
Fld	Field		WF-N	*Major & Mrs Holt's Battlefield Guide to the Western Front – North*
Fr	French			
Ger	German			

HOW TO USE THIS GUIDE

This book may be read at home as a continuous account, used en route as a guide to specific battles and battlefields, dipped into at any time via the index as a source of fascinating detail about the First World War or kept as a reminder of past visits to the sites described.

The Western Front First World War battles are included in chronological order and their historical significance is recounted through sections which precede the battlefield tours entitled 'Summary of the Battle', 'Opening Moves' and 'What Happened'. These are designed to remind readers of the salient features of each battle so that the later details may later be more readily understood and to provide a framework upon which the accounts that follow during the battlefield tours may be hung.

At the front of each chapter are one or more quotations from people who were involved in the war and these have been chosen to give a relevant personal flavour to the detailed accounts. We recommend reading them both before and after a tour. Your own viewpoint may have changed.

MILES COVERED/DURATION/OP/RWC/ TRAVEL DIRECTIONS/EXTRA VISITS

The battlefield tours cover features that during our many years of guiding and writing have been the most requested, as being the best-known, the most important, the most emotive. Added to them are the new sites that have recently been opened up. None is exhaustive – this is a *condensed* battlefield guide – but in combination with the specially drawn maps for each battle they provide a compact and hopefully illuminating commentary upon the events of the time, from glimpses of the 'Grand Designs', through individual acts of heroism to the memorials that now mark the pride and grief of a past generation.

A start point is given for each tour from which a running total of miles is indicated. **Extra Visits** are not counted in that running total. Each recommended stop is indicated by a clear heading with the running total, the probable time you will wish to stay there and a map reference to the relevant sketch map. The letters OP in the heading indicate a view point from which salient points of the battle are described. RWC indicates refreshment and toilet facilities. Travel directions are written in *italics* and indented to make them stand out clearly. An end point is suggested, with a total distance and timing without deviations or refreshment stops. 'Base' towns or cities are suggested which can provide convenient and comfortable accommodation and restaurants.

In addition **Extra Visits** are described to sites of particular interest which lie near to the route of the main itineraries. These are tinted light grey and boxed so that they clearly stand out from the main route. Estimates of the round-trip mileage and duration are given. Other **points of interest** which require a small diversion are prefixed by 'N.B.' and are boxed but not tinted.

It is absolutely essential to set your mileage trip to zero before starting and to make constant reference to it. Odometers can vary from car to car and where you park or turn round will affect your total so that it may differ slightly from that given in this book. **What is important, however, is the distance between stops.** Distances in the headings are given in miles because the trip meters on British cars still operate in miles. Distances within the text are sometimes given in kilometres and metres as local signposts use these measures.

Stout waterproof footwear and clothing, binoculars and a torch are recommended. Make sure you take adequate supplies of any medication that you are on. Basic picnic gear is highly recommended for remoter areas where restaurants are virtually non-existent or which close for lunch on unexpected days (and there is no greater pleasure than a crusty baguette filled with creamy cheese washed down with a drop of the beverage of your choice consumed on a sunny bank in a quiet corner of a battlefield). The boutiques in motorway stops can provide the wherewithal for a picnic if you are unlikely to pass a local supermarket or village shop (many now sadly permanently closed). It is also important to make sure that you have a full tank when you leave the motorway. Petrol stations are very rare in some localities. A mobile phone is a reassuring accessory.

MAPS/CHOOSING YOUR ROUTES/PARTICULAR VISITS

There are recommended commercial maps for each tour and it is suggested that the traveller buys them, or their nearest updated equivalent, and marks them before setting out. These maps, used in conjunction with the sketches in this book, make it possible not only to navigate efficiently but also to understand what happened where – and sometimes 'why'. For the battlefields of The Somme and parts of The Kaiser's Offensive the very detailed *Major & Mrs Holt's Battle Map of The Somme* is recommended. The sketch maps which accompany each battle described in the book use the same **colour coding system of mauve for war cemeteries, yellow for memorials, blue for museums, orange for Demarcation Stones, pink for bunkers.**

The battles are arranged chronologically and their descriptions are self-contained so that any individual battlefield may be visited in any order. An approximate distance from Calais is given to the start point of most battlefields. If they are to be visited in geographical sequence, then the large sketch map on pages 2 and 3 will help you plan your route.

It is strongly recommended that you pick up the free **Guide des Autoroutes** at the first toll booth you reach. This shows all the motorway systems that you will drive on the routes in this book, indicates the *Péage* sections, the refreshment stops etc.

There are many options for the visitor in choosing his or her itinerary, depending upon interest, time available etc. For practical reasons the geographical constraints will probably have to take precedence over the chronological order of the battles and it would obviously take several weeks to tour all the battlefields described. Studying the campaigns in any sort of meaningful order is further complicated by the fact that many of the battlefields overlap and were also fought over at several different periods. This particularly applies to the area covered by the battles of The Somme, The Kaiser's Offensive and Breaking the Hindenburg Line; The Aisne and the Chemin des Dames, 1914, 1917 and 1918 and the Marne 1914 and 1918. If none of the set itineraries exactly suits your interests you can 'Pick and Mix' your own route by using the Index.

Specific places to be visited may be found by reference to the Index and if a particular grave is to be located you should consult the **Commonwealth War Graves Commission**

Debt of Honour website or the **American Battle Monuments Commission website** before you set out (see below).

At the end of the book the 'Tourist Information' section gives tips on how to prepare for your journey, where to eat or stay, and where you will find information and help. The 'War Graves Organisations' section describes in brief some of the dedicated Associations which tend and administer the war cemeteries and memorials that you will visit following the tours or who work to keep the memory alive. Further advice is available at www.guide-books.co.uk.

A WARNING – THE IRON HARVEST

It is most unwise to pick up any 'souvenirs' in the form of bullets, shells, hand grenades, barbed wire etc. that may be found on the battlefield. They are often to be found temptingly piled up at the corners of fields awaiting collection by the French Army bomb disposal unit for controlled explosion. To this day unpleasant accidents and even fatalities are caused by farmers ploughing or builders digging foundations and even, regrettably, by souvenir hunters. Leaking gas shells are particularly dangerous and blood poisoning and tetanus can be caused by sharp and rusting objects. Safe souvenirs may be purchased at places such as the bookshop at Delville Wood on the Somme

'Iron Harvest' ready to be picked up by the bomb disposal unit.

FIRST BATTLE OF THE MARNE

SEPTEMBER 1914

'Blessed are those who died for carnal earth
Provided it was in a just war...
Blessed are those who died in great battles,
Stretched out on the ground in the face of God.'
Charles Péguy, *Blessed are Those*.

'The Germans were about 250 yards away, firing on us with machine guns
and rifles. The noise was perfectly awful. In a lull the C.O. said to the men:
"Do you hear that? Do you know what they are doing that for? They are doing that to
frighten you." I said to him: "If that's all, they might as well stop.
As far as I am concerned they have succeeded, two hours ago."'
Aubrey Herbert with the Irish Guards in the Rond de la Reine.

SUMMARY OF THE BATTLE

After the brief battle of le Cateau on 26 August the Germans pursued the retreating British and French armies towards Paris. On 3 September they forced crossings over the Marne thus threatening the Capital and prompting a French counter-attack that began on 5 September. Following fighting that stretched between Paris and Verdun the Germans withdrew towards the Aisne and by 12 September were back roughly where they had been at the end of August. Estimated losses for the French were 250,000 and for the Germans 200,000. British losses were just over 1,000.

OPENING MOVES

The Schlieffen Plan for the conquest of France had envisaged a swinging anti-clockwise advance through Belgium and then a rapid move to the south intending to cut off and surround the retreating French armies as well as taking Paris.

After the Battles of the Frontier and the British stand at le Cateau the Plan seemed to be succeeding, with the French 5th and 6th Armies and the BEF in full retreat. Co-operation between the British and the French (Gen Joffre) was at the best intermittent and Sir John French commanding the BEF, a man subject to dramatic lows and highs of spirit, decided that he would set off, apparently independent of any ideas that Joffre had, for the north-west of Paris, putting the River Seine between himself and the Germans. Learning this, Lord Kitchener made a rapid trip to France, cancelled the plan and ordered Sir John to cooperate with Joffre. Meanwhile the Germans were advancing rapidly.

The German 1st Army under Gen von Kluck (known to the British as 'Old One o'Clock) was at the extreme western end of the line. By 5 September, advancing on a line roughly via Fismes, Fère-en-Tardenois and Meaux, the Germans were within thirty miles of Paris and could see the Eiffel Tower. The allied armies having been retreating continuously for ten days were on the edge of exhaustion, the French government was evacuated to Bordeaux and some half a million citizens of Paris headed south. It looked very much as if the war could soon be over.

WHAT HAPPENED

The Germans advancing towards Paris formed the right wing of their invading forces. Von Kluck's 1st Army was in the lead with the 2nd Army about a day's march behind to the north and the 3rd strung out further back. It was not only the French and the British who were tired but the Germans too, some of whom had marched and fought over more than 150 miles in the last ten days. One German officer described his men much as the BEF saw their own soldiers: 'The men stagger forward, their faces covered in dust, their uniform in rags, they look like living scarecrows. They march with their eyes closed, singing in chorus so that they shall not fall asleep.'

This mass of German troops was aimed like a fist at the eastern flank of Paris but this fist was plunging into a yielding salient of French armies which gradually threatened to surround it (see Map 2). On 3 September Joffre determined that the Allied retreat should stop and, aided by aerial reconnaissance and wireless intercepts (probably the first time that they had been used in war), and although minded to remain on the defensive, he saw an opportunity to strike at von Kluck's flank. On 4 September he obtained a guarantee of full support from Sir John French who was no doubt chastened following the visit of Lord Kitchener.

Meanwhile in Paris its military commander, Gen Galliéni, also realised that von Kluck's exposed advance had opened his flanks and urged an immediate attack. Joffre, having discussed the troops' readiness with his army commanders, wanted to open the offensive on 7 September but Galliéni insisted that the opportunity was a fleeting one and that his **Army of Paris** would be ready on the 6th. Joffre agreed.

By the evening of 5 September von Kluck's force was in a perilous position. Situated just below Meaux and La-Ferté-sous-Jouarre and facing south-west, his 1st Army had to its front the BEF, on its right flank the French 6th Army under Manoury with Galliéni's Paris force in support and on its left flank the 5th and 9th Armies of d'Espérey and Foch.

Yet von Kluck was unaware of the danger and on 5 September his forces bumped into those of Manoury's army north-west of Meaux and were forced back. Von Kluck was taken completely by surprise and in the battle of the Ourcq which followed he moved part of his force to cope with Manoury. On 6 September the full Joffre counter-attack opened with the BEF (which until the day before had been still retreating on what was in effect the last day of 'The Retreat from Mons') and the French 5th Army finding that von Kluck's recent troop movements had opened a gap in the German centre, a situation monitored by air. Galliéni acted with vigour and sent forces from Paris to reinforce Manoury. One division detraining near the capital had no transport so some 600 Paris taxis were commandeered and during two journeys to the front carried over 6,000 troops. The process was not without difficulties, one of which was that the taxi drivers with Gallic enthusiasm took every opportunity to overtake each other thus mixing up the units in such a way that it took some hours at their destination to sort them out.

The Battle of the Marne became a confused struggle with temporary short gains and losses by each side but gradually the whole German line began to give way as far east as Verdun. The BEF found itself in a decisive position to exploit the growing gap in the German line but advanced slowly, partly due to the presence of a number of transverse rivers – the Grand Morin, the Petit Morin and the Marne. On 7 September Gen Haig recorded, 'I thought our movements very slow today in view of the fact that the enemy is on the run.' It was a criticism of his Commander-in -Chief and a year later, after Loos, he would take his place.

Nevertheless by 9 September the BEF was crossing the Marne ahead of the French, first below Château Thierry and then westwards as far as La-Ferté-sous-Jouarre (see Map 1). It was only at la Ferté that bridges were found to be blown (by the French in their earlier retreat) but the British 4th Division used a weir, a railway bridge and later a pontoon to make the crossing. Now the Germans were in full retreat and late in the evening Sir John French changed his orders from 'advance' to 'pursuit'. The outcome of the Marne battle was, according to Gen von Kuhl, Chief of Staff to von Kluck, due to 'the breakthrough of the British and the French 5th Army' though the reasons for, and the conduct of, the German withdrawal was the subject of a special enquiry in 1917 much as was to happen to Gen Gough over the retreat of his 5th Army in 1918.

The victory on the Marne was a major psychological bonus for the Allies, for up to this time the German armies had appeared to be invincible. Now the British and French soldiers and commanders knew that the enemy could be beaten, but the struggles that were to follow, with the Germans standing on the Chemin des Dames above the Aisne, would be quite different from those of movement that had been fought in the first two months of the war.

THE BATTLEFIELD TOUR

The front line along which the actions known as the 'First Battle of the Marne' took place was some 100 miles long. Clearly it is impossible for us to cover the entire line. We have concentrated upon the Allied right wing and in particular the southern part of the approximate route taken by the BEF following The Retreat which began at le Cateau on 26 August – Compiègne (the Armistice memorials and museum are clearly of the wrong period but as they were in the right location they have been included), Verberie, Néry, Betz, Meaux and La-Ferté-sous-Jouarre.

• **The Route:** The tour begins at Compiègne with the opportunity to visit sites of interest in the town. It then visits the Railway Carriage and Memorials at the Armistice Clearing; the site of 'L' Battery's famous engagement at Néry, its Memorials and the graves of the VCs and other officers and men of the Battery at Verberie and Néry; Villers-Cotterêts French National Cemetery; the unusual Guards Cemetery and the Memorial to 2nd Lt George Cecil in the Rond de la Reine and Gen Mangin's OP in the Villers Cotterêts Forest. It then moves south to Betz, the French National Cemetery and Army of Paris Monument; Etrépilly Local and National Cemeteries and Army of Paris and Col Dubujadoux Memorials; Chambry French National and German Cemeteries;

MAP 1: THE FIRST BATTLE OF THE MARNE: 5-12 SEPTEMBER 1914

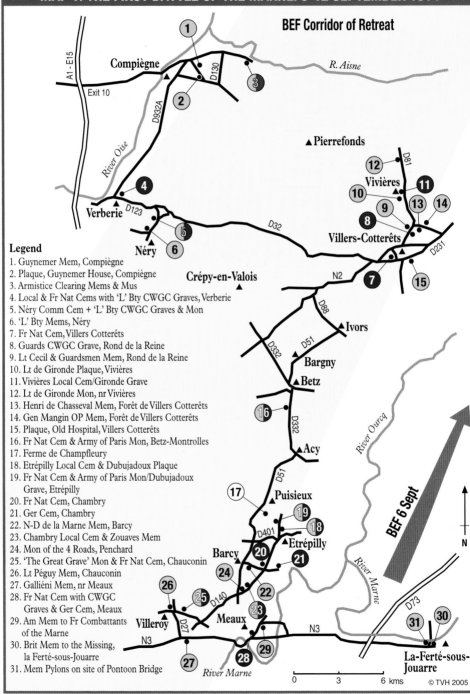

BEF Corridor of Retreat

Compiègne

R. Aisne

A1 - E15

Exit 10

D932A

River Oise

▲Pierrefonds

Vivières

Verberie D123

Néry

D32

Villers-Cotterêts

Legend

Crépy-en-Valois

N2

1. Guynemer Mem, Compiègne
2. Plaque, Guynemer House, Compiègne
3. Armistice Clearing Mems & Mus
4. Local & Fr Nat Cems with 'L' Bty CWGC Graves, Verberie
5. Néry Comm Cem + 'L' Bty CWGC Graves & Mon
6. 'L' Bty Mems, Néry
7. Fr Nat Cem, Villers Cotterêts
8. Guards CWGC Grave, Rond de la Reine
9. Lt Cecil & Guardsmen Mem, Rond de la Reine
10. Lt de Gironde Plaque, Vivières
11. Vivières Local Cem/Gironde Grave
12. Lt de Gironde Mon, nr Vivières
13. Henri de Chasseval Mem, Forêt de Villers Cotterêts
14. Gen Mangin OP Mem, Forêt de Villers Cotterêts
15. Plaque, Old Hospital, Villers Cotterêts
16. Fr Nat Cem & Army of Paris Mon, Betz-Montrolles
17. Ferme de Champfleury
18. Etrépilly Local Cem & Dubujadoux Plaque
19. Fr Nat Cem & Army of Paris Mon/Dubujadoux Grave, Etrépilly
20. Fr Nat Cem, Chambry
21. Ger Cem, Chambry
22. N-D de la Marne Mem, Barcy
23. Chambry Local Cem & Zouaves Mem
24. Mon of the 4 Roads, Penchard
25. 'The Great Grave' Mon & Fr Nat Cem, Chauconin
26. Lt Péguy Mem, Chauconin
27. Galliéni Mem, nr Meaux
28. Fr Nat Cem with CWGC Graves & Ger Cem, Meaux
29. Am Mem to Fr Combattants of the Marne
30. Brit Mem to the Missing, la Ferté-sous-Jouarre
31. Mem Pylons on site of Pontoon Bridge

▲Ivors

Bargny

▲Betz

D332

River Ourcq

▲Acy

D51

Puisieux

D401

▲Etrépilly

Barcy

River Marne

BEF 6 Sept

D73

Villeroy

Meaux

N3

La-Ferté-sous-Jouarre

N3

River Marne

N

0   3   6 kms

© TVH 2005

Barcy Notre-Dame de la Marne Monument; Chambry Local Cemetery and Original Wall Memorial; Four Roads Monument; The Great Grave and Péguy Memorial; Galliéni Statue; Meaux French National and German Cemeteries and American Monument. It finishes at the British Memorial to the Missing and the Pontoon Markers at La-Ferté-sous-Jouarre.

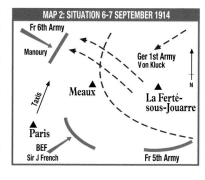

- **Extra Visit:** Lt de Gironde Grave and Memorials, Vivières
- **Special Visits:** Battles of the Marne Monuments at Dormans and Mondemont
- **Total time:** 6 hours 30 minutes
- **Total distance:** 100 miles
- **Distance from Calais to start point:** Approx 140 miles. Motorway Tolls
- **Maps:** IGN 1:25,000 – 2511 01 Forêts de Compiègne and 2512 01 Villers-Cotterêts
- **Base towns:** Compiègne, Meaux

Special Visits to French National Monument to the Victory of the Marne, Dormans, and Monument to the First Battle of the Marne, Mondemont.

N.B. The area covered by the First Battle of the Marne is so extended and points of interest on it so far apart that it was impossible to create a tight itinerary to include them all. For the sake of British readers there is inevitably a disproportionate emphasis on their participation in what was essentially a French battle – which we acknowledge and for which we apologise to our French Allies. There are, however, two important French Monuments which it is strongly advised to visit which lie far from any of our routes and to reach which, some map reading will be required.
Maps: Michelin 306 Local Aisne, Ardennes, Marne, 1:150,000 or IGN Carte de Promenade, Paris-Laon, 1:100,000

1. National Monument to the Victory of the Marne, Dormans (Map 10/32).

Dormans is mid-way between Château Thierry and Epernay on the junction of the N3/D18. [It could well be visited at the end of the Second Battle of the Marne Tour from Château Thierry.] It is well-signed in the town, is approached through the entrance to the Château, and has its own parking area.

The ornate Romano-Gothic 52m high Memorial Chapel, in which religious and military symbols are mixed, is approached up steps flanked by floral displays. At the top is an Orientation Table erected by the Touring Club of France in 1929 showing the points visible from this wonderful vantage point over the Valley of the Marne. To the left is a Lantern Tower and the cloistered Ossuary containing the ashes of

The National Monument to the Marne Victory at Dormans with floral tribute.

Special visits continued

1,500 WW1 soldiers, only eleven of whom are identified, together with the ashes of Déportés to Dachau and soil from Italian cemeteries where the remains of missing WW2 French soldiers lie. Along the cloisters are details of the First and Second Battles of the Marne with ORBATS and *bas-relief* portraits of Joffre and Foch. In the main building is a Crypt, a Lower Chapel and an Upper Chapel from the tower of which there is an incomparable view. The site was chosen by Foch with the Duchesse de la Rochefoucauld d'Estissac who formed a fund-raising committee to commemorate the battles.

Open: 11 November – 30 April: Sat 1430 to 1830, Sun 1000-1200 and 1430-1830, 1 May-15 September: every day except Tues 1430-1830. Sun: 1000-1200 and 1430-1830. Guided tours by appointment. Tel: + (0)3 26 57 77 87. The Château park is open every day from 1800 to 2000 when the exterior of the Chapel and the Colonnade may be visited. The Dormans Tourist Office is in the Château. Tel: + (0)3 26 53 35 86. Fax: + (0)3 26 53 35 87.

2. National Monument to the Victories of the Marne, Mondemont.
Mondemont is off the D951 above Sézanne along the D439. It is badly signed. In the village of Mondemont climb uphill to the large open space flanked by the Château and a farm, in the centre of which are the Monument and the Church. [See illustration on back cover.]

The 33m high monolithic Monument is absolutely stunning. Designed by architect Paul Bigot and sculptor Henri Bouchard, it was started in 1934, completed in 1939 and inaugurated in 1951. Its red-stone-covered 2,000 ton concrete pillar points to the skies and is engraved with rune-like characters dedicating it as a landmark to all who fought against the invader from ancient times, with the ORBAT of the Allies. On the front are *bas reliefs* of Allied Commanders: Sarrail, Langle de Cary, Foch, Franchet d'Espérey, French, Manoury and Galliéni. In their centre stands a larger scale figure of 'Papa' Joffre and a *Poilu*. Above them flies the figure of Victory and on the rear is a *bas relief* to Capt Chrissement, '*Fondateur des soldats de la Marne*'. Maréchal Foch chose the location on the site of one of the most crucial battles of the seven days of the 'Miracle of the Marne' when Paris was saved by heroic determination, spurred on by Joffre's immortal Order of the Day of 6 September 1914, when, as the salvation of the country was at stake, he ordered his troops to maintain conquered ground at all costs and be killed on the spot rather than fall back (an example that Haig was to follow in 1918).

In front of the Monument is a superb **Panorama/Orientation Table** with a magnificent view over the marshes of Saint-Gond. **Information Panels** in English, French and German describe the Monument and explain the stages of the Great War from the outbreak on 3 August 1914 through the retreat of late August, to the turn to the offensive on 6 September. The Battle of the Saint-Gond Marshes was hailed as the decisive point in the Battle when Cholet's 77th RI and Humbert's Moroccan Division saved the day against the 164th Hanoverian Regiment and the Imperial Guard of Von Hausen's German Third Army. Gen Humbert had his HQ in the Château nearby until it became untenable and then directed the battle from below the church. In the churchyard of the repaired

Special visits continued

church was buried Maj de Beaufort who commanded the attack and a headstone over the small Ossuary lists a Sous-Lieutenant, an Adjutant-Chef, an Adjutant, a Sergeant and four soldiers of the 77th RI, the 2nd Tir Algerien and the Zouaves. Three Plaques behind it describe **(1)** How on 5-10 September 1914 Gen Humbert's Moroccan Division stopped the rushing German tide and threw them back to the Marshes of Saint-Gond. **(2)** Then on 9 September Cholet's 77th RI arrived to retake the Château and the village in a brilliant assault. **(3)** On 9 September 1964, the fiftieth Anniversary of the Battle, there was a reunion between the 77th RI and the 4th Hanoverians to commemorate their glorious dead and their brave comrades.

On 5 September 2004, the ninetieth Anniversary, another great ceremony of commemoration took place here.

At the bottom of the hill is a small **Museum, open** every Sun June-September 1500-1800 hours. **Information/guided visits** contact Sézanne, Tel: + (0)3 26 80 51 43 or Col Claude Domenichi, President of Mondemont 1914 Les Soldats de la Marne, 6 Chemin des Carrouges, 51 120 Gaye. Tel/Fax: + (0)3 26 81 84 38. This is an extraordinarily powerful and moving site. Please visit it if you can.

From Calais take the A26/E15 direction Paris and, when the motorway splits to Reims, the A1 direction Paris/Arras. Take Exit 11 to Compiègne on the D935, cross the River Oise and drive straight to the centre of Compiègne by following signs to Centre Ville.

• *Compiègne*

Drive past the picturesque Town Hall to the left in the main square and continue to the parking in front of the Church of St Pierre on the left and walk back to the Tourist Office by the side of the Town Hall. **Tourist Office**, Place de l'Hôtel de Ville, Tel: + 33 (0)3 44 40 01 00. Note that there is a busy market on Saturdays so parking may be more difficult. Here you can pick up a town plan which will lead you to the following sites of interest:

1. **Monument aux Morts** by the Church of St Jacques (in which Joan of Arc came to pray when she was captured in 1430) sculpted by Real del Sarte (qv), inaugurated on 11 November 1922.
2. The splendid **Napoleonic Château**. Here Gen von Kluck had his HQ from 31 August 1914 when the Germans occupied the town until 14 September after the victory of the Marne when the town was recaptured. Gen Pétain moved his own HQ here on 15 May 1917 (when he succeeded Nivelle) until the German Offensive of 21 March 1918. Also the **Hotel Sessavalle-Soultrait** where he lived (opposite the *Sous-Prefecture*) and where Hitler stayed after he took the Armistice in June 1940.
3. **The Monument to the *Déportés*.**
4. **The Historical Figurines Museum** (to the right of the Town Hall). More than 100,000 lead figures including WW1.
5. In March 1918 Compiègne lay on the Germans' route towards Paris in their March 1918 offensive and most of the townspeople were evacuated. Between June and September 1918 almost 3,500 buildings were destroyed before the town was liberated. Compiègne also had a sad history in WW2, most of the old

town being razed to the ground by bombs in May 1940, with many civilian casualties. Some 48,000 prisoners were deported from the vast prison camp at Royallieu and the barracks in the Cours Guynemer and today there are **Monuments to the *Deportés*** at Royallieu, on the railway station platform and at the Bellicard roundabout.
You can also pick up a leaflet describing the multitude of restaurants (eighty-six are claimed!) and hotels to suit all pockets and tastes.
Continue by car up the rue Magenta, and the rue de Pierrefonds. At the corner with rue Victor Hugo to the left is

Guynemer Monument (Map 1/1).
This impressive group of statuary was sculpted by Henri Navarre and pays tribute to one of Compiègne's most famous sons, the French WW1 Ace, Georges Guynemer. Born in 1894 (actually in Paris – the family moved here in 1903), Guynemer scored fifty-four victories with his famous *Cigogne* (Stork) Squadron – their insignia is engraved on the memorial here. The Guynemer Memorial in Poelkapelle near Ypres, where he was brought down on 11 September 1917, is in the shape of a stork. The luxury motor car company Hispano Suiza adopted the emblem of the stork as it was Guynemer's favourite car. His motto *'Faire face'* (Face up to danger) is still that of the Military Aviation School.

Guynemer Monument, Compiègne.

Continue past the famous National Haras stud farm to No 112 rue St Lazare on the right.

Guynemer House (Map 1/2).
In this elegant old house Guynemer lived from 1903 until war broke out in 1914 and a marble plaque on the wall records how the Capt Aviator Georges Guynemer, Legendary Hero, fell from the skies in glory on 11 September 1917.
Continue to the roundabout and turn left following signs to Clairière de l'Armistice. Continue following signs to the car park.
Set your mileometer to zero.

• The Armistice Clearing Museum and Memorials, Clairière de Rethondes/0 miles/ 30 minutes/Map 1/3

In the clearing before the car park is

Monument to 'The Heroic soldiers of France, defenders of the Fallen and of the right, glorious liberators of Alsace and Lorraine' by E. Brandt. It depicts a fallen German Eagle, was destroyed by the Germans during WW2 and is now restored using the original stones brought back from Germany.

Follow the path to the Museum. On the left is

Monument to three members of the *Garde Général des Eaux et des Forêts* killed during the war.

Continue to the clearing.

Here **two sections of railway track** remain, parallel to each other. The one to the right is marked 'Maréchal Foch', the one to the left 'German Plenipotentiaries'. There is a large **Statue of the Marshal** by F. Michelet, erected in 1927, to the

Monument to Heroic Soldiers of France, Armistice Clearing.

left and a huge slab which records that 'on 11 November 1918 the criminal pride of the German Empire was vanquished by the free people whom they tried to subjugate'.

Charged with finding a discreet site for parking two trains, the railway engineer Emile Toubeau discovered this isolated clearing and the two little-known tracks leading from the station at Rethondes which were used by the Artillery. On 7 November Marshal Foch's train, comprising carriages for the French and British delegates led by Admiral Wemyss and Gen Weygand, a restaurant car, the Marshal's carriage and an office, arrived. The German train followed at 0530 on 8 November. It comprised a 'salon wagon' built for Napoleon III in 1867 complete with Imperial coat of arms. At 0730 Marshal Foch arrived from Paris bearing the text of

Foch Statue, Armistice clearing.

Foch's carriage site with tracks leading to the Museum, Armistice Clearing.

the Armistice and the first meeting took place at 0900 and continued over a period of three days. When the document was signed a telegraph message was sent to the Eiffel Tower. The news spread quickly and village bells all over France sounded.

After the war the carriage was for a short time again used as a restaurant car, then was displayed at Les Invalides. In 1927 it was restored with funds donated by the American Arthur Fleming and returned to the clearing. The clearing itself was inaugurated on 11 November 1922 by President Millerand.

On 21 June 1940 Adolf Hitler ironically and gleefully received the capitulation of France in the historic railway carriage here from Marshal Pétain and the clearing was then destroyed. The slab and the railway carriage were taken to Berlin and the carriage was destroyed by the SS as the Americans arrived in the city. On 11 November 1944, in the presence of civil and military authorities, the clearing was 'purified' by the Flame from the Tomb of the Unknown Soldier under the Arc de Triomphe in Paris. The stone was returned in 1946 but only a few fragments of the original coach were found in the Forest of Thuringen in April 1945 and the carriage in the Museum is an identical model.

Outside the Museum are **Information Panels** and a **Monument** which in 1950 replaced the one which was originally erected in 1927 'thanks to the generosity of **American Mr Arthur Henri Fleming**' and which was destroyed in 1940.

The Museum houses the railway carriage laid out as it was in 1918. There is also the eternal Flame of Memory and 1918 and 1940 exhibitions and some superb stereoscopic viewing machines. One emerges through a souvenir and book shop. **Open:** daily except Tuesday 15 October to 31 March 0900-1200 and 1400-1715 (but only in the afternoon during December and January); 1 April-14 October 0900-1200 and 1400-1815. Tel: + (0)3 44 85 14 18.

Leave the clearing and take the D546 direction Compiègne.

Your direction of travel now follows broadly that taken by the BEF as it continued its retreat and by bearing that in mind it is possible to have a general understanding of the juxtaposition of the forces involved in the various actions described.

Continue to the junction with the N31 and turn right, direction A1/Autres Directions. At the roundabout turn left signed Pierrefonds on the D130. [At this point you could go into Compiègne on the N31 if not visited before]. *Continue through the vast forest* (and beware 'large animals' suddenly crossing at twilight – this could mean deer or wild boars!) *and at the next roundabout turn right signed A1/Autres Directions on the D973. At the next roundabout take the Clermont/A1 road and at the next major junction (7 miles) turn left direction Senlis on the D932A. Continue following signs to Senlis through Lacroix and at the roundabout (12.6 miles) take the Verberie Centre road, drive over the railway and turn sharp left signed to the Gare on Route de Compiègne. Turn first right on rue Marcel Dourson and right at the stop sign on rue des Moulins and continue to the local cemetery on the left with a green CWGC sign.*

• *Local and French National Cemeteries with CWGC Graves, Verberie/14.2 miles/15 minutes/Map 1/4*

Opposite the cemetery is a **Memorial to the Indo-Chinese War.**

Inside the top gate to the Local Cemetery and to the left is a CWGC Plot with five headstones. They are of four R Inniskillings of 1 and 5 September 1914 and one 'Victim of the Great War'. At the front is a stone laurel wreath with the words, *'Pour les enfants de Verberie, soldats et Alliés, morts pour la Patrie.'*

Continue to the adjacent military cemetery.
The Military Cemetery was started during the 1918
Battle of the Oise and there is an **Information Panel**
about the Battles of the Aisne and the Oise. It
contains 2,600 burials, of which 2,506 are French
WW1, of whom 1,429 are in two ossuaries There are
also fifty-three British, of whom twenty-six are in
two ossuaries. The individual graves are of 5th
Dragoons of 1 September 1914 and 2 RAF graves of
1918. In the mass grave to the left there is a **large
stone commemorating twelve** (un-named) **men of
'L' Battery, RHA** who fell in the 'affair' of Néry 1
September 1914 of whom five are buried here and
seven at Néry (qv). There are ten headstones, with
twelve named members of the RHA and one which
commemorates eight Unknown.

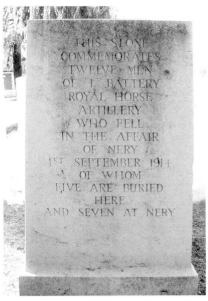

L Battery Burial Marker, French National Cemetery, Verberie.

Continue to the Stop sign and turn left on the D123.
Continue to Saintines and take the first (easy to miss,
15.8 miles) narrow road to the right to Fay. Continue
under a wonderful stone railway arch on the narrow
winding road, past the farm at Fay to the churchyard
on the right.

• Communal Cemetery, Néry with CWGC Graves & Monument/ 17.9 miles/10 minutes/Map 1/5

In the churchyard cemetery, which contains a wonderful **1870/'14-'18 Memorial**, is a
CWGC Plot with **a stone which commemorates twelve Men of 'L' Battery, RHA** (seven
of whom are buried here and five at Verberie (qv)) and sixteen named RHA stones. At
the back is an obelisk to **Maj John Stephen Cawley**, 20th Hussars, Bde Maj 1st Cav Bde,
age 34; **Capt Edward Kinder Bradbury, VC**, age 33; **Lt John Davies Campbell**, age 31,
'For gallantry and ability in organizing the defence of 'L' Battery against heavy odds at
Néry on the 1st September' and also to **Capt the Hon Oswald Cawley**, Salops
Yeomanry, killed near Merville on 22 Aug 1918, age 35. To the left are the headstones of
Campbell and the two Cawleys and to the right is Bradbury's.

The BEF retreat from Mons had continued in a south-westerly direction across a
front of some twenty-two miles bordered to the west by Compiègne, to the east by
Soissons and centered on Villers-Cotterêts (see Map 1). The 1st Cavalry Brigade and L
Battery had bivouacked at Néry with orders to continue the retreat at 0430 on 1
September, but thick mist reduced visibility to under 200 metres and it was decided to
delay the move. An hour later German cavalry chased a patrol of the 11th Hussars into
the village and L Battery came under intense fire from German artillery, machine-gun
and rifle fire from enemy barely 500 metres away to the east. The horses panicked with
guns still hooked, leading to chaos. Casualties were heavy. Capt Bradbury, helped by
those officers and men not killed or wounded, unlimbered three guns but one was
immediately destroyed by a direct hit. A second under Lt Giffard opened fire but it too
was hit and Giffard and his men were all killed or wounded.

Obelisk to 3 British Officers, Néry Local Cemetery.   Headstone of Capt Bradbury, VC.

Capt Bradbury at the third gun was joined by Lt Mundy and Lt Campbell and they continued to fire towards the east but Campbell was soon killed. Bradbury's gun came under attack from some twelve German guns and continued to reply. Meanwhile the German 4th Cavalry Division dismounted and attempted to approach the village from the east but were stopped by two dismounted squadrons of the 5th Dragoon Guards. At about 0800 British reinforcements now arrived from the direction of Saintines (1st Middlesex) and Verberie (where you were earlier – a Warwickshire and Dublin Fusiliers composite battalion). At L Battery BSM Dorrell joined Capt Bradbury and Sgt Nelson though Bradbury was killed at that very moment. Dorrell and Nelson continued to fire until they ran out of ammunition when artillery support from recently arrived I Battery, some 1200 metres to the south-west, forced the Germans to withdraw. The 1st Middlesex with a squadron of the 11th Hussars hastened their departure, capturing eight guns and seventy-eight prisoners. By 0845 the action at Néry was over. Five officers and forty-nine men of L Battery were killed or wounded and **Bradbury**, **Sgt Major David Nelson** (later a Major, was killed in Lillers on 8 April 1918 and is buried in Lillers Comm Cemetery) and **BSM George Thomas Dorrell** (later a Lt Col, died in Cobham in 1971) were all awarded the **VC**.

Continue through the village to the main road crossroads of the D554 with the D98 and park on the right .

• *Memorial and Plaque to 'L' Battery/18.3 miles/5 minutes/Map 1/6*

Here in 'Place 'L' Néry Battery' is a Memorial to the famous Battery and a Plaque on the wall behind commemorating the action of 1 Sept 1914 of the 2nd Dragoon Guards (Queen's Bays) who had been in the village on the morning of the 1st and played a conspicuous part in helping to repulse the German 4th Cav Div. 'The Battle of the Marne was won at Néry', it maintains! There are several other (French) contenders for that honour!

RHA Memorial, Néry, with 2nd DG Plaque.

Return through the village on the D98 signed to Vaucelles and turn right just before the local cemetery. You will then pass a
Memorial to Members of the FFI assassinated by the Germans on 20 August 1944. *Continue to Vaucelles, turn right on the small road signed to Béthisy on the D123, continue over the railway and turn right on the D123 signed to Crépy en Valois and pick up signs to Villers-Cotterêts. Continue to Gilocourt, take the D32 and keep on it.* You will now be driving along a most picturesque route following the course of the River Automne with winding roads, passing many beautiful stone buildings – Abbeys, Châteaux, fortified farms – and woodland.

At Largny the road becomes the D231. Continue under the dual carriageway towards Villers-Cotterêts and at the traffic lights turn left on the Avénue de Compiègne signed to the cemetery. Continue past the local cemetery to the National Cemetery on the left.

• ***French National Cemetery, Villers-Cotterêts/35.7 miles/10 minutes/ Map 1/7***
The cemetery was started in 1914 by the town hospital. It contains 3,411 French WW1 burials, of which 933 are in two ossuaries, four British and four Russian graves. There are ten WW2 French. Three of the CWGC headstones are among the French crosses but in the top left hand corner by the ossuary is the headstone of **Grenadier Guardsman J.E.**

Heslin, 14 September 1914, who is buried in the mass grave. There is a large plot containing Moroccan, Jewish and Indo-Chinese graves.

Continue onto the N2, turn right direction Soissons and take the first exit on to the D81, then cross the N2 direction Vivières on the D81 into the Forest of Retz.

This is the most majestic forest with acres of glorious mature beech trees and enticing walkways leading in all directions into the woods.

Continue to the Cross of Sacrifice on the right just after a right-hand bend.

• *The Guards' Grave, Villers-Cotterêts/38.2 miles/10 minutes/Map 1/8*

This tiny cemetery contains ninety-eight casualties of the Grenadier, Irish, Coldstream and Life Guards who fell in the forest 1-19 September 1914. Most are buried in the mass grave but to the left are what appear to be the individual graves of **2nd Lt George Cecil**, Grenadier Guards, age 18 (with no religious symbol), **Lt G. Lambton**, Coldstream Guards, age 26, **Maj C.A. Tisdall**, Irish Guards and **Lt Col the Hon George H. Morris**, Irish Guards, age 42. Headstones mostly bearing the names of two Guardsmen each line the wall. The layout is quite unique and utterly lovely. The Cross of Sacrifice also bears the legend usually found on the War Stone in large cemeteries, 'Their Name Liveth For Evermore', chosen by Rudyard Kipling. Steps with iron railings then lead down to the mass grave paved with grey stone. It has the atmosphere of a very special place and indeed one of the most poignant stories of the war was played out at this very spot involving some famous and interesting people.

One of the *dramatis personae* was the extraordinary eccentric Aubrey Herbert, later better known for his intervention with the Turks to negotiate an Armistice in Gallipoli for both sides to bury their dead after the dreadful battles of 20 May 1915. Herbert, who had become MP for Yeovil in 1911, had travelled extensively in Turkey and the Balkans and was offered the throne of Albania in 1913. In childhood he was practically blind but an operation when he was seventeen restored partial sight. He would never have passed an Army medical, so when war broke out in August 1914 Herbert took matters into his own hands, bought himself a uniform and when the Irish Guards marched from Wellington Barracks on 12 August to Nine Elms Station he slipped into the ranks and sailed with them to Le

Cross of Sacrifice, Guards' Grave Cemetery, Rond de la Reine.

Havre. Their CO, Col Morris, tolerated this unusual recruit who accompanied the Regiment to Mons and the Retreat, eventually finding himself in the Forest of Villers-Cotterêts on 1 September. There the CO gave the order, 'We are required to hold this wood until 2 o' clock in the afternoon. We may have to fight a rearguard action until a later hour if there is a block in the road. We are to retire upon Rond de la Reine' (your next stop). Herbert kept a diary and recorded the dreadful events of the day. He had acquired a racehorse that he called Moonshine and although an indifferent horseman was appointed Col Morris's 'galloper' (messenger) and spent the early part of the morning delivering messages through some lively fire from the enemy. By 1030 he was back in the wood and the Guards were soon subject to a terrific onslaught by the Germans with machine-gun and rifle fire. Several orders arrived, including one to hold on at all costs, one to charge – which was not heard amongst the din of the battle – and then the order to retreat arrived. Two of the gallopers were killed almost immediately after delivering their messages. Men were falling with accelerating frequency and Col Morris, who seemed to lead a charmed life, raced from one section of the wood to another, cheering up the men. The Guards were now virtually encircled and their casualty list grew alarmingly. Herbert was wounded in the mêlée, captured by the Germans and found himself in a German hospital in Vivières (see **Extra Visit** below), in the company of (Lord) Valentine Castlerosse and (Lord) Robin Innes Kerr who, in order to impress their captors, tried using their titles, while Aubrey used his clout as an MP. The French were approaching and the hospital was about to be abandoned. When the Germans decided they would have to take these three very important prisoners with them, the three heroes downplayed their status and were left with the other prisoners. There they learned that their beloved Colonel had died in the final charge, with all the seventy or so men who had charged with him.

Supporting the Irish Guards were the Grenadier Guards, among them 2nd Lt George Cecil, son of Lord and Lady Edward Cecil, (close friends of Rudyard Kipling) and John, son of Lord and Lady Manners. Manners was reported killed and young Cecil was posted as 'Missing' at first. His distraught mother enlisted the help of her famous author friend to help her find out what had happened to George. The quest became an ironic and unwitting rehearsal for the Kiplings in their search for their own son, John, posted 'Missing' in the Battle of Loos in September 1915 [the full story is described in our biography, *My Boy Jack? The Search for Kipling's Only Son.*] It was later recorded that George Cecil was killed leading a bayonet charge with his sword in his hand.

Lady Cecil had two famous brothers, Gen Frederick Maxse, who commanded 18th Division, and Leo Maxse, editor of *The National Review*. She was also a friend of Clemenceau. All possible strings were pulled at the highest level and Lady Cecil managed to get herself out to Villers-Cotterêts where she met the Mayor, Dr Mouflier and his wife, a nurse at the local hospital, but could find no concrete news. Then on 17 November a Red Cross Enquiry Department party including Col Morris's brother, Lord Killanin, visited the village to exhume the bodies that had been hastily buried after the disaster of 1 September. They identified the Colonel's body by his watch and George Cecil's from initials on his uniform. Lady Cecil's desperate search was over. For years after the Moufliers and other inhabitants of Villers-Cotterêts cared for the graves. On visiting them after the war Kipling wrote that the 'one long rustic-fenced grave is perhaps the most beautiful of all resting places in France'. The rustic fence has gone but the grave is still as beautiful.

Continue to the junction and stop on the right. On the left is

• Memorial to 2nd Lt George Cecil and Guardsmen/38.4 miles/5 minutes/ Map 1/9

This hauntingly lovely figure of a mourning female looking down on a British helmet bears an inscription on the back, 'In honour of the officers and men of the Grenadier, Coldstream and Irish Guards who fell near this spot on 1 September 1914. This memorial was placed here by the Mother of one of them and is especially dedicated to 2nd Lt George Edward Cecil.' Beneath the statue are the words, '*Passant, arrête-toi*' – Passerby, stop here.

Memorial to 2nd Lt George Cecil & Guardsmen, Rond de la Reine.

Extra Visit to de Gironde Memorials and Grave, Vivières (Map 1/10/11/12)

Round trip: 8.0 miles. Approximate time: 30 minutes

Take the D81 to Vivières and turn left into the village to the small crossroads with the Mairie to the right.

On the wall ahead on Rue de l'Escadron de Gironde is a **Plaque** which explains how in the night of 9-10 September the **2nd Squadron of the 16th Dragoons commanded by Lt de Gironde** on a reconnaissance mission behind the German lines made a surprise attack on a German airfield and put the planes out of commission.

Turn round and return to the Local War Memorial. Turn left on the C4 signed to Soucy. Continue to the Local Cemetery on the right with the CWGC green sign.

In the cemetery is a **CWGC Plot** with nine headstones, all from 23 April 1944. **They are Sqn Ldr C.W. Poulter**, age 30, **Sgt W. Heather**, Air Gunner, 21, **Sgt S. Glaister**, Air Gunner, ECAF, **Flt Sgt L.E. Amos**, Air Bomber, 20, **Sgt D.K. Ray**, Wireless Operator/Air Gunner, **Sgt D.B. Sheehan**, Flt Engineer, **Sgt A. Walker**, Navigator, 21, **Sgt N. Dobson**, Pilot and **Flt Sgt F.W. Lambert**, Air Gunner, 21.

At the back of the cemetery is the **Tomb of Lt Gaston Eugène Marie de Gironde** who fell on the field of honour on 10 September 1914 in Vivières, with a commendation on his valour by Gen Pelegier, 22 February 1921. Also buried here is Dragoon Maurice Neveux, killed in the same attack, and other soldiers' graves along the wall, mostly from 1915.

Extra Visit continued

Continue and rejoin the D81 and turn left. Continue to the monument on the left (park on the right).

Bronze plaques on the **Monument** surmounted by a cross record how **Lt de Gironde** was killed here. On the side are the names of the officers who were killed with him in the attack on a German airfield on this site. 'He was like his sword, straight, gentle, strong and brilliant. He had the character of a Christian soldier.' What a sight it must have been – the impetuous and gallant young cavalry officer charging the German aeroplanes at the head of his squadron and putting them out of action! After his death S/Lt Kérillis took command of the squadron, was soon wounded and was only saved by Dragoon Cossenet who was killed

Monument to Lt de Gironde.

protecting him. He was then taken to Montigny-Lengrain where his wounds were treated by l'Abbé Saincyr. Kérillis and his dragoons then managed to escape the Germans wearing civilian clothes. Two officers, de Villelume and Rollin, refusing to abandon their uniforms, were captured. The exploits of this dashing squadron were recounted in *Une Incroyable Odyssée* by the Comte Arnauld Doria.

Return to the Rond de la Reine and rejoin the main itinerary.

Turn right signed Tour d'Observation du Gen Mangin and continue through the beech forest on a somewhat causeway-like road.

The route of this track is roughly the defensive line adopted by the 3rd Coldstream (west of Rond de la Reine) and the 2nd Grenadiers (east) about 1100 on 1 September when, confused by order and counter-order, they attempted to cover the retreat of 2nd Division who were moving down from the north. The thickness of the woods led to confused fighting. The Irish Guards filtered in company by company to give support and Col Morris was killed early on in what was the first serious engagement that his regiment had had. Two platoons of Grenadiers were surrounded at Rond de la Reine where they fought to the last man, all being killed or wounded. John Manners was one of the platoon commanders. So mixed up were the three battalions that for some time there was no central control. Nevertheless the Guards fought their way back to Villers-Cotterêts where by 1400 they had put some space between themselves and the enemy. The 4th Guards Brigade lost over 300 officers and men in the fighting.

After some 1.1 miles there is a small **Memorial on the right to Henri de Chasseval (Map 1/13)** of the 11th Dragoons who fell here for France on 12 June 1918 age 25.

Continue some .2 mile to the sign to the left and park.

• Gen Mangin's Observation Tower/39.9 miles/15 minutes/Map 1/14

A five-minute walk up the track into the wood leads to a polished granite stone etched with a sketch of a high observation tower which was used by the General as he directed the attack of 18 July 1918 'which forced the victory' (see page 205).

Return to the road and continue to the N2. Turn right on the dual carriageway and filter left to take the D231 over the railway. Continue to Villers-Cotterêts following Centre Ville over two traffic lights and stop on the right by a park. Cross the road on the pedestrian crossing and walk back to the archway of the first large building, No. 32.

• Plaques, Old Hospital, Villers-Cotterêts /43.5 miles/10 minutes/ Map 1/15

Under the archway leading to what is now a retirement home, is a plaque to commemorate the old hospital, with a list of benefactors, and another plaque to the American Red Cross First Aid Post and to the *Union des Femmes de France* who endowed a bed here, 1918-1920. There were three main volunteer American ambulance organisations – the American Red Cross, the American Field Service (qv – see Pont à Mousson) and the Norton-Harjes Ambulance Corps. The latter was formed from the Harjes section of the American Red Cross and the American Volunteer Ambulance Corps founded in 1914 by Richard Norton. The latter two were absorbed by the US Army Ambulance Corps by the end of August 1917. Many of the volunteer ambulance drivers were writers, including Dashiell Hammett, Ernest Hemingway, Somerset Maugham, John Masefield and Robert Service.

Return to the crossing.

On the wall behind it is a **Plaque to Emile Anfroy** killed by the Germans 29 August 1944.

Continue to the Tourist Office to the left next to the cinema.

• Villers-Cotterêts Tourist Office/43.6 miles

Here you can pick a list of restaurants/hotels in this attractive and busy little town. Beware – it shuts for lunch at 1230.

Continue through the town, past the impressive local War Memorial, and join the N2 direction Paris, Compiègne. Continue to Vauciennes and keep to the left on the N2 as the road forks. Continue through Gondréville and after some 400m turn left past the Relais Routier du Virage on a small road (the D25). Continue to Ormoy le Davien and follow the winding road through the village to the crossroads. Turn right and after some 150m turn left before the Calvary on what you will find is the C7 into Bargny. Continue to the crossroads and turn right signed Betz on the D51. Continue into Betz and at the T junction turn left on the D332 signed Acy and then keep on the D922 in Betz where the D332 briefly becomes the D922 and then reverts to the D332.

While the Guards Brigade delayed the German advance at Villers-Cotterêts the 2nd Division continued its retreat and after a nineteren mile march reached Betz about 2300 on the night of the 1 September where they rested.

Continue along a beautiful tree-lined avenue on what is reminiscent of a Utrillo landscape of a French road and continue to the small cemetery on the right.

• *French National Cemetery Betz-Montrolles/Army of Paris Monument/ 56.6miles/10 minutes/Map 1/16*

The large obelisk **Monument** is to the **Soldiers of the Army of Paris** who died on the Battlefield of the Ourcq in September 1914. It bears the names of twenty-one soldiers who lie in the mass grave in front of it. On 25 August 1914 General Joffre was told to form an army of at least three corps to defend Paris. This he did by reinforcing Galliéni's command with elements of the 3rd and 6th Armies and a number of reserve divisions thus forming the Army of Paris. Nevertheless Joffre advised the government to leave Paris, which they did on 2 September.

Continue along the line of trees to Acy.

The tall steeple of the old church at Acy is pierced, perhaps a precedent for the 'fretwork' *Art Deco* churches of the Somme rebuilt in the 1920s.

Bear left on the D332 and then right on the D18 signed to Meaux. At Nogeon bear left on the D51 to Puisieux and on entering the village immediately turn left on a tiny road, ironically called the Grande Rue, just before the local War Memorial.

On the **War Memorial is the insignia of the** *Croix de Guerre* awarded to the village by Order of the Army, 1920.

Bear left past the church.

Note the rue de Poligny to the left. It leads to the **Ferme de Poligny** which was burned by the Germans. It is reported that they used the large wheat hangar as a funeral pyre for 2,000 of their dead, a practice it is claimed that they repeated in several hangars in the area.

Continue on the rue de Champfleury to the large farm on the left (64.5 miles).

The **Ferme de Champfleury (Map 1/17)** has commanding views over the rolling open countryside, dotted with isolated farms. Here von Kluck had his HQ for eight days at the beginning of September 1914 until he saw that the battle was lost and ordered a retreat. The owner had fled to Paris as the Germans approached and returned after the battle to find his cellar and billiard room (where the Germans left a 'jeering inscription') demolished. In the cherry tree at the front he found an iron chair wedged in the branches which had been used by the German command as an OP. The French 56th Division attacked from the right across the fields, carrying the farm on their third attempt. Once in possession of it they were subjected to a heavy bombardment from Etrépilly, suffering many casualties.

Continue to the main road and turn left on the D38. At the crossroads with the D401 turn left signed Etrépilly. Cross the Thérouanne River and enter the village keeping to the right and then turning left on the D146 just before the church signed to Vincy Manoeuvre and the National Cemetery on rue du Colonel Dubujadoux. Continue to the cemetery on the right.

• *Memorials Etrépilly Local Cemetery/67.7 miles/10 minutes/Map 1/18*

On the wall outside the cemetery is a **Plaque to Col Dubujadoux** who was killed, already twice wounded, at the head of his 2nd Zouaves as they chased the Germans from Etrépilly in a night attack with the bayonet. They were then repulsed from the village in a German counter-attack having lost half their strength and three-quarters of their officers.

French National Cemetery and Monument to Army of Paris, Etrépilly.

French National Cemetery and Army of Paris Monument, Betz-Montrolles.

The Ferme de Champfleury.

THE ZOUAVES

The original Zouaves were formed in 1831 in Algeria from members of a fierce Kabyli tribe and were totally indigenous. They fought with distinction in the Crimea, in Africa, in Mexico, in northern Italy and such was their reputation that in the American Civil War future Gen George B. McClellan formed a company of 'Zouaves' (the 5th New York Volunteer Infantry) who even sported the colourful Zouave uniform.

In France, where they fought in the Franco-Prussian War, more French personnel gradually joined the Zouaves (affectionately known as 'Zou-Zous') until they outnumbered the Algerians, but their distinctive Arabian, red or white baggy-trousered uniform with a long sash and tasselled fez, was retained for many years. The four regiments were distinguished by the colour of the trimmming round their waistcoats. By mid-1915 the exotic Zouave uniform was replaced with a practical khaki and a steel helmet.

The 2nd Zouaves had been formed at Montpellier on 20 August 1914 under Lt Col Dubujadoux. The Regiment comprised the 4th Bn under Cdt D'Urbal, the 12th Bn under Cdt de Marcy and the 14th Bn under Cdt Dechizelle. After their fearful losses here of 7 September 1914 (during which Cdt D'Urbal was also killed) they were moved, under Lt Col Dechizelle, to the Artois Front, then to Ypres – where they were victims of the April 1915 gas attack – and on to Monastir where Dechizelle was killed. They were dissolved at the end of 1918.

On the back wall of the cemetery is a **Memorial to the Soldiers of the Army of Paris** who fell in the Battle of the Ourcq, 6-10 September 1914 and the graves of **Henri Champain**, 35th RI, 7 September 1914, age 27 and **Cpl André Bican**, age 25.
Continue to the large memorial ahead.

Plaque to Col. Dubujadoux, Etrépilly Local Cemetery.

• National Cemetery and Monument to Army of Paris, Etrépilly, 67.8 miles/10 minutes/Map 1/19

The large monument bears a quotation from Victor Hugo, 'Glory to our eternal France. Glory to those who die for her' and a Plaque to commemorate the Battle of the Ourcq, September 1914. Under the first cross in the right hand plot is buried the gallant **Col Dubujadoux**. There is a mass grave at the rear containing 534 burials.
N.B. Be aware that workings for the new TGV line may cause diversions in this area.
Return to Etrépilly and turn right on the D401, recross the Thérouanne and immediately turn left on a very small road just before the Calvary. Continue to the cemetery on the right.

• French National Cemetery, Chambry/70.5 miles/5 minutes/Map 1/20

The cemetery was started in 1914 during the Battle of the Ourcq. It contains 1,331 burials, of which 990 are in four ossuaries. After the war bodies were brought in from surrounding battlefields, including a number of Moroccans. Many of the graves are from 1914. The cemetery was relandscaped in 1980.

The actual entrance to the cemetery is round the corner and opposite is a **1940 Memorial.**

Turn left at the crossroads signed to the German Cemetery and stop at the cemetery on the left.

• German Cemetery, Chambry/70.8 miles/5 minutes/Map 1/21

The monument in the centre of the cemetery, the entrance and the symbolic marker stones are of deep red stone. The 998 burials are in a mass grave, 985 of them unknown. Although tidy and well-tended, there are no flowers here.

Turn round and continue back on the D97 past the front of the French cemetery to the large monument on the left.

• Notre-Dame de la Marne Monument, Barcy/72.2 miles/10 minutes/ Map 1/22

Surrounded by a well-tended grassy area this large statue of the Virgin Mary with Child commemorates the thousands of men who fell on this plateau and also the man who inspired it, Monseigneur Marbeau, Bishop of Meaux. An **Information Panel** explains how the Bishop vowed to erect a memorial should the city of Meaux be spared from the impending German attack on 8 September 1914 (which by and large it was). Unfortunately he died on 1 May 1921. The monument, sculpted by L Maubert, was not unveiled until 9 June 1924 in the presence of Marshal Foch, the widow of Gen Manoury, Generals Pau, de Lamaze, Lavigne-Delville and the Colonel and Officers of the 23rd Dragoons, many other dignitaries and over 4,000 people.

Beneath the statue are the words, *'Tu n'iras plus loin'* – 'You will go no further' – reminiscent of Pétain's emotive cry at Verdun – *'Ils ne passeront pas'* – 'They will not pass'. The baby Jesus seems to be holding up his hand in admonition to the German forces.

On this site on 4 September, on the eve of the beginning of the Battle of the Marne, Gen von Kluck had his advance HQ. The plateau became the scene of bloody battles and under the Calvary de Barcy, on the site of the present flagpole, many of the soldiers killed between 3 and 7 September 1914 were originally buried. Other lone cemeteries dotted the whole of the plateau, charting the progression of the fighting. The first pilgrimage to their graves was on the Anniversary of 5 September 1915. A number of them now lie in the Chambry National Cemetery, recently visited.

For many years this site of such heroic resistance by the French was totally neglected. Because of the subject of the statue local people thought the monument was merely religious and the Bishopric of Meaux had no funds to maintain it. Then in 1982 a donation was finally made to the Commune of Barcy where local historians now realise the full significance of this powerful site and maintain it accordingly.

Continue to the crossroads with the D38 in Barcy.

On 4 September Barcy was a German divisional HQ and a small group of French civilians, among them the brother of Mgr Marbeau, had been arrested near Vareddes in the Monsigneur's car and brought before the General here. He told the group that he would keep the car and that they were to inform the citizens of Meaux that by tomorrow his troops would be in Paris. But the following day Gen Manoury's troops had begun their flank attack on the Germans (see Map 2) and Barcy was retaken the day after. The village then served as a start point for the attacks on Chambry and in the fierce fighting the 246th RI lost twenty officers, including their Colonel, and the 289th had to make three desperate assaults in one day. The village was badly damaged in the heavy bombardments.

Turn left towards Meaux. At the first fork take the small road to the left (C2). Enter Chambry, turn left and continue to the cemetery on the left.

• Chambry Local Cemetery & Original Wall Memorial/74.3 miles/ 10 minutes/Map 1/23

Inside the gate on the right is the grave of **Henri Allaire**, killed at Chambry on 7 September 1914, age 23. In the centre of the cemetery is part of the original cemetery wall which bears a **Plaque** explaining how Zouaves of the 45th African Division pierced the wall and stopped the enemy counter-attack at the price of very high losses and forced the precipitate defeat which contributed to the Victory of the Marne, 6 and 7 September 1914. In fact the village changed hands many times in the desperate fighting, much of it hand-to-hand, between 6 and 8 September and it was the Germans who had first occupied the cemetery, pierced the wall (and an original holed length of wall can be seen at the bottom of the cemetery) and rained fire down on the attacking French. When the Colonial forces managed to force them out they employed the same tactics. The small mausoleum in the cemetery served as a dressing station, but was soon overflowing with the wounded. The French then took shelter in a large trench constructed outside the cemetery walls where many of their dead remained. The cemetery and the trench became the focal point for pilgrimages as early as 1915.

Return to the village and take the D140 direction Penchard. Continue to the crossroads. On the right is

• Monument of the Four Roads/75.6 miles/5 minutes/Map 1/24

The monument to the soldiers of the Army of Paris bears the quotation from Victor Hugo seen on the Etrépilly Memorial (qv). The monument was erected on the crossroads here by the Engineers on the orders of Gen Galliéni and contemporary photographs show it covered in wreaths and standards on the Anniversary in September 1916.

Continue over the crossroads and over the railway through Penchard.

The woods around Penchard were scattered with the graves of the Moroccan Brigade who attacked the village on 5 September when bitter hand-to-hand fighting ensued. It is purported that the Germans left several spies in the woods to signal the position of the attacking French forces.

At the War Memorial fork to the right on a small (easily missed) road signed to Chauconin Neufmontiers and then turn right again on the D140 into the village of Neufmontiers, following signs to Paris.

The direction of Paris can easily be gauged in this area as it is on the flight path to Charles de Gaulle airport. The **War Memorial** to the left of the green in Neufmontiers les

Notre-Dame de la Marne Monument, Barcy.

View through one of the original loopholes, Chambry Local Cemetery.

Monument of the Four Roads, near Penchard.

The Great Grave, Chauconin with Monthyon behind.

Meaux bears a plaque to the heroism of the soldiers who stopped the German advance. On the *Mairie* ahead is a list of the names of villagers killed in the war. The Germans briefly occupied the village on 5 September, using the church as a first aid post.

Continue to the crossroads with the D129 and turn right towards Villeroy. Continue to the monument on the right.

• 'The Great Grave', French National Cemetery, Chauconin Neufmontiers/ 80.1 miles/5 minutes/Map 1/25

This brilliant memorial, the '*Grande Tombe*', with a colourful mosaic of sword and standards, is surmounted by a cross and commemorates the 133 Frenchmen of the 231st, 246th and 276th RIs and the 55th and 56th DI who are buried in the ossuary here. The grave was created in 1914 after the Battle of the Ourcq and the monument by Henri Faucheur, in 1932. Among them is the famous French writer **Charles Péguy**, a Lieutenant in the 276th RI who was killed at Villeroy on 5 September 1914, the first day of the Battle of the Marne. His name is on the right, on the top line of the list picked out in *Art Deco* style mosaic lettering.

Beyond the monument is a hill on which there are two radio relay towers. This is Monthyon and in September 1914 the hill was surmounted by a windmill which the Germans used as an OP and from which it is said that the Eiffel Tower could be seen on a clear day. It became a target for the French Artillery to destroy that view of the Capital. The advance guard of the German Reserve Corps had sited their own machine guns and artillery on these heights and the first shots of the Battle of the Marne had been fired on 5 September from here.

Continue to the crossroads and stop by the memorial on the corner ahead.

• Memorial to Lt Charles Péguy/80.4 miles/5 minutes/Map 1/26

The tall pillar records that Charles Péguy fell in these fields on 5 September 1914. On a stone behind the pillar is a quotation from his poem, *Heureux qui...*, quoted at the beginning of this chapter. Péguy was born in Orleans on 7 January 1873 to a semi-literate peasant family yet managed to enter the prestigious *Ecole Normale Supérieure*. He became a politically active Socialist, supporting Dreyfus in the anti-Jewish Dreyfus Affair and started a review called *Les Cahiers de la quinzaine* in 1900, gradually developing his highly nationalistic and religious views. The years from 1910 until his death saw a frenzy of creation starting with the first of his

Memorial to Lt Charles Péguy, Chauconin.

famous Mystery plays, *Le Mystère de la Charité de Jeanne d'Arc*. The obituaries that followed his untimely death gave him the fame that eluded him during his life and he achieved international cult status, especially in France during WW2 when he became an icon for the Resistance. 'His design', wrote Edmund Gosse in 1916, 'was to carry out in the twentieth century the sacred labour of Jeanne d'Arc'.

On top of the stone is a ceramic orientation table showing the French and German positions, enamelled by J. Serre in 1992. It describes how at 5 o'clock in the afternoon of 5 September 1914 the 276th RI, departing from Iverny Chauconin, attacked across the fields with the object of taking the heights of Penchard and Monthyon, held by the Germans. At the beginning of the attack Lt Péguy, at the head of his section, was killed outright by a bullet in the forehead (having told his men to lie down).

Take the D27 towards the N3 (not signed to anywhere!) and at the junction with the N3 turn left along the dual carriageway. Stop at the statue on the right.

• *Statue of Gen Galliéni/82.4 miles/5 minutes/Map 1/27*

The fine bronze statue, with its green patina, shows the General shading his eyes, his caped coat flying in the wind, as he looks into the distance. Its caption is '*La Ville de Paris à Général Galliéni*'. In front is a circular stone that obviously once held an orientation table but which is now missing and there is a general air of neglect about the site.

Continue on the N3 downhill towards Meaux. Keep to the left lane on entering the town following signs to Centre Ville and 'i'/Office de Tourisme. Continue to the car park to the left of the large war memorial. Behind is

• *Meaux War Memorial and Office de Tourisme/86.2 miles/10 minutes*

Unlike its fate in 1870 and earlier conflicts, Meaux mostly escaped the ravages of WW1 as its Bishop, Mgr Marbeau (qv) had prayed. British troops had rushed through the city during The Retreat on 2 and 3 September 1914, blowing up the old Market Bridge and the footbridge further downstream. The town's civil authorities, as well as some 13,000 out of its 14,000 inhabitants, evacuated the town, but Mgr Marbeau stayed behind to look after the wounded that poured in after the battles of 5 September. Several shells landed on the city but it sustained no serious damage.

The impressive War Memorial is surmounted by a winged statue of Victory and flanked by two lions. It commemorates the 1870 Franco-Prussian War, WW1 and WW2. Living in Couilly (five miles south of Meaux) in August 1914 was the American friend of Gertrude Stein, Mildred Aldrich, who kept a diary which she later published as *A Hilltop on the Marne*, which gives a fascinating picture of daily life during the fighting.

Behind is the **Tourist Office** which can provide lists of hotels, restaurants and other attractions in the town.

Exit the car park from the far end and continue following signs for Soissons. Skirt the ancient ramparts to the right and then the River Marne and leave Meaux turning left on the D405, signed to Soissons and then Vareddes.

To the right at 2 Ave Maréchal Foch is the interesting Chinese Restaurant, Délice de Hongkong. Tel: + (0)1 60 32 06 85.

Continue under the railway bridge to the cemetery on the left.

• *French National, CWGC and German Plots, Meaux Cemetery/88.2 miles/ 10 minutes/Map 1/28*

On the wall of the local Meaux Cemetery is a green CWGC signs and also a French War Graves sign. On the left as one enters is a French Military plot with four British headstones, including that of **Lt A.M. Smith Cumming**, Seaforth Highlanders, age 24, 3 October 1914. All the French crosses, solid Muslim exotically-shaped headstones and even the CWGC headstones bear the bright red, white and blue roundel of *Souvenir Français*. It is a striking, moving and unusual sight.

To the right is the drab **German Military Plot**. This contains sixty-five burials in individual graves under grey crosses and 998 in a mass grave. There are no *Souvenir Français* roundels on the headstones.

Continue a further .6 mile over the Canal de l'Ourcq to the parking for the memorial on the right.

• *American Memorial to French Combatants of the Marne/88.8 miles/ 10 minutes/Map 1/29*

This monumental statue is known as 'Hopeless Victory'. It is on the site where the on-rushing German Army was halted in September 1914. The heroic struggle by the French to save their *Patrie* and their Capital from the invaders was widely publicised in America, whose intervention was eagerly sought. After the 1918 Armistice the idea to erect a memorial to the Battle of the Marne resulted in a competition. The winner was the sculptor Frederick MacMonnies, with the architect Thomas E. Hastings and the builder Edmond Quattrochi, and it took fourteen years for his design to be realised. The final monument was 26 metres high, was made of 220 blocks of Lorraine stone and was in the classical style. The central figure of France is likened to a Spartan Mother, howling in grief over the bodies of her dead sons. It was unveiled in September 1932 by the French President, Albert Lebrun, President of the Council Edward Herriott and the American Ambassador Walter Evans Edge. It bears a quotation from Marshal Joffre, 'Here speak again the silent voices of heroic sons of France who dared all and gave all in the day of deadly peril, turned back the flood of imminent disaster and thrilled the world by their supreme devotion.' It was erected by the 'American Friends of France in Memory of the Battle of the Marne in September 1914.'

Continue to Vareddes on the D405.

The Germans were forced back from Vareddes, leaving their wounded behind – these were sheltered and tended in the *Mairie* – but taking with them twenty old hostages, including the *Curé*. The old men were forced to march seventeen miles on the first day, and several, who could not keep up the required pace, were shot. The survivors were despatched to Germany by train from Chaulny but were repatriated several months later.

Here is the 3-star Logis de France, l'Auberge du Cheval Blanc, 55 rue Victor Clairet, Tel: (0)1 64 33 18 03. Fax: + (0)1 60 23 29 68.

Statue of Gen Galliéni, west of Meaux.

The huge American Memorial to French Combattants of the Marne, Meaux.

Headstone of Lt A.M. Smith Cumming, Meaux Cemetery.

British Memorial to the Missing, La-Ferté-sous-Jouarre.

RE Pylon, River Marne, La-Ferté-sous-Jouarre.

Turn right on the D97 and then left into Germigny.

At the beginning of September the Germans had a heavy battery in Germigny, which fired on Meaux. On 8 September they recrossed the Marne, blowing the bridge below the village behind them. A French recce party consisting of a Sergeant and nine men had forced them out. On 9 September the British Engineers built a pontoon bridge under heavy fire and with great tenacity after seventeen unsuccessful attempts.

Continue on the D97 to Trilport and turn left on the N3 to La Ferté-sous-Jouarre. Enter the town and continue to the large memorial on the left.

British Memorial to the Missing and Pylons on Site of Pontoon Bridge, La-Ferté-sous-Jouarre/101 miles/15 minutes/Map 1/30/31

In the summer of 1926, to quote *The Unending Vigil*, the French had become 'disquieted by the number and scale of the Memorials which the Commission proposed to erect.' The contract, however, was already out for the monument at la Ferté, considered to be marking 'the most important battle of the war' and it went on to be inaugurated on 4 November 1928 by Gen Sir William Pulteney in the presence of Marshal Foch, Field Marshal Milne and Gen Weygand. The names of the missing, in regimental order, are inscribed all round the memorial, before which the flags of the UK, France, Belgium, Canada and the EEC fly. One name of note is that of **Rifleman Charles Frederick Banks** KRRC who was killed at Mons on 14 September 1914. His nephew is the author Arthur Banks whose *A Military Atlas of the First World War* is a prime work of reference. There is a Register box to the left but a notice explains that it is not possible to keep the book there and that it can be examined by telephoning the *Mairie* of la Ferté on + (0)31 60 22 25 63 during working hours.

The elegant memorial, designed by G.H. Goldsmith, records the 3,888 Missing who fell in the 1914 battles of Mons, le Cateau, the Marne and the Aisne. It is made of white Massangis stone and was erected on land donated by the de Jussieu family.

Walk to the bridge over the Marne and down a path to the river bank.

Pylons on each bank mark the position of the Pontoon Bridge built whilst under fire from the Germans who held the high ground on the northern bank, by 4th Division Engineers, thus allowing passage of the left wing of the BEF in its northward advance. They are surmounted by the Engineers' grenade mounted on a circular paving and describe how portions of the Division had already crossed by boat at the weir near Luzancy and below the destroyed bridge.

Views of the River Marne and its banks are quite beautiful from this point.

• End of First Battle of the Marne Tour.

ST MIHIEL SALIENT: THE FORMATION

SEPTEMBER 1914

'Il pleut, il pleut du fer. Chaque détonation est affreuse; chaque cri qui la suit est affreux; mais le plus affreux c'est la seconde de silence durant laquelle j'attends ce cri. Car il y aura un cri, je le sais. Il faut que quelqu'un crie sous le coup... Et le cri monte à travers les branches qui pleurent des gouttes d'eau glacées, sourd ou déchirant, sauvage ou plaintif, plein de révolte ou de reproche.
Où sommes nous? Quelle heure est-il? Est-ce le soir ou le matin? Est-ce le printemps ou l'automne? J'ouvre la bouche comme si le cri devait sortir de ma poitrine.
Mais dans ma poitrine je n'ai plus de coeur, je n'ai plus qu'une poignée de ces feuilles pourries dans lequelles nous marchons, nous marchons,
sans jamais sortir de ce bois.'
Paul Cazin, 29th RI in *Humanist à la Guerre,* about the fighting in the Bois d'Ailly.

'It's raining, it's raining steel. Every detonation is frightful, every cry that follows it is frightful, but the most frightful is the second of silence during which I wait for that cry. Because there will be a cry, I know it. Someone has to cry beneath that blow... And the cry ascends across the branches which weep drops of frozen water, deaf or heart-breaking, full of rebellion or reproach. Where are we? What time is it? Is it evening or morning? Is it spring or autumn? I open my mouth as if the cry would emerge from my breast. But there's no heart any more in my breast, only a fistful of rotten leaves in which we march, we march, without ever getting out of this wood.'

SUMMARY OF THE BATTLE

On 20 September 1914 the Germans launched an attack from Metz designed to outflank Verdun from the south. Although they crossed the Meuse at St Mihiel and held the town, they were unable to advance further. However, they occupied a triangular salient from Les Eparges in the west below Verdun, via St Mihiel in the south, to Pont-à-Mousson below Metz in the east, and it remained in German hands until retaken by the Americans four years later.

OPENING MOVES

As the Germans advanced into Belgium in August 1914 so the French crossed the German border into Alsace Lorraine and on 21 August they were defeated not far from Metz in what they called the 'First Battle of Nancy'.

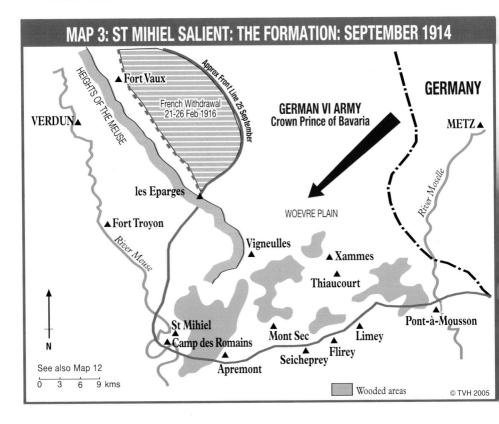

MAP 3: ST MIHIEL SALIENT: THE FORMATION: SEPTEMBER 1914

This was part of the series of engagements known as the 'Battle of the Frontiers' which in turn led to the French and British retreat to the River Marne. By 1 September Paris was under threat and two days later the Government moved out of the Capital to Bordeaux.

On 6 September the Allied armies under Joffre initiated a major counter-attack during which Gen Galliéni used some 600 Paris taxis to ferry troops to the front. Fierce fighting continued for several days but by 13 September the 'First Battle of the Marne' was over and the Germans were in general retreat between Paris and Verdun. It was time for the Germans to alter the point of their offensive. Now they looked not at Paris, but at Verdun, the strongest fort in the line beside the heights of the River Meuse, established by the French following their defeat of 1870. It was the heart of the French defences and seemingly impregnable but the Germans reasoned that if they could outflank Verdun to the south they could then threaten the rear of the Allied forces now engaged in pushing the main German force northwards in the 'Race to the Sea'.

It was a good concept but could it work?

WHAT HAPPENED

Halfway between Verdun and St Mihiel is the Fort of Troyon. All three are on the River Meuse. As early as 8 September the German 6th Army under the Bavarian Crown Prince had bombarded Troyon (See Map 3). Clearly even at this stage the Germans had it in mind to try to outflank Verdun by crossing the Meuse to its south but they must also have thought to pre-empt any attempt by the French to launch a 'Second Battle of Nancy'.

German infantry reached Troyon and Gen Sarrail, whose 3rd Army was defending Verdun, ordered the destruction of some of the bridges over the Meuse. However, as the German withdrawal to the north began on 13 September, following the end of the First Battle of the Marne, the pressure on Troyon and Verdun eased – but only for a week.

On 20 September four German Army Corps advanced from Metz accompanied by heavy artillery fire upon the Meuse forts. By 23 September they were at Seicheprey, on the 25th they entered St Mihiel, which was defended only by a single territorial battalion, and the following day they crossed the River Meuse.

This was a critical moment. The French XVI Corps was rushed up from Nancy and the Germans were stopped, but they held St Mihiel, the point of a salient that extended some thirteen miles into French territory and severed two main railway lines, thus cutting off Verdun and leaving it to be served by just a single track narrow gauge line from Bar le Duc.

The salient would hold for almost exactly four years, though extended somewhat above Les Eparges by the French withdrawal during the Verdun Battles. The French described it as a hernia and the Germans called it the *Sankt Mihiel Bogen*.

THE BATTLEFIELD TOUR

This is done in conjunction with St Mihiel Salient: The Recapture. See page 255, Map 12, page 258.

Statue in American Cemetery, Thiaucourt.

Statue in German St Mihiel Cemetery.

THE AISNE

13-30 SEPTEMBER 1914

'On the 13th [September 1914] when the divisions made a rather cautious
and leisurely advance, they should have been reminded, in spite of their fatigue
after over three weeks' continuous operations, that "sweat saves blood".'
The War Office, 1934

We first saw fire on the tragic slope
Where the flood-tide of France's early gain,
Big with wrecked promise and abandoned hopes,
Broke in a surf of blood along the Aisne.
The Aisne, Alan Seeger,
American poet fighting with the French Foreign Legion
and killed on the Somme on 4 July 1916

SUMMARY OF THE BATTLE

On 13 September 1914 the BEF, moving north from the Marne, crossed the River Aisne in pursuit of the Germans and for two weeks both sides fought tenaciously on and around the Chemin des Dames ridge. By the end of the month stalemate had been reached and trench warfare had begun. Had the BEF been just two hours earlier at the river the outcome could have been quite different. British casualties have been estimated at some 12,000.

OPENING MOVES

On 6 September the counter-attack planned by Joffre following the First Battle of the Marne began, catching the Germans by surprise. After three days of fighting during which the Allies gradually got the upper hand, the Germans began to retreat towards the Chemin des Dames beyond the River Aisne, leaving a gap, covered only by cyclists and cavalry, of some twenty-five miles between their First and Second Armies from Soissons to Cerny. Into this gap the BEF advanced. The Germans, aware of the gap, started to move their 7th Army down from Belgium where it had been investing Maubeuge which had held out until 8 September. The coming encounter was to be one of the most important of the early war, perhaps of the war itself, because an Allied break-through seemed eminently possible. Some even thought that it could decide the outcome of the war. This was a race to see who could get to the top of the Chemin first – the BEF or the 7th Army.

WHAT HAPPENED

The Allied line against the Aisne was, left to right, the French 6th Army west of and up to Soissons, the BEF from (including) Soissons to (including) Bourg and east of Bourg the French 5th Army (see Map 6). Facing them was the German 1st Army with the 7th Army moving rapidly south heading for the Chemin de Dames. General Joffre, commanding the Allied efforts, ordered that the pursuit from the Marne be continued across the river Aisne.

On 12 September 4th Division reached the high ground south of Venizel and Brigadier Hunter-Weston's 11th Brigade was ordered to seize the Venizel bridge. Hunter-Weston led the Brigade himself marching forward in pouring rain and reaching the bridge at 0100 on 13 September. The bridge had been blown by the Germans but not completely. Infantry could still cross with care and all four of the brigade's battalions were on the north bank by 0300 hours. They were the first British troops to cross the Aisne and they were ahead of the French. At dawn the Brigade took the crest of the hill immediately beyond the river by a bayonet charge. It was a splendid effort following a march of some thirty miles in heavy rain. *The Official History* says, 'Had other divisions been equally enterprising – and their marches on the 12th had been shorter than those of the 4th Division – the fighting on the 13th might have had a different result'.

A War Office report on the action later commented, 'HQ 4th Division was in a café near the south end of the bridge. A place more likely to be shelled could hardly have been chosen, but it remained untouched for some time!'

At Missy, immediately east of Venizel, 4th Division's Cyclist Company had seized the bridge undamaged at 0100 but lost it to a German counter-attack at 0400. The bridge had been allocated to 5th Division and when the Royal West Kents, the lead troops, arrived they found that, following the early morning recapture, the Germans had blown the bridge. Heavy machine-gun fire prevented any attempt at a crossing until nightfall when, using small boats, the RWK ferried men across. A German patrol was met and defeated and by daylight on 14 September both the RWK and the King's Own Scottish Borderers were established on the northern bank.

Further east at Vailly, where the bridges (along the full length of the BEF front the Aisne was accompanied by a canal and to make crossings to the north bank two bridges at each point had to be taken) had been allocated to 3rd Division, the Divisional Commander, Major General Hubert Hamilton, personally reconnoitred the crossings and ordered the Royal Scots to cross despite enemy shellfire. By 1600 on the 13th the RS were established on the north bank at Vauxelles Château, about one mile north-west of Vailly. Eventually both the 8th and 9th Brigades crossed the Aisne.

The far right of the BEF front was that of Haig's I Corps and neither it nor the Cavalry Division reached the Aisne on the night of 12 September. However, by building a temporary trestle span, and using a pontoon bridge, 2nd Division crossed both at Chavonne (advancing as far as Soupir) and Pont Arcy on 13 September. To the right, alongside the French, 2nd Cavalry Brigade led the 1st Division attack on Bourg on 13 September and using an aqueduct crossed, followed by the whole Division who were on the north bank by 1800.

Thus, by the end of the 13th, the BEF was over the river at each end of its line with other scattered crossings in between. It was now a matter of taking the high ground of the Chemin before the German 7th Army arrived. Further to the right the French had crossed at Pontavert and were fighting as far north as Corbény. Things looked good.

But von Zwehl, commanding the 7th Army, had force-marched his men forty miles in twenty-four hours, losing almost a quarter of his infantry to exhaustion en route and by 1100 on the 13th he had arrived on the crest of the Chemin des Dames and stood firmly in the path of the BEF. The Germans had won the race.

Nevertheless the Allies were determined to continue the assaults and the BEF, working closely with the French forces on its flanks, constructed pontoon bridges at Venizel (4th Division), Vailly (3rd Division) and Pont-Arcy (2nd Division) and continued its efforts to climb the heights. Below Cerny-en-Laonnois on 14 September, 3rd Brigade of 2nd Division, 1 Corps, (Haig), reached the road joining the two villages on the very crest of the ridge where the Loyal North Lancs Memorial now stands. But the Germans had constructed formidable defensive positions using trenches and barbed wire and their artillery commanded the valley and river crossings below so that the British were forced back to the valley that same day, the Corps suffering around 3,500 casualties.

The fighting continued until the end of the month (though as early as 16 September Sir John French ordered that the British positions should be strongly entrenched, suggesting that even then he saw an end to offensive actions), the French crossing the river in actions that some call the 'Second Battle of the Aisne'. The tail-end of the fighting was mostly artillery bombardment and counter-bombardment. The lines stabilised in essentially the positions that existed on the morning of 15 September, i.e. the BEF was strung along the north bank of the Aisne while the Germans held the heights of the Chemin and were constructing and improving intricate defensive positions making full use of the caves and woods found in the area. It was the beginning of the trench warfare that would last for four years.

THE BATTLEFIELD TOUR

This can be found on page 117 in conjunction with the Chemin des Dames Battles of 1917/1918.

Headstone of Conscientious Objector, Orderly H.H. Jackson, Vailly-sur-Aisne Cemetery.

Calvary at end of Chemin des Dames.

VERDUN

21 FEBRUARY-18 DECEMBER 1916

'Within our reach there are objectives for the retention of which the French General
Staff would be compelled to throw in every man they have.
If they do so the forces of France will bleed to death.'
Gen von Falkenhayn to the Kaiser.

'Courage – On les aura!' ('Courage – We'll get them')
The last phrase of General Pétain's *Order of the Day*
to the defenders of Verdun on 10 April 1916.

*'Ce que nous avons fait, c'est plus qu'on ne pouvait
demander des hommes, et nous l'avons fait.'*
('What we have done is more than one could ask of men, and we did it.')
French academician Maurice Genevoix, Founder and President of the
Association National du Souvenir de Verdun, who served as a Lieutenant in the 106th RI.

SUMMARY OF THE BATTLE

On 21 February 1916 the German 5th Army attacked the fortified French town of
Verdun in an operation called *'Gericht'* – 'A place of execution'. The battle lasted
for ten months, but Verdun never fell. French casualties were estimated at
540,000, German at 430,000.

OPENING MOVES

The classic invasion route into France from the east crosses two rivers, first the Moselle,
and then the Meuse. Above the Meuse to its east is a 1,500ft high ridge and in its
western shadow is Verdun. Attila came this way and destroyed the city, the Germans
conquered it in the tenth century and France took it back in the sixteenth. In the late
seventeenth century the great French military architect Vauban included Verdun in his
defensive scheme for the protection of France, but in the 1870 war Bismarck's armies,
though they followed tradition and crossed the Moselle, bypassed Verdun and went on
to Paris. Eventually Verdun, the last great fortress to capitulate in the Franco-Prussian
War, fell to von Moltke the Elder. The well-trodden invasion path across the Meuse
from Metz and between the two rivers is an area known as Alsace-Lorraine which, in
the peace treaty of 1871, was ceded to Germany, leaving in every French heart the
desire for revenge. Verdun thus became a border fortress town, the symbol of French
esprit which, together with the lost provinces of Alsace and Lorraine, assumed a
mystical significance dear to all Frenchmen. *'Ils ne passeront pas',* 'They shall not pass'
was its slogan.

After 1871 France built up her defences to the east and north of Verdun adding three dozen forts in two lines, the largest of which was Fort Douaumont, less than five miles from the centre of Verdun. Yet in 1916, after eighteen months of war, Douaumont was virtually unmanned. Why?

The reason is a logical one. In 1914 when the Germans invaded Belgium their route took them directly onto the fortified towns of Liège and Namur, and although stirring defence by the garrisons delayed the invasion, the towns were first by-passed and then reduced by the German heavy artillery. Furthermore, the Schlieffen Plan was only hinged on Alsace-Lorraine, the main forward effort of the German invasion being well north through Belgium. Gen Joffre concluded from the failure of the Belgian forts to stop the enemy that Verdun no longer had value as a fortress, and this view was officially promulgated in a memorandum of 9 August 1915. In addition, since the German threat was concentrated elsewhere, the defence of Verdun was given low priority and invested in a command known as the 'RFV' – the Verdun Fortified Area – which relied upon a thin line of trenches partially manned by over-age reservists. Steadily Joffre disarmed the forts, moving some of their weapons elsewhere and downgrading the quality of the garrison. However, knowing the country's almost religious belief in the invincibility of Verdun, he issued optimistic and reassuring propaganda about its defences.

Not all French leaders were happy about what was happening in Verdun. Gen Herr, commanding the RFV, repeatedly warned Joffre that the defences were too weak, but the most effective and consistent complaints were made by Lt Col. Emile Driant, a local political deputy. Joffre had taken offence at the steady increase in complaints against his policy at Verdun and ruled that no one in his command could directly approach their political representatives to express their views. Such actions were, he said, 'calculated to disturb profoundly the spirit of discipline in the army'. Complaints had to be made to the next senior officer in the military hierarchy – with predictable results for the future career of the complainant. Driant, however, as a Deputy himself, could maintain his political contacts. He had rejoined the colours at the outbreak of war and in 1916 commanded the 56th and 59th *Chasseurs à Pied* (infantry) based in the Bois des Caures, a wood some seven miles to the north of Verdun (see Map 4). He wrote to the President of the Chamber of Deputies in August 1915 complaining about the state of the Verdun defences, 'The sledge-hammer blow will be delivered on the line Verdun-Nancy. What moral effect would be created by the capture of one of these cities... if our first line is carried by a massive attack, our second line is inadequate and we are not succeeding in establishing it.' Galliéni, who had saved Paris and gone on to become Minister of Defence, learned of the letter and wrote to Joffre, 'Reports have come to me from various sources concerning the organisation of the front indicating that deficiencies exist in the conditions of the works at certain points. In regions of the Meurthe, Toul and Verdun notably, the line of trenches appears not to have been completed.' Joffre in his memoirs says, 'I confess that this letter impressed me disagreeably.' Four days later he sent a long reply to Galliéni repeating his oral mandate about soldiers not reporting to politicians and asking for the names of those whom Galliéni had described as 'various sources'. 'To sum up' wrote Joffre, 'I consider that nothing justifies the fears which, in the name of the Government, you express in your despatch.' However, Joffre did react to the situation and sent Gen de Castelnau to inspect the defences of Verdun. It was 20 January 1916, barely one month before the German hammer-blow would fall.

The German Chief of Staff, Gen Erich von Falkenhayn, was convinced that the heavily entrenched western front could not be broken, and in order to defeat France it was now a matter of breaking her will to fight. This could be done, he reasoned, by killing so many French soldiers that the nation would sue for peace. How then to kill enough Frenchmen to make his plan succeed without killing as many of his own men? His answer was artillery. If he could secretly assemble a huge array of guns and get the French army to stand in front of them he could shell it to death. How to make the French army rally to a particular place? Answer – threaten something that they value above all else, i.e. Verdun.

Thus the operation called 'A Place of Execution' was evolved and, during that same January that de Castelnau was inspecting Verdun, von Falkenhayn added to the already formidable artillery of the 5th Army. Into the narrow Verdun sector were brought over 500 heavy guns: 300 field guns, 150 giant mine throwers, 13 'Big Berthas' (420mm weapons that had been used against Liège) the list went on and on. Three million shells were stockpiled and six new infantry divisions stood by. On 8 February Joffre and the French Council for National Defence met in Paris and agreed that 'a German offensive in the near future was unlikely'. Thirteen days later, on 21 February, the Germans attacked.

WHAT HAPPENED

At 0715 hours on 21 February the German artillery opened fire over a fifteen-mile front and at 1645 hours six infantry divisions advanced on a narrow five-mile corridor on the east bank of the Meuse. They imagined that the advance would be a formality, that all French resistance would have been destroyed by the pounding of some 1,400 guns – a misconception repeated by the British six months later on the Somme. Shattered pillboxes, shapeless trenches and splintered stumps of trees in a moonscape of shellholes met the attackers, but so did French soldiers. In small disjointed actions the *Poilus* fought tenaciously, delaying the German advance so that only the front trench line was occupied before darkness fell.

On 22 February the attack widened. Lt Col. Driant and his men put up a valiant defence in the Bois des Caures (qv). Driant was killed and of his 1,200 men only 100 got out of the wood that day. The French defences began to crumble and on 24 February Joffre sent for a new man to take over RFV – Gen Pétain. His staff rushed to the Hotel Terminus at the Gare du Nord in Paris where the 60-year-old Pétain was spending the night with his mistress. Pétain told them to wait until the morning, a decision that is game, set and match to Drake's insistence on playing bowls when confronted by the Spanish Armada.

On 25 February Fort Douaumont fell without firing a shot. Late that night Pétain arrived and immediately reorganised the defence into four separate command and administrative areas and established the beginnings of the single-road supply system that became known as '*La Voie Sacrée*' ('The Sacred Way'). His positive, confident manner and precise orders steadied the French nerve and on 26 February Joffre concentrated all officers' minds by saying that he would court-martial anyone who ordered his men to withdraw.

In between short breathing spaces the German attacks continued. On 6 March the 5th Army turned its attention to the west (left) bank and attacked Mort Homme but failed to take it that day and 9 April saw what was to be the last all-out offensive by the 5th Army. Pétain continued to exercise firm control and instituted a policy of immediate counter-attacks against what progressively had been 'nibbling' offensives by the Germans. At the same time, however, he pestered Joffre to send him more and more reinforcements, troops that Joffre could not spare, and on 1 May Joffre moved Pétain and replaced him with Nivelle. Nivelle opened the throttle on offensive spirit and although Mort Homme fell to the Germans at the end of May and Fort Vaux on 7 June, the German resolve was weakening. The beginning of the Somme Battle on 1 July drew German reserves away from Verdun and the last German assault took place on 11 July. On 29 August von Falkenhayn was replaced by von Hindenburg and Ludendorff. Between 24 October and 18 December 1916 Gen Nivelle's offensive recaptured Douaumont and Vaux. Just before Christmas 1916 the longest battle of the war – for the French *the* battle – was over.

From 1917 the name Verdun was given to roads and squares throughout the land and on 12 April the small Normandy commune of Allemagne (a name which had become impossible to maintain) was changed to that of the heroic village of Fleury and became Fleury-sur-Orne.

THE BATTLEFIELD TOUR

The thorough student of military history could spend a week walking the battlefields around Verdun without exhausting all the marked footpaths. The less intense visitor can spend two full days following the road signs to places of military interest. The tour we propose does not pretend to be exhaustive. It offers the interested visitor a selection of important and relevant sites that match the commentaries and maps in this book and should lead to an overall understanding of the issues at stake, the sacrifice of the French and the horrendous conditions in which the soldiers fought.

- **Total distance:** 88 miles
- **Total time:** (excluding Verdun city memorials and museums) 8 hours 30 minutes
- **Distance from Calais to start point:** 242 miles
  Motorway Tolls on the Calais-Reims and Reims-Metz sections.
- **Base town:** Verdun
- **Maps:** IGN 3112 ET TOP 25 Forêts de Verdun et du Mort-Homme 1:25,000; IGN Carte de Promenade No 10 Reims-Verdun 1:100,000; Michelin 307 Local Meurthe-et-Moselle, Meuse, Moselle 1:175,000

- **The Route:** The tour begins at the Voie Sacrée Memorial, drives along that road to Verdun past the Liberty Roads Monument, visits the Tourist Office in Verdun and surrounding Memorials, the Victory Memorial, the World Centre for Peace and the Citadel before moving on to the **Right Bank Battlefield** via Faubourg Pavé National Cemetery and Memorials, Fort Vaux, the Lion Monument, the Maginot Monument, the Memorial Museum at Fleury, Douaumont Fort followed by the Ossuary, Cemetery and Memorials and The Trench of Bayonets. The **Left Bank Battlefield** tour visits the

MAP 4: VERDUN: 21 FEBRUARY – 18 DECEMBER 1916

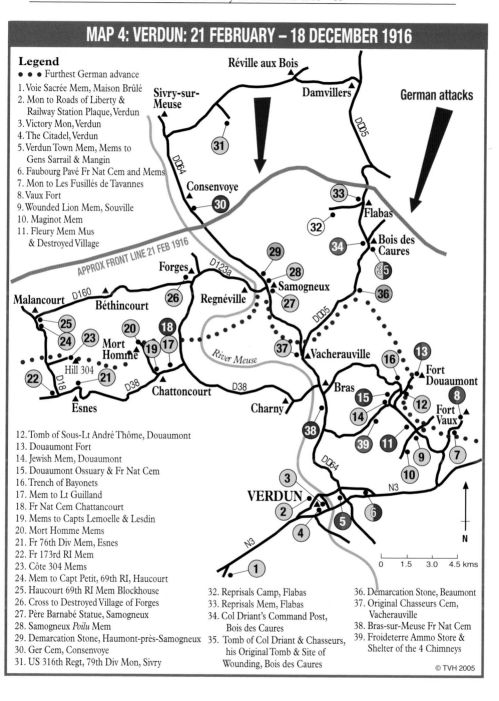

Legend

● ● ● Furthest German advance

1. Voie Sacrée Mem, Maison Brûlé
2. Mon to Roads of Liberty & Railway Station Plaque, Verdun
3. Victory Mon, Verdun
4. The Citadel, Verdun
5. Verdun Town Mem, Mems to Gens Sarrail & Mangin
6. Faubourg Pavé Fr Nat Cem and Mems
7. Mon to Les Fusillés de Tavannes
8. Vaux Fort
9. Wounded Lion Mem, Souville
10. Maginot Mem
11. Fleury Mem Mus & Destroyed Village

Réville aux Bois

Sivry-sur-Meuse

Damvillers

German attacks

Consenvoye

Flabas

Bois des Caures

Forges

Samogneux

Malancourt

Béthincourt

Regnéville

River Meuse

Vacherauville

Fort Douaumont

Mort Homme

Hill 304

Chattoncourt

Bras

Esnes

Charny

Fort Vaux

VERDUN

APPROX FRONT LINE 21 FEB 1916

12. Tomb of Sous-Lt André Thôme, Douaumont
13. Douaumont Fort
14. Jewish Mem, Douaumont
15. Douaumont Ossuary & Fr Nat Cem
16. Trench of Bayonets
17. Mem to Lt Guilland
18. Fr Nat Cem Chattancourt
19. Mems to Capts Lemoelle & Lesdin
20. Mort Homme Mems
21. Fr 76th Div Mem, Esnes
22. Fr 173rd RI Mem
23. Côte 304 Mems
24. Mem to Capt Petit, 69th RI, Haucourt
25. Haucourt 69th RI Mem Blockhouse
26. Cross to Destroyed Village of Forges
27. Père Barnabé Statue, Samogneux
28. Samogneux *Poilu* Mem
29. Demarcation Stone, Haumont-près-Samogneux
30. Ger Cem, Consenvoye
31. US 316th Regt, 79th Div Mon, Sivry

32. Reprisals Camp, Flabas
33. Reprisals Mem, Flabas
34. Col Driant's Command Post, Bois des Caures
35. Tomb of Col Driant & Chasseurs, his Original Tomb & Site of Wounding, Bois des Caures

36. Demarcation Stone, Beaumont
37. Original Chasseurs Cem, Vacherauville
38. Bras-sur-Meuse Fr Nat Cem
39. Froideterre Ammo Store & Shelter of the 4 Chimneys

0   1.5   3.0   4.5 kms

N

© TVH 2005

National Cemetery at Chattancourt, Mort Homme and its Monuments, Côte 304 and its Monuments, Haucourt Memorial and Blockhouse. It returns via the Père Barnabé Memorial, Samogneux War Memorial, Demarcation Stone, German Cemetery, Consenvoye, US Monument at Sivry, Reprisals Camp and Memorial at Flabas, Bois des Caures, and Col Driant Command Post Memorials, Bras National Cemetery, Froideterre and the Four Chimneys Bunker and back to Verdun.

From Calais take the A26 to Reims and then the A4 Autoroute de l'Est. Continue on the A4/E50 Autoroute de l'Est. Take the Voie Sacrée Exit No 30 direction Verdun on the NVS (National Voie Sacrée) 3/N35.

Set your mileometer to zero at the Péage.

N.B. On exiting there is a small **French National Cemetery, Les Souhesmes-Rampont,** to the right. It contains 1,067 French WW1 burials and one Russian. It was created in 1916 with the casualties from the Verdun battles. It also contains seven CWGC WW2 graves, 1 RAF and six RCAF, all of 408 Sqn, killed on 17 April 1943, mostly aged 20 or 21.

Continue on the N35.

N.B. After some 1.4 miles a *Voie Sacrée* **Marker Stone** (see below) is passed on the left. It is in superb condition and worth a photo stop.

Continue to just short of the junction with the N3 and the sign (easy to miss) to the right to the Memorial of the Voie Sacrée.

• *La Voie Sacrée & Memorial, Moulin-Brûlé/2.6 miles/10 minutes/* Map 4/1

You are now travelling along the lifeline to the beleaguered city of Verdun. The fate of the city rested on its ability to resupply the front with reinforcements, munitions and supplies and to bring out the wounded. Railway lines into the city were either cut or unable to bear heavy loads, so only this one road still in French hands leading to the city remained. On 19 February 1916 GHQ created a Commission under Commandant Girard to make good the surface of the road from Bar le Duc. Some 8,200 engineers and men of the *Regulatrice Routière* worked on the surface shovelling 900,000 tons of cobblestones into place. Then the movement of motorised vehicles (all that was permitted to use the road) was regulated. Speed was limited to 15-20kph and broken down vehicles had to be pushed into the ditch. During the battle some 6,000 vehicles made the circular trip transporting, each week, 90,000 men and 50,000 tons of materiel, clocking up a total of 1million kms. The system was called 'Noria', after the continuous North African water wheel. Drivers put in eighteen hour days, resting at the wheel over the intense ten-day period of the height of the battle. The various groups, each with their own emblem (swan, cock, club etc.) developed an incredible *esprit de corps* and pride in their gruelling work. The name *Voie Sacrée* was coined by the writer Maurice Barrès in April 1916.

Uphill to the right, with a parking area in front, is the Memorial, inaugurated in 1967 by Gen Boucaud, Président de la Féderation Nationale du Train, which pays tribute to the drivers of the 'Train' (Army Service Corps) of the *Voie Sacrée*. The fine cream stone monument bears superb *bas-reliefs* of scenes along the Sacred Way by the sculptor Barrois.

Continue towards Verdun on the N3.

On the way alternate 1944 Liberty Highway and *Voie Sacrée* Marker Stones are passed on the left.
Continue following signs to Verdun Centre Ville over the railway to the monument on the left. Stop on the right.

• Railway Station and Monument to the Roads of Liberty/8.1 miles/ 5 minutes/Map 4/2

The Railway Station is behind the monument. On it is a **Plaque** which commemorates the use of the station (built by Eiffel in 1868) which served as a hospital during the war and from which thousands of wounded were evacuated between 1915 and 1916. From it on 10 November 1920 the train carrying the Unknown Warrior (qv) left on its journey to Paris where the body was placed beneath the Arc de Triomphe.

In 1922 Raymond Poincaré inaugurated the series of Marker Stones which mark each kilometre of the *Voie Sacrée* and which start in Bar-le-Duc. Similar to the normal Demarcation Stones they are surmounted by a green French *casque* with a laurel wreath. The final stone is here in Verdun itself and is incorporated in the Monument to Liberty in which there is also a marker stone for the 1944 Liberty Highway.

Continue following signs to Verdun Centre. Then follow the tourist information signs, through the town and over the River Meuse to the Tourist Office in the Place de la Nation near the Chaussée Gate and park.

•Verdun Tourist Office/Memorials/9 miles/10 minutes/Map 4/5

The Verdun battlefield is a paradise for enthusiasts of fortifications and for ramblers. There are a dozen different, well-signed walking routes which cover many areas of the battlefield, the forts, casemates, batteries, trench lines, regimental memorials etc. which pepper the battlefield and which are far too numerous to be covered on the following driving tour. These route plans can be obtained at the Fleury Memorial Museum (see below).

[**N.B.** It is recommended that you buy the makings of a picnic in the town before you take off for the battlefields if you don't want to use time in coming back to Verdun for lunch, as apart from the Auberge des Pélerins Café at Douaumont, there are no refreshment facilities on the Right Bank tour. Don't forget a bag of the famous *dragées* for which Verdun is famous. Also fill up with petrol in the town.]

In recent years the main historic sites have been tidied up, grass cut, good parking areas built, reception areas cleaned and modernised, helpful and informative signing installed so that there is now an impression of good maintenance. However in the process, and during the change of emphasis from battlefield commemoration to promotion of Verdun as a City of Peace, one gets the impression that some of the 'soul' and tangible emotional links with the events of '14-'18 have been lost.

Available in the tourist office is a good selection of guide and history books, many translated into English or by English authors, videos, postcards etc. During your visit check the opening times of the Citadel, the museums and forts on this itinerary, which vary bewilderingly from season to season and may well differ from those printed below which were correct at time of going to press. **It is essential to pick up a town plan in order to locate the memorials and museums in the town.** You can also

Monument to the Voie Sacrée.

Voie Sacrée Marker Stone.

The Five Defenders of Verdun.

The Victory Monument.

purchase an entrance Pass here to various museums and monuments in and around the city which gives you a 20% reduction.
Open: times change according to season but mostly from 0900-1200 and 1400-1700, Mon-Sat. Off-season Sun and holidays 1000-1300. High season 0830-1830. Tel: + (0)3 29 86 14 18. Fax: + (0)3 29 84 22 42.

Inaugurated in 1993 a spectacular *son et lumière* evocation of the battle, called *'Des Flammes... à la lumière'* (From the flames to the light), takes place in the old Quarry at Haudainville each Friday and Saturday evenings from 13 June-26 July in which 300 French and foreign (including German) actors, accompanied by projected images, play out the suffering and the courage of the men of 1916 and the aspirations towards peace. Reservation in advance recommended. Tel: + (0)3 29 84 50 00.

Immediately outside the office is a **Statue of Gen Sarrail** who, while commanding the French 3rd Army defending Verdun in 1914, ignored Joffre's instructions to withdraw and thereby saved the town. Across the road are the *bas-relief* statues of five soldiers, making a wall with their bodies to defend Verdun, symbolising the cry, *'Ils ne passeront pas!'* This is the **Town Memorial** sculpted by Grange and beside it is a **Memorial Tablet to Gen Mangin**. Across the river is the **Chaussée Gate**, built in the fifteenth century and which is said to have been the inspiration for the badge of the US Corps of Engineers. To its right, past the Gendarmerie and by the large car park is a large statue, **La Défense**, based on a model by Rodin, showing a winged figure of France supporting a naked soldier. The Quay along this bank of the Meuse is known as the **Quai de Londres** in gratitude to the London Committee which 'adopted' Verdun after the war, as a **Plaque** on the wall at the end of the quay to the left records: bringing together 'the heart of the British Empire' and the centre of the French fighting. Along it are many bars and snack bars whose tables in the summer months spill out onto the quay making it a very pleasant lunch stop.

Using the Tourist Office map, make your way to the memorials and museums described below.

• The Victory Monument/Map 4/3
Cut into the old wall of the town is a steep flight of seventy-three steps flanked by a pair of field guns captured on the Russian front. At the top is a 90ft high column surmounted by a soldierly knight, inaugurated on 23 June 1929. Raymond Poincaré, President of the Republic from 1913-1920, is intimately associated with the Department of the Meuse. He was born in Bar-le-Duc where he started his political career and is buried there. He was highly emotionally involved with the Battle of Verdun and frequently visited the battlefield. His speech of 14 September 1916 was taken as the basis of the renovation of Verdun and its text is inscribed on the monument. At the base of the column is a small crypt in which is kept the Golden Book of the Medals of Verdun, France, America and Germany. The monument is the focal point for the annual June commemorations which are always attended by very important personalities. From 1920-1939 it was Pétain and from 1945 to 1952 military personages such as de Gaulle and de Lattre. From 1953 politicians have been the guests of honour and on each tenth anniversary it is the President of the Republic: Coty, de Gaulle, Giscard d'Estaing, Mitterand and Chirac. In 1984 there was an historic meeting of reconciliation here between Pres Mitterand and Chancellor Kohl. It is open from Easter-11 November. 0900-1200 and 1400-1800.

• The Cathedral

Between the two world wars when the crypt was being restored the sculptor, le Bourgeois, created a series of images of the battles, including a heart-breaking depiction of a blind-folded soldier about to be executed.

• The World Centre for Peace, Liberties and Human Rights

This was created in the old Episcopal Palace next to the Cathedral and officially inaugurated by Prime Minister Edouard Balladur on 30 June 1994. There are permanent exhibitions on the '14-'18 War and 'From War to Peace', using many modern audio-visual techniques, as well as changing temporary exhibitions. The WW1 section contains some fascinating ephemera and artefacts which are imaginatively presented and in which technology does not overwhelm humanity. In the vestibule is a powerful sculpture by Brian Mercer inspired by Wilfred Owen's poem *Dulce et Decorum Est*.
Open: 1 February-31 May: every day from 0930-1200 and 1400-1800; 1 June-15 October 0930-1900; 16 October-20 December 0930-1200 and 1400-1800.
Tel: + (0)3 29 86 55 00. Fax: + (0)3 29 86 15 14. Website: www.centremondialpaix.asso.fr
There is free parking in the courtyard.

• The Town Hall

In 1927 a small museum was created in the Town Hall showing the twenty-six decorations received by the town – the most-decorated in France – with standards, presentations by Allied countries, private possessions of Maginot and other dignitaries, '*Livres d'Or*' containing the names of the 200,000 French and American soldiers who were killed in the battles for Verdun etc. Opened on days of official ceremonies or by appointment. Tel: + (0)3 29 86 18 39.

• The Citadel/Map 4/4

Building of this fortress began in 1624 and fifty years later Vauban added to it. In the late-nineteenth century nearly five miles of underground passages were built and during the First World War it had its own commander and artillery defences, a chapel, a baker (producing 28,000 rations of bread per day), a hospital etc. Over 10,000 people – military and civilian – sheltered here during the war and there was even the birth of a baby girl, christened 'France'. Today it houses a museum and offers both a film show and a slide presentation relating to life in the Citadel and the battles. It was in the Citadel that the French Unknown Soldier was chosen in the presence of André Maginot, and the scene is re-created in the room where it took place. It is advisable to wear a jacket inside as the temperature is always cold. 'Claustrophobics' are warned not to enter! A '*petit train*' departs every five minutes and takes the visitor through fifteen successive galleries with commentaries in five different languages. Allow at least thirty minutes. Inside the main entrance there are WCs, book/souvenir stall and some fascinating 1914 shop windows.

   Nearby on the 'Carrefour des Maréchaux' are sixteen large statues of famous French Marshals and Generals of the Napoleonic, 1870 and First World War periods.
Open: every day at least from 0930-1200 and 1400-1700. No lunchtime closing from

April to end September when it also opens half an hour earlier and closes up to an hour later. Tel: + (0)3 29 86 14 18. Entrance fee payable.
Drive out of Verdun on the N3 following signs to Toutes Directions, Champs de Batailles and then Douaumont and Vaux. Just before leaving the outskirts of Verdun there is a military cemetery on the left flying the Tricolore.

• *Faubourg Pavé National Military Cemetery & Memorials/9.9 miles/ 10 minutes/Map 4/6*

To the left of the cemetery is the Aviators' Memorial. It commemorates pre-war pioneers who were killed over Verdun as well as WW1 and WW2 pilots. In front of the cemetery is a circle of the famous rapid fire **French 75mm guns** and to the right a dramatic **Statue with plaques to those executed by the Germans** in both wars. This is by Léon Cuvelle and is a stone replica of the bronze statue he created to commemorate the prisoners of the Camps de Représailles at Flabas where he was imprisoned in 1917 (qv). There are some 5,000 burials here under somewhat stark rows of crosses unrelieved by flower beds. Below the cross in the centre are seven Unknown Warriors from among whom the eighth was chosen to lie under the Arc de Triomphe in Paris to symbolise the 1,700,000 Frenchmen who fell in the war. The traffic in the Champs Elysées leading to the Arc is stopped every evening to allow a procession to the grave of the Unknown Soldier where the Eternal Flame is rekindled. Surely we could do something similar in London?

Near the side entrance to the cemetery is a **CWGC Plot** with seven WW2 CWGC graves. Three are of the RAF, four of the RCAF.

Continue, following signs to Longwy and Metz then uphill to the battlefields and then left signed to Fort Vaux on the D913. Continue to the junction with the D913a signed to Fort Vaux to the right and turn.

N.B. To the left after turning is the entrance to the Tavannes Tunnel. This tunnel served as a shelter, munitions dump and first aid post during the battle and on the night of 4-5 September 1916 an explosion of a store of grenades caused 500 deaths of the 24th and 18th RI. Here too is the shelter of the Tunnel Battery built in 1888 to hold three huge guns. The actual Fort of Tavannes was constructed in 1874-6 and when Vaux and other more modern forts were built it was relegated to a second-line fortification.

Continue to a sign to the right of a clearing in the trees down a steep path.

• *Monument to Les Fusillés de Tavannes/13.8 miles/10 minutes/Map 4/7*

This Memorial commemorates sixteen members of the French Resistance who were brought here and shot by the Germans in 1944.

Continue and park at Fort Vaux

• *Fort Vaux/15 miles/30 minutes/Map 4/8*

Building work began here in 1881 and the basic fort was completed in three years, but around the turn of the century it was strengthened with 7ft of steel-reinforced concrete laid on top of a 5ft thick shock barrier of sand. This was then covered with a thick layer of earth. The fort, surrounded by a moat, had its own water reservoir, kitchen and

Entrance to the Citadel.

Léon Cuvelle's Statue to 'Victims of German Barbarism', Faubourg Pavé Cemetery.

The Wounded Lion of Souville.

Vaux Fort.

The Maginot Memorial.

dormitories for a garrison of 250 men. The fort did not come under direct attack until March 1916, but during a bombardment by 420mm Big Bertha artillery in February the one-ton shells damaged the water reservoir, filled the moat with debris and destroyed the one 75mm gun turret.

During May the garrison in the fort grew to 670 men, made up by stragglers from the battlefield and by June 2,000 shells per hour were falling on and around it. The Germans occupied the upper corridors, driving the defenders into the lower levels. There cordite fumes and concrete dust created by the explosions exacerbated the *Poilus'* thirst brought on by heat and lack of water. On 1 June water was down to 1 litre per man per day, on 4 June to ¹/₂ litre and on 5 June to zero. Maj Raynal, the fort commander, sent out his last message by pigeon on 4 June and on 7 June at 0350 hours the fort surrendered. The Germans honoured the defenders and the German Crown Prince asked to meet Maj Raynal.

There is a well-stocked book and souvenir shop and a guided, or sometimes self-guided (with an English script), tour around the interior of the fort, which takes about half an hour. There is an entrance fee. It is always chilly and damp inside – take a sweater. **Open:** very variable according to season. Closed January & February, then 0930-1200 and 1400-1700. No lunchtime closing May to end August and open until 1830.

On the exterior of the fort is a plaque to the brave pigeon who flew from the fort to Verdun with Maj Raynal's last message, despite being gassed. He died after delivering his message and was decorated for his gallantry. There is a stuffed pigeon inside the fort to represent him.

Walk to the top of the fort.
Look for the distinctive finger shape of the Douaumont Ossuary which is clearly visible to the north-west.
Return to the junction and turn right following signs to Fleury and Memorial Museum. Continue to the crossroads where there is a recumbent stone lion on the left.

• The Wounded Lion of Souville Monument/17.9 miles/5 minutes/ Map 4/9

The crossroads is called Chapelle Sainte-Fine and marks the site of a destroyed Chapel as well as the closest point to Verdun reached by the Germans (on 23 June 1916) who were attacking from your right.
Turn left and continue to the monument on the left.

• Maginot Memorial/18.3 miles/5 minutes/Map 4/10

André Maginot, like Lt Col. Driant (qv), was a local Deputy and enlisted at the outbreak of war. On 9 November 1914 Sgt Maginot was wounded and disabled. In 1916 he returned to Parliament and became Minister for War when, influenced by the fact that the fortress of Verdun had proven invincible, he supported the building of a defensive wall of forts to guard against a future war. His efforts in raising government money to build the system caused it to be named 'The Maginot Line'. The memorial was erected by his friends and consists of a shield in front of which is a bronze group of soldiers sculpted by Gaston Broquet. The memorial was pictured on fund-raising posters just before the Second World War.

Turn round, return to the crossroads, turn left and continue to the museum 200 yards further on and park in the car park.

• The Fleury Memorial Museum/19.1 miles/45 minutes/Map 4/11

In front of the museum, which was opened in 1967, is an array of artillery and a number of shells including a German 420mm giant.

At the museum boutique inside the entrance it is advisable to buy the English 'Souvenir Guidebook' which guides the visitor around the exhibits describing each display in turn including continuous video displays and timed film shows. Here twelve walking tour leaflets (qv) may be picked up (free of charge). In the museum there is a large wall map which, at regular intervals, sets out to explain the battle with multi-lingual commentary, signs and coloured lights. In the centre of the floor is a realistic reproduction of a battlefield, complete with debris, and overhead – and often overlooked – are a reconstructed, full-size Nieuport Bébé and a Fokker Elli. There are further displays on the ground floor. There are toilets. Entrance fee payable.

Open: Every day from 15 March-15 September 0900-1800. From 16 September-14 March 0900-1200 and 1400-1700. Closed January. Tel: + (0)3 29 84 35 34.

A walk to the site of the **village of Fleury**, where small markers indicate where buildings once stood, is likely to take up to twenty minutes there and back, but it is a telling witness to the absolute destruction that took place here in 1916. At the end of the trail is a Memorial Chapel. The woods tend to attract mosquitos, so take precautions.

Return to your car and continue to the crossroads. Turn right along the edge of the National Cemetery, signed to Fort Douaumont. Continue to the recumbent statue on the right.

• Tomb of Sous-Lieutenant André Thome/20.4 miles/5 minutes/Map 4/12

Like Maginot and Driant, Thome was a local Deputy who enlisted in the 6th Dragoons. He was killed at Verdun on 10 March 1916 at the age of thirty-six. He was awarded the *Légion d'Honneur* and the *Croix de Guerre* and was known as the 'Soldier of the Right'.

Continue on the D913D to the car park at Fort Douaumont.

• Fort Douaumont/21.2 miles/30 minutes/Map 4/13

If you didn't climb on top of Fort Vaux, you should certainly climb onto Douaumont. You may be able to make out Fort Vaux (look for the *Tricolore* to the south-east) and the Fleury museum (to the south-west) and by using Map 4 you can now get a good idea of the size and shape of the battlefield.

The fort was built in 1885 and like Vaux was improved up to 1914. Following the failure of the Belgian forts to stop the German invasion, Douaumont was stripped of its garrison, though its main guns remained. On 25 February 1916, four days after the battle opened, a patrol of the 24th Brandenburgers entered the fort unopposed and captured it together with its garrison of about a dozen. Just how this happened is not clear. Some accounts say that the garrision was asleep, but that seems unlikely at 1600 hours in the middle of a battle. Other reports say that the Germans had disguised themselves in red uniforms as French Zouaves.

Fighting around the fort continued and at the end of May the French got into the northern part but were driven out. It was not until Gen Mangin's offensive of 24 October that the fort was recaptured and held despite strong German counter-attacks. The workings of the fort's 75mm and 155mm gun platforms can be seen and are familiar to those who have visited the Maginot Line. (The conference that led to the building of the Maginot Line was held in Verdun after the war.) On 8 May 1917 a grenade store inside the fort exploded and 679 German soldiers were killed and are buried in the fort in a walled gallery where today there is a memorial chapel.

There is a souvenir bookshop in the fort and a tour, often self-guided like Vaux, which can also be chilly, even in mid-summer. Entrance fee payable.

Open: similar times to Vaux. Tel: + (0)3 29 84 18 85.

Return to the Douaumont National Cemetery, drive along the bottom of the Cemetery and turn right.

On the left is passed the **Jewish Monument** (qv) (Map 4/14).

Park in the car park behind the Ossuary building.

• *Douaumont Ossuary & National Cemetery/22.7 miles/45 minutes/ Map 4/15*

This dramatic and original building, with its *Art Deco* overtones, immediately demands the visitor's attention and reaction. Visible through small windows at ground level are the bones of 130,000 French and German soldiers whose remains were collected from around the battlefield. The ossuary, or mass grave, was begun in 1919 and transferred to the monument in 1927. The building was the idea of Monseigneur Ginistry, Bishop of Verdun, who raised money (some of it from the United States) for its construction. The foundation stone was laid in 1920 and the Memorial was officially inaugurated on 7 April 1932. Below and in front of the building is the National Cemetery in which are buried 15,000 identified French soldiers, and the comfortable conformity and familiarity of the white crosses and red roses of the cemetery contrast with the uneasiness that most Anglo-Saxons feel when confronted by the Ossuary.

On the 450ft long façade are the names and coats of arms of the towns that contributed to the building and inside is a nave with eighteen alcoves, each corresponding to sectors of the battlefield where bones were found. Individual soldiers are commemorated on panels paid for by the families. In the centre of the building, opposite the entrance, is the Chapel, with four small SGWs commemorating sacrifice, stretcher-bearers and field medical services. At one end of the nave is a vault in which a flame of remembrance is lit when services are held.

Above it is a 150ft high tower which can be climbed for a small charge and on top of which is a lantern and a victory bell. The whole mixture of visible bones, religious symbolism and commercial souvenirs, combined with the powerful architecture of the memorial, can disconcert the visitor. Perhaps that is a more appropriate reaction than a feeling of wellbeing, bearing in mind what took place here. It is said that if all the soldiers who were killed at Verdun tried to stand up there would not be room enough here for them to do so.

Below (and approached from the car park at the rear) is a bookshop, and a comfortable theatre in which a most effective and moving 20-minute film, describing the life of the French soldier at Verdun and making a convincing plea for peace, can be

The Fleury Memorial Museum.

*The Ossuary,
Douaumont.*

*Tomb of S/Lt
André Thome,
Douaumont.*

Cupola on Fort Douaumont.

*Muslim and Christian Graves,
Douaumont Cemetery.*

seen. There is an entrance fee. There are WCs in the car park.
Open: every day from 1 May-4 September from 0900-1830. Winter months 0900-1200 and 1400-1700, other months variable! Tel: + (0)3 29 84 54 81.

Four different religions were planned to be commemorated here: Catholic, Muslim, Jewish and Protestant. The main building is obviously Catholic, the **Jewish Memorial** to the left of the main building was not inaugurated until 1938 when anti-semitism was rising in France. It is in the form of a 31m long wall on which the tables of the law are engraved. During WW2 it had to be protected by a wooden fence which hid it from view. The small nearby **Muslim Memorial** was built only in 1959 and from time to time there are plans to make a more important memorial. There is still no Protestant memorial.

Return to your car and follow signs to the left to 'Tranchée des Baionettes', passing local and regimental monuments on the way and the Abri des Pélerins *on the right.*

This café which also used to serve as a first aid post for pilgrims is closed on Mondays and for the winter from 15 November. Lunch 1200-1500. Closes at 1900. Tel: + (0)3 29 85 50 58.

• *The Trench of Bayonets/23.3 miles/10 minutes/Map 4/16*

This memorial commemorates an action of 23 June 1916 when two battalions of the 137th Infantry Regiment were buried alive in their trenches by German artillery fire. The story, one of the great French myths of the war, has it that a number of the *Poilus*, who were standing in their trench with fixed bayonets waiting to go over the top, died as they stood there and when the fighting stopped a row of bayonets remained visible above the filled-in trench. The mass grave was completed by the Germans and in 1919 Col Collet of the 137th erected a small wooden monument over the row of what were actually projecting rifles – rather than the bayonets of the legend. On 3 August 1920 Gen Bataille actually reported that exhumations had been made at the site and seven bodies were found, of which four were identified – these were reburied in a special row in the Fleury cemetery. The Unknowns were reburied at the site. None of the bodies was standing upright! George Rand, a wealthy American, hearing of the story which

The line of Bayonets.

Exterior of the Trench of Bayonets.

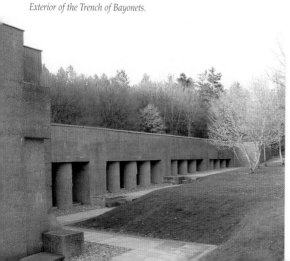

was taken up with the enthusiasm by the press, hungry for heroes, funded the building of the present monument (inaugurated on 8 December 1920 by President Millerand). The simple, massive 'pharaonic' style of the design by André Ventre of Paris emphasises the significance of what is commemorated rather than the self-importance of the architecture. The bayonets are the object of souvenir hunters and may or not be in evidence.

Continue downhill to Bras-sur-Meuse and at the T junction turn right on the D964 and then left on the D115 direction Charny, crossing the Canal and then the River Meuse to **the left bank**. *Continue through Charny and turn right on the D38 signed to Marre. Continue through Marre following signs to Mort Homme on the D38 to Chattancourt and then turn sharp right uphill on a very rough track, bordered by a glorious array of wild flowers in the summer, to the Cimetière Nationale.*

• Lt Guilland Memorial/French National Cemetery, Chattancourt/ 32.4 miles/10 minutes/Map 4/17/18

On the path to the cemetery is a **Memorial to Lt Pierre Guilland**, age 25 of the 38th RA, an aviation observer of the Moroccan Division, Squadron C34, who was killed in aerial combat with 3 enemy planes when flying low to protect an infantry attack at Mort Homme on 20 August 1917. This well-maintained monument commemorates what was obviously a very special man, decorated with the *Légion d'Honneur* and the *Croix de Guerre et Palme*. The memorial bears his citation by Gen Guillaumont.

The cemetery contains 1,699 WW1 burials from the nearby fighting, concentrated here between 1920 and 1925 and has a magnificent view over the valley below. (Standing with one's back to the gate the tip of the Douaumont Ossuary can be seen at 11 o'clock.) It also contains twenty-seven burials from WW2. It was re-landscaped in 1987.

Return to the main road, continue through Chattancourt and turn right on the D38b signed to Mort Homme.

N.B. To the right are then passed Memorials to **Capt Lemoelle** (in the form of a fountain) who gloriously fell at the head of his company on 10 March 1916 attacking the Bois des Corbeaux crying *'En Avant'* and **Capt R. Lesdin** (in the form of an obelisk) of the 36th RI, 22 April 1916 (**Map 4/19**).

Continue to the summit of Mort-Homme.

• Mort Homme/Monuments/34.1 miles/15 minutes/Map 4/20

The German attack here began on 6 March 1916. In three days the enemy had arrived at the foot of this famous hill and it took them more than a month to reach the summit and there they were isolated. On 20 August 1917 the 31st DI retook the position and pushed the front back to the stream at Forges. On the right is a **Memorial to the 40th Division** and beside it a **wooden cross** erected in 1984 to Franco-German Friendship through the tombs. The dramatic **Mort Homme Monument** which now crowns the summit of the hill (from which it lost twelve metres in the combat) recalls the events of March 1916. It is in the form of a corpse standing by his tomb. In his right hand he holds his shroud, in his left a standard. There are several plaques on the base below the legend commemorating the dead of the 69th Division, *'Ils n'ont pas passé'* [They did not pass]. On the reverse the horrific individual losses of the Regiments engaged 12 April-13 May 1916 are listed: 251st RI – 930, 254th RI – 767, 267th RI – 759, 287th RI – 1,040, 306th RI – 513, 332nd RI – 537, Arty & Eng – 202. To the right is an **Information Panel** to mark the entrance to the Mort Homme Tunnel built by the Germans who called it the **Gallwitz Tunnel**. A French veteran recalls how he and his comrades found '600 nervous men caught in a trap' here in the sophisticated shelter that had ventilation, lighting and fresh water.

Return to Chattancourt and turn right on the D38. Continue to Esnes.

The **Local War Memorial** was constructed from the stones of the old ruined church and on it is a *bas-relief* demonstrating the difficulties of reconstructing the villages. A peasant is shown sowing seeds on a tomb.

Continue to the local cemetery on the right.

N.B. Just past the cemetery are **Memorials** to the **76th Division** and a **1940 Memorial** to the **3rd** and **23rd RIC** and **Capt Paul Cresson**, *Croix de Guerre* (**Map 4/21**).

Continue to the turning to the D18 signed to Côte 304.

[**N.B.** By continuing some 500 metres along the road the **French National Cemetery, Esnes-en-Argonne** would be reached. There are 6,661 WW1 burials in the cemetery, of which 3,000 are in two ossuaries. The concentrations from the surrounding battlefields were made between 1920 and 1925. More bodies were moved here in 1982 and the cemetery was re-landscaped in 1987.]

Turn right on the D18.

N.B. At the turning on the left is a **WW1/WW2 Memorial** to the **173rd RI** (**Map 4/22**).

Continue to the junction with the D18A and turn right.

N.B. In the woods to the left after some 400 metres is a path leading to the isolated **Tomb of J. Delépine**.

Continue to the monument on the crest.

• Côte 304/Monuments/39.9 miles/10 minutes/Map 4/23

When the Germans' first assault on Mort-Homme failed they turned further west and flung themselves against this hill known as '304'. The first attacks of 20 March and 9 April 1916 failed but at the beginning of May after a fearsome bombardment the Germans managed to get a grasp on the northern slopes. They did not manage to occupy the very summit until 29 June 1917 and on 24 August a powerful French counter-attack retook the hill. During this fierce combat the village of Esnes was totally destroyed.

In a clearing, approached by a long avenue of black pines on the summit of the hill, is a great truncated obelisk on which is a cross. It was inaugurated on 7 June 1934 and commemorates the 10,000 heroic dead whose blood impregnated this land and whose units are recorded round the memorial. It was erected by subscription on the initiative of the veterans whose Président d'Honneur was Maréchal Pétain.

To the left is the **Tomb of S/Lt Georges Fabre**, 3rd Mixte Regt Zouaves Tirailleurs, *Légion d'Honneur, Croix de Guerre*, 18 May 1916, age 40, erected by his wife and daughter, Hélène. A sign to the right leads to the **Memorial to Joseph Girard**, 1940.

Return to the D18, turn right and continue through the site of the ancient village of Haucourt.

The dramatic Mort Homme Monument.

ILS N'ONT PAS PASSE

AUX MORTS DE L'AGS DIVISION

The Côte 304 Monument.

1916

11'	45'
39'	123'
153'	126'
17'	38'
18'	55'
152	64'

DIVISIONS
D'INFANTERIE

UNITES RATTACHEES

A LA MEMOIRE
DU S/LIEUTENANT GEORGES FABRE
MIXTE REGT. ZOUAVES TIRAILLEURS
LEGION D'HONNEUR CROIX DE GUERRE
TOMBÉ A LA COTE 304 LE 18 MAI 1916
A L'AGE DE 40 ANS
SOUVENIR
DE SA FEMME MME GEORGES FABRE
ET DE SA FILLE MELLE HELENE FABRE

Tomb of S/Lt Georges Fabre, Côte 304.

N.B. At 43.3 miles there is a neglected **Memorial to Capt Maurice Petit** of the 69th RI, age 21, 5 April 1916, St Cyrien, *Croix du Drapeau, Croix de Guerre, Légion d'Honneur*, in the bank to the right (Map 4/24).

Continue to Malancourt-Haucourt. On the right is

• Haucourt 69th RI Memorial/Blockhouse/43.4 miles/5 minutes/ Map 4/25

On the ruins of a blockhouse (l'Abri de Malancourt) surmounted by a cross and some artefacts (helmet, shell etc.) is the **Memorial to six Coys of the 69th RI** who entirely disappeared between 30 March and 5 April 1916 in the defence of the villages of Malancourt and Haucourt and to the **79th US Division** fallen in the same place in September 1918. Beside it a plaque to the 69th who ended the war with six citations and the colours of the *Médaille Militaire*. During the battle half of the men were reduced to fighting with only spades and picks as their rifles, bayonets and machine guns had been destroyed in the attack.

Continue to Malancourt.

[**N.B.** At the junction with the D160 the American Memorial at Montfaucon and Cemetery at Romagne are signed to the left. These are approached from the A4 in the Meuse-Argonne Tour below.]

The village was taken by the Germans on 31 March 1916 during their attack on Côte 304 and was not retaken until the American offensive of September 1918. It was rebuilt on its original site.

Turn right past the church in Malancourt on the D160 and continue through the ancient village of Béthincourt to the existing village.

Haucourt Memorial Blockhouse.

Béthincourt was at the centre of operations on the Left Bank. The French offensive of August 1917 brought the front to the south of the village when all the houses were obliterated by the bombardment. The modern village was reconstructed some 400m to the east and is surrounded by the Forest of Mort Homme. In the village square is the imposing **Local Memorial** on the left. By its side on an octagonal base is the bell of the old church, found in the ruins. It is pierced by two bullet holes.

Continue on the D160 to the junction at the site of the ancient village of Forges just before a bridge to the right.

The destroyed village was once marked by **four crosses** which are almost impossible to locate today. One, however, may be seen over the road to the left here (**Map 4/26**).

Bear right over the bridge and then left on the D123 towards Forges-sur-Meuse and then right on the D123A before the village.

The forest around Forges was occupied by the Germans and the village was taken on the first day of the assault. The ruins were retaken by the Americans in September 1918 and after the war the village was rebuilt nearer to the Meuse.

Continue through Regnéville, direction Samogneux, over the river and canal on the D123A to the T junction at Samogneux. Turn left and stop immediately. Behind you is the

• *Père Barnabé Statue/51.7 miles/5 minutes/Map 4/27*

The **Statue of Père Barnabé**, an old peasant leaning on his stick, symbolises the refugees of the Meuse. Behind him is a sign, 'Here was Samogneux'. The statue was 'due to the generosity of Mrs Horace Gray. After the work by Henri Frémont.' Mrs Gray, a wealthy American, was so moved by the book *Père Barnabé* which told of the courage of the villagers, by Henri Frémont a Verdun publisher, that she had it translated and distributed in America. She was able to raise 230,000 francs in less than five years which she sent to M. Frémont and agreed with him that it could go towards the rebuilding of Samogneux, in particular the bridge.

The village was occupied by the Germans on 24 February 1916 and retaken on 21 August 1917.

Continue a short distance along the D964 to the pull-in on the right and stop. Walk up the grassy slope.

• *Samogneux War Memorial Poilu/51.8 miles/10 minutes/Map 4/28*

At the top is the ancient ruined village cemetery. In it is the most beautiful statue of a young *Poilu* complete with his rifle and gas mask. It was erected thanks to Mrs Gray of Boston, 'benefactor of Samogneux' and to Mr Henri Frémont, author of *Père Barnabé*, 1933. The sculptor was Gaston Broquet. There is also a 1939-1945 plaque on the base of the memorial.

Continue to a parking area and picnic site on the right and pull in.

• *Demarcation Stone/52.1 miles/5 minutes/Map 4/29*

There is a sign to the right here to Haumont-près-Samogneux Destroyed Village.

Continue parallel to the River Meuse on the left to a sign on the right to

• *German Cemetery, Consenvoye/54.3 miles/10 minutes/Map 4/30*

Here lie 11,148 German soldiers under black crosses interspersed with the occasional Jewish headstone in this cemetery completely devoid of colour apart from the red stone entrance gate and wall.

Continue to Sivry and turn right in the village on the C1 signed to US Monument. Continue along the winding road uphill, following signs to La Grande Montagne and Monument to the US 316th Inf Regt to a track to the right at the top and then right again along an avenue of fir trees.

In the springtime you will be driving through blossoming thorn bushes and fruit trees – a delightful route.

• *US 316th Regiment, 79th Division Monument, Sivry/60.3 miles/ 10 minutes/Map 4/31*

The gracious cream stone monument is surrounded by a yew hedge and stands in a commanding position with spectacular 360° views. On the skyline over the Valley of the Meuse a tall wireless mast with flashing lights can be seen and just to its right amongst woods is the tower of the US Monument at Montfaucon. The Monument here was erected in 1928 and around it is written the Divisional history and battle honours – Troyon, Montfaucon, Sector 304 and this site, La Grande Montagne. Broadly speaking the heights that you see beyond the D964 and across the Meuse were taken by the 79th on 26 September 1918, the opening day of the Meuse-Argonne Offensive (see Map 13 and note the position of the D964 road on Maps 4 and 13). During October the Americans prepared for a major offensive against German positions here, to begin on 1 November. It was to be their last of the war. The 5th Division forced crossings over the Meuse on 6 November (see Meuse-Argonne Tour, Extra Visit, page 314) and by the Armistice of 11 November the 79th Division had cleared this hill. During the last eleven days of fighting the twelve American divisions involved had had over 18,000 casualties. The Divisional emblem is the Cross of Lorraine.

The next stop is near the village of Flabas and the most direct way of reaching it is to return to the small metalled road from Sivry and turn right. At the next junction fork right on the D102D to Damvillers and take the D65[905] to the junction right with the D125 signed to Moirey. Turn right and continue to Flabas. [The mileages from now assume that that is your route. If for any reason the small road looks difficult to negotiate, you can return to the D964, turn left and then left again on the D19 to Damvillers, then right on the D65 to Moirey and from there take the D125 at the fork (the left fork is signed to Verdun) to Flabas.] Drive past the church and through the village past a small chapel on the left along a track which can be muddy when wet. Bear left towards a group of firs and stop at the nearest point on the track to them. The monument is in the group of firs to your right. When walking to it you must take care not to damage any crops in the field.

• *Reprisals Camp, Flabas/71.7 miles/10 minutes/Map 4/32*

In the group of seven fir trees is a small stone with the inscription *Ici furent des Camps de Représailles 1917* (Here were Reprisal Camps, 1917). Behind it is a large **Information Panel** erected by young German firemen in a spirit of reconciliation on 18 July 2001. It

Statue of Père Barnabé, Samogneux.

The red stone entrance, German Cemetery, Consenvoye.

The fine **Poilu** *Memorial, Samogneux.*

records the appalling details of life in the Reprisal Camp here. On 21 December 1916 the Germans, with the backing of the US Ambassador, demanded that the French should keep to the recognised rules of behaviour in regard to prisoners of war, in particular to the rule that prisoners should not be kept within 30kms of the front line. They gave an ultimatum which expired on 15 January 1917 and when this was not observed they hastily built POW camps near the firing zone like the one that existed here. Its 50 x 30 metres circumference was enclosed by barbed wire and 500 French prisoners were crammed into the space. It contained one small hut, only big enough for 200 prisoners to huddle in for warmth in the cold winter nights. At daybreak the prisoners were marched to labour camps which were under French fire, mainly to repair roads for bringing up supplies, notably at Samogneux and in the Bois des Caures. Food and drink were totally inadequate and to add to the misery of the prisoners they were regularly beaten with truncheons by a sadistic Feldwebel and his guards. Many died of malnutrition, dystentry, typhus and from French Artillery fire. Only one man tried to escape and when he was recaptured he was submitted to the punishment depicted on the Panel – tied to the barbed

US 316th Regt, 79th Div Monument, Sivry.

wire fence with barbed wire. The incident was depicted by one of the six officer prisoners of the camp, Léon Cuvelle, in 1934 in the form of a bronze sculpture known as 'the Iron Man' and erected in Flabas. It was destroyed by the Germans in 1940 but a stone statue by Cuvelle in the French Faubourg Pavé Cemetery in Verdun (qv) reproduces the incident, although the barbed wire restraints are replaced with rope, as in the Flabas Reprisals Memorial visited next. Cuvelle also wrote a book, *Leurs*

Site of Reprisals Camp, Flabas.   *Information Panel and Memorial Stone.*

Représailles, in 1929 about his experiences and tells how, when the French finally acceded to the German requests, the surviving 300 prisoners were marched to Malmédy station, showered and put on trains to various camps in Germany where they were first quarantined (because of the outbreak of typhus in the Reprisal Camp). The survivors returned at the end of the war.

Return to the village.

The small chapel you pass on the right is the Chapelle St Mau.

At the fork downhill past the church turn sharp right on the D125 and stop immediately. To the left at this point are signs to the road you have come down to Camps de Représailles and Chapelle St Mau and

• Reprisals Memorial, Flabas/72.3 miles/5 minutes/Map 4/33

The Memorial in the form of a stone statue of a bound *Poilu* is similar to that in the Faubourg Pavé French National Cemetery (qv). Its caption reads, 'To the prisoners, martyrs, victims of Reprisals, Verdun Front, 1914-1916'.

Continue towards the Bois des Caures and stop on the left by the sign to the right to Col Driant's Command Post and follow signs into the wood.

• Col Driant's Command Post/73.7 miles/10 minutes/Map 4/34

Constructed in WW1 this huge bunker received massive artillery hits and was classified as an historic monument in 1931 and preserved in its 1918 state. Inside many individual plaques have been erected by the families of the Chasseurs. Around it thirty-two markers have been erected in a semi-circle with the insignia of the Chasseurs battalions who bore the brunt of the first attacks of 20 February 1916.

Continue over the junction to the car park and picnic site on the left.

Here there are **Information Panels** and a handy picnic site. '*Caures*' means hazel nut trees and the authors were pleased to see a small hazel tree by their picnic table. The wood is an emotional part of the tragedy of Verdun and walking to the memorials off the metalled road into the woods, undulating with old trenchlines and craters, gives one a sense of empathy with the fated Colonel and his brave Chasseurs. In the car park is a sign *Sentier de Découverte.* This leads over a wooden bridge and through the woods to a clearing. Note the signs that there is firing in the wood from 0800-2200, Mon & Tues. Over the road is

• Monument to the Chasseurs/Tomb of Col Driant/Site of Col Driant's mortal wound/Original Tomb of Col Driant/73.9 miles/15 minutes/ Map 4/35

In 1922 a committee of old Chasseurs, presided over by Gen Castelnau, erected this imposing mausoleum in which Col Driant was buried with, according to his oft-expressed wish, several of his Chasseurs. The thirteen Unknown crosses of men of the 56th and 59th BCP are in a semicircle behind his tomb above which are diminishing crosses in *bas-relief* leading to a large cross.

Return to the clearing over the road.

The *Sentier de Découverte* then leads through the woods to the site of Driant's mortal wound (130m). A small monument marks the site with the inscription, 'They fell silently beneath the shock like a wall.' Beyond (380m) is the spot from which Driant's body was exhumed in 1922. The site is marked by a simple cross. Here in the Bois des Caures the gallant 61-year-old Col Driant (qv), a Saint-Cyrien married to the daughter of Gen Boulanger, who left the army to become a writer then a politician (he was MP for Nancy), and his Chasseurs à Pied, withstood the first German onslaught of the campaign in February 1916. He anticipated disaster and had already in his usual forthright manner criticised the organisation of the Verdun defences. The shallow water-filled trenches in the marshy wood were in the direct line of the German attack and on 20 January he issued a Despatch urging his men to prepare for action. It ended with the words, 'Chasseurs do not surrender.' The next morning he took off his wedding ring and gave it to his secretary with the instructions that should he die it should be given to his wife. At 0645 Driant rode into the wood, where a reserve company was constructing a communication trench, to speak to the two officers in command. A shell fell among them and the Colonel was killed. His Chasseurs continued to resist until death.

Continue on the D905 through the Bois des Caures to a turning to the left to the ancient village of Beaumont.

N.B. Just before the turning is a traditional **Demarcation Stone** (**Map 4/36**) on the left erected by the Touring Club of France

Continue to the D964 and turn right. Continue to just before the sign for Vacherauville. On the left is

• First Cemetery & Monument to the 'Chasseurs de Driant'/78.7 miles/5 minutes/Map 4/37

The Chasseurs à Pied fought in the area of the village of Vacherauville from 1914. Here their first dead were buried. In November 1915 a monument was erected in the centre of the cemetery which was destroyed in the bombardments of 1916. A maquette of the monument is to be found in the *Mairie* of the village. After the war the bodies of Chasseurs not claimed by their families were reputedly buried in the Military Cemetery of Bras (you pass it later) and in 1926 the veterans erected a memorial here to mark the original cemetery.

Turn round and continue on the D964 towards Verdun. Continue through the village of Bras-sur-Meuse to the cemetery on the right

• French National Cemetery, Bras/80.2 miles/10 minutes/Map 4/38

This was started in 1916 during the battle. It contains 6,386 soldiers, of which 2,000 are in two ossuaries. An exhaustive search through the register found no named members of 56th and 59th Chasseurs killed on 22 February 1916 and said to be reburied here. Perhaps they are among the Unknowns in the mass graves. There are also 151 burials from WW2. The cemetery was totally re-landscaped in 1990.

Continue to the junction with the D913b and turn left through the Bois des Vignes. Continue to the sign to the left to Munition Store, Froideterre and stop just beyond it by the sign to Les 4 Cheminées on the right.

Col Driant's Command Post, Bois des Caures.

Ammunition Store, Froideterre.

Col Driant and Chasseurs' Tomb Monument.

• Froideterre: Shelter of the Four Chimneys, Ammunition Store/83.2 miles/20 minutes/Map 4/39

This huge underground bunker on the edge of the Les Vignes Ravine was used as a shelter and secure rest halt for the relief troops and those bringing up equipment onto the Thiaumont Plateau and Fleury Ridge, and also as a Field Hospital, over a period of ten months during the bitter fighting of 1916. The shelter was originally built in 1890 to accommodate 300 troops but its long gallery was converted into a field hospital in June 1916. On 20 June the hill of Froideterre was hammered with a brutal artillery bombardment and the vaulted roof of the shelter trembled under the onslaught. On 22 June more than 100,000 gas shells were fired onto the sector and penetrated into the bunker. The wounded who could not be evacuated, few of whom had gasmasks, were asphyxiated by the gas and died in terrible agony. At 0600 hours on 23 June German soldiers of five Bavarian Regiments, equipped with smoke bombs and flamethrowers, reached Froideterre at 0930 hours. They threw grenades down the ventilation shafts of the shelter, which was cut off from its lines of retreat, totally

Top of Shelter of the Four Chimneys, Froideterre – showing three!

devastating it. But at this point the Germans, themselves totally exhausted and unable to hold the position against a grenade and bayonet attack, retreated. Today **Information Panels** tell the story of the Bunker and the four ventilation chimneys stand intact.

A few metres back up the road is the **Ammunition Store Bunker**, with an iron grille and No Entry signs. This may be found to be forced open but it would be most unwise to enter the bunker. Beside it is a large **Information Panel** describing the route of the *Sentier de Froideterre* walking path (1 hour 30 minutes) and a sketch map of the points on the route.

Turn round, return to the D964, turn left and return to the Tourist Office at Verdun. This is a city now dedicated to Peace, rather than to the commemoration of War.

• End of Verdun Battlefield Tour
(approx 88 miles).

THE SOMME

1 JULY-17 NOVEMBER 1916

'You must know that I feel that every step in my plan has been
taken with the Divine help.'
Sir Douglas Haig to Lady Haig before the battle.

'The news about 8 a.m. was not altogether good.'
Sir Douglas Haig on 1 July.

'Our battalion atttacked about 800 strong. It lost, I was told in hospital,
about 450 the first day, and 290 or so the second. I suppose it was worth it.'
NCO of the 22nd Manchesters.

SUMMARY OF THE BATTLE

On 1 July 1916 a mainly volunteer British Army of 16 divisions in concert with five French divisions attacked entrenched German positions in the Department of the Somme in France. Over-reliance by the British on the destruction of enemy defences by preparatory artillery bombardment led to almost 60,000 British casualties on the first day and more than 400,000 before the fighting ended on 17 November 1916. The maximum advance made in all that time was six and a half miles. Total German casualties are estimated to have been about the same as the British and the French were almost 200,000.

OPENING MOVES

Few campaigns of recent history provoke such emotive British opinions as 'The Battle of the Somme'. Those who study the First World War tend to fall into two main camps: those who are anti-Haig and those who are pro-Haig. But there are those who move from one opinion to the other, according to the quality of debate. Was the C.-in-C. a dependable rock, whose calm confidence inspired all, whose far-seeing eye led us to final victory and who deserved the honours later heaped upon him? Or was he an unimaginative, insensitive product of the social and military caste system that knew no better: a weak man pretending to be strong, who should have been sacked? Doubtless the arguments will continue and more space than is available here is needed for a fair consideration, but there are some immovable elements: for instance the misjudgement concerning the artillery's effect upon the German wire and the appalling casualties on 1 July 1916. Those casualties, while not sought for by the French, may well have been hoped for by them. At the end of 1915 the French and British planned for a joint offensive on the Somme, with the French playing the major role. Masterminded by Joffre, the plan was (as far as Joffre was concerned) to kill more Germans than their pool of manpower could afford. But when the German assault at Verdun drew French forces away from the Somme, the British found themselves with the major role, providing sixteen divisions on the first day to the French five.

It was to be the first joint battle in which the British played the major role and, in the opinion of some French politicians, not before time. There was a growing feeling that the British were not pulling their weight and a bloody conflict would stick Britain firmly to the 'Cause'. It was to be the first major battle for Kitchener's Army following their rush to the recruiting stations in the early days of the war.

It was also to be the first battle fought by Gen Haig as C.-in-C. There was a great deal riding on the outcome of the Battle of the Somme. The British plan was based upon a steady fourteen-mile-wide infantry assault, from Serre in the north to Maricourt in the south, with a diversionary attack at Gommecourt above Serre. One hundred thousand soldiers were to go over the top at the end of a savage artillery bombardment. Behind the infantry – men of the Fourth Army, commanded by Gen Rawlinson – waited two cavalry divisions under Gen Gough. Their role was to exploit success.

WHAT HAPPENED

The battle may be divided into five parts:

Part 1.	The First Day	1	July
Part 2.	The Next Few Days	2	July +
Part 3.	The Night Attack/The Woods	14	July +
Part 4.	The Tank Attack	15	Sept
Part 5.	The Last Attack	13	Nov

Part 1. The First Day: 1 July

At 0728 hours seventeen mines were blown under the German line. Two minutes later 60,000 British soldiers, laden down with packs, gas mask, rifle and bayonet, 200 rounds of ammunition, grenades, empty sandbags, spade and water bottles, clambered out of their trenches from Serre to Maricourt and formed into lines fourteen miles long. As the lines moved forward in waves, so the artillery barrage lifted off the enemy front line.

From that moment onwards it was a life or death race, but the Tommies didn't know it. They hadn't been 'entered'. Their instructions were to move forward, side by side, at a steady walk across No Man's Land. It would be safe, they were told, because the artillery barrage would have destroyed all enemy opposition. But the Germans were not destroyed. They and their machine guns had sheltered in deep dugouts, and, when the barrage lifted, they climbed out, dragging their weapons with them.

The Germans won 'the race' easily. They set up their machine guns before the Tommies could get to their trenches to stop them, and cut down the ripe corn of British youth in their thousands. As the day grew into hot summer, another 40,000 men were sent in, adding more names to the casualty lists. Battalions disappeared in the bloody chaos of battle, bodies in their hundreds lay around the muddy shell holes that pocked the battlefield.

And to what end this leeching of some of the nation's best blood? North of the Albert-Bapaume road, on a front of almost nine miles, there were no realistic gains at nightfall. VIII, X, and III Corps had failed. Between la Boisselle and Fricourt there was a small penetration of about half a mile on one flank and the capture of Mametz village on the other by XV Corps. Further south, though, there was some success. XIII Corps attacking beside the French took all of its main objectives, from Pommiers Redoubt east of Mametz to just short of Dublin Redoubt north of Maricourt.

The French, south of the Somme, did extremely well. Attacking at 0930 hours they took all of their objectives. 'They had more heavy guns than we did', cried the British generals, or 'The opposition wasn't as tough', or 'The Germans didn't expect to be attacked by the French'. But whatever the reasons for the poor British performance in the north they had had some success in the south – on the right flank, beside the French.

Part 2. The Next Few Days: 2 July +
Other than the negative one of not calling off the attack, no General Command decisions were made concerning the overall conduct of the second day's battle. It was as if all the planning had been concerned with 1 July and that the staffs were surprised by the appearance of 2 July. Twenty-eight years later, on 7 June 1944, the day after D-Day, a similar culture enveloped the actions of the British 3rd Division in Normandy. Aggressive actions were mostly initiated at Corps level while Haig and Rawlinson figured out what policy they ought to follow. Eventually, after bloody preparation by the 38th (Welsh) Division at Mametz Wood, they decided to attack on the right flank, but by then the Germans had had two weeks to recover.

Part 3. The Night Attack/The Woods: 14 July +
On the XIII Corps front, like fat goalposts, lay the woods of Bazentin le Petit on the left and Delville on the right. Behind and between them, hunched on the skyline, was the dark goalkeeper of High Wood. Rawlinson planned to go straight for the goal. Perhaps the infantry general's memory had been jogged by finding one of his old junior officer's notebooks in which the word 'surprise' had been written as a principle of attack, because, uncharacteristically, he set out to surprise the Germans and not in one, but in two, ways.

First, despite Haig's opposition, he moved his assault forces up to their start line in Caterpillar Valley at night. Second, after just a five-minute dawn barrage instead of the conventional prolonged bombardment, he launched his attack. At 0325 hours, 20,000 men moved forward. On the left were 7th and 21st Divisions of XV Corps and on the right 3rd and 9th Divisions of XIII Corps. The effect was dramatic. Five miles of the German second line were overrun. On the left Bazentin-le-Petit Wood was taken. On the right began the horrendous six-day struggle for Delville Wood. Today the South African Memorial and Museum in the wood commemorate the bitter fighting.

But in the centre 7th Division punched through to High Wood and with them were two squadrons of cavalry. Perhaps here was an opportunity for a major breakthrough at last. Not since 1914 had mounted cavalry charged on the Western Front but, when they did, the Dragoons and the Deccan Horse were alone. The main force of the cavalry divisions, gathered south of Albert, knew nothing about the attack. The moment passed, the Germans recovered, counter-attacked and regained the wood.

There followed two months of local fighting under the prompting of Joffre, but, without significant success to offer, the C.-in-C. began to attract increasing criticism. Something had to be done to preserve his image, to win a victory – or both.

It was: with a secret weapon – the tank.

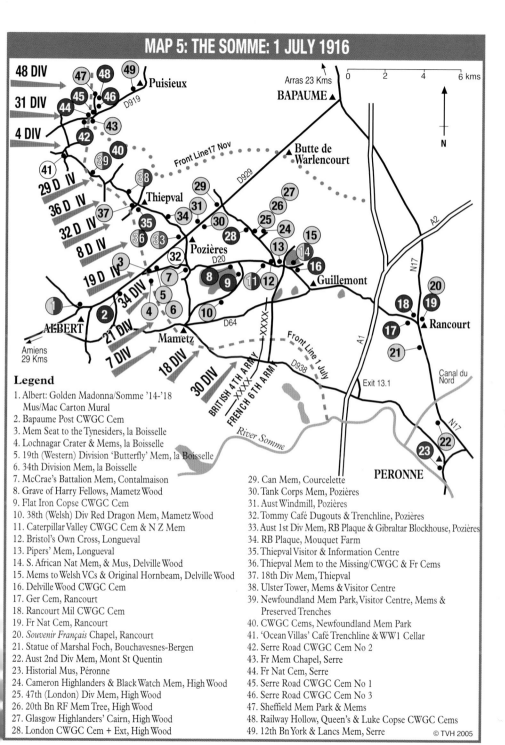

MAP 5: THE SOMME: 1 JULY 1916

48 DIV

31 DIV

4 DIV

29 D IV

36 D IV

32 D IV

8 D IV

19 D IV

34 DIV

21 DIV

7 DIV

18 DIV

30 DIV

BRITISH 4TH ARMY

FRENCH 6TH ARM

Puisieux

D919

Thiepval

Pozières

D20

Mametz

D64

Front Line 17 Nov

D929

Butte de
Warlencourt

Guillemont

Rancourt

Front Line 1 July

D938

Exit 13.1

River Somme

PERONNE

Canal du
Nord

ALBERT

Amiens
29 Kms

Arras 23 Kms

BAPAUME

A2

N17

A1

N17

0   2   4   6 kms

N

Legend

1. Albert: Golden Madonna/Somme '14-'18 Mus/Mac Carton Mural
2. Bapaume Post CWGC Cem
3. Mem Seat to the Tynesiders, la Boisselle
4. Lochnagar Crater & Mems, la Boisselle
5. 19th (Western) Division 'Butterfly' Mem, la Boisselle
6. 34th Division Mem, la Boisselle
7. McCrae's Battalion Mem, Contalmaison
8. Grave of Harry Fellows, Mametz Wood
9. Flat Iron Copse CWGC Cem
10. 38th (Welsh) Div Red Dragon Mem, Mametz Wood
11. Caterpillar Valley CWGC Cem & N Z Mem
12. Bristol's Own Cross, Longueval
13. Pipers' Mem, Longueval
14. S. African Nat Mem, & Mus, Delville Wood
15. Mems to Welsh VCs & Original Hornbeam, Delville Wood
16. Delville Wood CWGC Cem
17. Ger Cem, Rancourt
18. Rancourt Mil CWGC Cem
19. Fr Nat Cem, Rancourt
20. *Souvenir Français* Chapel, Rancourt
21. Statue of Marshal Foch, Bouchavesnes-Bergen
22. Aust 2nd Div Mem, Mont St Quentin
23. Historial Mus, Péronne
24. Cameron Highlanders & Black Watch Mem, High Wood
25. 47th (London) Div Mem, High Wood
26. 20th Bn RF Mem Tree, High Wood
27. Glasgow Highlanders' Cairn, High Wood
28. London CWGC Cem + Ext, High Wood
29. Can Mem, Courcelette
30. Tank Corps Mem, Pozières
31. Aust Windmill, Pozières
32. Tommy Café Dugouts & Trenchline, Pozières
33. Aust 1st Div Mem, RB Plaque & Gibraltar Blockhouse, Pozières
34. RB Plaque, Mouquet Farm
35. Thiepval Visitor & Information Centre
36. Thiepval Mem to the Missing/CWGC & Fr Cems
37. 18th Div Mem, Thiepval
38. Ulster Tower, Mems & Visitor Centre
39. Newfoundland Mem Park, Visitor Centre, Mems & Preserved Trenches
40. CWGC Cems, Newfoundland Mem Park
41. 'Ocean Villas' Café Trenchline & WW1 Cellar
42. Serre Road CWGC Cem No 2
43. Fr Mem Chapel, Serre
44. Fr Nat Cem, Serre
45. Serre Road CWGC Cem No 1
46. Serre Road CWGC Cem No 3
47. Sheffield Mem Park & Mems
48. Railway Hollow, Queen's & Luke Copse CWGC Cems
49. 12th Bn York & Lancs Mem, Serre

© TVH 2005

Part 4. *The Tank Attack: 15 September*

Still very new and liable to break down, thirty-two tanks out of the forty-nine shipped to France in August assembled near Trônes Wood on the night of 14 September for dispersal along the front, and the following morning at 0620 hours, following a three-day bombardment, eighteen took part in the battle with XV Corps. Their effect was sensational. The Germans, on seeing the monsters, were stunned and then terrified. Nine tanks moved forward with the leading infantry, nine 'mopped up' behind. Barely over three hours later, the left hand division of XV Corps followed a solitary tank up the main street of Flers and through the German third line. Then Courcelette, too, fell to an infantry / tank advance.

The day's gains were the greatest since the battle began. But there were too few tanks and, after the initial shock success, the fighting once again degenerated into a bull-headed contest. The opportunity that had existed to use the tank to obtain a major strategic result had gone. Many felt that it had been squandered. Yet the tank had allowed 4th Army to advance and the dominating fortress of Thiepval finally fell on 26 September, helped, it was said, 'by the appearance of 3 tanks'. At last the British were on the crest of the Thiepval-Pozières-High Wood ridge. But Beaumont Hamel in the north still held out.

Part 5. *The Last Attack: 13 November*

At the northern end of the battlefield, seven divisions of the Reserve (5th) Army assaulted at 0545 hours on 13 November. Bad weather had caused seven postponements since the original date of 24 October. V Corps was north of the River Ancre and II Corps was south. The preparatory bombardment had been carefully monitored to see that the enemy wire had been cut, but this eminent practicality was offset by the stationing of the cavalry behind the line to exploit success. Apart from the overwhelming evidence of past battle experience that should have made such an idea absurd, the weather's effect on the ground alone should have rendered it unthinkable. The generals were as firmly stuck for ideas as any Tommy, up to his waist in Somme mud, was stuck for movement.

The attack went in with a shield of early morning dark and fog, the troops moving tactically from cover to cover. Beaumont Hamel and the infamous Y Ravine were taken by the 51st Highland Division and their kilted Highlander Memorial stands there today in memory of that achievement. Fred Farrell, the official artist attached to the Divisional HQ, sketched in detail the taking of the main German position at Y Ravine, identifying the men involved. The drawing is included in a collection published by T. C. and E. C. Jack in 1920. Fighting went on for several more days, and 7,000 prisoners were taken – though Serre did not fall. But at last enough was enough. The attack was stopped and the Battle of the Somme was over.

THE BATTLEFIELD TOUR

There are more than 100 sites of particular interest to be seen on the Somme battlefield of 1916 – excluding those associated with the Kaiser's Offensive of 1918. Here we have selected those places whose names or memorials feature in the top requests made to us over the years (see Map 5).

[A more detailed tour can be made using our *Major & Mrs Holts' Battlefield Guide to the Somme* with our *Battle Map of the Somme*].

• **The Route:** The tour begins in Albert, visits the Golden Madonna and the Somme '14-'18 Museum; Bapaume Post CWGC Cemetery; la Boisselle – Tyneside Memorial Seat, the Lochnagar Mine Crater, the 19th (Western) and 34th Divisional Memorials; Contalmaison – McCrae's Bn Monument; Mametz Wood – Harry Fellows' grave, Flat Iron Copse CWGC Cemetery, 38th (Welsh) Division Dragon Memorial; Longueval – Caterpillar Valley CWGC Cemetery, Bristol's Own Cross, Pipers' Memorial, the South African Memorial, Museum and CWGC Cemetery at Delville Wood; High Wood – Cameron Highlanders & Black Watch, 47th (London) Division, 20th Bn RF Tree and Glasgow Highlanders' Memorials, London CWGC Cemetery; Courcelette Canadian Memorial; Pozières – Australian Windmill and Tank Memorials, Tommy Café recreated trenches, Australian 1st Division Memorial and Gibraltar Bunker; Thiepval – Visitor & Education Centre, Memorial to the Missing of the Somme and Anglo-French Cemetery, 18th Division Memorial; The Ulster Tower Visitor Centre and Memorials; Beaumont Hamel Newfoundland Visitor Centre, Memorial Park, preserved trenches, Memorials and CWGC Cemeteries; Serre – CWGC Cemeteries Nos 2 and 1, French Cemetery and Chapel, 12th Bn York & Lancs Memorial.

• **Extra Visits:** Rancourt *Souvenir Français* Chapel, British, French & German Cemeteries; Foch Statue, Bouchavesnes; Australian 2nd Division Memorial, Mont St Quentin; The Historial Museum, Péronne; Serre Road No 3, Queen's and Railway Hollow CWGC Cemeteries, Sheffield Memorial Park and its 'Pals' Memorials.

• Planned duration, without stops for refreshments or extra visits: 8 hours

• Total distance: 26.5 miles

• Distance from Calais to start point via A26 to Arras and A1 to Bapaume and D929 to Albert: 100 miles. Motorway Tolls

• Base Towns: Arras, Albert, Amiens

• Maps: *Major & Mrs Holt's Battle Map of the Somme*; Michelin 286 France Nord Flandres-Artois – Picardie: 1:200,000

*From Calais take the A16/A26 direction Paris/Reims then the A26 direction St Omer. Continue to the motorway junction with the A1 beyond Arras Centre and take the A1 signed Paris/Arras-Est to Exit 14, Bapaume. At the roundabout follow signs to Albert on the ring road and then on the D929 via Warlencourt and le Sars. You will then pass several sites of interest that will be visited later in the tour. Enter Albert and turn right following signs to Amiens and drive down the rue Birmingham towards the Basilique which is surmounted by a golden figure holding aloft a baby. If possible stop in the parking area in the square. **Set your mileometer to zero.***

• *Albert/Golden Madonna/Somme '14-'18 Museum/Mac Carton Mural/0 miles/45 minutes/RWC/Map 5/1*

Fierce fighting around Albert began in the early months of the war, the first enemy shelling being on 29 September 1914. By October 1916, when the Somme offensive had pushed the German guns out of range, the town was a pile of red rubble. On 26 March 1918, during their final offensive, Albert was taken by the Germans and retaken by the British on 22 August, the East Surreys entering the town at bayonet point. Albert was a major administration and control centre for the Somme offensive, and it was from here that the first Press message was sent announcing the start of the 'Big Push'.

The golden figure above you is the Virgin Mary holding aloft the baby Jesus. It stands on top of the Basilique of Notre-Dame des Brébières. Before the war thousands of pilgrims came annually to see the black Madonna inside the church which, legend says, had been discovered locally by a shepherd in the Middle Ages (hence the church's name, from *brébis,* the word for ewe). In January 1915 German shelling toppled the **Golden Madonna** on the steeple to an angle below horizontal, but it did not fall. Visible to soldiers of both sides for many miles around, the statue gave rise to two legends. The British and French believed that the war would end on the day that the statue fell (it is said that the Allied Staff sent engineers up the steeple at night to shore it up to prevent raising false hopes). The Germans believed that whoever knocked down the Madonna would lose the war. Neither prediction came to pass. During the German occupation from March to August 1918 the British shelled Albert and knocked down the Golden Virgin. The figure was never found and today's statue is a replica. The townspeople strongly resisted the suggestion to remount it in its wartime leaning position. The Basilique was rebuilt to the original design by the son of the original architect, Duthoit, with sculptures by Albert Roze. Most of the town (notably the station) was rebuilt in the 1920s in the distinct *Art Deco* style then in vogue. The idea to declare it a *Zone Rouge* (too dangerous to rebuild, like some of the battlefields around Verdun) was also strongly resisted by the inhabitants of Albert.

To the right of the church is the entrance to

Somme '14-'18 Trench Museum

This interesting and well-presented museum has been made in the subterranean tunnels under the Basilique and other parts of the town. To either side of the main corridor are realistic scenes and sound effects of 1914-18 trench and dugout life – British, French and German – with informative captions in all three languages translated by Paula Flanagan Kesteloot. They are full of authentic artefacts and weapons. Visitors emerge through a souvenir/book shop into the pleasant arboretum public gardens. **Open:** every day 1 February-15 December 0930-1200 and 1400-1800. June-September 0930-1800. Entrance fee payable. Tel: + (0)3 22 75 16 17. Fax: + (0)3 22 75 56 33. E-mail: musee.des.abris.somme.1916@wanadoo.fr   Website:www.musee-somme-1916.org/ www.somme-trench-museum.co.uk

On the wall opposite the top exit to the park is a striking **Mural by Albert Mac Carton** showing the Basilique with the Madonna, leaning perilously, and the figures of Allied soldiers. In the small garden in front of it is a **Plaque** to commemorate the inauguration of the mural on 29 June 1996.

Return up rue Birmingham and turn left on the D929 signed A1/Lille/Bapaume.

You are now moving along the axis of the British attack of 1 July 1916.

Continue to the second large roundabout.

On top of the roundabout a controversial 4-metre high **statue of a British Tommy** clambering out of his trench holding his rifle is planned for 2005. Made of resin and painted in lifelike colours he charges towards the German lines. The statue was the initiative of the Albert Museum and is funded by the Museum, the town of Albert and the Somme *Conseil Général*. The *Conseil* is among sponsors (including Lions, Rotary,

Entrance to the Somme '14-'18 Museum.

Maquette of the proposed Tommy Statue, Albert.

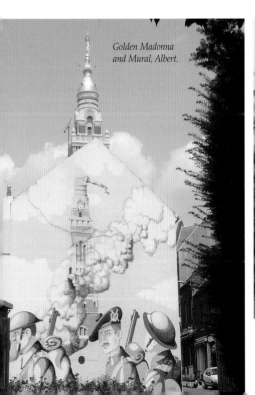

Golden Madonna and Mural, Albert.

Diorama, Somme '14-'18 Museum.

Airbus and Crédit Mutuel) for a Poppy Country Marathon, to be run on 3 July 2005 starting from Albert, to raise money for charity. It was the brainchild of Paul Chaplin, a British teacher living on the Somme. For details see www.somme-marathon.com
Continue following Bapaume signs to the cemetery on the right.

• Bapaume Post CWGC Cemetery/1.3 miles/10 minutes/Map 5/2

One of the first cemeteries in this sector to be completed, it contains two battalion commanders of the Tyneside Brigade: **Lt Cols William Lyle** and **Charles Sillery**, lying side by side in Row IG, both killed on 1 July.

Continue up and then down over the hill (known as the Tara-Usna line), passing the Poppy Restaurant on the right, *to the junction in la Boisselle.*
This was the British front line and here there is a **Memorial Seat to the Tynesiders (Map 5/3)**. (Those who are fortunate enough to possess a copy of John Masefield's classic *The Old Front Line* will find many of its descriptions still valid from this point onwards.)

Fork right on the D20 before the seat and turn first right following signs to la Grande Mine on the C9.

• Lochnagar Crater & Memorials, La Boisselle/2.7 miles/20 minutes/ Map 5/4

The land containing the crater was purchased in 1978 and is maintained privately by Englishman Richard Dunning as a personal memorial to all those who fought in the Battle of the Somme and in particular to those, of both sides, killed in the crater. Other memorials have subsequently been erected there: a **Stone in Memory of Pte Tom Easton** of the 2nd Bn Tyneside Scottish; a **Memorial Seat 'Donated by friends** who visit in memory of friends who remain'; **Memorial Seats to veteran Harry Fellows** and to the **Grimsby Chums**; a wooden **Cross in memory of Pte George Nugent** whose remains were found on the spot on 31 October 1998 and a **Plaque to Gnr W.G. Noon.** At the entrance is a **CGS/H Information Panel.**

Richard, who is intensely aware of the historical and spiritual value of the crater, of its ability to shock and evoke the violence of war through its sheer size, has also raised a simple 12ft high **Cross** made from church timber originating on Tyneside. Much work has recently been undertaken to enhance the feeling that one is entering a very Special Memorial area and a 'living' Garden of Remembrance. One passes through large stone curbs and 'knife-rests' along duckboards and a hedge bounds the site.

Richard may be contacted on 01483 810651. On 1 July each year at 0728 a simple but very moving and involving memorial gathering takes place at the crater. There is also a ceremony here on 11 November. All members of the public are able to attend either ceremony.

N.B. It is forbidden to climb down into the crater because of the damage it causes to this fast-eroding precious remnant of the war.

Mine warfare had been carried on in this area well before July 1916 and there were many craters in No Man's Land. In June, along the Western Front as a whole, the British had blown 101 mines and the Germans 126. In this area some of the shafts dug, from which tunnels then reached out to the enemy line, were over 100ft deep with tunnels at up to four levels.

When dug, the mine here was known as Lochnagar, and had been started by 185th Tunnelling Company in December 1915. It was finished by 179th Tunnelling Company and packed with two charges of 24,000 and 36,000 lb of ammonal. Seventeen British mines, including Lochnagar, were exploded at 0728 hours along the front on 1 July and the circular crater here measured 300ft across and was 90ft deep. Debris rose 4,000ft into the air and, as it settled the attack began. It failed. The attacking battalions of Tyneside Scottish followed by the Tyneside Irish were reduced to small parties of survivors.

Following the failure of the attack by the Tynesiders of 34th Division, the 10th Worcesters were ordered to move up from beside Albert to make an assault at dawn on 2 July. So chaotic were conditions in the communication trenches that the battalion got lost, and the attack did not go in until 3 July. The Worcesters took the crater area and the village, **Pte F.G.** Turrall winning a **VC** in the process, but the battalion lost a third of its fighting strength and the Commanding Officer was killed.

Return to the village and turn right on the D20. Continue to the church on the left.
It was in la Boisselle on 2-3 July that the extraordinary Belgian-born officer, **T/Lt Col Adrian Carton de Wiart,** commanding the 8th Gloucesters, won his **VC** for forcing home the attack and controlling the commands of three other battalion commanders who had been wounded while exposing himself fearlessly to the enemy. He was wounded eight times during WW1 (including the loss of an eye and his left hand) went on to become Lt Gen Sir Adrian Carton de Wiart, KBE, CB, CMG, DSO, with many foreign awards and distinguished service that took him to Poland, Norway, Yugoslavia, Italy and China in WW2.

In front of the church is

• 19th (Western) Division 'Butterfly' Memorial/3.2 miles/5 minutes/ Map 5/5

This Memorial, with its butterfly emblem carved on the top, commemorates their casualties of 2 July-20 November at la Boisselle, Bazentin le Petit and Grandcourt. The Divisional Units are inscribed on the base. The Division took the village on 4 July 1916.

Continue to the end of the houses on the left. Up a track to the left is

• 34th Division Memorial/3.3 miles/10 minutes/Map 5/6

The figure of Victory (minus her original laurel wreath) commemorates the Division's exploits here on 1 July 1916. It incorporates their distinctive checkerboard emblem and the composition of the Divisional Units. Beyond the memorial the top of the Thiepval Memorial and Ovillers CWGC Cemetery may be seen.

Continue to Contalmaison, passing a sign to Gordon Dump CWGC Cemetery on the right. In the village, after passing a sign to Contalmaison Château CWGC Cemetery to the left, turn right on the D147 and stop by the church.

Tynesiders Memorial seat, la Boisselle.

The Lochnagar Crater.

First of July Ceremony, Lochnagar Crater.

German trumpeter at the ceremony.

Cairn to McCrae's Bn, Contalmaison.

• *Memorial to McCrae's Battalion, Contalmaison/4.9 miles/5 minutes/ Map 5/7*

Dedicated on 7 November 2004 this 10ft high cairn of Elgin stone commemorates the remarkable Battalion of Lt Col Sir George McCrae, the 16th Royal Scots, who on 1 July 1916 captured the German strong point known as Scots Redoubt in the ruins of Contalmaison. Their story is told on superb bronze relief plaques on the cairn showing the 34th Division's chequerboard insignia, a cartoon that was the regimental Christmas card for 1916, the figure of Sir George, the Heart of Midlothian Football Club's sacrifice and details of the unveiling and local cooperation. The full story of Sir George and his brave battalion and Jack Alexander's efforts to resurrect 1920 memorial plans was told in the Spring 2004 edition of *The New Chequers*, the Journal of the 'Friends of Lochnagar'.

Return to the junction and turn right following signs to Bazentin and Longueval on the D20, skirting Mametz Wood on the right.

> N.B. At the end of the wood is a track to the right (6.3 miles) which leads to the **Grave of Harry Fellows** (qv) (**Map 5/8**) some 100 metres into the wood (which is private property).

Continue to the next small track to the right signed to 'Flat Iron Copse CWGC Cemetery' and turn down it.
N.B. The following two visits may be difficult by car if the weather has been particularly wet.
Continue to the cemetery on the right.

• *Flat Iron Copse CWGC Cemetery/7.1 miles/15 minutes/Map 5/9*

The cemetery was begun by the 3rd and 7th Divisions on 14 July 1916 as they cleared Mametz Wood after its capture by the 38th (the wood is immediately behind the rear wall of the cemetery). There are over 1,500 burials, including two pairs of brothers, each serving with the RWF. **Cpl Thomas Hardwidge** of the 15th RWF was injured on 11 July and when his brother **L/Cpl Henry Hardwidge** went to give him water they were both shot and killed. Four days earlier, on 7 July, the **Tregaskis brothers**, **Leonard and Arthur, both Lieutenants** in the 16th RWF were killed under similar circumstances. A particularly notable burial is that of **Cpl Edward Dwyer**, **VC** of the 1st Battalion, East Surreys. Dwyer received his award for 'conspicuous bravery and devotion to duty at Hill 60 [in the Ypres Salient] on 20th April 1915' and when back in Britain gave lectures to help the recruiting effort. In the 1980s Pavilion Records of Sussex produced a remarkable pair of records, now available on cassette and CD, GEMM 3033/4, which feature original recordings from the 1914-18 period. Track 2, side 2 of the first record is a monologue by Dwyer, most probably the only extant contemporary recording of a First World War VC.

Headstone of Cpl Dwyer, VC, Flat Iron Copse, CWGC Cemetery.

Continue down the track (which deteriorates significantly from this point) which follows the eastern edge of Mametz Wood until you reach the magnificent red Welsh Dragon at the south-eastern corner.

• *38th (Welsh) Division Red Dragon Memorial/ 7.5 miles/10 minutes/ Map 5/10*

To a first approximation the dragon faces the wood as did the attacking Welsh. On the morning of 7 July 1916, one week after the first day of the Battle of the Somme, two British divisions began a pincer attack on Mametz Wood, a German stronghold held by the

Prussian Guard. The two divisions were the 17th, attacking from the west, and the 38th (Welsh), attacking from the east. The attack was a failure. German machine guns, apparently unaffected by the preparatory artillery bombardment, inflicted heavy casualties upon the attackers, approaching across the open ground. Battlefield communication broke down and a covering smokescreen failed to appear. At the end of the day neither division had even reached the wood, let alone captured it. Three days later, just after 0400 hours on 10 July the two divisions were ordered in again. The main thrust this time was towards the southern face of the wood by the Welsh – a frontal assault. The leading battalions were the 13th, 14th and 16th RWF and despite the hail of German small-arms fire they made it to the wood. The struggle became increasingly bitter in the thick undergrowth beneath the splintered trunks. More and more Welsh battalions were committed to the struggle until almost the whole division was in among the trees. The bloody contest, often bitter hand-to-hand fighting, continued for two days until, on the night of 11 July, the Germans withdrew.

The cost to the 38th (Welsh) Division, proudly raised by Lloyd George and inadequately officered by his cronies and protégées, was high – some 4,000 men were killed or wounded. Although they did capture the wood they came under severe criticism for having taken five days to do so and in 1919 Lt Col J.H. Boraston, co-author of *Sir Douglas Haig's Command*, effectively accused them of a lack of determination which prevented a significant Fourth Army advance on the Somme. The extraordinarily high proportion of literate, articulate writers serving with the RWF chronicle the Division's side of the story. Lt Wyn Griffith, author of *Up to Mametz*, served with the 15th Bn RWF and fought in the wood, his young brother, a dispatch runner, being killed when Griffith sent him out with a message in a desperate attempt to stop our own barrage which was falling on the Welsh. Pte David Jones chronicles the epic struggle in what is probably the war's most original work of literature – the poem *In Parenthesis*. Robert Graves and Frank Richards, both of the 2nd Bn, describe the horror of mopping up in the wood a few days after the attack and Siegfried Sassoon watched it go in from Pommiers Redoubt. Inspired by their accounts, Colin Hughes wrote the definitive account of the raising of the Division and the attack on the wood in *Mametz* (Orion Press, 1982).

The exuberant and emotional Welsh Dragon Memorial, designed by sculptor-in-iron David Peterson, was raised mostly through the tireless fund-raising and organisational efforts of Cardiff Western Front Association member **Harry Evans and his wife Pat**. It was unveiled on 11 July 1987 and although not an 'official' national memorial, is the focal point of Welsh remembrance on the Western Front.

Beside it is a **bronze relief map** and short account of the battles and behind it a **Seat presented by Maj Huw Rodge.**

Return to the D20 and continue in the direction of Longueval, passing a sign to Thistle Dump CWGC Cemetery to the left. Continue to the cemetery on the right.

• *Caterpillar Valley CWGC Cemetery & New Zealand Memorial/9.9 miles/10 minutes/Map 5/11/OP*

This is the second largest cemetery on the Somme (the largest being Serre Road No 2), containing 5,197 UK burials, 214 NZ, 98 Australian, 19 SA, 6 Canadian and 2

The glorious red Welsh Dragon Memorial overlooking Mametz Wood.

The Delville Wood Memorial with the Museum behind.

Newfoundland with 38 Special Memorials. The majority are unknown. On the left hand wall is the **NZ Memorial to the Missing**.

OP. The cemetery is on the Longueval Ridge and is an excellent vantage point. With your back to the entrance, the NZ Memorial Obelisk is straight ahead at 12 o'clock across Caterpillar Valley. At 2 o'clock is Longueval Church with Delville Wood behind. At 3 o'clock is the Bristol's Own Cross. At 11 o'clock is High Wood with the London CWGC Cemetery to the left. Just before 10 o'clock is the wireless mast at Pozières and at 9 o'clock the Bazentin Woods. **OP.** From the shelter at the rear of the cemetery Montauban Church is straight ahead at 12 o'clock, at 10 o'clock is Trônes Wood, at 11 o'clock is Bernafay Wood and at 3 o'clock is Mametz Wood.

Continue to the cross on the left at the junction with the D107 just before the village.

• Bristol's Own Cross/10.2 miles/5 minutes/Map 5/12

This Memorial was raised by British and French volunteers under the leadership of Dean Marks, then a technician with Dupont UK. In the seventieth Anniversary year of the Battle of the Somme his two-year-old daughter Amy, his father Roy, the Mayor of Longueval plus a party of helpers put up the new cross. It stands where the 12th Battalion Gloucestershire Regiment set off to battle and commemorates those who fell around Longueval and Guillemont between July and September 1916.

Continue to Longueval village. On the left at the crossroads is

• Pipers' Memorial, Longueval/10.5 miles/5 minutes/Map 5/13

Unveiled on 20 July 2002 this white statue of a piper with black pipes was the inspiration of Ian C. Alexander of the War Research Society and the Somme Battlefield Pipe Band. It perpetuates the memory of the Pipers of various regiments who fought in WW1 and many of whose badges are on the wall behind the Piper. On the base are lines from the poem, *Cha Till MaCruimein* by Lt E.A. Mackintosh, MC of the Seaforth Highlanders – 'The pipers in the street were bravely playing...'. Longueval was chosen for the site as it was captured by the 9th Scottish Division in July 1916 and through it many pipers marched.

Continue through the village following signs to the South African Memorial, Delville Wood.

The Pipers' Memorial, Longueval.

• Delville Wood: South African National Memorial, Museum, Memorial to Welsh VCs and Original Hornbeam, CWGC Cemetery/ 10.8 miles/40 minutes/Map 5/14/15/16/RWC

On the right of the road is Delville Wood Cemetery, Longueval, which was made after the Armistice and contains over 5,200 burials and almost two-thirds are unknown. One grave of note is that of **Sergeant Albert Gill**, KRRC, who won a posthumous **VC** when rallying his platoon by standing up in full view of the enemy. There are 151 South African graves. On the left of the road is Delville Wood itself, the South African National Memorial and behind it the Museum built in 1985-6. The memorial (unveiled by the widow of Gen Louis Botha on 10 October 1926) is topped by a sculpture of Castor and Pollux clasping hands. The sculpture, designed by Alfred Turner, symbolises the unity of the English and Afrikaans-speaking peoples of South Africa. A replica overlooks Pretoria from the terrace of the Government Buildings designed, as was the Memorial, by Sir Herbert Baker, ARA.

The **Museum** is a beautifully designed building with delicately engraved glass windows around an inner courtyard and dramatic *bas-reliefs* in bronze depicting the bitter days of fighting for the wood. To the left and rear of the building are **Memorials to an original hornbeam** which has survived since the terrible fighting of 1916 **and a small stone to two Welsh VCs, Cpl Joseph Davies and Pte Albert Hill**, 20 July 1916.

In the large car park there are clean toilets and a shop serving snacks which also has an exceptional range of First World War books, postcards and collectables. **Open: February-March and mid-October-11 November 1000-1545 and 1 April-mid October 1000-1745.** Closed Mondays, December and January and French holidays. Tel: + (0)3 22 85 02 17.

The battle for the wood was a complex one and is well told in the Museum and in booklets available there. The South African Brigade was attached to 9th Scottish Division, and when the latter took Longueval village on 14 July, the Springboks were given the task of taking the wood. At dawn on 15 July the assault began with a fearsome artillery duel. Five days of hand-to-hand fighting followed. It rained every other day and enemy artillery fire reached rates exceeding 400 shells a minute. The landscape was a tangled mess of broken tree stumps, huge shell holes, mud and water overlaid with bodies of soldiers of both sides (many of whom still lie in the wood). Though the South Africans were told, and tried, to take the wood 'at all costs', they couldn't quite do it, and when they were relieved by 26 Brigade on 20 July only 143 men of the original 3,150 came out of the trenches. It was not until 25 August 1916 that 14th (Light) Division finally overcame all enemy resistance in the wood.

A great-uncle of one of the authors survived being buried alive by a shell for several days, though he never fully recovered from the horrific experience. Lord Moran, later to become Churchill's doctor, but then serving with the 1st Bn the Royal Fusiliers in the trenches immediately south of Delville Wood during the battle, described in his book, *The Anatomy of Courage*, the burials of some of his men. 'Shells were bursting all around and in the black smoke men were digging. Muffled appeals for help, very faint and distant, came out of the earth and maddened the men who dug harder than ever, and some throwing their spades away, burrowed feverishly with their hands like terriers. It was difficult to get the earth away from one place where they said someone was buried without piling it where others were digging also. We were getting in each other's way. We were afraid too of injuring those buried heads with the shovels and always through our minds went the thought that it might be too late. Then there was a terrific noise, everything vanished for a moment, and when I could see, Dyson and the two men working beside him had disappeared. They were buried.' The Royal Fusiliers had been under 'friendly fire' during this incident, a phenomeon that is all too common in warfare – see *The Lost Battalion* – including the Second Millenium conflict in Iraq.

In the 1918 battles the Germans overran the area on 24 March and 38th (Welsh) Division retook the wood on 28 August.

Extra Visit to Rancourt German Cemetery (Map 5/17)/Rancourt Mil CWGC Cemetery (Map 5/18)/French National Cemetery (Map 5/19) & Souvenir Français Chapel (Map 5/20)/Statue of Marshal Foch (Map 5/21)/Aust 2nd Div Memorial (Map 5/22)/ Historial Museum, Péronne (Map 5/23).
Round trip: 25 miles. Approximate time: 2 hours 30 minutes

Take the D20 through Guillemont and Combles, pass under the A1 Motorway to Rancourt.

As you approach the N17 you will pass on the right the **German Cemetery** (3,930 individual graves, 7,492 in a mass grave). To the left on the N17 is a *Souvenir Français Chapel* raised by the du Bos family in memory of their son **Lt Jean du Bos,** *Légion d'Honneur, Croix de Guerre,* age 26, 25 September 1916, which is full of interesting personal memorials and beside which is a **CGS/H Information Panel.** Behind it is the **French National Cemetery** (the largest on the Somme with 8,566 burials, 3,240 of which are in four ossuaries) and opposite is **Rancourt Military CWGC Cemetery** (76 known, 17 unknown and 3 WW2 burials).

Continue on the N17/N37 direction Péronne.

N.B. After approx 1 mile you will pass on the right an imposing **Statue of Marshal Foch** at Bouchavesnes-Bergen.

N.B. At approx 4 miles further you will pass the fine **Australian 2nd Division Memorial** in the form of a typical 'Digger' at Mont St Quentin. The Australians took the bitterly-fought-for hill on 31 August 1918, losing 3,000 casualties in the often hand to hand fight. They captured 14,500 prisoners and 170 guns in their campaign from 8 August. They continued to pursue the Germans and by the night of 3 September they had taken Péronne.

Continue into Péronne following signs to the Historial.

Historial de la Grande Guerre/RWC. This costly and ambitious project, which aims to show WW1 in an entirely new light and act as a centre for documentation and research as well as an exhibition centre, was funded by the *Département de la Somme* and opened in 1992. Its façade is the medieval castle, behind which is the modern building, designed by H.E. Ciriani. There is a book and souvenir shop inside the entrance and then the great exhibition halls chart the years before the war, the war years (and in particular 1916) and the post-war years, from the

Extra visit continued

British, French and German points of view. There are many audio-visual presentations with some rare contemporary footage and changing temporary exhibitions. On the ground floor is a basic cafeteria. At the entrance is a **Ross Bastiaan bronze plaque** inaugurated in 1993.

Open: every day 1000-1800, (except Monday, 1 Oct-31 May). Annual closing mid-December-mid-January. Tel: + (0)3 22 83 14 18.

E-mail: df17@historial.org Website: www.historial.org

Return to Longueval and pick up the main tour.

The imposing entrance to the Historial, Péronne.

Interior view, Historial.

Return to Longueval village and follow signs to Bazentin on the D20, then turn right on the D107 signed to Martinpuich and Bois des Fourcaux (High Wood). Continue to the edge of the wood ahead, which is High Wood, and turn up the track to the right. Continue some 400m to

• Cameron Highlanders & Black Watch Memorial/12.6 miles/10 minutes/Map 5/24

This commemorates the Cameron Highlanders who fell here in September 1916 and throughout the war. On the reverse is the inscription to the Black Watch. Behind the memorial are the water-filled craters from mines dug by 178th Tunnelling Coy on 3 and 9 September 1916.

Return to the D107, turn right and continue some 100m to

The Australian 2nd Division Memorial, Mont St Quentin.

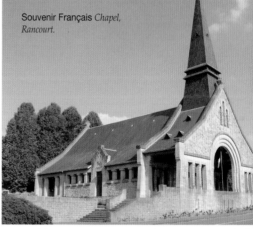

Souvenir Français *Chapel, Rancourt.*

The German Cemetery, Rancourt.

• 47th (London) Division Memorial/12.9 miles/5 minutes/Map 5/25

This is the third version of the Memorial to commemorate the action of the Division on 15 September 1916 when it finally took High Wood, one of its assault formations being the 1st POW's Own Civil Service Rifles. Two tanks were promised to support the attack at 0550 hours instead of the traditional artillery barrage. The tanks did not materialise and although the Wood was won by midday only 150 men of the Battalion reached it. The unit history records, 'Meanwhile the tanks had not shown up though one of them later on, after nearly smashing up Battalion Headquarters, got stuck in a communication trench and materially interfered with the removal of the wounded. Its pilot got out and going into Battalion Headquarters asked the Commanding Officer where High Wood was.' The CO's reply is not recorded.

A further eighteen paces along is

• 20th Battalion Royal Fusilier Tree/12.9 miles/5 minutes/Map 5/26

The oak tree at the edge of the wood, on which there is a small plaque, was planted in memory of the Public Schools Battalion killed here on 20 July 1916.

Continue a further 200m to the cairn on the right.

• Glasgow Highlanders' Cairn/13.00 miles/5 minutes/Map 5/27

This commemorates the unsuccessful attack of the 9th Glasgow Highlanders. It is constructed from 190 stones from near Culloden, is 5ft 7in high, the minimum height for the battalion, and is surmounted by a Glasgow paving stone. The inscription translates, 'Just here, Children of the Gael went down shoulder to shoulder on 15 July 1916.' It was erected in 1972 by Alex Aiken, whose book *Courage Past* deals with the attack.

Continue to the British cemetery on the left.

• London Cemetery & Extension/13.1 miles/15 minutes/Map 5/28/OP

The original cemetery was begun in September 1916 by the burial of forty-seven men 'in a large shell hole' by 47th Division, and was later enlarged by the addition of other graves to make a total of 101. That area is immediately to the left of the main entrance. The cemetery was further extended after the Armistice and is the third largest on the Somme, containing over 3,330 graves of which more than 3,100 are unknown. There is a 1939-45 plot in the cemetery too.

Death makes no political distinction and just as Herbert Asquith, Liberal Statesman and Prime Minister until December 1916, lost a son (Raymond) on the Somme, so did Arthur Henderson, leader of the Labour Party at this time (later to win the Nobel Peace Prize in 1934). **Capt David Henderson** of the Middlesex Regiment, attached to 19th London Battalion, was killed in High Wood on 15 September 1916, age 27, and is buried here.

OP. From the rear of the cemetery looking forward you will be standing in the German 'goal', the goal posts being the woods of Bazentin to the right and Delville to the left. Beyond Bazentin is the northern end of Caterpillar Valley from where the cavalry launched an attack on 14 July, heading for the goal. Very few made it. Clockwise can be seen Longueval Church spire at the edge of Delville Wood; Caterpillar Valley Cemetery on the ridge; the unusual silhouette of Montauban Church on the skyline; Bazentin-le-Grand Wood straight ahead and to the right the wireless mast at Pozières Windmill. The valley ahead is where the Cameron Highlanders formed up for the September attack on High Wood and, up the shallower valley running towards Delville Wood to the left, the Deccan Horse charged in July.

Continue through Martinpuich to the D929 Albert to Bapaume road and turn left.

After 150m on the right is

• Canadian Memorial, Courcelette/15.1 miles/5 minutes/Map 5/29

This simple octagonal block of granite (the standard Canadian memorial) commemorates the actions of the Canadian Corps from September to November 1916. The 2nd (Canadian) Division drove the enemy from this position on 15 September aided by a tank called 'Crème de Menthe'. Their assault was broadly towards you along the line of the road.

Continue to the tall wireless mast on the left before Pozières and stop by the memorial on the right.

• Australian Windmill Memorial/RB Plaque/Tank Corps Memorial, Pozières/16.0 miles/10 minutes/Map 5/30/31

The ruins of the old windmill can still be seen sticking out of the mound of earth. This was the high point of the Pozières Ridge, so bitterly and bloodily fought for by the Australians. Over the month of August when Haig, pushed by Joffre, was indulging in piecemeal attacks, it was the three Australian Divisions that hammered towards the high ground of the ridge along the Albert-Bapaume road (the one along which you are driving). In forty-five days the Australians launched 19 attacks and lost 23,000 officers and men. The site was bought by the Australian War Memorial Board and the inscription on the bronze plaque by **Ross Bastiaan** reads, 'The ruin of Pozières windmill which lies here was the centre of the struggle in this part of the Somme Battlefields in July and August 1916. It was captured on 4 August by Australian troops who fell more thickly on this ridge than on any other battlefield of the war.' Ten days after the Australians left the Somme the tank made its debut.

In Pozières the ebullient **2nd Lt Bert Jacka** was gravely wounded and added an **MC** to his Gallipoli **VC**, the first **AIF VC**, in an astounding feat of bravery, killing some dozen of the enemy whilst hit seven times. He died in 1932.

Walk across the road to the other memorial. Beware the traffic.

It was at the battle of Flers-Courcelette, Part 4 of the Somme offensive, that tanks went into action for the first time. This obelisk, with its four superb miniature tanks, is a memorial to the fallen of the Corps, and its fence is constructed from tank 6-pounder gun barrels and early driving chains. This point was one of several where the tanks mustered ready for the attack after assembling behind Trônes Wood on the night of 14 September.

Continue down the hill into Pozières. On the left is

20th Bn. RF Memorial Tree, High Wood.   *The Glasgow Highlanders' Cairn, High Wood.*

London Cemetery.

Detail of Gun-carrier Tank Mk 1, Tank Memorial, Pozières.

Section of Trenchline, Tommy Café.

• *Tommy Café/Trenchlines & Dugouts/16.7 miles/15 minutes/Map 5/32/RWC*

The café offers snacks and meals throughout the day and in the garden is a recreated German and Allied trench/dugout system complete with uniformed models and sound effects and many weapons and artefacts from the superb collection of M Carreele Antoine de Mortemer. In 2006 a 2-star, twelve ensuite bedroom, hotel is due be opened here. Tel: + (0)3 22 74 82 84. E-mail: cafe@letommy.com
Website: www.tommy-battlefield-hotel.com

Continue for about 200 yards.

[**N.B.** Some 400m straight ahead on the right is the Pozières 4th & 5th Armies Memorial and CWGC Brit Cemetery.]

Turn right along a small road signed to the 1st Aust Div Memorial.

• *Australian 1st Division Memorial/RB Plaque & Gibraltar Blockhouse/16.9 miles/10 minutes/Map 5/33*

The village was captured on 24 July 1916 by the 1st Australian Division and the British 48th Division, the main German trench defended by the 117th Division being along the line of this small road. Across the road opposite the Memorial (in front of which is a **RB**

Plaque) is a German bunker known as Gibraltar now maintained by the CGS/H, complete with observation platform and **CGS/H Information Panels.**

Continue to the T junction by the church, turn left and follow the D37 to the bronze memorial on the right.

• Mouquet Farm RB Plaque/18.1 miles/5 minutes/Map 5/34

This **RB Plaque** was unveiled near the site of Mouquet (known to Tommy as 'Mucky' and to the Diggers as 'Moo Cow') Farm in 1997. It commemorates the Australians who fell in August-September 1916 in the struggles for Thiepval and is close to the line of the German 'Constance' Trench.

Continue to Thiepval village, turn left just past the church and continue to the car park on front of the building on the right.

• Thiepval Visitor and Education Centre/19.8 miles/30 minutes/Map 5/35/RWC

A Visitor and Education Centre was opened here in September 2004 by one of its Patrons, HRH the Duke of Kent. The nearly £2 million required was funded half by British donations and half by the Conseil Général de la Somme and EU Regional Funds. It is run by the Département and the Historial at Péronne and supported by Madame Geneviève Potié, Mayor of Thiepval. It is the inspiration of Sir Frank Sanderson who has fund-raised energetically to find the fifty per cent from some 2,000 different donors and worked with determination to see the challenging project through with the French builders. The idea was regarded as somewhat controversial by purist regular visitors who feared that the building would detract from the classical Lutyens Memorial and that the proliferation of information centres in the area was tending to create a Somme 'theme park'. Sensitive to these feelings the designers have created a discreet sunken building with a glass façade and original Lutyens bricks which is shielded by the wood and which will blend into the environment. It is served by a new road to separate it from traffic to the Memorial with a large car and coach park. The Centre contains a book shop, refreshment and toilet facilities, as well as offering historical **Information Panels** (by Professor Peter Simkins, Brother Nigel Cave and Michael Steadman) and a databank to enable visitors to trace where relatives – Allied and German – are buried or commemorated. Part of the exhibition is devoted to personal details of some of the 72,000 men who are commemorated on the Memorial and there is a striking montage of some of their portraits. Another section is devoted to Sir Edwin Lutyens. There are facilities for student groups and for bus drivers.

An accurate 1:25 scale model of the Lutyens Memorial stands inside the entrance. It was constructed by Andrew Ingham and Assocs.

During the excavations, the Durand Group (qv) established that no significant vestiges of the war were disturbed other than a few shells and the remains of six Germans who were taken in charge by the German authorities.

Open: Every day (except mid-December to end of January): 1000-1700.
Tel: + (0)3 22 74 60 47. Fax: + (0)3 22 74 65 44.
website: www.thiepval.org.uk

Walk to the entrance to

• *Thiepval Memorial & Anglo-French Cemetery/19.8 miles/30 minutes/ Map 5/36*

The structure is both a Battle Memorial and a Memorial. As the former it commemorates the 1916 Anglo-French offensive on the Somme and as the latter it carries the names of over 73,000 British and South African men (the Australians, Canadians, Indians, Newfoundlanders and New Zealanders are commemorated on their own national memorials or elsewhere) who have no known grave and who fell on the Somme between July 1915 and 20 March 1918. One hundred and forty feet high, it was designed by Sir Edwin Lutyens and has sixteen piers on whose faces the names of the missing are inscribed. It stands on a concrete raft 10ft thick built 19ft below ground and is the largest British war memorial in the world. It was unveiled on 31 July 1932 by HRH the Prince of Wales in the presence of the President of the French Republic. During the 1980s it had to be refaced owing to deterioration of the original bricks chosen by Lutyens. Behind the Memorial is a small Anglo-French Cemetery, which symbolises the joint nature of the war. Its construction was paid for equally by both governments and 300 dead of each nation are buried there, the French graves marked by crosses, the British by their traditional headstones.

This area was captured by the 18th Division on 27 September 1916 in Part 4 of the Somme Battle and a memorial to them stands at the road junction behind Thiepval. There is another in Trônes Wood. Thiepval fell to the Germans again on 25 March 1918 and was recaptured by the 17th and 38th (Welsh) Divisions on 24 August 1918.

The 73,000 names include musicians (like **Lt George Butterworth, MC**, of the DLI), **writers** (like **Lce Sgt Hector Hugh Monro, known as 'Saki'**, of the 22nd Royal Fusiliers), poets (like **Lt T. M. Kettle** of the Dublin Fusiliers) and **Victoria Cross Winners T/Capt E. Frankland Bell**, 9th RIF, **Pte W. Buckingham**, 2nd Leicesters, **T/Lt G. Cather**, 9th RIF, **Pte 'Billy' McFadzean**, 14th RIR, **Rifleman W. Mariner**, 2nd KRRC, **T/Lt T. Wilkinson**, 7th LNL and **Sgt Maj A. Young**, Cape Police, SAF, and the inspiration for P.G. Wodehouse's admirable butler, Jeeves, was **Pte Percy Jeeves**, 15th R Warwicks, age 28, 22 July 1916, a professional cricketer who played for Warwickshire. It is worth looking in the registers for your own family name – many visitors have been surprised to discover a forgotten relative on the memorial.

A formal service of remembrance open to the public is held here each 1 July organised by the RBL, complete with military band and diplomatic presence.

Return to your car and continue round to a T junction 100m further on.

• *18th Division Memorial/19.6 miles/5 minutes/Map 5/37*

The obelisk commemorates the Division's victory at Thiepval. Behind it is Thiepval Wood and the Ulster Tower may be seen to the right.

Turn right and at the Thiepval crossroads by the church take the D73 to the left.

The **Connaught Cemetery** is passed on the left and behind it Thiepval Wood – now owned by the Somme Association – apply to the Ulster Tower for details. The path to the right leads to **Mill Road Cemetery**.

Continue to the tower on the right.

The book shop, Thiepval Visitor & Education Centre.

RB Plaque, Mouquet Farm.

The poignant faces of some of the Missing of the Somme, which confront you as you enter.

July 1st Ceremony, Thiepval Memorial.

• Ulster Tower Memorials & Visitor Centre/20.4 miles/15 minutes/ Map 5/38/RWC/OP

This is a replica of the tower known as Helen's Tower on the estate of the Marquis of Dufferin and Ava at Clandeboye in County Down where the 36th (Ulster) Division trained before coming to France. There is a small chapel on the ground floor and in 1990 it was rededicated by Princess Alice, Duchess of Gloucester (who died in 2004). There are **Memorials** in the grounds to the **36th (Ulster) Div's VC Winners,** to the **Division (known as 'the Orange Order Memorial'), a bench to the VCs of the Orange Order** and **a flagpole** donated by the Women of Ulster. Behind the tower is a Visitor Centre and small book stall manned by the Somme Association who in 1994 declared the Tower to be Northern Ireland's National Memorial. **Open: every day** except Monday, end February-end November. Tel: + (0)3 22 74 87 14.

Stand on the road with your back to the entrance gates.

OP. Straight ahead at 12 o'clock is Thiepval Wood (now shown on modern French maps as Authuille Wood). At 9 o'clock is Connaught Cemetery and beyond it the Thiepval Memorial. At 2 o'clock on the horizon is Beaumont Hamel Memorial Park.

On 1 July the Ulsters walked, and then charged, from the forward edge of Thiepval Wood, across the road, up past where the Tower stands and on to the crest and beyond. They were the only soldiers north of the Albert-Bapaume road to pierce the German lines. Some say their achievement was due to a mixture of Irish individualism, alcoholic bravura and religious fervour. It was also the emotive anniversary of the Battle of the Boyne (on the old calendar). Whatever the reason, it was a magnificent feat of arms. Within an hour and a half, five lines of German trenches had been overwhelmed. Some

The Ulster Tower.

small parties of 8th and 9th Royal Irish Rifles penetrated the German second line, but unsupported by advances on their left or right, shelled by their own artillery, exposed to enemy machine guns on their flanks and subject to fierce counter-attacks, they were forced to withdraw at the end of the day. Fourteen hours after the assault began the lines finished virtually where they started, but the Irish, unlike most, had won the race at 0730. If the rest of the 4th Army had advanced at the same speed it is certain that the outcome on 1 July would have been totally different. Four **VCs** were won by Ulstermen that day: by **Capt Eric Bell** of the 9th Bn, Royal Inniskilling Fusiliers; **Lt Geoffrey Cather,** 9th Bn Royal Irish Fusiliers; **Pte William (Billy) McFadzean,** 14th Bn Royal Irish Rifles and **Pte Robert Quigg** of the 12th Bn, Royal Irish Rifles.

Continue down the hill, over the River Ancre and the railway.

[To the right is **Ancre CWGC Cemetery**. In it are buried some of the men of the Royal Naval Division killed in November 1916 and remembered by A.P. Herbert in his poem *Beaucourt Revisited,* e.g. **Vere Harmsworth**, son of the newspaper magnate. To the left is the area described by Edmund Blunden in *The Ancre at Hamel: Afterwards.*]

Turn left, following signs up the hill to the Newfoundland Memorial Park, Beaumont Hamel. Stop at the large car park on the left. Walk into the park.

• *Newfoundland Memorial Park/Visitor's Centre/Memorials/ Cemeteries/Preserved Trenches/22.4 miles/45 minutes/Map 5/39/40/WC*

The park covers eighty-four acres and was purchased by the Government of what was then Newfoundland as a memorial to their soldiers and sailors killed in the Great War. It was officially opened by Earl Haig on 7 June 1925. **Plaques** to either side of the entrance, erected in 1997, describe how the site was conceived by Padre Thomas Nagle and constructed under R.H. Cochus, landscape artist, with funds raised by the Government and women of Newfoundland.

The attack on 1 July was in the direction in which you are walking. The assault division was the 29th. The first brigade to go in, the 87th, was cut down and the 88th was ordered up. One assault formation was the 1st Battalion of the Royal Newfoundland Regiment. They made their attack across the area of the park you are now entering. It lasted less than half an hour. Every officer who went forward was either killed or wounded. Of the 801 that went into action, only sixty-eight members of the regiment were unwounded, one of the highest casualty counts for any regimental unit on 1 July.

The **Visitor's Centre** is on the right. In the form of a typical Newfoundland wooden building it has some interesting displays and a small bookstall. **Open every day** except Christmas & New Year's Day. April-December 1000-1800 and January-March 0900-1700. Guides available January-mid-December. Tel: (0) 3 22 76 70 86.

N.B. Because of the erosion caused by the increasingly large number of visitors it is essential to keep to the prescribed paths and not to climb into the trench lines. Archaeological explorations are being undertaken here by the Durand Group (qv).

Returning to the main path the first **Memorial** to be seen is that to **29th Division**, its distinctive red badge displayed on a stone cairn, which is on the left of the path a few metres from the entrance. Then almost immediately on the left is the bronze box containing the Visitors' Book and a **Plaque** on the right carrying a verse by **John**

Oxenham. Further on is the striking figure of a **Caribou**, the emblem of the Newfoundland Regiment (there are three others in France – at Gueudecourt, Masnières (qv) and Monchy-le-Preux). A path leads to a parapet around the Caribou on which are orientation arrows identifying various parts of the battlefield, including the three British cemeteries in the park: **Hawthorn Ridge No. 2, Y Ravine** and **Hunters** – a circular cemetery which had originally been a large shell hole. At the bottom of the mound on which the Caribou stands are **bronze Plaques** on which are named 591 officers and men of the **Royal Newfoundland Regiment**; 114 of the **Newfoundland Royal Naval Reserve**; 115 of the **Newfoundland Mercantile Marine** who lost their lives during the war and have no known grave; the **Staff of the Imperial Tobacco Coy of the 1st Newfoundland Regiment.**

Also visible are the '**Danger Tree**', a twisted skeleton of an original trunk which marks the spot where casualties were heaviest on 1 July (about halfway to Y Ravine), and in the distance at the bottom of the slope, the **kilted Highlander of the 51st Highland Division** bearing the Gaelic inscription, 'Friends are Good on the Day of the Battle'. It stands on a platform of Aberdeen granite and commemorates the action of the Division in taking Beaumont Hamel and the natural feature of **Y Ravine** (a main German support position then riddled with tunnels) on 13 November during Part 5 of the Somme Battle. The figure is some 35m from the Ravine (about 20m deep) and between them is a **Celtic Memorial Cross.**

Continue to Auchonvillers.

On the left is the welcoming **guest house run by Avril Williams** and the '**Ocean Villas**' tearooms run by her daughter, Cathy, serving snacks and meals. Under the building is a well-preserved **cellar** used as a dressing station during the war. Behind is an excavated **trench line (Map 5/41)**. Tel/Fax: + (0)3 22 76 23 66 or Tel: + (0)3 22 76 19 93. E-mail: avril@avrilwilliams.com / tearooms@avrilwilliams.com

Turn right after some 200m on the D174 signed to Beaumont Hamel and then left (still on the D174) to join the D919. Turn right towards Arras on the D919 and stop at the first British cemetery on the right.

• Serre Road CWGC Cemetery No 2/Val Braithwaite Memorial/25.6 miles/10 minutes/Map 5/42

This cemetery is one of three named Serre Road. They were begun by V Corps in the spring of 1917, overrun by the Germans in March 1918 and retaken in August. Here are over 7,100 burials, including some Germans. At the Serre end of the cemetery, outside the wall by the roadside, is a **Private Memorial** to **Lieutenant VA Braithwaite, MC**, of the SLI, a regular officer who had served in Gallipoli and who was killed on the first day of the Somme battle, along with his Commanding Officer, Adjutant and fourteen other officers of the 1st Battalion. Their attack had been made along the line of the road, and to its right, against the German stronghold known as Quadrilateral Redoubt, which was on the site of the cemetery. As well as winning the MC, Braithwaite had twice been MiD. His son fought as a Company Commander with the Regiment in the Normandy campaign in 1944. Also killed here on 1 July was Brig Gen C.B. Prowse, GOC 11th Infantry Brigade, also SLI, who gave his name to 'Prowse Point' Cemetery, Plugstreet Wood. He is buried in Louvencourt Mil Cemetery.

The Visitors' Centre, Newfoundland Memorial Park.

The mourning Caribou.

Memorial to 13th, 14th Bns, York & Lancs, Sheffield Memorial Park.

The imposing entrance to Serre Road No. 2 CWGC Cemetery.

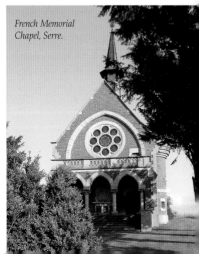

French Memorial Chapel, Serre.

Beyond the cemetery was the German fortified trench system called Heidenkopf, part of which stuck out towards the British Front Line. It was in a dugout in No Man's Land near this position that the poet Wilfred Owen experienced the events that led to the writing of one of his most famous poems, *The Sentry*. In the spring of 2003 the BBC, with a group of experienced battlefield archeologists co-ordinated by Andy Robertshaw and Owen's nephew Peter, set out to try and find that dugout. The farmer who owned the field gave the team nine days to conduct their exploration. During that time they did in fact discover the German trenches and in them three sets of human remains, one of them with a clearly identifiable name tag. He was Wehrmann Jakob Hönes of 7 Kompanie, 121 RIR killed on 13 June 1915. Another was a Würtemburger NCO and the third was a soldier of the King's Lancaster Regt. Owen's dugout was not, however, discovered.

Continue to

• French National Cemetery, Memorial Chapel, Serre Road No 1 CWGC Cemetery/25.9 miles/15 minutes/Map 5/43/44/45

The French Cemetery contains more than 800 graves of men from two infantry regiments – the 243rd and the 327th – both raised in Lille. It was constructed in 1921 and opposite, on the right of the road, is a **Memorial Chapel** at the entrance to which is a **Plaque to the 1st Bavarian Reserve Infantry Regiment.**

Next to the French Cemetery is **Serre Road No. 1.** This was begun in May 1917 by V Corps but was enlarged after the Armistice by concentration of over 2,000 graves from other parts of the Somme battlefield. There are some 2,100 burials, including seventy-one French soldiers. On 1 July 1916 it was the Leeds and Bradford Pals who attacked here, i.e. the 15th, 16th and 18th West Yorks.

On the other side of the road are signs to **the Redan Ridge cemeteries**, **Waggon Road and Munich Trench.**

Continue to a track to the left signed to CWGC Cemeteries.

Archway Sheffield Memorial Park.   *12th Bn. York & Lancs Memorial, Serre.*

Extra Visit to Serre Road No. 3 (Map 5/46), Sheffield Memorial Park & Memorials (Map 5/47), Railway Hollow, Luke Copse & Queen's CWGC Cemeteries (Map 5/48).
Round trip: .8 miles. Approximate time: 45 minutes

Turn left up the track noting that it is an active agricultural pathway. If it is very dry it may be possible to drive as far as Serre Road No 3.

Serre Road No 3 CWGC Cemetery. This tiny cemetery contains eighty-one burials, mostly W Yorks from 1 July with four Special Memorials.

Continue to the enclosed area to the left.

Sheffield Memorial Park. This contains **Memorials to the Accrington, Barnsley, Chorley and Sheffield Pals, to Pte A.E. Bull of the 12th York & Lancs** and to **Alister Sturrock**. The grassed park area covers some of the trenches from which the northern Pals received their baptism of fire on 1 July 1916. At the bottom is **Railway Hollow CWGC Cemetery** containing 107 burials, mostly York & Lancs of 1 July, plus one French grave.

Straight ahead with your back to the entrance up a grassy path is

Queen's CWGC Cemetery. This small cemetery contains 311 burials mostly from July and November 1916, including Accrington Pals.

To the left is

Luke Copse CWGC Cemetery. This contains seventy-two burials including men of the Sheffield City Bn, with two brothers, **L Cpl F and Pte W Gunstone** and a **Memorial to the 2nd Suffolks**, 13 November 1916. Originally there were four copses here named after the Apostles.

Return to the main road and pick up the main itinerary.

Continue into the village of Serre. On the left is

• *12th Bn York & Lancs Memorial, Serre/26.5 miles/5 minutes/Map 5/49*

This was raised by Sheffield to her Pals. The village was a German fortress and there were no significant gains here during the July or November 1916 fighting. The Germans eventually withdrew on 24 February 1917 and the Manchesters moved in the following morning.

• *End of Somme Battlefield Tour*

N.B. The road continues on into Arras for R/WC.

THE CHEMIN DES DAMES: THE SECOND BATTLE OF THE AISNE

16 APRIL 1917-23 OCTOBER 1917- MAY-NOVEMBER 1918

'Adieu la vie, adieu l'amour,
Adieu toutes les femmes!
C'est bien fini, c'est pour toujours
De cette guerre infâme.
C'est à Craonne, sur le plateau,
Qu'on doit laisser sa peau,
Car nous sommes tous condamnés.
Nous sommes les sacrifiés.'

'Goodbye life, goodbye love,
Goodbye all the girls!
It's really the end, forever,
Of this infamous war.
It's on the plateau, at Craonne,
That we have to leave our skins,
Because we're all condemned.
We're being sacrificed.'

Anonymous. *Song of Craonne*. Sung during the mutinies of 1917.

The Credo of the 4th French Tanks
'I believe in everything we are told by Capitaine Lemaire.
In the superiority of military services
In the all-powerfulness of the Schneider
In the value of Hébert's gymnastics
In the power of green peppermint
In the 'Crucifix' brand of port
And in everything that makes up the Tank Corps!
Amen.'

A.S. Vignol, 4th (Bossut's) Unit

'Grave mistakes were made in the course of our last offensive.
We must have done with rash plans whose grandiose conception
hardly hides their emptiness and lack of preparation.'
Painlevé, French Minister for War after the Second Battle of the Aisne

SUMMARY OF THE BATTLE

On 16 April 1917 the French 5th and 6th Armies under Nivelle launched an attack on a front of 40kms north from the Aisne towards the high ground between Soissons and Reims with the aim of breaking out beyond it. The combined effects of accurate and heavy German artillery fire, the loss of surprise and atrocious weather of sleet and snow stopped the French offensive on the Chemin des Dames ridge. Nivelle was removed. French casualties are estimated at 187,000, German at 163,000.

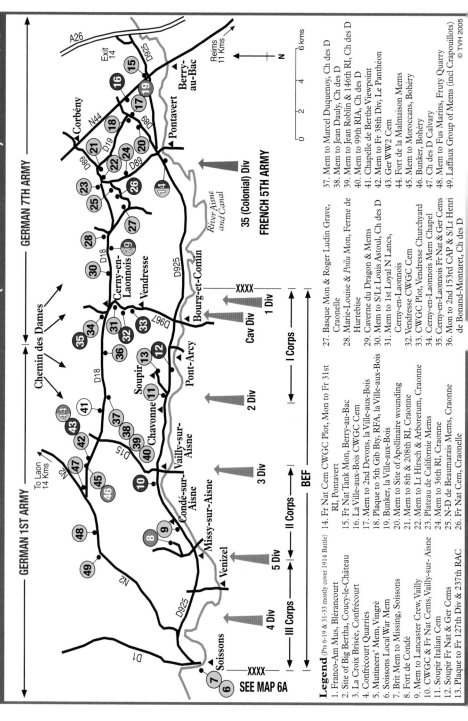

MAP 6: AISNE/CHEMIN DES DAMES: 12-13 SEPTEMBER 1914 (SHOWING FORMATIONS)/APRIL 1917/1918

© TVH 2005

Legend (Pts 6-19 & 31-33 mostly cover 1914 Battle)

1. Franco-Am Mus, Blérancourt
2. Site of Big Bertha, Coucy-le-Château
3. La Croix Brisée, Confrécourt
4. Confrécourt Quarries
5. Mutineers' Mem, Vingré
6. Soissons Local War Mem
7. Brit Mem to Missing, Soissons
8. Fort de Condé
9. Mem to Lancaster Crew, Vailly
10. CWGC & Fr Nat Cems, Vailly-sur-Aisne
11. Soupir Italian Cem
12. Soupir Fr Nat & Ger Cems
13. Plaque to Fr 127th Div & 237th RAC

14. Fr Nat Cem CWGC Plot, Mon to Fr 31st RI, Pontavert
15. Fr Nat Tank Mon, Berry-au-Bac
16. La Ville-aux-Bois CWGC Cem
17. Mem to 2nd Devons, la Ville-aux-Bois
18. Plaque to 5th Gib Bty, RFA, la Ville-aux-Bois
19. Bunker, la Ville-aux-Bois
20. Mem to Site of Apollinaire wounding
21. Mem to 8th & 208th RI, Craonne
22. Mem to Lt Hirsch & Arboretum, Craonne
23. Plateau de Californie Mems
24. Mem to 36th RI, Craonne
25. N-D de Beaumarais Mems, Craonne
26. Fr Nat Cem, Craonelle

27. Basque Mon & Roger Ludin Grave, Craonelle
28. Marie-Louise & *Poilu* Mon, Ferme de Hurtebise
29. Caverne du Dragon & Mems
30. Mem to S/Lt Louis Astoul, Ch des D
31. Mem to 1st Loyal N Lancs, Cerny-en-Laonnois
32. Vendresse CWGC Cem
33. CWGC Plot, Vendresse Churchyard
34. Cerny-en-Laonnois Mem Chapel
35. Cerny-en-Laonnois Fr Nat & Ger Cems
36. Mon to 2nd 153rd CAP & S/Lt Henri de Bonand-Montaret, Ch des D

37. Mem to Marcel Duquenoy, Ch des D
38. Mem to Jean Dauly, Ch des D
39. Mem to Jean Roblin & 146th RI, Ch des D
40. Mem to 99th RIA, Ch des D
41. Chapelle de Berthe Viewpoint
42. Mem to Fr 38th Div, Le Panthéon
43. Ger WW2 Cem
44. Fort de la Malmaison Mems
45. Mem to Moroccans, Bohéry
46. Bunker, Bohéry
47. Ch des D Calvary
48. Mem to Fus Marins, Fruty Quarry
49. Laffaux Group of Mems (incl Crapouillots)

OPENING MOVES

In December 1916 General Joffre handed over command of the French forces to General Nivelle, a genial though often angry, positive-speaking man who, having done well at Verdun (qv) both believed, and appeared to be, the 'man to win the war'. He promoted what he called the 'Nivelle System' of warfare which involved the rapid concentration of forces at vital points without the use of prolonged pre-bombardments, a method that needed both complete secrecy and battlefield mobility. The German line bulged south between Arras and Soissons and Nivelle created a plan to pinch out the salient with three armies 'in 24 to 48 hours'. He took ten copies of his plan to London to show Lloyd George, who responded to the General's enthusiasm and instructed Sir Douglas Haig to cooperate fully in the attack, the British to be responsible for the assault at the northern end of the front around Arras (see **Vimy Ridge, Arras** WF-N). Nivelle promoted his plan at every opportunity, winning over the politicians if not all of his fellow Generals with the assertion that 'victory is certain'. In writing to his three Army Commanders he commanded them to 'rupture' the enemy lines and to take their forward and artillery positions with an offensive characterised by 'violence, brutality and rapidity.'

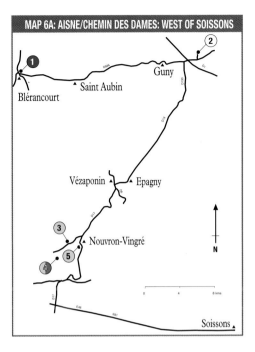

MAP 6A: AISNE/CHEMIN DES DAMES: WEST OF SOISSONS

On 9 February the Germans began a surprise withdrawal to the Hindenburg (Siegfried) Line in Operation Alberich and by 5 April the salient that Nivelle had planned to invest had effectively disappeared. Clearly not aware of the adage that, 'no plan survives contact with the enemy', Nivelle insisted that Alberich had not made any difference, despite the fact that what had been a flank attack now became a frontal attack against a concentrated enemy in prepared defensive positions. Many Generals who had been unhappy with the original plan felt even more doubtful over Nivelle's indifference to the changed circumstances, Pétain in particular saying that the Allies did not have sufficient strength to carry out the plan. Nivelle threatened to resign but President Poincaré and the politicians that he had charmed, though uneasy, felt unable to gainsay his confidence and the attack, which had become known as 'the best publicised secret of the war', went ahead.

WHAT HAPPENED

At 0600 on 16 April, between Soissons and Reims, 19 Divisions of the French 5th (Mazel) and 6th (Mangin) Armies went into the attack with an enthusiasm generated by their Commander's confidence and with the belief that a great victory would soon be theirs.

They were supported by thousands of artillery pieces (estimates vary from 3,000 to 5,000) and with a new innovation – a creeping barrage planned to move ahead of the infantry and thus keep down the heads of the German defenders, the German 7th Army under General von Bohm. Then, too, there were some 200 tanks, spotting and fighter aircraft and overall more than 1 million men. Could such an assault fail? It could and did. The 16th of April 1917 was to be for the French what the 'First Day on the Somme' is to the British.

On the night of 15 April Nivelle's message was read out to his troops, 'The hour has come! Courage and confidence! Long live France!' The Kaiser meanwhile had sent a message to the Crown Prince of Bavaria, 'The great French infantry attack is hourly awaited... all Germany is expectantly watching her brave sons... my thoughts are with them.'

As the infantry climbed out of their trenches in pouring rain and the rolling barrage and the tanks moved forward, the German artillery and machine guns rained destruction upon them. The attack, so publicised by Nivelle, had been expected and the Germans had planned for it, even having a copy of the attack orders which had been found in the satchel of a sergeant of the 3rd Zouaves captured on 4 April. Of the 200 tanks, 132 were Schneiders (developed by the Schneider company in conjunction with Colonel Estienne (qv) and inspired by the design of the American Holt tractor) which were in action for the first time. Most of the Schneiders were put out of action, fifty-seven being totally destroyed. The crew of six had little hope of surviving a direct artillery hit as the petrol tanks were alongside the hull machine-gun positions.

The infantry bravely pushed on but the creeping barrage moved too quickly, the troops struggling through the mud could not keep up with it. At 1430 the Germans began carefully planned counter-attacks and by the end of the day the French had had 40,000 casualties. Mangin's command had a high proportion of Colonial troops (some 40,000 served on the Chemin and 10,000 became casualties) and chilled by the cold weather many found the conditions unbearable and ran back into the rear areas spreading alarm and uncertainty. Instead of being some six miles beyond the Chemin the French were stuck on, or struggling up, its lower slopes. In their trenches, wet and demoralised, the *Poilus'* morale plunged from the highs to which Nivelle's boasting had taken it, to the level of despair. By the evening of the first day it was clear that the planned break-through would not be possible. Nivelle had promised to end the assault if success had not been achieved within forty-eight hours but he did not do so and he continued the attacks. A small gain was achieved in the first week in May when a five kilometre stretch of the Chemin around Craonne was taken but the affair ground to a halt on 9 May, ten days after the first French troops mutinied.

The first mutiny occurred on 29 April. The 2nd Battalion of the 18th Infantry Regiment had suffered 600 killed, wounded and missing out of 800 on the first day of the battle. The survivors moved to supposed rest billets near Soissons and the battalion was rebuilt with re-inforcements from other battalions in anticipation of transfer to the 'quiet' Alsace front. Nivelle, however, had no reserves to call upon and became increasingly desperate to snatch success from the disaster which faced him. The soldiers were no fools and they knew that the repeated orders to attack were Nivelle's attempts to save face and when the 2nd Battalion was ordered back to the front on 29 April it was too much for them.

Buoyed by alcohol they refused to go back to the trenches though eventually most of them did – some of them ironically baa-ing like lambs to the slaughter. As the column marched through the dark the military police selected about a dozen men, seemingly at random, to suffer by example for the sake of future discipline. All were tried and five were sentenced to death. Of the five one escaped but the other four were shot.

The actions of the 2nd Battalion became the stuff of rumour and fantasy, casualty figures in the absence of official numbers were greatly exaggerated, feeding the anger of the soldiers, and unrest spread. Almost 24,000 troops would eventually mutiny and fifty-five would be shot though, extraordinarily, for almost a decade little news of the mutinies got out to the Germans, Allies or the general public. On 15 May Pétain replaced Nivelle. It was now Pétain's job to rebuild the French army.

On 27 May 1918 the third of the German offensives, often known collectively as the 'Kaiser's Battles', struck along the Chemin des Dames against General Duchêne's 6th Army. Two German Armies took on twelve Allied Divisions of which three were British – the 8th, 21st and 50th – whose defensive positions were only lightly held (see OPENING MOVES – THE SECOND BATTLE OF THE MARNE) stretching roughly fifteen miles from the area of the Caverne du Dragon east to the N44. Three days later the Germans reached the Marne having crossed both the Aisne and the Vesle, but just above Pontavert, at the eastern edge of the Chemin fifteen miles north-west of Reims, one British Battalion of 8th Division stood firm and the record of their stand is there to see today.

THE BATTLEFIELD TOUR

(This covers the Aisne 1914, and the Chemin des Dames 1917, 1918)

• **The Route:** The tour begins at the Franco-American Museum, Blérancourt, visits Soissons and the French and British Memorials, follows the course of the Aisne through the British crossing points at Missy-sur-Aisne, Vailly-sur-Aisne, Condé-sur-Aisne, Chavonne, Soupir (with its French, Italian and German Cemeteries), Bourg-et-Comin (CWGC Plot in the Local Cemetery) to Pontavert (French Cemetery with CWGC Plot and Memorials to the French 31st RI) to Berry-au-Bac (French National Tank Memorial). Ville-aux-Bois CWGC Cemetery, and 2nd Devons/5th Bty, RFA Memorials and Apollinaire Memorial; Craonne Arboretum and French Memorial; California Plateau, Old Craonne & Orientation Table; Basque Monument; Hurtebise French Monument; Caverne du Dragon; Chemin des Dames Memorials; Cerny-en-Laonnois Loyal N Lancs Mem, Memorial Chapel, French National and German Cemeteries; Vendresse British and Local Cemeteries; Fort de Malmaison; Chapelle Sainte-Berthe; Laffaux Memorials incl National Crapouillots Monument.

• **Extra Visits:** Site of Big Bertha, Coucy-le-Château; the Mutineers' Memorial, Vingré; WW1 Quarry Art, Confrécourt; Fort de Condé; 36th RI Memorial, Craonne.

• **Total time:** 8 hours 15 minutes

• **Total distance:** 85.0 miles

• **Distance from Calais to start point :** 145.5 miles

• **Base Towns:** Soissons, Laon, Lac d'Ailette

• **Map:** Michelin 511 Regional NORD Flandres, Artois, Picardie

From Calais take the A16-A26 direction Paris to Exit 11, St Quentin Sud then take the D1 direction Soissons.

N.B. An alternative to starting the tour at Blérancourt would be to continue on the A26-E17 motorway from St Quentin and exit at Laon. Then take the N2 direction Soissons to the junction with the D18 and drive the itinerary in reverse. This makes challenging use of our directions!

At the junction at Terguier with the N32 to Soissons keep on the D1. The Franco-American Museum is now signed to Blérancourt. Take the D934 and continue to the T junction. Turn right and right again at the Hôtel de Ville. Pass the local memorial on the right and continue to the entrance to the Château and park outside the archway.

Set your mileometer to zero.

• *Musée National de la Coopération Franco-Américaine, Blérancourt/ 0 miles/45 minutes/ Map 6/1/RWC*

This unique museum was inspired by Americans Anne Murray Dicke and Anne Morgan (daughter of the steel magnate) who arrived in the town in 1917 to help the war effort and the local population. With Pétain's help they installed themselves in the remains of the Château (close to the front line) which had been built by Salomon de Brosse for Bernard Potier de Gesvres in the seventeenth century. The main section of the Château had been destroyed during the Revolution and only the entrance arch and 'pavilions' remained. These remarkable women erected prefabricated wooden huts in the empty central area (and a recreated hut stands there today) and from there their teams of doctors and social workers (all female) sallied out to succour the wounded in their model T Ford ambulances. The ambulances were donated by the American Field Ambulance Service whose drivers were recruited from university students, mainly from the East Coast.

After the war, in an ambitious programme known as CARD (*Comité américain pour les régions dévastés*) they turned their attention to the problem of looking after the health, of feeding, clothing, housing and educating the pitiful refugees of Picardy as they returned to their shattered homeland. Five free libraries were set up, with children's sections and today there is a recreation of a 1920s children's library in the museum. Two

The Château de Blérancourt with the reproduction wooden hut through the entrance arch.

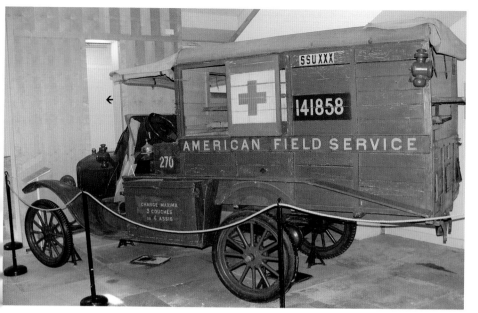

AFS Ambulance, Blérancourt Museum.

of the pavilions were converted to house the original museum (today they contain Anne Morgan's extraordinary collection of photographs and film and the archives). In 1930 the museum was taken over by the State.

In 1989 a superb, award-winning wing, the Gould Pavilion, using marble and delicately-coloured sycamore wood, was built by architects Yves Lion and Alain Levitt. It contains a remarkable collection of paintings by American artists who all had connections with Europe, some on loan from other important museums in France. There are also changing temporary exhibitions of paintings, drawings or photographs. In 2003, for example, there was an exhibition of the war-time drawings in the cubist style, by Jean Hugo (Victor Hugo's great-grandson). It also has a superb model T Ford ambulance and documentation about the Lafayette Squadron.

The buildings are surrounded by the unique 'Gardens of the New World', with three different seasonal sections. In the garden is a statue of George Washington, identical to the ones in Richmond, Virginia, and in Trafalgar Square, London. A line of fine poplar trees is a memorial to the ambulance drivers who were killed in the war.

There are plans for further expansion into a new wing to be opened in 2006.

Opening times: every day except Tuesday (plus 1 May, 25 December, 1 January) 1000-1230 and 1400-1800. Entrance fee payable. Gardens open all year 0800-1900, entry free. Handicapped facilities. Tel: + (0)3 23 39 60 16. Fax: + (0)3 23 39 62 85.

N.B. As the museum may be closed for the new works it is important to telephone in advance, also if an English-speaking guide is required. Tel: + (0)3 44 38 47 02.

At the reception there is a small boutique and WCs. Adjoining the entrance arch of the museum is the delightful hotel/restaurant Le Griffon, with eleven rooms with ensuite facilities and excellent cuisine. Tel: + (0)3 23 39 23 39. Fax: + (0)3 23 39 11 20.

Extra Visit to Site of the Big Bertha, Coucy-le-Château (Map 6/2) Round trip: 16.0 miles. Approximate time: 30 minutes

Return to the junction with the D1, go straight over and follow signs to Coucy-le-Château and Emplacement de Grosse Berthe. After 7.8 miles turn left up a muddy track through the woods.

The large circular gun emplacement is some .3 mile up the track and is only visible when one is about to fall into it. On it could be mounted one of the four huge guns with a range of 110kms which the Germans situated around the Aisne and pointed at Paris (hence the name 'The Paris Gun'). The French nicknamed them 'Berthes' after Krupp's daughter. At 0720 on 23 March 1918 the first shells fell on the 19th Arrondissement of Paris from a gun situated at Montoir, Crépy-en-Laonnois. Twenty-five minutes later a shell landed on the Gare de l'Est, but panic was at its highest when on 29 March 1918 a shell fell on the Church of Saint Gervais killing 75 and wounding ninety. Altogether the massive guns fired 300 125kg shells, killing 256 and wounding 620 people over distances of up to 140kms, taking four minutes to reach Paris. They could not fire with any accuracy upon a specific target but were designed to cause terror. In this they were highly successful. At the beginning of April 1918 nearly a million Parisians fled the city. The last shell was fired on 9 August 1918 and the monsters were then silenced as Gen Mangin retook the Forest of Saint-Gobain.

Return to the main road and back to Blérancourt.

[OR Continue uphill passing the ruins of the Château de Coucy to the picturesque square at the top.

The castle was built in the early thirteenth century, demolished by Mazarin in 1652. The still grandiose ruins, with the remains of the historic keep, were seriously damaged during WW1.

Here is the charming 2-star Logis de France Hotel/Restaurant Belle Vue, Tel: + (0)3 23 52 69 70, with seven modest bedrooms and an excellent restaurant with a variety of menus to suit all budgets.]

Leave Blérancourt on the D6 south and continue to the junction with the D17 at Vézaponin.

Extra Visits to Croix Brisée and Demarcation Stone (Map 6/3), The Wartime Wall Art, Confrécourt Quarries (Map 6/4) & Monument to Shot Mutineers, Vingré (Map 6/5) Round trip: 12.0 miles. Approximate time: 1 hour 30 minutes

This is a quite extraordinary Extra Visit and well worth the deviation.

Turn right on the D17 towards Nouvron Vingré. Just before the village turn right on the D2020 and continue to the large farm complex with massive gates on the right.

This is the **Ferme de Confrécourt,** rebuilt on this site some distance from the original after the war. One should apply well in advance to the owner, M. Pamart, Address: Ferme de Confrécourt, 02290 Nouvron-Vingré, Tel: + (0)3 23 74 25 90, for an appointment if you wish to visit the quarries.

During the war the quarries near the ancient ruined farm here sheltered thousands of men who left some extraordinary sculptures, engravings and drawings on the walls. In the Aisne district there are some 400 of such quarries and underground shelters

Extra visit continued

which still bear the traces of their wartime occupants and the future preservation of these fragile and moving reminders of the war is being threatened. The Association "Soissonnais '14-'18" has been formed to make an inventory of those that remain. Gradually their dedicated and enthusiastic volunteers are mapping their positions, cleaning them out and placing protective iron grilles at their entrances.

You will be conducted down the road to the left to the **Croix Brisée**, the start point for the quarry tour. This stone monument recalls the original cross that stood here before the war and which was fractured by shellfire and surrounded by the dead of the 298th RI in September 1914. It was erected in 1929 and was recently renovated by members of the Association. Opposite the Cross is a **Demarcation Stone**, also erected in 1929 – two years after the Touring Club de France initiative had finished. Both monuments were financed by Jean, Marquis de Croix.

A track then leads down to the ruins of the fortified **Ancienne Ferme de Confrécourt** built by the Benedictines of the Abbey of Saint-Médard of Soissons in 893. This vast edifice was 110m long by 80m wide and included a huge barn in the courtyard. On 11 September the Germans took the farm but after pillaging it abandoned it that night pursued by the Chasseurs Alpins. It was then subjected to four years of bombardment and gradual ruin. Around it the 1st Battle of the Aisne, 13-30 September 1914, raged. Gen Manoury insisted that the plateau should not be abandoned and 400 men faced two German Regiments in the defence of the farm. In the fight for the plateau the 6th Army was decimated. In the month of September alone 38,500 men were killed, wounded or missing. The Germans suffered similar losses. By November the French dead had risen to 454,000 men – one-third of the losses of the entire war. A mass grave for 500 French and German soldiers was made by the farm and later two cemeteries were made to take more of the dead.

The mobile war then settled down to the static war of the trenches and men dug in or sheltered in the old quarries of the plateau. From 16 September 1914 the medics of the 216th RI set up their hospital in the quarries of Confrécourt and it was used as a shelter for men coming out of the front line. The officers made a comfortable billet with some furniture and a fireplace, but the men lay on filthy straw, plagued by rats, fleas and the all-prevalent humidity. Stonemasons and amateurs alike of successive regiments left their mark on this extraordinary shelter: the 1st Zouaves had their own entrance to their quarry, the 35th and 298th RI carved a beautiful chapel, complete with altar and cross near a flight of stone steps which led to the front. Several repetitive themes emerged: women, religion, patriotism, caricature and regimental insignia. Here at Confrécourt these outpourings of human art by men sheltering from the horrors of the war are truly outstanding.

Also remarkable is the kilometre of Decauville narrow gauge track that runs in front of the warren of quarries.

Return to the D2020 and turn left. Continue into Nouvron Vingré and turn left at the T junction. Continue to the memorial at the edge of the field on the right on the D138.

Although the mutinies of 1917 are well-documented, there were serious mutinies as early as 1914. They were caused by waves of panic that swept through the French Army and were brutally and often unjustly repressed. Gen de Villaret ordered a tightening of discipline. On 27 November 1914 the 19th Coy of the

'Big Bertha' gunpit, Coucy-le-Château.

Decauville track, Confrécourt.

DANS CE CHAMP
SONT TOMBÉS
GLORIEUSEMENT
le Caporal FLOCH
les soldats
BLANCHARD, DURANTEL, GAY
PETTELET et QUINAULT
du 298° R.I.
FUSILLÉS
LE 4 DÉCEMBRE 1914
RÉHABILITÉS SOLENNELLEMENT
PAR LA COUR DE CASSATION
LE 29 JANVIER 1921

Memorial to Executed
Men, Vingré, with detail
of the plaque.

The Chapel to 298th & 35th RIs, Quarry de
Confrécourt.

Eric Kennington's powerful British Memorial, known as 'The Soissons Trinity'.

Extra visit continued

298th RI held the line here at Vingré (and it is their Chapel in Confrécourt Quarry that is illustrated). Their first line trenches were lost to a German *coup de main* attack and to serve as an example for lack of determination, five soldiers and a corporal were shot on 4 December 1914. The men, accused of disobeying the orders of their squadron commander, 2nd Lt Paulaud, were chosen by lot and spent their last night in a quarry in the bank over the road from the memorial. There they wrote their pathetic last letters to their families and on houses throughout the village these poignant messages are reproduced on perspex boards. The next day they were shot in the field behind the **Monument** by a firing squad in parade-ground order. Their comrades pursued their case with dedicated enthusiasm and were vindicated when the men were rehabilitated on 29 January 1921.

They were not the first to be shot. On 13 November soldier Leymarie of the 305th RI, wounded by an enemy bullet, was accused of self-mutilation and shot. Soldier Bersot of the 60th RI was shot for refusing to take the trousers from his dead pal.

Ironically Gen de Villaret was gravely wounded some 500m from this spot on 11 March 1915 and the same shot tore out the left eye of Gen Manoury, GOC 6th Army, who died, blind, in 1923. He was posthumously appointed a Marshal of France.

The story of the mutineers of Vingré was the inspiration for Stanley Kubrick's powerful film *Paths of Glory*, starring Kirk Douglas as a sympathetic officer.

The first people to be executed at Vingré were the farmer Monsieur Léopold Amory and his wife, shot by the Germans on 20 September 1914.

Return to Vézaponin and pick up the main itinerary.

Return to the D6 and continue towards Soissons. Join the N31-E46 into Soissons, following signs to Centre and 'i' for the Office de Tourisme in Place F. Marquigny.

• Soissons: Local & British War Memorials/ 23 miles/30 minutes/Map 6/6/7/RWC

N.B. The length of stay given here simply allows time to visit the main memorials. Obviously, having negotiated the route into the City, you may well wish to linger longer. It makes a convenient lunch break.

There is good parking in the square and you can pick up lists of local hotels, restaurants, city plan etc. The Cathedral of Saint-Gervais-Saint-Protais stands in this square which was completely reconstructed after the war to give a good view of this historic building. Opposite it is the Eglise Saint-Pierre, behind which is the British Memorial.

a. **French Monument aux Morts, Place Fernand-Marquigny.** This impressive memorial, designed by R. Lamourdedieu, finished in 1927 but not formally inaugurated until 1935 (by President Lebrun), shows a tableau of historic events in the city from Carolingian times. A winged figure of Victory surmounts the WW1

Soissons War Memorial.

bas-reliefs and statues and memorials to later conflicts have been added.

b. **British War Memorial, Place Saint-Pierre.** This imposing memorial (near the Pont des Anglais) was the subject of a competition won by sculptor Eric Kennington with Gordon Holt while the overall design was by Vernon Owen Rees. Kennington, who had enlisted with the 13th London Regt on the outbreak of war, was badly wounded in June 1915 and started his brilliant series of soldier portraits during his convalescence. He was invalided out in 1917 and then employed by the War Propaganda Bureau to produce pictures of the Western Front. After the war Kennington won acclaim for his 24th Div Memorial in Battersea Park which led to the Soissons commission. The monument was inaugurated on 22 July 1928 (Kennington just finished his carvings in time) by Lt Gen Sir Alexander Hamilton Gordon who had commanded the British forces on the Aisne in 1918. It became known as 'The Soissons Trinity' as it represents three young soldiers who are, according to Capt H.A. Taylor in *Goodbye to the Battlefields*, 'grim, but very peaceful and impressive, standing at the foot of a grave of a newly buried comrade.' It was constructed from a 22-ton block of local Euville stone and won much critical acclaim and local admiration for its boldness and strength. On the screen at the rear of the memorial are inscribed the 3,987 names of the Missing of the Marne and the Aisne. The memorial register is kept at the *Mairie*.

The nearby Pont des Anglais was the setting of a poem called *The Hell Gate of Soissons* which recounts how 'in 1914 during the Retreat from Mons, twelve British soldiers, one after another, were killed in their efforts to light the fuse which would demolish a section of the bridge, and deny to the advancing enemy, the passage of the Aisne.'

c. **Reconstruction Monument, Place Saint-Christophe** (see city plan – it is within walking distance). This concrete memorial by the brothers Joel and Jan Martel is 20m long and consists of 8 columns and is surmounted by enormous wings and the statue of Capt Aviator Guy de Lubersoc who was a leading light in the post-war reconstruction. *Bas -reliefs* show the combats, the evacuation and the reconstruction. On the reverse the inscription recalls the thousands of buildings, private and municipal, that had to be rebuilt.

Follow Toutes Directions then turn right direction Laon, over the Aisne past Crouy on the D925, by-passing the turning to Bucy-le-Long take the D925 and parallel the course of the Aisne (to the right).

N.B. By turning right on the D95 the wide Venizel crossing may be visited. It was to Venizel that Hunter-Weston led 11th Brigade on 12 September 1914 and by using the partially destroyed bridge he had his brigade over the river by 0300 the following morning led by the 1st Hampshires. The battalions then fixed bayonets and set off for the high ground, reaching the spurs, which run to the left alongside the D925 between Bucy and Sainte Marguerite, just as dawn broke.

Continue to Missy-sur-Aisne.

d. **Missy-sur-Aisne.** The 5th Division had been allocated the bridges at Condé and at Missy for its crossings but because of the exposed approach to Condé it was decided to concentrate upon Missy alone. The bridge was taken briefly by 4th Division's Cyclist Company but the 1st RWK (13 Inf Bde) overcame German machine guns to secure the partially destroyed Missy bridge at about 0300 on 13 September. However, accurate German artillery fire directed from the air prevented any real use of the crossing and some units which got over by raft on 15 September were forced to withdraw south of the river.

> ## Extra Visit to the Fort de Condé (Map 6/8). Round trip: 4.5 miles. Approximate time: 1 hour
>
> *Go left into the village of Missy and turn right on the D53, signed Fort de Condé into Chivres-Val and turn right up a narrow winding road (planned improvements will allow coaches to reach the Fort).*
>
> This is a visit of particular interest to fortification enthusiasts. This late nineteenth century military fort in the shape of a pentagon formed part of the defensive system of the distinguished military architect, Gen Séré de Rivières (qv), after the Franco-Prussian War of 1870. It was then covered with three metres of turfed earth, rendering it virtually invisible from a distance, and surrounded by a deep ditch. What distinguishes this huge stone fort (which covers five hectares) is its architectural beauty with many features, like vaulted ceilings and elegant galleries, which would grace a Château. After the turn of the century de Rivières's forts fell into disuse as modern ammunition was deemed to make them redundant. During WW1 it was occupied by the Germans and partially destroyed. They were dislodged during the Nivelle Offensive of 1917. In May 1918 it was retaken by the German 7th Army and finally retaken by the French 54th RI on 7 August 1918.
>
> For many years later it lay abandoned and was bought by the Commune of Chivres-Val in 1959 and for a while was used as a stone quarry. Then in 1979 an Association to save the Fort was formed and finally in 2001 the grouping of sixty-three Communes of the Val de l'Aisne acquired the Fort and it is now undergoing an ambitious and expensive (4 million euros) renovation. It is now used for concerts and other events – particularly effective are the Saturday night *son et lumière* shows. **Open:** daily from April-November 0930-1200 and 1330-1800. Telephone in advance for a guided visit in English. Tel: + (0)3 23 54 40 00. Fax: + (0)3 23 54 40 04. There is a small boutique at the entrance and modern WCs.
>
> *Return to Missy and pick up the main itinerary.*

By-pass Missy and continue towards Vailly-sur-Aisne on the D925.

N.B. At 7.3 miles from Soissons Centre is a granite **Memorial (Map 6/9)** at the side of the road on the left to the memory of the English and Canadian **Crew of a Lancaster of 405 Sqn**, brought down here on 23 April 1944. It names the seven crew members. On the 60th Anniversary the site was cleared and planted with flowers and a wreath-laying ceremony took place here.

Continue through Condé-sur-Aisne to

• Vailly-sur-Aisne CWGC and French National Cemeteries/33.1 miles/ 15 minutes/Map 6/10

Here the British 3rd Division began crossing the river from your right on 13 September 1914. The village fell to the Germans in 1915, was retaken by the French on 18 April 1917, lost again 1 June 1918 and finally captured by the French on 15 September 1918.

Continue to the cemetery on the left.

The Cemetery, designed by Sir Edwin Lutyens, was made after the Armistice and the majority of burials are from September 1918 with many others from 1918. It contains 650

The River Aisne at Vailly.

graves, of which nearly half are Unidentified. There are Special Memorials to three soldiers and one German grave. Among the interesting burials here are **Brig-Gen N.D. Findlay**, CB, RA, CRA 1 Div, age 55, 10 September 1914 (the first British General to be killed in the war) and **Capt Theodore Wright**, VC, RE, (among the first **VCs** of the war) age 31, 14 September 1914. Wright won his VC at Mons on 23 August 1914 trying to connect up a lead to demolish a bridge whilst wounded in the head. Here at Vailly he assisted the passage of the 5th Cavalry Brigade over the pontoon bridge and was mortally wounded whilst helping a wounded soldier to shelter. Here too is buried **Orderly H.H. Jackson** of the Friends Ambulance Unit, age 28, 27 May 1918. The FAU was formed with Quaker and other Conscientious Objectors who were allowed to serve in non-combative situations.

Headstone of Capt Theodore Wright, VC.

Beside it is a **French Cemetery** which contains 1,559 burials from the WW1 and seventeen from WW2. It was started in 1917 during the Battle of the Chemin des Dames and enlarged at several different periods by burials from nearby small cemeteries. At the top is a grey polished granite **Memorial to Sgt Felix Germain Jacquinot**, 120th BCP, 8 July 1917, *Croix de Guerre* and **Col Joanny**, 68th BCP, 23 October 1917, killed on the Chemin des Dames in the battles at Le Panthéon.

Continue to the crossroads.

[N.B. By turning right signed Chassémy and continuing over the River Aisne, on the right can be seen a **Memorial to Robert Whalen**, an American soldier who fell on 29 August 1944 in the Liberation of Vailly. For the 13 September 1914 (almost exactly thirty years earlier) crossing, 3rd Div was allocated Vailly. The canal bridge had not been damaged but the river bridge had a gap in it which was crossed by planking. At 1500 8th Brigade began to cross under shellfire and within an hour the 2nd RS were established at Vauxelles Château north-west of the village and that night the RE began constructing a pontoon bridge.]

Turn left and continue following the road as it bends to the right.

You then pass the impressive **Local Memorial of this 'Martyrs' Town'**. The war destroyed the town, killed its children, soldiers and civilians but their courage did not flinch.

Continue and turn right on the D925 towards Chavonne.

By going straight on here on the D14 you would reach the high ground around Vauxelles Château which the RS occupied on the night of 13 September.

Go through Chavonne.

At 1200 on 13 September the 2nd Coldstreamers (4th Gds Bde, 2nd Division – in which many years later one of the authors was proud to serve), using a middle trestle section, crossed the partially destroyed bridge against German rifle fire and by 1730 had advanced to the top of the ridge some 500 metres to your left. However, orders came down from I Corps to withdraw and this was done, leaving just one company of Coldstreamers to guard the bridge. The reason for the order to withdraw was never discovered.

Continue and stop on the left at the Italian Cemetery.

• *Soupir Italian, French and German Cemeteries, Chavonne/37.6 miles/ 15 minutes/Map 6/11/12*

The 2nd Italian Army Corps arrived in Champagne on 25 April 1918 where it was engaged in the 2nd Battle of the Marne on 23 June. They fought in the area until 1 August and then after a period of rest they went into the line again on 22 September on the River Aisne. On 30 September they attacked and took Chavonne and the following day Soupir, but subsequently they incurred heavy losses. By the end of the war the Italians had lost 4,375 killed and 10,000 wounded, including some Italian

The entrance to the Italian Cemetery at Soupir, the Italian flag proudly flying.

The dramatic sculptures on the Monument at the top of the Cemetery.

prisoners used as labourers by the Germans and who died in captivity. The cemetery contains 592 burials beneath white crosses and in it the French flag flies to the left, the Italian to the right. In the centre is a cross with bronze books on either side inscribed to the II Corps of Gen Alberico Albricci from April-November 1918. At the top is a striking black sculpture of three heads, erected on 20 September 1921. The cemetery is immaculately maintained, the gates and the sculptures being regularly painted in black.

Continue on the D925 to the two cemeteries, French on the right, French and German on the left, in Soupir (38.2 miles).

Gen Pétain had his HQ in the Château of Soupir in 1917 when he 'took the army in hand' after the mutinies (qv). The British also used the grounds as a Field Dressing Station. Today only a ruined arch remains where the magnificent building once stood. **French National Soupir Cemetery No 1** has 7,806 French burials, of which 2,822 are in three ossuaries and 266 in a collective grave, plus one Belgian and one Russian burial.

The German Cemetery has 5,125 individual graves and 5,958 in a mass grave. Over the road is **Soupir No 2 Cemetery** with 2,216 French WW1 burials, of which 250 are in an ossuary, plus five Belgians, two British, one German and twenty-seven Russians. There are 545 French soldiers and thirty-three Belgian civilians from WW2.

Turn left by French Cemetery No 1 into the village (the ruined arch of the Château can be glimpsed from time to time on the right) *and continue to the church. Beside it is* The local Memorial with a **Plaque (Map 6/13)** to the 127th French Division (who from Soupir conquered Chavonne and liberated the plateau to Aizy) and the 237th RAC.

Return to the D925.

Ahead at Pont Arcy the Engineers built a pontoon bridge on 13 September and at 1630 under fire 5th Inf Bde completed their crossing there and the 2nd Connaught Rangers were able to move west to Soupir where, joined later by the 2nd Grenadier Guards of 4th Bde, they resisted strong German counter attacks. One of the officers with the Grenadiers was Prince Alexander of Battenburg, known in the regiment as 'Drino' who, having caught jaundice, was returned to base. One of his fellow officers described him as, 'not a heaven-born soldier and ... rather a responsibility to have on one's hands' (*Fifteen Rounds a Minute* by J.M. Craster). His brother Prince Maurice was killed on 27 October 1914 in the Ypres Salient and is buried in Ypres Town CWGC Cemetery. As the fighting after 14 September moved from offence to defence the villages such as Soupir at the bottom of the slopes became administrative areas with medical facilites, billets, supply dumps, water points etc.

Continue to Pont-Arcy.

Pont-Arcy. The iron bridge is similar to that crossed by the 5th and then 4th Bdes. It was blown by the Germans after First Marne. On 13 September 5th and 11th Fd Coys RE constructed a pontoon bridge here.

Continue on the D925 through Bourg-et-Comin.

Bourg. 2nd Cavalry Bde helped by 2nd Inf Bde crossed the river at Bourg via the tow path (the bridge was destroyed) and the canal bridge, on the 13th, and by 1300 were on top of the Bourg spur (visible to your left). The D967 that you will cross leads past eastern edge of the spur to Cerny (see Map 6) and the action there is described at Cerny.

Continue via Oeuilly and Beaurieux towards Pontavert and stop before the village at the French Cemetery on the right.

• *French National Cemetery with CWGC Plot/Monument to French 31st RI/Pontavert/49.9 miles/10 minutes/Map 6/14*

This unusually well-maintained cemetery, with flower beds along the rows of crosses and flanked by pink flowering cherry trees in the springtime, contains 6,694 French burials, of which 1,364 are in an ossuary, sixty-seven British and fifty-four Russian burials.

Information Panels at the entrance describe in detail, with clear sketch maps, the violent combats in the area to dislodge the Germans from the strongly fortified '*buttes*' in the hillside to the left that they took in March 1916. The attackers finally succeeded on 17/18 April, taking many prisoners but with heavy losses. The 31st RI won a 5th Army Citation for their gallantry. The cemetery was started in 1915 and after the Armistice was enlarged from other small cemeteries along the Chemin des Dames. It was completely relandscaped in 1972. At the top is a **Memorial** to the dead of the 31st RI, 1914-1918. In it is buried the **son of Aristide Briand,** the Socialist Statesman and journalist.

The CWGC Plot at the top contains over sixty graves, half of which are unidentified. Among them is **Pte H. Withrington**, DLI, 29 May 1918 and two soldiers who died as PoWs.

Continue into the village and turn right to the River Aisne. Stop

On 13 September the French 35th Div crossed here at about 1030 and later that day were attacking towards Corbény, Craonne and Craonelle on the Chemin des Dames (see Map 6).

Turn round and return to the D19 and continue to the right to the crossroads with the N44 above Berry-au-Bac.

N.B. In the French Cemetery over the river to the right is a **CWGC Plot** with some thirty WW1 burials of 27-29 May 1918, of which about half are unidentified, and a small number of WW2 burials.

By turning right here towards the town the conveniently sited Restaurant de la Mairie, with a great *hors d'oeuvres* buffet and a variety of menus, is reached after a few hundred metres. Tel: + (0)3 23 79 95 15.

Go round the roundabout and stop in the large car park.

[**N.B.** By continuing some 2 miles on the D925 one may join the A26 motorway to Reims (some 12.5 miles distant) for RWC (See Tourist Information below)].

• *French National Tank Monument, Berry-au-Bac/54.3 miles/10 minutes/ Map 6/15/OP*

The Memorial, on the site of the Ferme de Choléra, commemorates the first engagement by tanks in the Nivelle Offensive – on 16 April 1917 – and those killed in tanks. It was inaugurated on 2 July 1922 by Marshals Foch and Pétain and Generals Mangin, Weygand and Estienne (qv) who was known as the 'father of the tanks' and of whose head there is a *bas-relief*. It is the focal point of remembrance for tank veterans who hold an annual ceremony here each April and **Information Panels** give the history of Motorised Warfare. A modern tank and an armoured car stand in the car park.

Stand with your back to the back of the monument.

OP. The French attack of 16 April 1917 came broadly from your left towards the German lines which were over to your right. The tanks, led by the popular

The Tank Monument, Berry-au-Bac.   *Headstone of Lt Col C.G. Buckle, DSO, MC.*

Commandant Bossut, crossed the German lines broadly along the road that runs to your right behind you and he was killed as his tank approached the German second line, short of the village of Juvincourt. On the back of the monument is a memorial to the taking of this position, Le Choléra, by Col Moisson of the 151st RI reinforced by Bossut's tanks. Three-quarters of the 128 tanks broke down or were destroyed and many of their crews burned to death.

Take the N44 direction Corbény and continue to the CWGC Cemetery on the left.
N.B. After about a mile there is a large **Bunker** on the right.

• *La Ville-aux-Bois British CWGC Cemetery, La Musette/56.2 miles/ 10 minutes/Map 6/16*

The cemetery was created after the Armistice from the May 1918 Battles. It contains 548 burials with eighteen Special Memorials.

In the small plot to the left as one enters the cemetery lies **Lt Meredith P. Lewis**, RAF, age 22, 15 July 1918, who entered the RFC in February 1917 from the USA. Here too is buried **Lt Col Christopher Galbraith Buckle, DSO, MC**, 2nd Northants, age 30, 27 May 1918, the son of Maj-Gen Christopher Buckle, CB, CMG, DSO. He had won his awards at Loos in 1915 and on the Somme in 1916 and he had been wounded five times but by April 1918 he appeared tired and depressed, pessimistic about the chances of survival of a Colonel of the Infantry.

Across the N44 lies the village of Juvincourt. From just beyond the village at 0415 on a misty 27 May the Germans launched a strong attack supported by some tanks, gas shells and preceded at 0100 hours by a bombardment by the heavy artillery of Col Bruchmüller. They met with fierce resistance at some points along the line – notably by the Devons of 8th Division in the Bois des Buttes (qv) and the 50th Division around Craonne and at the 'Outpost Line' held by the 2nd Northants. The latter fought until virtually surrounded and their Commander, Lt Col Buckle, was last seen at the entrance to his HQ dugout, pistol in hand, overwhelmed by the enemy.

In November 1918 Maj-Gen Buckle, commanding the 2nd Army Artillery near Nieuport, travelled to the Aisne to find his son's grave. He was able to locate the HQ dugout with a small cross nearby and in it his son's message pad with a defiant final message written at 1300 hours. It read, 'All platoon commanders will remain with their platoon and ensure the trenches are manned immediately the bombardment lifts. Send a short situation wire every half hour. No short bombardment can possibly cut our wire and if sentries are alert it cannot be cut by hand. If they try, shoot the devils.'

In July 1919, Christopher's mother, to whom he had been extremely close, made one of the earliest pilgrimages to the mostly uncleared battlefield of the Aisne, probably accompanied by her husband. This poignant journey of love is movingly described in an article, *A Mother's Pilgrimage*, by author and military historian, Tony Spagnoly. It was a gruelling journey by a very frail old lady. Passport procedures were lengthy and exhausting, the Channel crossing and long train journey from Boulogne to Amiens (where she stayed at the famous Hotel du Rhin) and then the eighty miles by car through the devastated battlefields and the deserted homes of the shattered villages to Ville au Bois, gruelling. From there she walked the mile or so, across the rusting barbed wire and the old trenchlines, to her son's old HQ dugout and saw the cross above the grave of 'the joy of our life, the pride of our hearts', with his bullet-riddled helmet slung over it. The site was ablaze with wild flowers, amidst which the butterflies flittered and the song of birds filled the air. Mrs Buckle returned with a feeling of content at such an appropriate resting place for her nature-loving son.

At the junction with the D89 just beyond the cemetery turn left and continue to the crossroads in La Ville-aux-Bois. Turn left signed Pontavert on the D89. Continue to the Mairie on the right.

• Memorials to 2nd Devons & 5th Gibraltar Battery RFA, La-Ville-aux-Bois/57 miles/10 minutes/Map 6/17/18

The Devons' Memorial on the left commemorates their action of 27 May 1918. In Tournai on 5 December 1918 the Battalion was awarded the *Croix de Guerre* and Palm by the French Divisonal Gen Languishe in the presence of Generals Birdwood and Butler. It was an impressive ceremony during which the whole of 8th Division was on parade. The medal was pinned to the Battalion's Colours and a citation recorded how 'On 27 May 1918, North of the Aisne, at a time when the British trenches were being subjected to fierce attacks, the 2nd Battalion Devonshire Regiment repelled successive enemy assaults with gallantry and determination and maintained an unbroken front till a late hour. Inspired by the *sang froid* of their gallant Commander, Lt Col R.H. Anderson-Moorhead, DSO, in the face of an intense bombardment, the few survivors of the Battalion, though isolated and without hope of assistance, held on to their trenches North of the River and fought to the last with an unhesitating obedience to orders. The staunchness of

The Memorial at La-Ville-aux-Bois to the 2nd Devons, recounting their gallant action of 27 May 1918.

this battalion permitted the defences south of the Aisne to be organised and their occupation by reinforcements to be completed. Thus the whole Battalion, Colonel, twenty-eight Officers and 552 non-commissioned officers and men, responded with one accord and offered their lives in ungrudging sacrifice to the sacred cause of the Allies.' Signed 'Berthelot, General Commanding Fifth Army.' The Memorial bears the Maltese Cross of the *Croix de Guerre*.

Over the road on the wall of the *Mairie* is a Plaque to commemorate the members of 5 (Gibraltar) Fld Bty Artillery who gave their lives at La-Ville-aux-Bois on 27 May 1918. During the offensive of May 1918 the Battery was attacked by an overwhelming force. The guns continued to fire and resistance did not cease until every man was killed or injured. For this action the Battery was awarded the *Croix de Guerre*.

Extra Visit to Memorial to Site of Wounding of Guillaume Apollinaire & Bunkers (Map 6/19/20)
Round trip:1.6 miles. Approximate time: 15 minutes

Continue over the next junction.

N.B. Just past it is a large Bunker on the left. This was built by the Germans in 1916 and taken and held by the Devons in May 1918.

Continue.

On the right is the Bois des Buttes which still contains the traces of the war. In it the Devons fought their desperate battle, immortalised by the painting *Faithful Unto Death*.

Continue some 300m to the grey granite memorial on the right.

N.B. If you are coming up the D89 from Pontavert, this is clearly signed.

In the woods behind the **Memorial** the poet **Guillaume Apollinaire** (the *nom de plume* of Wilhelm de Kostrowitzky) was severely wounded. Born in Rome in 1880, he was educated in Nice and Monaco, moved to Paris in 1899 and started to write poetry at an early age. In 1911 he was wrongly arrested for the theft of the Mona Lisa and only gained French nationality when he enlisted as an artilleryman 2nd Class in the 38th RA. In August 1915 he transferred to the 96th RI and was promoted to 2nd Lt. In March 1916 he was in the front line here when he was hit by shrapnel from a 150mm shell. He was progressively moved back until he was treated in the Italian Hospital in Paris where his friend Picasso sketched him with a bandage around his wound. As a volunteer he was refused the *Légion d'Honneur* for his brave action but was awarded the *Croix de Guerre*, which he referred to as a 'cross of heavy torment'. Apollinaire's experience at the front inspired many powerful poems, notably *L'Adieu du Cavalier*, which contains the famous line (and pun – *Adieu*, Farewell and *Dieu*, God),

Ah Dieu! Que la guerre est jolie (Oh God! What a lovely war) and the long poem *Zone*, interestingly translated by Samuel Beckett. He died in the flu epidemic on 13 November 1918 and is buried in Père Lachaise Cemetery in Paris. The Memorial was erected on the initiative of the writer Yves Gibeau who lives nearby. It bears these lines of poetry,

---

Extra Visit continued

Dis l'as tu vu Gui au Galop	*Say have you seen Guy at the Gallop*
Du temps ou il était militaire	*During the time he was a soldier*
Dis l'as tu vu Gui au Galop	*Say have you seen Guy at the Gallop*
Du temps qu'il etait artiflot à la Guerre	*When he was a gunner in the War*

Continue to the end of the wood.

N.B. There is a large, unusually shaped **Bunker** on the right, built by the Germans in 1916 and used by HQ 23 Inf Bde on 27 May 1918.
Turn round and return to the Devons' Memorial.

Turn round, return to the crossroads and turn left signed to Caverne du Dragon. Continue to the junction with the D19 and turn right and immediately left following signs to the Chemin des Dames. Continue to the junction with the D18.

• *Memorial to the 8th & 208th RI, Craonne/59.8 miles/10 minutes/ Map 6/21*

The Regimental Memorial is on the bank to the left just before the junction. They saw action here in April 1917 and at Craonne-Chevreux, 1914-1918.

Turn left on the D18 signed to Craonne and continue to the junction with the D985. Just before the junction on the left is

• *Monument to Lt Joseph Adolphe Hirsch/Arboretum Old Craonne/ 60.4 miles/5 minutes/Map 6/22*

The Lieutenant of the 2nd Engineers fell at Craonne on 5 May 1917. He was awarded the *Croix de Guerre* and the *Légion d'Honneur*. On the opposite corner is the local Craonne War Memorial.

Turn right.

The village of Craonne was completely destroyed during the horrific fighting of 1914-1918. To the right a beautiful seven-hectare **Arboretum** now marks the undulating site of the village. There is a large car park with **Information Panels** beside it.

Continue to the next car park on the right.

• *Orientation Table, & French Memorials, Plateau de Californie/60.8 miles/15 minutes/Map 6/23*

Above the car park is a striking modern sculpture, showing soldiers' heads entangled in the stylised barbed wire, which symbolises the bloody battles that took place here and the fearsome casualties. The sculptor was Haim Kern and the inscription is *'Ils n'ont pas choisi leur sépulture'* – 'They didn't choose their burial place'. To some French the Chemin des Dames and its controversial mutinies is still a politically sensitive area and this strikingly emotional monument was vandalised (but now repaired) soon after its unveiling in 1998.

From the monument there is a walking tour of about fifteen minutes, with **Information Panels** along the route which illustrate the appalling conditions in which the men fought. It passes old trench lines and shell holes and a German bunker on which is a **Plaque to the 68th RI** and beside it some more **Information Panels.**

Haim Kern's dramatic modern Memorial to the Dead of the Chemin des Dames.

Detail of one of the heads in the Memorial.

The orientation table across the road shows the start line of the 16 April 1917 Nivelle Offensive. From here there is a magnificent view over the Plains of Champagne towards Reims. **Information Panels** describe Nivelle's infamous Plan and discuss whether it was daring or foolish. Although Nivelle had promised to call it off if it was not successful on the first day, he relentlessy pursued it until 25 April. Although the French took 22,000 prisoners, 180 artillery pieces and 1,000 machine guns, they lost 30,000 killed, 54,000 wounded and 4,000 taken prisoner.

The name 'Californie' comes from a nineteenth century Champagne producer, Henri Vannier, who sold his wine in America and who brought back some native seeds from his trip to the USA.

> **N.B.** By continuing along the D18 you would reach the Statue of Napoleon on the site of the mill which he used as an OP on 7 March 1814 during the Battle of Craonne. Though Napoleon defeated the rearguard Russian Corps of Blücher's forces, the Allied invasion of France was near to success and a month later he abdicated and was then exiled to Elba.

Turn round, return to the junction and turn right downhill to Craonne.
Continue to the junction with the D894 to Pontavert.

Extra Visit to French 36th RI Memorial (Map 6/24). Round trip: 1.9 miles. Approximate time: 10 minutes.

Take the D984 and continue to the memorial on the left, which is just past a junction to the right.

As you drive out of the village the tall Basque Memorial may be seen on the crest to the right.

This sadly uncared for **Memorial** commemorates the Chapel of Jeanne d'Arc established by Cdt Chassery of the 36th RI for the worship of his men. It bears the Maltese Cross insignia of the *Croix de Guerre* (an award created in 1915). Only two of the four 155mm shell cases that surrounded it now remain. The inscription was 'I ring for prayer. I ring when enemy aircraft are coming. I will ring for victory and Peace.'

Return to the junction with the D18.

Continue into Craonne.

The town was rebuilt here with financial help from Sweden as the French were reluctant to rebuild this village on the very site of the infamous mutinies. The foreign assistance was motivated by the Swedish soldiers who fought here with the French Foreign Legion.

Information Panels opposite the imposing Town Hall explain the reconstruction. When the evacuated inhabitants of the area returned to what had been their homes or farms, the task of clearing, de-mining and generally making safe this scarred lunar landscape was formidable. Then came the monumental task of rebuilding houses, businesses, public buildings and churches. The fashionable *Art Deco* style of the Twenties is evident in much of this reconstruction. Certain areas of the Chemin des Dames were declared *Zones Rouges* – so dangerous that they could never be built upon or cultivated again. These areas have been afforested.

Continue uphill on the D18 to a small shrine on the right.

• *Shrine to Notre Dame de Beaumarais/62.7 miles/5 minutes/Map 6/25*

Below the shrine is a Cross which commemorates Capt Marqué who fell on 30 May 1917 at Blanc Sablon, Mgr Douillard, Padre of the 73rd RI, the 46th RI and Col Le Coq, Cdt 18th CA.

Continue to Craonelle and the cemetery on the right.

• *French National Cemetery, Craonelle/63.2 miles/10 minutes/Map 6/26*

This moving cemetery is laid out on a slope, giving the impression of a body of men marching up the hill. Amongst the white French crosses, arranged with geometric precision on the green grass, unrelieved by any flowers, are several CWGC headstones. They are to men of the 5th E Yorkshires who in May 1918 fought here to the last man. They include **Pte Norman Gibson**, 27 May 1918, age 18, with the inscription, 'We miss him most who love him best.' There is also a French cross bearing the names of the two brothers **Chrisostome**, one a Corporal who was killed in 1914, the other a Sergeant killed in 1915. There are also the ornately shaped headstones of the Muslim

The Basque Memorial.

British headstones among their French Allies in the National Cemetery, Craonelle.

Colonial Forces (but whose graves do not face Mecca) and a Jewish headstone with the Star of David. At the top is an Ossuary with 1,809 burials, 1,738 of them Unknown.

Continue uphill to the small cross roads.

This was known as *Le Carrefour de la Mort* (The Crossroads of Death) as, like Hellfire Corner in the Ypres Salient, the German artillery was ranged on it and it was a deadly place to cross.

Turn right and continue to the large memorial.

• *The Basque Monument/64.5 miles/10 minutes/Map 6/27*

This impressive and sympathetic Monument with a statue of a Basque peasant in traditional costume, complete with his beret, his coat nonchalantly slung over his left shoulder, and leaning against an obelisk, commemorates the important role played by the 36th Division in the conquest of the bloody Plateau de Californie in May 1917 under murderous fire from the Prussian Guard. He has his back to the Plateau, from which you have just come and looks down on the scene of the Basques' attacks. The fine and unusual monument was designed by the architect Forest and sculpted by Grange. Veterans of this action talk of their comrades going mad with thirst and from the cacophony of the guns, and having to be shot to put them out of their misery.

The 36th Div was mostly made up from men from the Pyrenees and the south-west of France – the Basque region. The Basque people have a unique language and have an obscure origin. They settled in the north-east of Spain and the Gascony area of France in the eighth century. During the Spanish Civil War and following the bombing of Guernica they lost the limited independence that they had had and formed a separatist movement (ETA) which uses terrorism as a method of regaining it. But the Basques' independence of spirit made them a formidable fighting force and they were heavily engaged on the Chemin in September 1914 and May 1917 (when they took the Plateau de Californie) when casualties were so heavy that two brigades had to be disbanded for lack of reinforcements. Nevertheless the Division was back in action on the Chemin the following month and again in September 1918.

Standing with one's back to the rear of the statue the red roof of Hurtebise Farm can be seen on the horizon at 12 o'clock and there is a magnificent 360° sweeping view round the monument. Below it are the vestiges of trench lines and craters and behind it runs the start of the Chemin des Dames. There are **Panorama Boards** and **Information Panels** in front of the statue (overlooking the Valley of the Aisne) and behind it (overlooking the Chemin des Dames). The Panels describe the efforts of the 36th Division, the Monument, the Role of Padres and the involvement of Napoleon in the area in 1814.

Turn round, return to the crossroads and turn very sharp right downhill to the two yew trees on the right.

• *Grave of Roger Ludin/65.1 miles/5 minutes/Map 6/27*

A few metres into the woods, this small white cross marks the resting place of a soldier of the 280th RI, 20 July 1917.

Continue downhill through Oulches-la-Vallé-Foulon then take the first right and continue winding uphill to the D18.

You will then pass through the site of the completely destroyed village of **La Vallée Foulon**, never rebuilt, and of which only the empty communal washing pool remains on the left.

At the D18 turn left. Stop at the memorial on the right.

• *Farm and French Monument, Hurtebise/67.2 miles/10 minutes/Map 6/28*

The farm was rebuilt after the war, during which it was completely destroyed, on the site of the ancient Cistercian Farm of Vauclair. During the war this was an important strategic position as it was the key to the narrow strip (virtually the width only of the old road) of the crest whose dominating position was so bitterly fought for by both sides.

Beside the farm is the magnificent statue showing the 1814 'Marie-Louise' (the name of Napoleon's wife) of Napoleon's troops and the 1914-1918 *Poilu*. The work commemorates both the Craonne battle and the fighting on the Chemin 100 years later. Hurtebise is an appropriate spot for the memorial because in March 1814 the opposing French and Allied (Russian and Austrian under Blücher) Armies faced each other astride the Chemin right here.

From this point to the large crucifix at the corner with the N2 (which you visit later) one is driving along the very crest of the historic **Chemin des Dames**, a road which stretches about twenty kilometres along the top of the plateau, which rises some 200 metres in parts. It is a natural barrier and an enviable defensive position which has seen conflict from Roman, Frankish and Napoleonic times through to the dreadful struggles of the '14-'18 War. Its name came from the route taken by the daughters of Louis XV, Adelaide and Victoire, from Paris to the Château de la Bove, which was cobbled for the ladies' comfort. To the right here on the D886 are the ruins of the ancient Cistercian **Abbey of Vauclair**, founded in 1134 by St Bernard. Used as an ammunition dump by the Germans it was heavily bombarded by Nivelle. Now by the ruins is a botanical garden with 400 medicinal plants and an orchard containing 150 old species of apple trees. The Château de la Bove is a few kilometres further along the road.

Continue to the large car park on the right.

• *Caverne du Dragon/Regimental Memorials/67.9 miles/40 minutes/ Map 6/29*

In the car park are **Information Panels** about the Chemin des Dames and the Caverne du Dragon.

In 1997 the Conseil Générale de l'Aisne launched a major campaign to improve and promote the WW1 sites of the Chemin des Dames. The focal point of this historical area is this extraordinary and unique museum (which was the property of *Souvenir Français* and is now leased from them for thirty years) which was extensively refurbished at that time and officially reopened in July 1999. It is housed in a vast underground quarry that dates back centuries and which was in use until the nineteenth century. From January 1915 the Germans occupied the quarry (giving it its name *Drachenhöhle* because of its seven exits which belched fire like the legendary animal – although there are in fact many more exits) and converted it into underground barracks with special command and firing posts, a hospital, a chapel, a first aid post and dormitories and an electrical system. The cavern, with its 2.5 kms of galleries which lead towards Vauclair, was

The entrance to the Caverne du Dragon.

continually disputed and frequently changed hands. At times French and German troops co-habited in it and the Germans built strong walls to protect their territory, to defend the exits and to prevent gas attacks. It was finally retaken by the 152nd RI under Lt Col Barrard who took 300 prisoners after a fearsome battle in the dark.

The museum charts the daily life of the men who lived here with the use of modern production techniques, artefacts and collections, sound effects, videos and archive images. At the entrance is a topographical model of the Chemin des Dames with special lighting effects and archive images projected on two screens. In the reception area is a magnificent panoramic view over the Valley of the Aisne, a boutique (which sells the haunting *Song of Craonne* (qv)) and cafeteria.

Open: Closed Mondays and throughout January. Guided visits (duration 1 hour 30 minutes) start every half an hour with the last visit 1 hour and 30 minutes before closing time. February-December: 1000-1800. July-August: 1000-1900. Closed for lunch. Tel: + (0)3 23 25 14 18. Fax: + (0)3 23 25 14 11. E-mail: caverne@cg02.fr

N.B. A visit to this important site is a 'must' for the background information you will gain on the Chemin des Dames campaigns and for the unique atmosphere of this vast underground battlefield and shelter. Please be aware, however, that for safety reasons, one has to be accompanied by a guide. It is important during weekends and busy holiday seasons in particular, to book an English-speaking guide (and they are quite superb) in advance.

Beyond the Reception buildings are three memorials, all in a rather sorry state, as are the majority of monuments and memorials in the area – the battlefield tourism campaign sadly did not extend to refurbishing the many poignant reminders, personal, regimental and divisional, to the men who fought and died here. They are to:

1. The **4th Zouaves** with the Citation for their brave and energetic conduct at the Ferme de la Creute that they held for seven days under a violent cannonade and incessant rifle fire and repeated assaults. By Order No 20 of 29 September 1914, Gen Maud'huy.
2. The **164th Division**, Chemin des Dames 1917 (on a large boulder).
3. The **41st BCP** who fell in the Caverne and on the Chemin des Dames May-June 1917. A grey polished granite monument erected on 27 May 1982.
   Continue on the D18.

After 1.7 miles a **Memorial to 'our beloved son' S/Lt Louis Astoul (Map 6/30)** of the 70th Senegalese, *Croix de Guerre*, age 24, 16 April 1917, is passed on the right.

N.B. There is a superb view in the valley ahead of Vendresse CWGC Cemetery visited later.

Continue to the junction with the D967 in Cerny-en-Laonnois and turn left.
Immediately on the right is

• Memorial to the 1st Loyal N Lancs/70.9 miles/ 5 minutes/Map 6/31

This elegant memorial in the form of a tall Greek pillar with a coat of arms, commemorates the Battalion and all its officers, NCOs and men who laid down their lives 1914-1918. It is surrounded by railings.

The road which you are on, the D967, runs downhill past the small farm of Troyon (on the left at the first right-hand bend) through the village of Vendresse to Bourg (see Map 6). The details of the crossing at Bourg were given earlier and by 1800 on 13 September the whole of 1st Division was across the river. It was known that the Germans occupied the sugar factory which stood about 350 metres ahead of you on the left and it and Vendresse were shelled by the divisional artillery. At 0300 the following morning 2nd Inf Bde set off from Bourg in pouring rain heading for Vendresse and then Troyon which the KRRC reached about 0445. One company was sent up to the Chemin des Dames. Thus the actions which are now being described took place just in front of you (looking downhill) with the Germans occupying the heights and the BEF trying to fight their way up the hill and onto the Chemin.

Initially the Germans had been caught by surprise and some had surrendered, but by 0800 the fighting had become intense. The Royal Sussex took on the enemy in the sugar factory and established a machine-gun post in it thus

The graceful column to the 1st Loyal N Lancs, Cerny

Vendresse Brit CWGC Cemetery in the Valley of the Aisne.

enfilading the enemy still opposing the KRRC at Troyon. Now 1st Guards Brigade moved up, attacking towards you on the right of the road as you look downhill and not long after 0800 the 1st Coldstreams, Camerons and Black Watch all reached the Chemin to your right but with heavy losses. The Sussex and KRRC were also under great pressure and the 1st Loyals (1st Div, 2nd Bde) were sent up to help. The morning was very foggy making it impossible to provide effective artillery support and about 0900 Lt Col Ponsonby, commanding the Coldstreams, led a company-strength party to where you now are, but due to poor visibility it remained isolated for the rest of the day. The BEF's hold on the heights was tenuous and the Germans launched many counter-attacks. One at 1300 hit the entire force now clinging to the slopes, driving the R Sussex out of the sugar factory and the rest part-way downhill. By 1630 all the infantry of 1 Div was in action and General Haig ordered a general advance, but little progress was made. The isolated Coldstream force here at Cerny made its way out at midnight guided by an officer with a compass and carrying their Colonel who had been wounded.

The attempt to take the Chemin ridge had failed and the BEF got no further. The enemy opposing them had been fortified by the 'just arrived' 7th Army. It has been calculated that the seventy-eight British battalions that crossed the Aisne were opposed by at least 100 German battalions. If the Allies had been quicker off the mark at the Marne, and the BEF as a whole had had the energy displayed by Hunter-Weston on the night of 12 September, the result would have been quite different. The Loyals, Coldstream, Grenadiers and KRRC each lost over 350 men each on the 14th alone while I Corps (the formation we have been involved with here) lost some 3,500 altogether. One casualty of note was Lt Col Adrian Grant-Duff commanding the 1st Black Watch who was killed on 14 September and is buried in Moulins New Communal Cemetery thirteen kilometres north of Fismes. He, as Assistant Secretary of Imperial Defence 1910-1913, had designed the 'War Book' that defined the actions to be taken in the event of war.

Continue downhill to the cemetery on the right.

• Vendresse British CWGC Cemetery/71.9 miles/10 minutes/Map 6/32

This was the scene of repeated and severe fighting in 1914 and again in 1918. The cemetery, designed by Sir Edwin Lutyens, was made after the Armistice by concentration from many small cemeteries in the region. It now contains over 700 burials, of which more than half are unidentified and there are several special memorials to three soldiers and to fifty men buried elsewhere whose graves were destroyed by shell fire. Here is buried **Brig Gen Ralph Hamer Husey**, DSO + Bar, MC, four times MiD, Order of Merit, 4th Class (Montenegro), commanding 25th Inf Bde, who died on 30 May of wounds received on 27 May 1918, age 36. He landed in France on 4 November 1914 and was wounded four times.

Also buried here is **Lt the Hon Herbert Lyttleton Pelham**, Adjt 2nd R Sussex, age 30, *Légion d'Honneur,* son of the 5th Earl of Chichester, killed on 14 September 1914 'who held aviator's and pilot's certificates'. **Maj Alexander Kirkland Robb**, DLI, age 42, killed 20 September 1914, was described by one of his men, Pte T. Warwick (who purportedly won the VC, though no record can be found of him), thus, 'The Germans were entrenched not eighty yards away on the other side of a hill, their trenches being far more formidable than ours. We had not very long to wait before shells and bullets began to fly about us in all directions. Our men tried to rush up the hill, but first one and then the other fell under the hail of fire. The Germans were at least twelve to one, but our men held their own, fighting as I have never seen men fight before. We had a great leader in Maj Robb. He led the men splendidly.' Robb was then obviously hit and Warwick, who had brought two other wounded soldiers back under fire, recounted, 'My last journey was the most difficult of all. I had to travel over the crest of the hill to within thirty yards of the German trenches, and how I escaped being killed I really do not know. I crawled on my stomach and got along as best I could and I am glad to say that I succeeded in bringing Maj Robb back right as it were from the very noses of the Germans. It was a hard job to get him, and in my effort I was shot through the back and fell.'

Continue downhill into the village and turn right on the D88 signed Moussy, follow the road round past the Mairie and stop by the church.

• Vendresse Churchyard Cemetery/72.3 miles/10 minutes/Map 6/33

At the rear of the church, surrounded by a small hedge, is a plot of over eighty CWGC burials, half of which are unidentified. There are special memorials to thirty-five soldiers known to be buried here. Unusually men are buried eight, six, three and two beneath one headstone – hence the surprising number of burials in this small space. Here is buried **Capt Riversdale Nonus Grenfell,** twin brother of Capt the Hon Frances Octavious Grenfell, one of the first VC winners of the war, and cousin of the poet, Capt the Hon Julian Grenfell.

In the adjoining grave is **Lt G.V. Naylor-Leyland**, R Horse Guards, age 22, 21 September 1914, MiD. His inscription reads, 'His Colonel wrote he was the bravest of officers and loved by his men.' These words are particularly touching as it shows how impressed the grieving and proud parents were of the words written by a caring CO – a message that he and his peers would have had the sorrow to write, comfortingly, to the bereaved families, many, many times – whether it was fully deserved or not. As this book is being written, Donald Rumsfeld the American Secretary of Defense is under severe criticism for the letters that his department has been sending to those families who have lost loved ones in Iraq and Afghanistan. Mr Rumsfeld was using a machine to sign the letters.

Return to the D18 and turn left. Continue to the Chapel on the right and stop.

• Cerny-en-Laonnois Memorial Chapel, French and German Cemeteries/ 74.0 miles/15 minutes/ Map 6/34/35

This junction with the D967 is the main crossroads of the Chemin des Dames. The Chapel here is the focus of official commemorations of the battles along the crest. Like a small version of St George's Church in Ypres its walls are covered with commemorative plaques – to individuals and units. On 17 April 2003, for example, the family of Sgt Paul Léon Emery of the 146th RI, killed at Vendresse on 17 April 1917, erected a plaque to

Information Panels along the walls of the stylised trench, Royère.

Memorial to S/Lt Henri de Bonand-Montaret, 2nd 153rd CAP, 16 April 1917.

Cerny-en-Laonnois Memorial Chapel and Pillar.

The faded glory of the Moroccan Regiment Monument, Ferme de Bohéry.

him. The white stone altar is carved with rows of receding crosses. Outside are **Information Panels** describing the French burial procedures and the National War Cemeteries. Another tells of the meeting here on 8 July 1962 when Charles de Gaulle met Konrad Adenauer in a symbolic gesture of reconciliation. The top of the tall pillar in front is illuminated at night and the Chapel is floodlit, providing an evocative picture.

Over the road the French National Cemetery contains 5,150 French burials, of which 2,386 are in an ossuary, plus fifty-four Russians. It was started in 1919 from concentrations of burials along the Chemin des Dames and completed in 1925. In 1972 it was completely relandscaped. **Information Panels** inside the entrance show photos of the Chemin des Dames with sketch maps of the Caverne du Dragon sector and descriptions of the battles.

The entrance to the German Cemetery is behind the French one with a long, and in summer colourful, shrub-lined path leading to the cemetery itself where beneath drab grey crosses lie 3,533 soldiers in individual graves and 3,993 in a mass grave. There is no colour there at all.

Continue on the D18 to a memorial on the left up the bank just before the crossroads with the D883.

N.B. There now follow a series of memorials to individuals who fell in April-May 1917, erected by their parents and comrades whose monuments overlook the site of their death. Their condition is generally poor, although *Souvenir Français* maintain some of them. Unfortunately they are all sited in the banks of the Chemin des Dames at places where it is dangerous to stop.

N.B. The **Monument (Map 6/36)**, approached by steps, is to the **2nd 153rd CAP** 'who bravely assaulted Malval after thirten months of a cruel war to wrench back their countryland from an injust enemy'. Among them was **S/Lt Henri de Bonand-Montaret**, a history graduate and volunteer who fell here at the age of 19 for the love of France, of Montaret town and his French men. The inscription finishes with a quotation from one of Montaret's own letters: 'Fear nothing but pray to God for the battalion.' 16 April 1917. Their objective, Malval Farm, was in the valley to the right by the Ailette River.

Continue 1.6 miles to a crest.

N.B. On the bank to the left is a **Memorial (Map 6/37)** to **Marcel Duquenoy** of Calais, age 20, Cadet with the 350th RI, with the inscription 'In memory of our son who disappeared on 6 May 1917 in the wood opposite.'

Continue .1 mile.

German Bunker at Bohéry.

N.B. On the bank to the left is a **Memorial (Map 6/38)** to **Jean Dauly**, age 20, 350th RI, killed on 6 May 1917 in the wood opposite. 'Missed by his mother and all his family. Pray for him'.

Continue .2 mile to a bend to the left.

N.B. On the bank is a **Memorial (Map 6/39)** to **Jean Roblin** who died for France at the age of 19 and to his comrades of the 146th RI who fell with him on 8 May 1917. It bears the roundel of *Souvenir Français*.

Continue .4 miles to a memorial in the bushes on the left.

N.B. The monument **(Map 6/40)** is to the **99th RIA**, 20 May 1917 and 8 June 1940.

Continue to the large parking area on the right.

• Chapelle de Berthe Viewpoint, Royère/79.7 miles/10 minutes/Map 6/41

In the car park is a narrow sunken walkway, like a stylised trench, on whose walls are extremely interesting **Information Panels.** It was in this area that the Colonial troops in whom Gen Mangin had such confidence acquitted themselves with exceptional bravery and honour. The panels describe 'The French Melting Pot', the 600,000 men recruited from the Colonies during the war, 500,000 of whom came to Europe and 72,000 of whom were killed. The Germans mounted a propaganda campaign to discredit them, inventing stories of 'black outrages'. Other panels describe the Malmaison Offensive in clear detail. The French attacks were going in the direction ahead of the viewpoint and the wooded promontary to the left is the site of the Fort de Malmaison.

Up the slope is a superb viewpoint with **Information/Panorama Panels,** over the Ravine des Bovettes and as far as the tip of the Cathedral of Laon (visible between two Panoramas), with trench maps and aerial photos over the Chapelle de Berthe and Fort de Malmaison.

The Chapel beyond, on the site of an ancient chapel by a spring whose waters reputedly cured fever, damaged by Blücher's forces in 1870 and completely razed in '14-'18, was rebuilt in 1932.

Continue into Le Panthéon and the cemetery on the right at the crossroads.

N.B. On the right hand corner is a **Memorial to the 38th Div (Map 6/42)**, 23 October 1917, who left here for the assault. In one rush the 4th Zouaves attacked the Fort de Malmaison, achieving all their objectives and taking 600 prisoners, seventeen cannons and many machine guns.

• German WW2 Cemetery/Fort de la Malmaison Memorials/92.7 miles/10 minutes/Map 6/43/44

The large German WW2 cemetery contains 11,808 burials. The dead were concentrated from many parts of France and buried on this symbolic site. Beside the cemetery are **Information Panel**s explaining the strategic importance of the area.

Behind it are the ruins of the old fort which was made into a strong defensive position by the Germans and attacked by the Moroccans in October 1917 when the 2nd and 5th Divisions of the German Imperial Guard were decimated. The undulating grassed ground of the Fort, covered with flowering wild fruit trees in the springtime, can be seen through the fence. For a guided visit, apply to the Caverne du Dragon (qv). **Information Panels** in the car park describe the Fortification System designed by Séré de Rivières (who built the Fort de Condé visited earlier), the Malmaison Fort and the testing of explosives.

Continue .4 miles.

N.B. Here on the right is what was obviously once a splendid **Memorial to the Moroccan Regiment (Map 6/45)** with a bronze badge on the side and their anchor device with Arabic script. It records how the Regiment, under its energetic Commander, Lt Col Debailleul, received its 6th Army Citation. It was for their audacious and remarkable execution of a dangerous and difficult manoeuvre to take the Quarries of Bohéry and trenches on the Chemin des Dames, held by the Prussian Guard, 'at all cost'. They took 950 prisoners (including fourteen officers) and ten cannons. An arrow on the side of the monument points ahead to Bohéry which is beyond the large **Bunker (Map 6/46)**, some 300m over the road. This is a German blockhouse, probably built in 1916, and taken by the Moroccans in the attack of 23 October 1917.

Continue past the Ferme de Bohéry on the left, through La Malmaison, to the junction with the N2.

N.B. A deviation could be made at this point to the historic and spectacular city of **Laon** by turning right and continuing some fifteen kilometres on the N2. The focal points are the famous Cathedral of Notre Dame and its eight kilometres of intact medieval ramparts, though the city boasts eighty historic monuments! The magnificent Gothic Cathedral was built with locally quarried stone. On the towers are statues of oxen, in theory to commemorate the legend of a miraculous white ox which appeared to help the workmen haul the heavy material up to the top of the 100m high hill. Today a small cable railway links the upper and lower towns.

On the right is

• *Monumental Calvary, Chemin des Dames/82.4 miles/5 minutes/ Map 6/47*

In 2004 this imposing cross which guards the entry to the Chemin des Dames was crumbling and neglected. However work was in progress to widen the N2 at this point and it is to be hoped that when it is completed the memorial, raised by National public subscription, will be restored to its former glory. It is to perpetuate the memory of 'our valiant soldiers fallen on the Chemin des Dames and in the Combats of Malmaison'. It was last renovated in 1977. On it are several individual plaques.

Turn left on the N2 direction Soissons and continue to the memorial on the right.

• *Memorial to Fusiliers Marins/Fruty Quarry/84.3 miles/15 minutes/ Map 6/48*

The monument, on a large block of stone, shows the crossed anchors insignia and their battle honours: Dixsmude 1914, Yser '14-'15, Poesele 1917, St Jansbeek 1917, Hailles 1918 and Laffaux 1918.

Behind the memorial, in the trees, is the entrance to a quarry in which carvings, of various vintages, can be found. It was taken by the Fusiliers Marins after the bitter fighting of 14 September 1918.

Monument to the Fusiliers Marins, Fruty.

Monument to Gen Estienne, 'Father of the Renault FT Tank', Laffaux.

Entrance to the Fruty Quarry.

Continue to Laffaux. Park by the café-restaurant-hotel on the right.

• *Laffaux Group of Memorials (incl Crapouillots)/85.0 miles/ 15 minutes/ Map 6/49/RWC*

On the site of the old Moulin de Laffaux, the scene of many bitter struggles during the war, have been gathered a variety of '14-'18 monuments, many in a very neglected state of repair. The most important, in the centre of the site, is the huge **French National Monument aux Crapouillots** in the shape of a mortar bomb. *Crapouillot* is French soldiers' *argot* dating from the 1880s for a small trench mortar. The monument was badly damaged by fire in the Battle of June 1940 and was rebuilt on 22 June 1958. To the right and left of the monument are plaques erected by the *Anciens Combattants* of the Cavalerie and Chars de l'Aisne and the Lefèbre Groupe of tanks.

To the right are **Monuments and Memorials** to
1. **Gen Jean-Baptiste Eugène Estienne** (qv), who conceived the Renault FT Tank, but who experienced much opposition to his revolutionary idea until he eventually convinced Joffre to authorise a pilot programme. The monument is made up from bits of tanks and bears a message from the General (who died in 1936) applauding the success of the newly built tanks in the 5-6 May 1917 Battle.
2. **Sgt Pilot Damez,** *Croix de Guerre* + 2 Citations of SM106 Sqn who was brought down at Vauxrains, some three kms along the N2, with his plane in flames after a dogfight on 19 August 1917.

The impressive Monument to the Crapouillots, Laffaux.

3. **Cuirassier Thiriez** who fell here on 7 May 1917.
4. **Frédéric Taillefert** of the 4th Mixed Regt of Zouaves, a crack machine gunner who was killed on 23 October 1917 while showing rare bravery at Chavignon in the attack on Fort Malmaison. Citation dated 9 April 1919 from Marshal Pétain.

To the left, beyond the café are memorials to **French and Allied Stenographers** with a **Plaque** from the *'Transmetteurs du 58 Regt de Transmissions'*; to the **4th, 9th & 11th Cuirassiers** and to **Henri Dupouy,** 7th RIC, who fell on 7 May 1917 age 25.

Beside the café is a sunken monument to the **1940 Moulin de Laffaux** and beyond a **Cross to Capt René Chasteigne,** and **Lt Michel Wagner,** both *Croix de Guerre* and *Légion d'Honneur* and to **5th Squadron, 9th CAP** on their victorious assault of the Moulin du Laffaux of 5 May 1917.

• *End of Chemin des Dames/Aisne Battlefield tour*
OR return to Soissons or Laon for RWC

CAMBRAI

20 NOVEMBER – 6 DECEMBER 1917

'Has not the Irish girl from the south, whose husband is in Egypt
and whose lover is in the Ulster Division, written to say there
is to be a mighty attack at Cambrai next month?
She should know! Many military secrets slip out between the sheets in war!'
Brig Gen F.P. Crozier, CB, CMG, DSO, GOC 119th Bde

'A tank, like a warship, is nothing more than a moving fortress.
The idea was so simple that by many it was not seen and when
observed by a man of the 'Haig' type of mind, its potentialities
became so terrifying that his one idea was to scrap it.'
Maj Gen J.F.C. Fuller, *The Army In My Time*

'The infantry, tanks and artillery working in combination were to endeavour
to break through all the enemy's lines of defence on the first day. If this
were successfully accomplished. . . cavalry were then to be passed through.'
Sir Douglas Haig's *Dispatches*

SUMMARY OF THE BATTLE

At 0630 hours on 20 November 1917 the British 3rd Army launched a surprise attack on Gen Marwitz's German 2nd Army using a total of almost 400 tanks. It was the first mass use of tanks in history. On the first day a six-mile-wide hole was punched in the Hindenburg Line south-west of Cambrai. It was not exploited. Two weeks later the British were back almost where they had started. Casualties on each side were about equal at 40,000.

OPENING MOVES

In December 1915 Winston Churchill wrote a paper on how the new British secret weapon, the tank, was to be used. In February 1916, Col Ernest Swinton, who had originated the tank idea, expanded on Churchill's paper. The core of Swinton's argument was that the tank should not be used until it could be employed en masse. Despite this, Gen Haig used the tank in small numbers during the Battle of the Somme in 1916 and the opportunity to overcome the enemy through the surprise use of the new weapon was lost. Yet the tank proved that it had arrived to stay and a Tank Corps was formed that set about defining the role of the new arm, its tactics and operating procedures.

At Tank Corps Headquarters in France in August 1917, Col J.F.C. Fuller (later Maj Gen), seeing how the Passchendaele offensive was bogging down in the mud of the Ypres Salient, proposed that an attempt to take St Quentin should be made, using large numbers of tanks. After discussion his idea was amended to be 'a tank raid south of

Cambrai' and this won the approval of Gen Byng whose command (3rd Army) included the Cambrai area. However, Haig's staff felt that it was important to concentrate upon the Ypres offensive and the Cambrai 'raid' was turned down. Nevertheless Byng and the Tank Corps continued to press the idea, upgrading their proposal from a one-day operation, which had no intent to capture ground, to a large-scale offensive which included the capture of Cambrai. By mid-October the Passchendaele offensive was looking ever more like a costly failure and perhaps GHQ saw in Fuller's idea the possibility of the redemption of British prestige. In any event the plan was then accepted. Gen Byng allocated the opening phase of the battle to two corps. On the right III Corps had the 6th, 12th, 20th and 29th Divisions plus the 2nd and 3rd Tank Brigades. In IV Corps were the 36th (Ulster), 51st (Highland) and 62nd (West Riding) Division, 1st Cavalry Division and the 1st Tank Brigade. Throughout the preparations for the battle great care was taken to ensure secrecy. All training took place way behind the lines which meant that units due to move up to take part in the battle had to send recce parties forward to see the ground. Those from the 51st (Highland) Division even wore trousers instead of kilts on their visits so that the enemy would not know that they were coming.

The same attention to detail was applied to the plan of attack which, much like the successful offensive at Vimy, had clear cut and limited objective lines – blue, brown and red.

The 3rd Army Commander set out three main aims for the offensive:

1. to break through the Hindenburg Line between the Escaut Canal and the Canal du Nord;
2. to capture Cambrai and Bourlon Wood;
3. to exploit towards Valenciennes.

On 19 November, the day before the battle was due to begin, Brig Gen Hugh Elles commanding the Tank Corps issued Special Order No. 6. It contained five paragraphs. The first and last were:

'1. Tomorrow the Tank Corps will have the chance for which it has been waiting for many months – to operate on good going in the van of the battle.

5. I propose leading the attack of the centre division.'

Some 400 tanks would lead with him.

On the German side the Hindenburg Line was certainly not just a line but a wide complex system of trenches, strong points, pillboxes and barbed wire defences constructed in depth. Before Cambrai were three main ribbons of defences facing the British: first that known as the Hindenburg Line, then some 400m-1,000m behind that the Hindenburg Support or Siegfried Line I, and third, about 200m-500m further still, the Siegfried Line II.

Machine guns provided mutual fire support between the lines with trench mortars hidden in covered fire positions. In all the German defences looked impregnable. Could the tank overcome them?

WHAT HAPPENED

At 0620 hours on Tuesday, 20 November 1917 the British guns opened fire and simultaneously the tanks led off into No Man's Land followed by the infantry. In front of the 6th Division was Gen Elles in his tank, 'Hilda', flying the green, red and brown battle standard of the Tank Corps. The Germans were taken completely by surprise. Tanks trailing grapples drove through the enemy wire tearing wide holes in it for the infantry to pour through. Other tanks carrying huge 2-ton bundles of wood called fascines, dropped

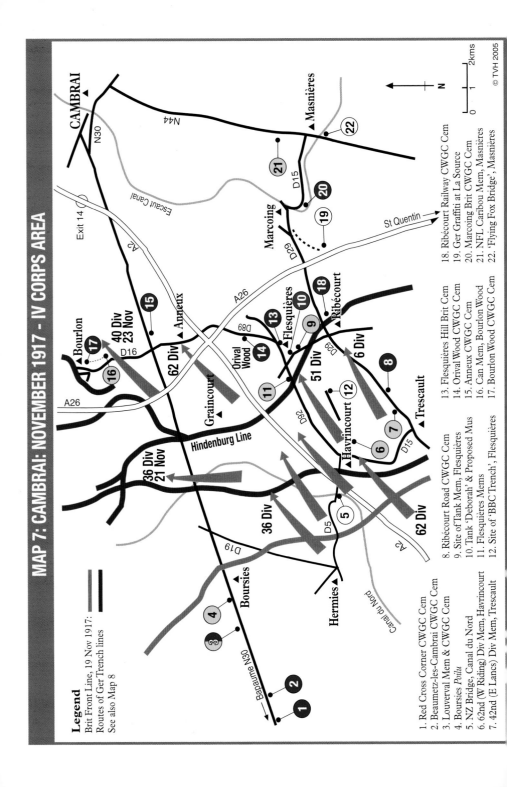

MAP 7: CAMBRAI: NOVEMBER 1917 - IV CORPS AREA

CAMBRAI

▲ Masnières

Marcoing ▲

St Quentin ➔

Escaut Canal

Exit 14

N30

N44

D15

A2

A26

D29

▲ Bourlon

40 Div
23 Nov

62 Div

Anneux ▲

D16

A26

Graincourt ▲

Hindenburg Line

Orival Wood ▲

D89

Flesquières ▲

Ribécourt ▲

51 Div

6 Div

D92

D28

Havrincourt ▲

▲ Trescault

D15

36 Div
21 Nov

36 Div

62 Div

D5

D19

Bapaume N30

Boursies ▲

Hermies ▲

Canal du Nord

© TVH 2005

N

0   1   2kms

Legend

Brit Front Line, 19 Nov 1917:
Routes of Ger Trench lines
See also Map 8

1. Red Cross Corner CWGC Cem
2. Beaumetz-les-Cambrai CWGC Cem
3. Louverval Mem & CWGC Cem
4. Boursies *Poilu*
5. NZ Bridge, Canal du Nord
6. 62nd (W Riding) Div Mem, Havrincourt
7. 42nd (E Lancs) Div Mem, Trescault

8. Ribécourt Road CWGC Cem
9. Site of Tank Mem, Flesquières
10. Tank 'Deborah' & Proposed Mus
11. Flesquières Mems
12. Site of 'BBC Trench', Flesquières

13. Flesquières Hill Brit Cem
14. Orival Wood CWGC Cem
15. Anneux CWGC Cem
16. Can Mem, Bourlon Wood
17. Bourlon Wood CWGC Cem

18. Ribécourt Railway CWGC Cem
19. Ger Graffiti at La Source
20. Marcoing Brit CWGC Cem
21. NFL Caribou Mem, Masnières
22. 'Flying Fox Bridge', Masnières

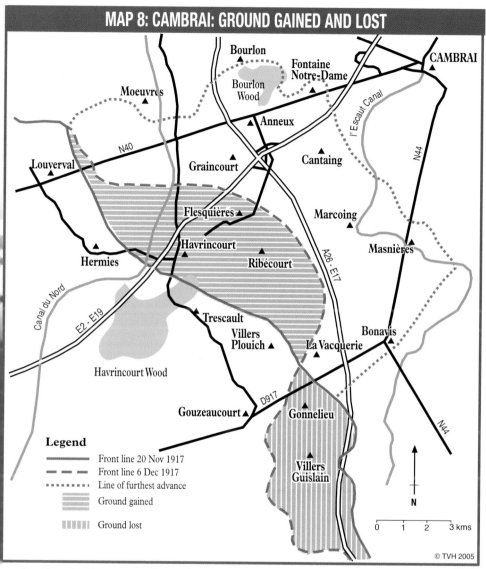

MAP 8: CAMBRAI: GROUND GAINED AND LOST

Bourlon

Fontaine
Notre-Dame

CAMBRAI

Bourlon
Wood

Moeuvres

l' Escaut Canal

Anneux

N40

N44

Louverval

Graincourt

Cantaing

Flesquières

Marcoing

Havrincourt

A26 - E17

Masnières

Hermies

Ribécourt

Canal du Nord

E2 - E19

Trescault

Bonavis

Villers
Plouich

La Vacquerie

Havrincourt Wood

D917

Gouzeaucourt

Gonnelieu

N44

Legend

Front line 20 Nov 1917
Front line 6 Dec 1917
Line of furthest advance
Ground gained

Ground lost

Villers
Guislain

N

0   1   2   3 kms

© TVH 2005

them into the German trenches to form bridges over which they and others could drive. The effect of so many of the metal monsters looming up, seemingly unstoppable through the early morning mist, was too much for many of the defenders who turned and ran.

On the first day III Corps achieved all of its initial tasks, breaching the Hindenburg Line and moving up to the St Quentin Canal. It also forced crossings over the canal at Masnières and Marcoing and it was across these that the 2nd and 5th Cavalry Divisions were planned to advance and sweep round and behind Cambrai. Gen Elles's 'Hilda', however, had come to grief before Ribécourt and he had to return to his HQ. Of the two assault divisions of IV Corps, the 62nd (West Riding) made excellent progress aided by its support force, 36th (Ulster) Division. Havrincourt, Graincourt and Anneux were taken and by the end of the day 186th Brigade had reached the Bapaume-Cambrai road (N30). At Flesquières, however, the other assault division, the 51st (Highland), was stopped dead (see Map 7).

Due to poor communications and the stationing of the main cavalry forces too far in the rear on the first day, the six-mile-wide and five-mile-deep hole in the German lines remained unexploited. Flesquières was taken on the 21st and so was Fontaine-Notre-Dame, but Bourlon Wood became a scene of bloody conflict. Little further advance was made that day. Gen Haig had initially limited the offensive to forty-eight hours. The time was now up. What to do: carry on the attacks or consolidate the gains and be satisfied? Gen Haig knew that he had no reserves with which to exploit any success because they were either stuck at Passchendaele (where less ground had been gained in three months than in one day at Cambrai), or had gone to help the Italians after Caporetto. Hope must have sprung eternal in the C.-in-C.'s breast because he continued the attack, which developed into a slogging match, particularly around the dominating feature of Bourlon.

Most unsportingly the Germans counter-attacked in force. Just after dawn on 30 November, following a short 'hurricane' bombardment with gas and smoke shells, they attacked with infantry moving in small groups and bypassing centres of resistance which were left to low-flying aircraft and close support artillery. It was a technique that had been developed in Russia by Gen Oskar von Hutier and which had been used to such effect at Caporetto. It was now the British turn to be surprised, and they were. After a week of hanging on grimly the British fell back to a 'winter line' on 6 December. The Cambrai adventure was over (see Map 8).

On 14 December 1917 GHQ issued a note saying that the BEF would cease aggressive operations and take 'a defensive posture'. Perhaps the scale of casualties was beginning to tell on the C.-in-C., or perhaps he had one eye on the Prime Minister, Lloyd George, whom he knew had half a mind to sack him if he lost many more men.

THE BATTLEFIELD TOUR

• **The Route:** The tour begins at Bapaume and visits Red Cross Corner & Beaumetz-les-Cambrai Mil CWGC Cemeteries; the Louverval Memorial; Boursies *Poilu*; the Canal du Nord; Havrincourt Château; 62nd W Riding Mem; 42nd Territorial Division Memorial; Ribécourt Road CWGC Cemetery; Flesquières & Tank Memorial, Flesquières Hill CWGC Cemetery; Orival Wood & Anneux Brit CWGC Cemeteries; the Memorials & CWGC Cemetery at Bourlon. It ends near Cambrai.
• **Extra Visits** to German Graffiti at La Source, Ribécourt Railway CWGC and Marcoing Brit CWGC Cemeteries, Masnières Newfoundland Caribou and St Quentin Canal Bridge (of 'Flying Fox' fame) and to the BBC Trench Line.
• **Total distance:** 21 miles
• **Total time:** 4 hours 30 minutes
• **Distance from Calais to start point:** Approx 90 miles. Motorway Tolls
• **Base towns:** Cambrai, Bapaume
• **Maps:** IGN Série Bleu 1:25,000 Cambrai 2507 E, 25070 O and 2607 O and Michelin 302 Local 1:150,000
  From Calais take the A26/E15 and then the A1/E15 (note that the same E road numbers can be attached to different A road numbers). Take Exit 14 on to the N30 direction Bapaume. (Do not take the Cambrai Exit!). Continue following signs to Bapaume Centre.

• *Bapaume*

Bapaume has had a checkered history, having been burnt or razed over thirteen times. It was the Allied objective on 1 July 1916. It had been occupied by the Germans as they pushed westwards on 28 August 1914 and was held by them until 17 March 1917 when they retreated to the Hindenburg Line. It was then occupied by the Australian 2nd Division, who found German fires still burning. The Germans left behind them a trail of devastation, having started 400 different fires, even leaving a delayed-action bomb which exploded on 25 March in the Town Hall, killing the Deputies Albert Tailliandier and Raoul Briquet. There is a memorial to them in *Art Deco* style to the left of the Town Hall entrance. The French journalist Serge Basset wrote, 'It is a town to cry over. Pillage preceded fire in each house. A stench of burning and of corpses envelopes this assassinated and violated town.' The Town Hall, in the main square, Place Faidherbe, was rebuilt between 1931 and 1935. In it are several memorials, frescoes and paintings which commemorate the '14-'18 War. In the square is the statue which gives it its name – to Gen Faidherbe. This is a replica of the statue, sculpted by the Parisian Jules Dechin that was inaugurated in 1891. Luckily he kept the model for it as on 29 September 1916 the statue was hit by shellfire. The Germans then took it for its scrap value, leaving the base. Dechin made the new statue, which was unveiled on 18 August 1929, placing it on the original base which still bears the scars of war.

The Germans returned to the town, which they had totally destroyed in 1917, during the March Offensive of 1918 until ejected by the New Zealand Division and Welsh troops on 19 August.

After the war the town was 'adopted' by Sheffield. It now makes a useful lunch break (but don't leave it much beyond 1300 hours) or base (see Tourist Information.)

Take the N30 north-east out of Bapaume and after some 3.7 miles stop at the well-tended grass path leading to the small British cemetery on the right hand side.
Set your mileometer to zero.

• *Red Cross Corner CWGC Cemetery/0 miles/10 minutes/Map 7/1*

The cemetery contains 190 UK Army, three UK Airmen, twelve Unknown, four S. African and one German prisoner of war. It was built where a light railway crossed the main road in mid-April 1917 and used until March 1918 by Field Ambulances. From March to August 1918 the Germans buried 350 of their casualties and ten British soldiers here. It was then known as Beugny No 3. After the Armistice the Germans were removed. Buried here is **Maj P.N.G. Fitzpatrick**, 71st Siege Bty Heavy Arty, 14 December 1917, 'son of Sir Percy and Lady Fitzpatrick of Amanzi S. Africa. Volunteered 4 August 1914 and served in the Rebellion and German SW Africa.'

Continue through Beugny with its beautifully painted golden Poilu to the cemetery sign on the right and stop by the track.

• *Beaumetz-les-Cambrai Military Cemetery No 1/2.9 miles/10 minutes/ Map 7/2/OP*

A fine uncut flint wall surrounds this cemetery which contains seventy-five UK Army and 182 Unknown burials. It was started by the Germans after the fighting of March 1918 and was known as No 9 Military Cemetery. After the Armistice 307 Germans were removed. Now it largely contains men of the 51st (Highland) Division with some men

Red Cross Corner CWGC Cemetery.

of the 6th, 19th and 25th Divisions. The headstone of **Pte W.R.O. Smith** of the Seaforths, 23 March 1918, age 20, bears the personal message, 'They paid the price to reach their goal across a world in flame.' **Lt F.C. Shackell** served in both the Army Cyclist Corps and the RFC. Beside him lies **2nd Lt W.F. Macdonald**, RFC. Both died on 23 May 1917.

OP. Stand facing the Cross and take it as 12 o'clock. At 11 o'clock on the horizon is the long shape of Bourlon Wood. The town of Cambrai is in the distance beyond the spire of Boursies Church straight up the road. Between 1 and 2 o'clock on the skyline is the distinctive church of Hermies with its dome and spire. To the right of the church is a large white silo. Halfway between the church and the silo is a short run of thick trees to the right hand end of which is a V cut. Behind this is the site of the proposed new Tank Memorial and it was across the slopes (from right to left towards Cambrai) between you and the trees that the tanks went into battle. Between 2 and 3 o'clock on the skline behind the left hand end of the near wood is Havrincourt Wood where the tanks lagered.

Continue to the memorial on the left.

• *The Louverval Memorial & CWGC Cemetery/4.2 miles/20 minutes/ Map 7/3*

The memorial is also known as 'The Cambrai Memorial' since it records the names of the 7,048 officers and men of the 3rd Army who died between 20 November and 3 December 1917 who are missing and have no known grave. They fell mostly in the fighting that followed the dramatic advances of the first day. The memorial bears the inscription, 'THEY ALL DIED IN FAITH.' It was unveiled by Sir Louis Vaughan on 4 August 1930. During 2003 and 2004 major refurbishment work was undertaken to

The Cambrai Memorial, Louverval.

replace many of the worn panels.

The names are inscribed on a semi-circular wall which has a cloistered walk and amongst the names are **Private Frederick George Dancox, VC**, who won his award near Langemarck in October 1917 and **the Queripel brothers** of the Channel Island's Militia (Capt Lionel Queripel of the same family would win a posthumous VC at Arnhem in 1944). There is also **Lt Gavin Patrick Bowes Lyon**, 3rd Bn Grenadier Guards, a cousin of the late Queen Elizabeth, the Queen Mother. (Her brother, Fergus, is commemorated at Dud Corner, Loos.) On the end memorial are fine *bas-relief* panels by **C.S. Jagger**, ARA showing graphic cameo details of life in the trenches. Jagger, who studied at the Sheffield School of Art and the Royal College of Art and who had learnt silver-engraving with Mappin & Webb before the war, joined the Artists' Rifles at the outbreak, first serving in Gallipoli where he was wounded in November 1915. Returning to the Western Front he was gassed and in April 1918 took part in the Battle for Neuve Eglise when he was again badly wounded, but survived to win the MC. After the war he returned to sculpting and amongst other masterpieces created one of the most evocative war memorials – the Royal Artillery Memorial at Hyde Park Corner. He died on 16 November 1934 at the age of 48, probably worn out by the combination of the pressure of work he undertook (completing some forty-five works between 1918 and 1934) and the effects of his war wounds.

Bas-relief of trench scene by C.S. Jagger

The Louverval Memorial itself was designed by H. Charlton Bradshaw and stands in the same grounds as the cemetery, which was begun in April 1917. Commemorated here are two men who have Private Memorials: **2nd Lt C.F. Hartley**, 2 Coldstream Guards, 27 November 1917, and **Lt H.W. Windeler**, 4 Grenadier Guards, 27 November 1917. Details of their somewhat difficult-to-reach memorials appear in *Private Memorials of the Great War on the Western Front* by Barrie Thorpe, published by the WFA. Among the 118 known burials in the cemetery (there are six unknown) is **Surgeon F.P. Pocock** who took part in the Zeebrugge Raid in April 1918 on the ferry boat *Iris* and was killed here five months later.

The road along which you have travelled was a main forward axis of the British assault and the German defences are ahead of you broadly astride the Canal du Nord which can be seen on Map 7. The preparations for the attack were carried out in the greatest secrecy with all forward area movements taking place at night. Some 1,000 guns were brought up and camouflaged, their sights being set without preliminary ranging fire. The tanks were brought up on thirty-six special trains to a Corps collecting area near Bray-sur-Somme and then moved to just behind their associated battalions. One at a time battalions were withdrawn to practice infantry/tank cooperation tactics.

The final moves to the front began on the night of 17 November. The tanks moved slowly in low gear to keep the noise down, following white tapes and the glowing cigarette tips of battalion guides, while aircraft flew overhead to mask the activity.

Continue along the Cambrai road to the village of Boursies. Almost at the bottom of the hill in the village (just before the church on the right) is a war memorial on the left.

• *Boursies Poilu/4.9 miles/5 minutes/Map7/4*

The village was immediately behind the British front line of 20 November 1917 (see Map 7). Axes such as this road were important arteries for the supplies and stores needed to initiate and sustain great offensives. In order to keep routes open, infantry battalions were rotated on 'pioneer duties' which were basically 'humping and lifting' activities. One such battalion that was working in exactly this area was the lst/5th Cheshire Regiment. Its history records the following: 'At the beginning of November it soon became evident that something was brewing as the Battalion was employed nightly with two Field Companies (Royal Engineers) of the 62nd Division on widening the main Cambrai road by corduroying, [re-inforcing the surface with logs], the north side of the road from Beugny [you drove through it just before Louverval] to Boursies. This work which was pushed on with feverish haste, was completed on the 20th.'

Four days later the Cheshires had to move back. 'The action of the enemy became much more lively and aggressive, so much so that the Battalion had to evacuate Boursies which had become a shell trap. The cook-house received a direct hit from a shell which killed a Sergeant cook . . . one field cooker was completely put out of action and a second considerably damaged.'

The village memorial is a *Poilu* standing on top of a column and the figure is brightly repainted from time to time in contemporary 'Horizon' blue – as bad a colour to fight in as a red coat. One interesting detail is the gas mask, which is rarely seen on memorial figures.

Continue out of the village and head towards the church. At the next crossroads turn right on the D34B-D19 through Demicourt to Hermies.

In the distinctive rebuilt church is a SGW showing St Theresa distributing roses to some *Poilus* and beneath the building was an underground shelter used by the Germans during the war. In 1917 the village square was merely a gigantic mine crater.

Continue and at the T junction turn left to Havrincourt Road on the D5 out of the village.
Running to the right of the road is the clearly visible line of the old railway which is shown on trench maps. Beyond the shrine on the right and the pylons marking the old railway line is Havrincourt Wood where the tanks massed in secret prior to the Cambrai attack.

Continue and stop just before the bridge over the Canal du Nord.

• *New Zealand Bridge, Canal du Nord/9.9 miles/10 minutes/Map 7/5*

The German forward defensive line ran towards you along the Canal to about 1km north of here where it bent eastwards to envelop the village of Havrincourt ahead and then bent even further east, excluding Havrincourt Wood which was in British hands (see Map 8). At the time of the battle this part of the canal was dry as it was still under construction. The present metal bridge over this highly embanked section with superbly built brick walls was erected by the New Zealand Tunnelling Coy under Capt J.D. Holmes in 1918, purportedly the longest bridge to be replaced in the war. The original bridge had been destroyed by the Germans and in September 1918 a new one was essential. The dry canal presented an obstacle about 180ft wide and 90ft deep and the area was under German shellfire, being virtually the front line. Work began on 27 September and the bridge structure was assembled on this bank. It was made 60ft longer than necessary to bridge the gorge so that the whole span could be slid on rollers across the gap. Eight days later the bridge was ready.

Continue over the bridge and the motorway to a junction with a small road to the right (10.2 miles).

Here was a great mine crater, marked on contemporary trench maps and known as Vesuvius. A similar crater some 350 metres to the right was known as Etna.

Continue to Havrincourt village to the gates of the grand Château on the right.

• *Havrincourt Château/10.8 miles/5 minutes*

Outside the Château, which was used by the Germans as a command post and visited by the Kaiser, then blown up by them in February 1917 to prevent the Allies from using it, is a green **Information Panel** in the 'Paths of Reconstruction after the Great War' Series erected by the Haut-Escaut Valley Tourist Board. This is **No 4.** The Château was rebuilt after the war in the Louis XIII style.

Continue round the Château wall downhill past the church and Poilu on the right and follow signs to Grand Ravine CWGC Cemetery to the large obelisk on the right.

• *62nd (W Riding) Division Memorial, Havrincourt/11.00 miles/ 10 minutes/Map 7/6*

Steps lead up to this imposing memorial which commemorates the Division whose axis passed through here in November 1917 and who also retook the village in 1918 after the Kaiser's Offensive. It lists the Division's battle honours and at three of its corners are plinths, two of which bear the divisional emblem of a pelican. Sawn-off stumps indicate former iron railings which were perhaps taken for the war effort in WW2. The Division had seventy-six tanks (only fifty made it to the start line) and split into two companies they led 187th Brigade on the left and 185th Brigade on the right. Within two

The flamboyantly painted Poilu War Memorial at Boursies.

The elegant rebuilt Château at Havrincourt.

The New Zealand Bridge over the Canal du Nord, Havrincourt.

The 62nd (W Riding) Division Memorial, Havrincourt, with the Division's Pelican insignia (inset).

The 42nd (E Lancs) Territorial Division Memorial, Trescault.

hours the 2/5th KOYLI were through Havrincourt village. The general direction of the Cambrai attack may be taken approximately as the route north-east followed by the A2-E19 Motorway, and on the first day the 62nd Division reached Anneux by which time only nineteen tanks still worked. The small road here continues to the area where the 'BBC Trench' (Map 7/12) was established.

Turn round, return to the Château and turn left on the D15 towards Trescault, passing through Havrincourt Wood.

The preparations and initial movements of the 51st Highland Division were typical of each of the divisions involved in the attack and this wood played a major role in the maintenance of secrecy. All rehearsals for the attack were carried out on a full scale model of the ground some nine miles west of Arras, including practice in infantry/tank cooperation. The plan involved moving the artillery up on 17 November, the tanks on 18 November and the infantry a day later – all to be done at night. The Royal Engineers and the Pioneer battalions constructed roads forward, supply and ammunition dumps, water points (some able to supply 7,000 horses per hour – a cavalry division had 10,000 horses) and camouflaged shelters. The Division had 4,000 men hidden in the wood and another 5,500 in the ruined village of Metz below the wood.

The Division's objectives were defined by the blue, brown and red lines and on each line a separate phase of the attack began. In the first phase the plan was to attack on a two-brigade front with each brigade on a two-battalion front. In front of the infantry were three waves of tanks, the Rovers or Wire-Crushers, the Fighting and then the Reserve, distributed roughly with one section of three tanks per infantry platoon – about 150 yards of front – with the first wave of infantry some 200 yards behind. The route which you will take from Trescault follows approximately that of the 5th Seaforth Highlanders, the right hand battalion of the right hand brigade (the 152nd) of the 51st Division.

In Trescault turn left at the crossroads on the D17 signed to Ribécourt la Tour. Continue to the white stone memorial on the left just before the village exit sign.

• 42nd (E Lancs) Territorial Division Memorial, Trescault/13.8 miles/ 10 minutes/Map 7/7

This pristine Memorial is in memory of all ranks of the Division who gave their lives for King and country during the Great War and in commemoration of the attack and capture of the Hindenburg Line at Trescault on 28 September 1918. Trescault had remained in British hands until the German advance of March 1918.

Continue along the road (which becomes the D29) to the cemetery on the right.

• Ribécourt Road CWGC Cemetery/14.00 miles/10 minutes/Map 7/8/OP

The cemetery was used chiefly by the 51st Highland and 59th (N Midlands) Divisions from February 1917-November 1918 (Plot I) and in October 1918 by the 42nd Division who originally called it 'The Divisional Cemetery'. It now contains 255 graves including six New Zealanders and a large block of Manchester graves of 27 September 1918 as well as men from the Cambrai battle.

OP. Stand with your back to the cemetery entrance. At 12 o'clock straight ahead are the red roofs of Havrincourt and to their left the bulk of Havrincourt Wood. The 62nd Division Memorial is just out of sight below the red roofs. Look right to the village with the distinctive square tower at 2 o'clock. That is Ribécourt. At 1 o'clock is a long wood in the middle foreground, almost in the centre of which is a gap. Halfway between the gap and the right hand end of the wood is the site of the proposed Tank Memorial on Flesquières Ridge. On the left hand end of the wood on the far horizon is Bourlon Wood and in the middle horizon on a line with the left hand edge of Bourlon Wood is a small wood shaped like a poodle lying down and facing left. This is close to the site of the BBC Trench.

The British forward line was just beyond the cemetery. The direction of attack of the 51st Division was towards the site of the future Tank Memorial which is on Flesquières Ridge, the axis passing to the left of Ribécourt ahead. The line of attack of all of the divisions is skewed right to left from the line of the roads rather than following the directions of the roads themselves, which sometimes makes it difficult to reconcile the actions and objectives of different formations. Thus Ribécourt ahead, which might look to be the natural target for the 51st Division, was actually the objective for 6th Division on the right of the 51st.

In the cemetery are buried **three Pte Williams (O.H., T., and T.R.)** of the 1st/8th Lancashire Fusiliers, 27 September 1918.

Continue over the River Riot into Ribécourt and stop in the main square in front of the church.

• Ribécourt Church & Town Hall/15.7 miles/5 minutes

Information Panel No 2 in the Paths of Remembrance and Reconstruction Series describes how the Germans made use of an underground shelter constructed in the Middle Ages, putting in a telephone exchange and electricity generator. Some galleries were equipped with rails which carried small wagons full of weapons and equipment. The church was used as a hospital.

Ribécourt was the 'Blue Line' (behind the German forward defences) for 'H' Battalion which was supported by the infantry of 71st Brigade (6th Division). On 20 November Gen Elles, commanding the Tank Corps, led off the attack in his tank 'Hilda'. The first German defences before Ribécourt were broken by 0700 hours, but 'Hilda' became stuck in a trench before the village was entered around 0800 hours. Gen Elles returned to his headquarters while the others continued towards the 'Brown Line' in the direction of Marcoing.

As the 51st Division passed to the left of Ribécourt they came under machine-gun fire from the village. **L/Cpl Robert McBeath** of the 5th Seaforths took out a patrol to investigate and found and killed the gunner with a revolver. A tank then arrived and drove a number of Germans into a deep dugout. McBeath followed them down and took prisoner three officers and over thirty other ranks as well as putting out of action five machine guns. McBeath was awarded the **VC**. After the war he emigrated to Canada where he joined the Vancouver police force but was killed in a pistol battle with an errant motorist on 9 October 1922.

The village, which remained in Allied hands up to 23 March 1918, was left in ruins after the battle but its reconstruction after the war was described as 'exemplary – as witnessed by the delightful Town Hall which incorporates the boys' and girls' schools, and the distinctive church.

It is believed that there is still a buried tank in the vicinity of Ribécourt.

Extra Visit to Ribécourt Railway CWGC Cemetery, German Graffiti at La Source of L'Eauette, Marcoing British CWGC Cemetery, Masnières Newfoundland Caribou and Canal Crossing of 'The Flying Fox' (Map 7/18/19/20/21/22).

Round trip: 12 miles. Approximate time: 1 hour 15 minutes.

Take the D29 direction Marcoing out of the village, turn first right following the green CWGC sign and stop just beyond the small cemetery on the left.

Ribécourt Railway CWGC Cemetery.

This tiny cemetery (too small for a Stone of Remembrance or a box for Visitor's Book and Cemetery Report) contains forty-five graves, mostly from October 1918. The mix of regimental and corps badges is extraordinary: RFA, RGA, RE, RAMC, MG Corps, Tank Corps, King's Liverpool, King's Shropshire Light Infantry, R Fusiliers, R Scots, Irish Guards, Gordon Highlanders, Devonshire, Suffolk, Duke of Wellington's, York & Lancaster, NZ Wellington.

The personal message on the headstone of **Pte L Thornber MM,** Suffolk, 1 Oct 1918, age 24, is gently more questioning than most, 'Thy will not mine o Lord'. The cemetery is as lovingly cared for as any of the large 'showcase' cemeteries that receive many more visitors.

Turn round, return to the D29 and turn right.

Note that the line of the old railway can be discerned in the valley to the right.

Continue over the motorway until you reach a sign just before the Marcoing village sign to 'La Source' to the right and follow it along a wood-lined track which parallels a stream to the left (L'Eauette). Continue to a fork in the track with a sign on a tree 'Non potable' (not drinking water) and stop. Walk along the left hand path to just before a picnic area.

Down a flight of stone steps to the left is the Source of the small l'Eauette stream which then flows through Marcoing. The site is on the German support line and there were artillery positions here. The Germans constructed the steps and the concrete frame to the pool where the Source emerges. They used the water for drinking, for watering their horses and in the mixing of concrete. To the left of the steps two sets of graffiti can be discerned – 'JR31 1917' and 'SKpz 2/84 1940' – with a swastika below. This quiet and now beautiful spot is redolent with memories of bygone conflicts.

The motorway is at the end of the main track and beyond it is the Bois Couillet. The advance of 6th Division after taking Ribécourt led them through Couillet Wood en route to Marcoing.

Turn round, return to the main road and turn right. Continue into Marcoing.

It was here that the tanks rallied, where there was an HQ and where many reports were written.

Continue into Marcoing, turn right on the D15, continue over the L'Eauette, past the splendid Hôtel de Ville and the War Memorial and turn left on the D15 over the L'Escaut, over the Canal de St Quentin and turn right towards Masnières. Continue over the level crossing.

It is on the site of what was a railway bridge during the battle.

The pristine Mairie at Ribécourt.

Headstone of 2nd Lt W.S. Haining, 'E' Bn Tank Corps, 20 November 1917, Ribécourt Road, CWGC Cemetery.

German 1917 graffiti at the Source.

The Source of the L'Eauette.

Extra visit continued

Continue to the CWGC sign just after the Marcoing exit sign and stop by the cemetery on the right.

Marcoing British CWGC Cemetery.
Marcoing and Masnières were captured by the 29th Division on 20 November 1917, the first day of the Cambrai Battle. On 30 November/1 December Masnières was held by the same Division against repeated attacks but it was evacuated under orders on the night of 1-2 December. Marcoing was left a few days later not to be retaken until 28 September 1918 by the 62nd (W Riding) Division who retook Masnières the following day.

The cemetery, which has an interesting stone and wrought iron entrance shelter, was made after the Armistice by concentration from local battlefields and the Rumilly German Cemetery. Almost all its nearly 400 burials are from November 1917 and September-October 1918. There are 191 Unknown and 181 Identified graves with Special Memorials to nineteen UK, four Canadian and one New Zealand. At the back of the cemetery in Row G lie a row of Newfoundlanders, all killed on 20 November 1917, including **Pte Hugh Pierson, MM**, age 21, who enlisted in St John's in August 1914, served in Gallipoli and was wounded in Ypres. Their Memorial Caribou is the next visit.

Headstone of Sgt J.H. Carter, R Newfoundland Regt, 20 November 1917.

Continue with the Canal de St Quentin to the right and enter Masnières. At the roundabout continue to the right following Toutes Directions on the D15 and stop on the left just past the large black sign to the Newfoundland Memorial.

Newfoundland Battle Memorial.
This is in the form of a **Caribou**, the emblem of the Newfoundland Regiment (there are three others in France (at Beaumont Hamel (qv), Gueudecourt and Monchy-le-Preux) baying in mourning for her dead sons. The date at the entrance is 20 November 1917. The memorial marks the ultimate advance of the Allies in the Battle of Cambrai.

Bourlon Wood is clearly visible on the skyline to the right behind the Caribou.

Beside it is **Information Panel No 10** in the *Chemins et Mémoires* series. It has an excellent sketch map of the battle with eleven marked points and tells the story of the Flying Fox at the Canal Bridge (visited next).

Turn round.

The Newfoundland Caribou Memorial, Masnières.

[**N.B.** On leaving the Caribou, signed to the right along a small road, is **Masnières Brit CWGC Cemetery**. In it is buried **L/Sgt Thomas Neely, VC, MM**. Neely won his VC award in Flesquières on 27 September 1918 when, his company being held up by heavy machine-gun fire, he dashed out under point-blank fire with two men, took the garrisons and captured 3 machine guns. On two successive occasions he rushed concrete positions, killing or capturing the occupants.]

Extra visit continued

Return to Masnières. Drive straight downhill over the traffic lights and park opposite the Hôtel de Ville just short of the bridge. Walk up to the bridge.
To the left is a park in which is the impressive stone **Local War Memorial,** with a statue of a *Poilu*, behind which is the school partly financed by the American family Hotstetter in memory of their aviator son, Lt Theodore, serving with the RAF, shot down over Masnières on 27 September 1918. He is buried in the US Somme Cemetery at Bony (qv). Unusually Hotstetter is listed on both the CWGC and the ABM websites. Also of interest is the church, designed by Pierre Leprince-Ringuet using the 'new' material, reinforced concrete. After ten fierce attacks Masnières was described as 'a tragic funeral pyre' by the time it was evacuated by the Allies in December 1917. After the war it was declared a *Zone Rouge* and uninhabitable – but the determined citizens thought otherwise and the town was rebuilt.

Beyond the Canal de St Quentin is a bridge over the River L'Escaut. The Canal bridge is now made of concrete with metal railings.

Here on 20 November 1917 Maj Philip Hammond with about twelve tanks of 'F' Bn entered Masnières in order to set up a bridgehead on the St Quentin Canal, but he was stopped by intense machine-gun fire from the opposite bank. **Tank 'Flying Fox II'** forced a way through the hail of bullets and tried to cross the bridge, which was mined, and collapsed, dropping the tank in the Canal. That afternoon the Newfoundland Infantry, accompanied by Canadian Cavalry, managed to cross the Canal, reaching the heights above Cambrai, but were halted by strong German batteries. They held their position throughout the night, isolated and without reinforcements, and were forced to withdraw the following morning.

Turn round and follow signs back to Ribécourt on the D15 and the D29. Pick up the main itinerary.

Bridge over the Canal du Nord where the 'Flying Fox' fell in.

Take the D89 towards Flesquières (the attack of the 51st Division came from your left along this road) and stop at the crossroads, at the right of which is the distinctive Château Farm gateway with miniature towers. Opposite is

• *Flesquières Tank Memorial/16.5 miles/5 minutes/Map7/9/OP*

The Flesquières Tank Association (see below) has chosen this site (in the 51st Division area) with its commanding views over the battlefield for their planned important and imaginative memorial to the Tank Battle of Cambrai of November 1917. It is on the old German support line. On the ground has been laid out the shape of the Union Flag and the stripes will form paths named after the various places of the battlefield. On a wall will be the names of all the regiments which took part in the battle and in the centre (the remains of an old windmill) the original tracks of Tank D.51 (Deborah) will be placed. At each corner are roses from the old 51st Highland Cemetery (which disappeared after the war) and the flags of all the Allies will fly here. There will also be a *Table d'Orientation*.

Standing with your back to the memorial, on the skyline to the right of the track ahead of you is the bulk of Havrincourt Wood through which you have driven and around which the tanks gathered prior to the battle. The line of attack was directly towards you. Standing here on top of the ridge it is clear that advancing tanks would make prime targets.

The track which runs between the memorial and the Farm gates leads down to Flesquières Hill Cemetery and would make an interesting walk or drive by 4-wheel-drive vehicle. Behind the memorial site is a line of trees along a cart track behind a watertower. To the left of the track is the wall of the Château Farm along which the Germans had a signalling post which sent messages to Cambrai, visible on the horizon to the right. In the field to the right behind the tree line it is believed that the famous Unter offizier Theodore Kruger of 8 Batterie Feld-Artillerie-Regiment 108, 54 Infanterie-Division, the sole remaining member of his field battery, fought on until he too was killed, but not before he had knocked out five tanks. This was reported by Capt Dugdale, the Observation Officer of 6th Division and the story so caught the imagination that it was repeated by Maj Gen Harper. In his *Dispatches* Gen Haig wrote, 'Many of the hits upon our tanks at Flesquières were obtained by a German artillery officer who remaining alone at his battery, served a field gun single handed until killed.'

The British press then blew up the story of the 'Hero of Flesquières' out of all proportion. Conan Doyle, for instance, increased the number of tanks to sixteen and it was decided to bury this hero with honour – but 'although a search was made all round the gun emplacements no trace of such a person could be discovered'. The Germans tried to identify him with no apparent success but years later a memorial was erected in Cologne to the German artillery. It showed the solitary figure of Theodor Kruger manning a field gun.

Some authorities doubt the existence of the German gunner, who came to be known as 'the Phantom Major'. Others, like Airman Arthur Gould Lee, were certain. He wrote in his diary for 28 November 1917, 'We walked to Flesquières and examined the scene at the corner of the Château wall where the Hun artillery major and a handful of men

The distinctive gateway of the Flesquières Château Farm opposite the site of the new Tank Memorial.

The recovered tank D.51, 'Deborah', Flesquières.

had held up the advance on the 20th by catching the tanks at point blank range as, one by one, they topped the brow of the slope to his front. It was an amazing sight. In a crescent, a few hundred yards long, facing his grave, lay a whole line of disabled tanks.' Between them the various authorities say the number of tanks destroyed was between seven and sixteen, a feat unequalled in European fighting until the exploits of Wittman in Normandy in 1944. Jean-Luc Gibot and Philippe Gorczynski in their magnificent work, *Following the Tanks. Cambrai 20 November-7 September 1917*, show E.17, E.18 and two other tanks knocked out right here. They had approached the ridge up the track opposite known as the Chemin des Vaches.

Continue into the village.

Note the blue railings of Flesquières Château on the left. The damage was caused during the battle.

Continue to the large barn on the right with flags flying.

• *Tank D.51, 'Deborah/16.7 miles/10 minutes/Map 7/10*

After the Battle of Cambrai the Germans systematically photographed and documented the tanks abandoned by the British and recovered any in working order, repaired them and some were re-used near St Quentin on 21 March 1918. Working parts were recovered from tanks too badly damaged to be repaired, for re-use, and the remainder were left in situ. After the war the British rescued some and brought them back to the UK, some were presented to towns in France where they were displayed for many years and others were melted down for scrap. The remainder gradually sank into the earth and were lost. A dedicated association of local enthusiasts was formed with the aim of locating and charting as many of the lost tanks as possible, to research the battle in depth and the men who fought in it. The results were published in *Following the Tanks* (qv). Other projects include the restoration of Deborah, the creation of a museum in this barn and the erection of a Tank Memorial (qv). Association research indicated that there was a tank buried in Flesquières and, with the help of the Arras Archaeological Society, they eventually succeeded in finding it on 5 November 1998 (the actual site is passed later in the tour) and on 20 November that year (the 81st Anniversary of the Battle) it became fully visible. The Royal Tank Regiment assisted in the lifting of the tank when it was brought to its present resting place. A series of happy coincidences then led to the identification of the tank as D.51, the tank of 2nd Lt Frank Gustave Heap which passed through Flesquières at 1015 on 20 November and came under fire from a battery of enemy field guns which scored direct hits on the tank, killing four members of its crew. Heap then collected the remainder of his crew and brought them back to safety. The following day the wreck of D.51 was found by the Scottish Infantry who buried the four dead crew members beside their tank.

To stand before this totally original relic of a battle fought some ninety years ago, complete with the holes made by the German field gun, its interior and engine clearly visible, is an awesome experience. Beside it are a 1916-17 77mm German Field Gun, a US Army truck and the chain beam of the tank A.2, 'Abou ben Adam' (from the poem by James Leigh Hunt). This tank was hit by a mortar shell during the attack on the 2nd objective, the 'Brown Line', and two crew members were killed, the others severely wounded. **Capt Richard William Leslie Wain**, commander of the Tank Section, seized a Lewis gun and charged the enemy, capturing the strong point and taking about half of the garrison prisoners. Although Wain was killed, his act of bravery allowed the infantry to continue their advance on Marcoing and he was awarded a posthumous **VC**. He is commemorated on the Louverval Memorial (qv). The chain beam was discovered when the motorway was made.

Flesquières is at the very heart of the Cambrai Battle and the Flesquières Tank Association plan to convert the barn in which Deborah now resides into a museum and Interpretative Centre about the battle and to mark the battlefield around it with appropriate and sympathetic **Information Panels**. The barn is normally locked and to visit this very special tank, apply to the Association, 3bis rue du Moulin, Flesquières, Contact: Philippe Gorczynski, Tel: + (0)6 14 30 01 65. E-mail: TankofFlesquiere@aol.com
Continue to the crossroads.

• *Flesquières WW2 Memorials/WW1 Information Panel/16.8 miles/10 minutes/Map 7/11*

On the left hand corner is another **Information Panel** (No. 3). It describes how at 0920 on 20 November 1917 tanks of 'G', 'D' and 'E' Battalion were stopped in their approach to Flesquières. Acting on information gained from prisoners taken from the 36th Division on 18 November, the Germans rushed six gun batteries of Field Artillery Regiment 213 to the area south of Flesquières and in front of Graincourt, adding to the firepower of the resident Field Artillery Regiment 108 (Kruger was in the 108th Regiment). Fierce fighting lasted all night and the next morning Flesquières was in the hands of the Allies, but they had sustained heavy losses. It was claimed that over fifty tanks were destroyed but Gorczynski (qv) puts the number as nearer to forty. Gen Harper had not stuck firmly to the recommended tactics for the tank use, particularly in having the 51st Division infantry 200 yards behind the tanks, too far to give immediate support. The delay at Flesquières prevented the forward movement of the 62nd and 6th Divisions, the flanking formations, and thus prejudiced the capture of Bourlon Wood.

Ahead are two memorials. One was erected by the Cambrai Branch of *Souvenir Français* and is to **17 soldiers** who fell heroically for France on 19 March 1940 and next to it, with a well-tended flower bed in front, is a **Memorial to Johannas Bergman**, 113th Recce Cavalry, US 2nd Armoured Division, killed near Flesquières on 2 September 1944. They stand in Place des Combattants where there is also a **Commemorative Tree** planted on 11 November 2003 with the French equivalent of 'Lest We Forget'.

Extra Visit to the BBC Trench Line (Map 7/12). Round trip: 2.0 miles. Aproximate time: 25 minutes.

Turn left and continue to the local cemetery. Turn left again downhill into the valley along a track best negotiated by 4-wheel-drive but with extreme caution by ordinary car. Continue to a T junction in the track and park. Walk up the track to the left. The entrance to the trench is to the right.

Note that the trench line is owned by the Association of the Flesquières Tank and the entrance to it is locked. As it has not been maintained since the programme, for safety's sake visitors must be accompanied through the trenchline. Contact: same as to visit 'Deborah' above.

Over the Easter 2002 period three episodes of a well-intentioned but inevitably controversial TV programme entitled *The Trench* were shown on BBC2. It aimed to recreate the everyday life of Tommy in a WW1 trench in as authentic a manner (without enemy fire!) as possible. Although the well-respected Khaki Chums were among the twenty-five volunteers who trained for and were eventually chosen to act as the Hull Pals there was some fear that the programme would trivialise what the men of '14-'18 had endured for real. After undergoing some hard training at Catterick the men moved to France. There following another week's training in situ, they alternated between the recreated trenches and a simulated behind-the-lines environment for three extremely hard weeks of iron rations, cold uncomfortable nights, often in the company of rats, boredom, primitive latrines and other '14-'18 harsh realities. Perhaps the major achievement of the experiment is as an educational tool and

Extra visit continued

it will inevitably stimulate interest in the Great War and the sacrifices of those who really took part in it. The IWM mounted an exhibition, sponsored by the BBC, to coincide with the programme. The trench line has a very authentic feel, complete with sandbags, duckboards, dugouts, fire steps, ladders for going over the top, latrines etc. However it is dangerous to enter the area without a guide. *Return to the crossroads in Flesquières.*

Note that to the left is the rebuilt **village church.** This was designed by the award-winning Parisian architect, Pierre Leprince-Ringuet, who was responsible for much of the reconstruction of Cambrai (qv), in 1924. Using the new medium of concrete it is built in an exuberant mixture of Romanesque and the then fashionable *Art Deco* style. He also designed the rebuilt Château.

Turn right on the D89 and continue to the British Cemetery on the right. Stop.
On the left, just before the cemetery on the right, is a house and opposite it a small ornamental park complete with windmill. It is there that Tank D.51 Deborah was discovered in November 1998. Support for the raising of it came from the Conseil Général du Nord and the Conseil Régional Nord-Pas-de-Calais and the town of Lincoln where the tanks were designed and built. The actual lifting was done with the help of members of the Royal Tank Regiment and information about the commander, 2nd Lt F.G. Heap, was given by his grandson William Heap.

• *Flesquières Hill CWGC Cemetery/17 miles/20 minutes/Map 7/13/OP*

The only significant delay on the first day was around Flesquières in the 51st Division sector as mentioned above. The *Divisional History* describes the German defences thus, 'The area through which the Division was destined to advance was traversed by three separate trench systems each forming integral parts of the Hindenburg system. Of these the first . . . was composed of a maze of wide, heavily wired trenches . . . in rear of the front system and just south of the village of Flesquières lay the Hindenburg support system, composed of two lines of heavily wired deep trenches connected with each other and with the front system.'

The 51st broke through the first part of the Hindenburg Line on 20 November but didn't penetrate the Support Line here until the following day, a 'failure' that has three simplistic explanations. First, Gen Harper, commanding the Division, did not follow the drill which had been worked out for tank/infantry cooperation. He had his tanks advance in fours, line abreast, instead of in threes in 'V' formation, and his infantry advanced behind the tanks in extended order, not in file as laid down. This may have resulted in heavier casualties, but a second and more serious mistake was that, having broken the first line, Gen Harper stopped to reorganise and his tank crews switched off their engines and got out. This had been part of the original plan, but the other divisions had exploited their initial success and continued to advance. After a twenty minute delay the 51st started to advance towards Flesquières Ridge at 0855 hours but by this time the friendly artillery support had moved on and enemy fire was coming down on the attacking force.

Third there was the devastating effect of the German 'Phantom Major' – see above – whose fire from Flesquières Château Farm area was steadily knocking out the Division's tanks.

The BBC Trench, Flesquières.

'Hull Pals' (Khaki Chums) in the BBC Trench.

Flint Wall at the entrance to Flesquières Hill CWGC Cemetery.

Headstones of the Crew of 'Deborah'.

The cemetery, approached up steps and with magnificent flint walls, is triangular in shape. The great cross is roughly central on the road side and standing beside it you have views across the ground over which the 51st and 62nd Divisions advanced.

OP. Taking the church on the skyline at Graincourt-lès-Havrincourt as 12 o'clock, at 9 o'clock is the direction of the start line for the attack, at 1 o'clock on the skyline Bourlon Wood is visible on its hill beyond Orival Wood and Orival Cemetery (the next stop) at 2 o'clock. Bourlon clearly commands the entry into Cambrai, whose spires can be seen at 3 o'clock in the distance on a clear day.

At the back of the cemetery at the apex of the triangle is a Special Memorial to men of the 63rd Royal Naval Division whose graves have been lost. Burials were started here by the 2nd Division in 1918 alongside a German cemetery. The German burials were removed after the Armistice. An idea of the degree of confusion in the fighting that followed the Cambrai attack may be gathered from the fact that of the over 900 graves here 74% contain unidentified bodies. There are thirty-one UK Navy (RND), 481 UK Army and seven Airforce, 303 Unknown, two Australian, eight Canadian, sixty New Zealanders and five Unknown and twenty-four Unknown Canadians.

Buried in a row together to the right of the shelter at the top of the cemetery are thought to be the four crew members killed on 20 November 1917 in Tank D.51, Deborah (qv): **Gunners Cheverton, Galway and Tipping and Pte Robinson**. One unique headstone lists '**Ernest George de Latham Hopcraft** (with no rank), BA Jesus College Cambridge served as Second Lieutenant 13th Bn Middlesex Regiment' (no date of death). He is listed in the Cemetery Report as a Private with the date of death 27 September 1918.

Continue to the next road junction turning left towards Bourlon Wood which is visible on the horizon. At the British cemetery on the left stop.

• Orival Wood CWGC Cemetery/17.6 miles/20 minutes/Map 7/14

The cemetery is beside a small wood that has the same shape today as it had at the time of the battle. It was begun during the fighting for Cambrai and enlarged after the war by burials brought in from around Flesquières. On the left is a Special Memorial to those who were originally buried in Flesquières Château Cemetery and at the back are twenty German graves including men from the German Naval Division. In the far right hand corner is the grave of **Chang Te Hsun** of the Chinese Labour Corps.

The most notable headstone here is that of the poet **Lt Ewart Alan Mackintosh MC**, 24, of the Seaforths, 21 November 1917, author of the collections *A Highland Regiment and War, the Liberator*. Regarded as a typical 'Gael', he was a popular and sensitive officer (see also the Arras section of the Vimy tour in WF-N), who became engaged to Sylvia Marsh in 1916 while teaching 'bombing' to the Cambridge Corps of Cadets. His most moving and heartfelt poem is *In Memoriam*, written in memory of Pte David Sutherland (qv) who died of his wounds during a

*Headstone of
Lt E.A. Mackintosh, MC, Orival Wood
CWGC Cemetery.*

trench raid which Mackintosh led in May 1916 and who had to be left in the German lines. His feeling of guilt is almost unbearable.

> *'Oh, never will I forget you,*
> *My men that trusted me,*
> *More my sons than your fathers',*
> *For they could only see*
> *The little helpless babies*
> *And the young men in their pride.*
> *They could not see you dying,*
> *And hold you while you died.'*

He was equally tender with his fiancée:

> *'The days are long between, dear lass.*
> *Before we meet again,*
> *Long days of mud and work for me,*
> *For you long care and pain.*

> *But you'll forgive me yet, my dear*
> *Because of what you know,*
> *I can look my dead friends in the face*
> *As I couldn't two months ago.'*

These were the words he wrote *To Sylvia*, on returning to the front from a 'cushy' job in Cambridge – only to be killed here on 21 November, the second day of the battle, shot in the head.

Continue on the D15, under the A2 motorway to Anneux.

N.B. To the left, over the A26 motorway, is the village of Graincourt-lès-Havrincourt. It was in a vault in the catacombs of the ruined church of Graincourt that Brig-Gen F.P. Crozier, GOC 119th Bde, made his headquarters prior to the attack on Bourlon Wood. The Germans had recently vacated the somewhat malodorous hideout which they had made into a telephone exchange for the Hindenburg Line. Their electric light was still burning when the 'cavalcade: colonels, company commanders, machine-gun officers, the staff grooms and gunners, [which] make up a troop of sixty-odd' took over the position. The Brigadier learnt later that it was the tomb of the Havrincourt family and that the Germans had used the lead from the family coffins.

Continue to the crossroads with the N30 main Cambrai road. Turn right and continue to the cemetery on the right.

• *Anneux British CWGC Cemetery/19.9 miles/10 minutes/Map 7/15*

Anneux was captured by the 62nd Division on 20-21 November 1917 and remained in British hands until the following 6 December. It was recaptured on 17 September 1918 by the 5th (W Lancs) and 63rd (RND) Division with the 52nd (Lowland) Division, whose men are all represented in the cemetery. It was originally made by the 57th Division's Burial Officer in October 1918 with 131 graves. It was increased after the Armistice by concentration from the surrounding battlefield and other small cemeteries and now contains 830 graves with 459 Unknown. There is a Special

Memorial to seven UK soldiers. It includes the grave of **2nd Lt Frederick George Wheatcroft**, East Surreys, 26 November 1917, age 35, 'Schoolmaster, Amateur International and Professional Footballer'. It was the East Surreys who kicked a football towards the German lines on the first day of the battle of the Somme and one wonders if Wheatcroft was involved. Also in the cemetery are three Chinese Labourers who died in March and August 1919 known only by their numbers. In one row five Lieutenants of the 102nd Battalion Canadian Infantry lie side by side, all killed on the same day – 27 September 1918.

Turn round, return to the crossroads and turn right on the D16 signed to Bourlon. Continue towards the church and turn right, following signs to the Canadian Memorial Bourlon Wood and park by the entrance.

• *Bourlon Wood & Canadian Memorial/20.7 miles/20 minutes/Map 7/16*

This wooded hill commands the routes to Cambrai and although it was a first-day objective it was here the Cambrai offensive finally foundered. Here too a valiant band of little men proved themselves worthy of every adjective for bravery and in so doing were destroyed. They were the Bantams, the 40th Division.

There were originally two Bantam Divisions, the 35th and the 40th. They were made up of small but sturdy men, 5ft to 5ft 3in tall and with a minimum chest measurement of 34in, but, owing to a lack of suitable reinforcements, the 35th lost its Bantam status at the end of 1916. When the 40th moved up from pioneering duties (having continued the earlier work of the Cheshires) four of the battalions were of normal-sized men.

On 21 November the church bells rang out in London in celebration of the news of the great victory at Cambrai. It was a mistake. Bourlon had not fallen. On 23 November the 40th (Welsh) Bantam Division was ordered forward to take over the offensive on Bourlon Wood and the Prussian Guard from the 51st Division. In three days of intense hand-to-hand fighting the Welsh took the wood but never managed to take the village. At the end of seventy-two hours the Division had lost 4,000 men. It was destroyed. Although the 40th then lost its Bantam status, in recognition of its magnificent record at Bourlon, the C.-in-C. allowed the Division to retain its cockerel emblem, together with two acorns symbolizing its sacrifice in the wood.

The Canadian Memorial, built on land donated by the Count of Francqueville, is approached by an imposing flight of eighty-five steps flanked by magnificent old chestnut trees said to have been planted in honour of Napoleon. At the top of the slope in a landscaped garden is a Canadian granite block of the standard pattern seen at Courcelette on the Somme and at Hill 62 in the Ypres Salient. It commemorates the Canadian Corps' crossing of the Canal du Nord on 27 September 1918 during the Hindenburg Line offensive and the subsequent advance to Mons and Germany.

In the woods surrounding the manicured Canadian Memorial area are many vestiges of the war – trench lines, shell holes etc. There are two **Private Memorials** near Bourlon Wood, to **2nd Lt Hartley and Lt Windeler,** both kia 27 November 1917. They are both commemorated on the Louverval Memorial. Their memorials are very hard to find and interested readers should refer to Barrie Thorpe's *Private Memorials of the Great*

The octagonal Canadian Memorial, Bourlon Wood.

War on the Western Front for directions.

    Return to the path at the bottom and if very dry it is possible to drive up the bumpy unmade road to the cemetery signed to the left – otherwise it is a .2 mile stroll. Continue to the fork in the path, to the right of which the path leads off into the woods.

N.B. Straight ahead at this point is a **French WW2 Cruciform Memorial to Frenchmen killed on 11 June 1944.**

    Continue along the left fork to the cemetery on the left.

• *Bourlon Wood CWGC Cemetery/21 miles/10 minutes/Map 7/17*

It was begun by the Canadian Corps in October 1918 and has some 245 burials, mostly Canadian. It was erected on land donated by the Count of Francqueville to the Canadian Government. The register reveals that many of the soldiers were of UK origin, being second or even first-generation Canadians, like **Cpl William Gibbs** of the 78th Battalion (Manitoba) Regiment who had fought in the Boer War with the 2nd Bn Royal Scots Fusiliers.

• *End of Cambrai Battlefield Tour*

OR Return to the N30, turn left and continue to Cambrai for RWC

(approx 27 miles total).

THE KAISER'S OFFENSIVE

21 MARCH – 25 APRIL 1918

'It will be an immense struggle that will begin at one point,
continue at another and take a long time. It is difficult, but it will be succesful.'
Ludendorff to the Kaiser.

'We move through St Quentin at a trot and the British are hardly firing.
Everything has gone brilliantly.'
Lt Herbert Sulzbach (German Artillery Officer),
Diary entry, 21 March, 1918.

'You must admit, General Gough, that your troops
sometimes left their positions before they should have done.'
Lord Milner to Gen Gough GOC 5th Army.

'With our backs to the wall and believing in the justice of our cause
each one of us must fight on to the end.'
From Field Marshal Haig's *Order of the Day, 11 April 1918.*

SUMMARY OF THE BATTLE

Following a five-hour bombardment by over 6,000 guns, one million German soldiers attacked along a front of nearly fifty miles opposite the British Third and Fifth Armies. Gough's Fifth Army, between Amiens and St Quentin, gave way and when the offensive was finally halted, in fighting that involved the world's first tank versus tank battle, Ludendorff had penetrated forty miles into the Allied lines, taken over 1,000 guns and inflicted more than 200,000 casualties. German casualties, however, were also nearly 200,000. Gen Gough was made the scapegoat for the near defeat of the Fifth Army.

OPENING MOVES

After the failure at Cambrai the BEF went into a defensive mode and began to construct positions in depth similar to the Germans. A forward lightly-held zone was meant to delay the attacker, while behind it was a main battle zone held in strength and depth. In both zones small redoubts (defended positions) and machine-gun posts were to be scattered like cherries in a madeira cake. The battle zone was generally to be separated from the forward zone by a gap of two to three miles and was to be 2,000 to 3,000 yards deep. Four miles further back still was a rear zone, effectively a second position to which the defence could retire if need be. All of these positions had to be prepared and, as it attracted the lowest priority, the rear zone in many places was hardly more than a belt of wire known as the Green Line.

The British C.-in-C., Haig, reasoned that the most critical part of his line was in the north, shielding the Channel Ports, and he put forty-six divisions to cover what amounted to two-thirds of his front. The remaining third, on the right, was covered by Gough's Fifth Army which mustered fourteen divisions. Already thinly spread compared to the north, the Fifth Army was given a further twenty-five miles to cover which were taken over from the French early in 1918. Foch also wanted Haig to contribute nine divisions to a central Allied reserve to be controlled by Foch. Haig refused. Instead he made a 'gentleman's agreement' that each would come to the other's aid with six divisions after five days' notice if the need arose.

On 29 November 1917 hostilities ceased on the Russian Front. A week later Rumania stopped fighting. The Germans now had spare forces which they could move to the Western Front. In the period up to the opening of the Kaiser's Offensive their strength rose by 30%. British strength, compared with the summer of 1917, fell by 25%.

Ludendorff held a conference, ironically in Mons on 11 November 1917, at which the plans for the *Kaiserschlacht* were discussed. He decided to strike first in the area of Arras and St Quentin where the ground would be firmer than in Flanders. He also chose to attack the British whose forces, he believed, had been weakened by Passchendaele and whose generals, he felt, were more inept and less flexible than the French. In addition he introduced a wholly new tactical philosophy. Ludendorff adopted an attack concept, originated by Capt Geyer, of a light tactical assault unit, the infantry group, made up from a few riflemen, mortar teams, engineers and light machine guns. These groups of 'storm troopers' incorporated in a thin screen would move forward to probe and penetrate enemy defences, by passing any centres of opposition according to circumstances and not limited by a rigid timetable. The main attack force, following behind and reinforced with its own under-command field artillery, would overcome any resistance remaining. In addition, artillery tactics were also revised. Von Hutier had introduced the idea of silent registration on the Eastern Front and it had been used with great effect at Caporetto. His chief gunner was Oberst Georg Bruchmüller and he now became the great conductor for the battle and orchestrated a score for the March artillery programme that was to confirm his nickname, 'Breakthrough Bruchmüller'.

Bruchmüller's plan began with silent registration and consisted of seven phases, six of them between 0400 and 0940 hours, the jump-off time. The seventh was a creeping barrage. He defined the targets to be hit, the intensity to be achieved, the explosive/phosgene gas mixture to be used, and the duration of each phase. Training for the attack, 'Operation Michael', was intensive and thorough. Steadily Ludendorff built up his strength. By the night of 20 March the German superiority in infantry was four to one, and the more than 6,000 guns standing by for Bruchmüller's overture were a larger assembled force of arms than those of the British on the Somme on 1 July 1916, the British at El Alamein in October 1942 and the Allies against Saddam Hussein in February 1991 all added together: *Der Tag* was about to dawn.

WHAT HAPPENED

At 0930 hours on 21 March 1918, after five hours of Bruchmüller's itemised bombardment, 3,500 mortars opened rapid fire on the British front line defences. Five minutes later in thick mist the storm troopers advanced. 5th Army communications had been destroyed, battalion positions and redoubts were cut off and by passed. Not only did the defenders know little about what was happening, they could see little. By nightfall, the Germans had penetrated the forward zone on both 4th and 5th Army fronts and were consolidating in the battle zone. Gough withdrew his right wing seven miles to behind the Crozat Canal (shown on modern maps as the St Quentin Canal between Ham and Chauny) and asked the French for permission to blow the railway bridges. They refused.

The following morning the Germans continued their assault, the mist still protecting them. By the end of the day the Fifth Army's centre had been broken and all of its meagre reserves committed. On the night of 22 March Gough decided that he must pull his remaining forces behind the line of the River Somme and make a stand there (see Map 9). The line held for three days but the German tide would not be denied. The Fifth's retreat continued. On 23 March German long-range railway guns started to shell Paris. The French considered pulling back to defend their capital and Haig looked at the possibility of abandoning the Fifth Army and moving the Third Army north to protect the Channel Ports. But the German advance was slowing. Their roads forward were clogged with traffic and constantly harassed by the RFC. Their soldiers, who had been on short rations for many months and whose clothing and equipment was of poor quality, were overwhelmed by the richness of captured British food and supplies and engaged in wholesale looting. Rudolph Binding, the German writer who took part in the advance, recorded in his diary on 28 March, 'There were men driving cows... others who carried a hen under one arm... men carrying a bottle of wine under their arm and another open in their hand... men staggering... men who could hardly walk... the advance was held up and there was no means of getting going again for hours.'

On 26 March, in emergency sessions, Clemenceau, Foch, Milner, Haig and others conferred under the chairmanship of President Poincaré at Doullens. The initial mood of impending defeat was shattered by Foch, who proclaimed, 'I will never surrender.' Haig promised Poincaré that he would hold Amiens and when Foch was appointed Supreme Commander of the Allied Forces on the Western Front, Haig willingly acquiesced to the position of Number Two. The headlong retreat of the Fifth Army, however, needed a scapegoat. Ignoring the fact that Gough had warned of his shortage of men both for fighting and for preparing defences, had warned of the too-extended frontage that he had to hold, had warned of the certainty of the location of the coming attack and had asked repeatedly for reinforcements, he was relieved of his command. Two days later Rawlinson took over from him in the field with the HQ staff of the Fourth Army. On that same day the German advance was virtually spent. The Third Army north of the Somme threw back the German efforts against Arras. Ten miles in front of Amiens, just to the east of the village of Villers Bretonneux, the tired Germans were fought to a standstill by the 1st Cavalry Division.

On 3 April Gough met Haig before returning to England. The meeting was brief. Haig said that the orders for Gough's removal had not come from him, that there would be an enquiry into the actions of the Fifth Army and its Commander and that Gough would have 'every chance' to defend himself. Haig concluded by shaking hands. 'I'm sorry to lose you Hubert,' he said. 'Goodbye'.

Already Australian troops, rushed down by Haig from the north, were arriving around Villers Bretonneux. When the Germans attacked again at dawn on 4 April it seemed momentarily as if the village must fall, but an Australian bayonet charge tipped the scales. The forty miles advance was over.

The Germans paused to gather their strength. At GHQ Haig realised that the situation was critical and asked Foch to take over some part of the front held by the

British and Commonwealth forces. Foch agreed to move a large French force towards Amiens and on 11 April Haig, worried about the morale of his tired and overstretched troops, issued a 'Special Order of the Day' which was addressed to 'All Ranks of the British Army in France and Flanders'. It said, 'Three weeks ago today the Enemy began his terrific attacks against us on a 50 mile front. Many amongst us now are tired. There is no other course open to us but to fight it out! Every position must be held to the last man: there must be no retirement. With our backs to the wall, and believing in the justice of our cause, each one of us must fight on to the end. '

In the dawn mist of 24 April the 4th (Ger) Guards Division and the 228th Division supported by thirteen tanks came down the hill from Villers Bretonneux towards Amiens. Again the Australians took them on, pinching out the village on the morning of Anzac Day, 25 April, just hours after the first ever tank-versus-tank battle. The advance was over. Amiens was safe and the Germans switched their attention to Flanders. But the signs were there that the end was nigh.

Three days earlier the Australians had buried Baron Manfred von Richthofen, the 'Red Baron', at Bertangles, with full military honours. An Australian anti-aircraft battery claimed the victory – so did the Canadian pilot, Capt Roy Brown, and the dispute continues to this day. Von Richthofen had had eighty kills and was a symbolic figure of German military prowess. His death was a great blow to military morale at a time when back home workers' strikes were crippling the German economy.

An extraordinary insight into the desperate attempts to stem the German tide is portrayed in R.C. Sherriff's play, *Journey's End*. It is set in an officers' dugout near St Quentin between 18-20 March 1918. The attack is anticipated, and a suicidal raid is undertaken into enemy lines to secure a prisoner for intelligence purposes and, because it is written from personal experience – Sherriff served with the East Surreys and fought in the battles of St Quentin, the Somme Crossings, the Battles of Rosières and Avre throughout March and April 1918 – it is searingly realistic. First produced in December 1928 at the Apollo Theatre it starred the unknown actor Laurence Olivier in the pivotal role of the company commander, Capt Stanhope. A brilliant revival, produced by David Grindley, and with the most superb cast who seem to 'be' rather than to act their roles, was put on in the Playhouse Theatre, London in 2004/5. The raw feelings and authentic sets and sound effects transcended the outmoded language and attitudes of '14-'18 to project a genuine empathic experience.

THE BATTLEFIELD TOUR

The attack took place along a broad front. In this concise tour we concentrate on the axis of the N29, St Quentin-Villers Bretonneux road, dealing initially with the German jump off, then their rapid advance and finally where it petered out. Other sites of the offensive are covered in some detail in *Major & Mrs Holt's Battlefield Guide to the Somme*.

• **The Route:** The tour begins at St Quentin and the French Cemetery and from there moves to the German jump-off trenches and Memorials at Fayet, past the Enghien Redoubt, the Manchesters' Memorial at Francilly-Selency and Manchester Hill. It returns to St Quentin and the German Cemetery. It then follows the retreat of a typical

Map 9: THE KAISERS OFFENSIVE: 21 MARCH 1918 – 25 APRIL 1918

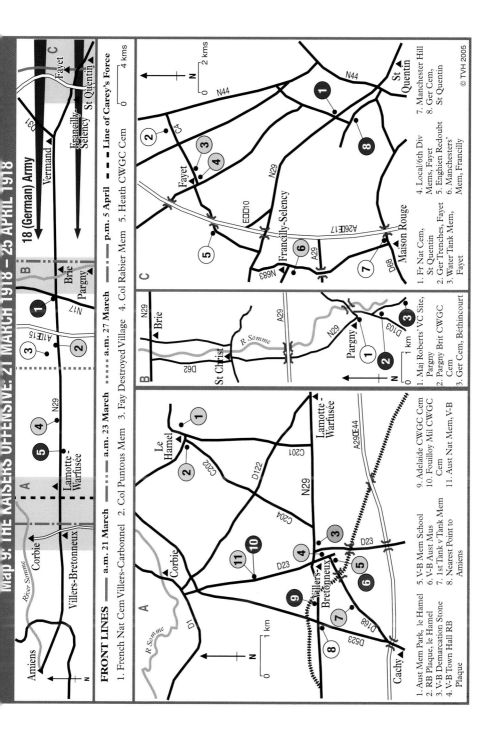

18 (German) Army

FRONT LINES —— a.m. 21 March —•— a.m. 23 March —••— a.m. 27 March —•••• p.m. 5 April – – Line of Carey's Force

1. French Nat Cem Villers-Carbonnel 2. Col Puntous Mem 3. Fay Destroyed Village 4. Col Rabier Mem 5. Heath CWGC Cem

© TVH 2005

A

1. Aust Mem Park, le Hamel
2. RB Plaque, le Hamel
3. V-B Demarcation Stone
4. V-B Town Hall RB Plaque
5. V-B Mem School
6. V-B Aust Mus
7. 1st Tank v Tank Mem
8. Nearest Point to Amiens
9. Adelaide CWGC Cem
10. Fouilloy Mil CWGC Cem
11. Aust Nat Mem, V-B

B

1. Maj Roberts' VC Site, Pargny
2. Pargny Brit CWGC Cem
3. Ger Cem, Béthincourt

C

1. Fr Nat Cem, St Quentin
2. Ger Trenches, Fayet
3. Water Tank Mem, Fayet
4. Local/6th Div Mems, Fayet
5. Enghien Redoubt
6. Manchesters' Mem, Francilly
7. Manchester Hill
8. Ger Cem, St Quentin

British infantry battalion to the Somme at Pargny and there traces the details of an action which led to the winning of a VC. The tour continues via Villers Carbonnel French Cemetery, Heath CWGC Cemetery, to Villers Bretonneux, the Franco-Australian Museum, the School and the Town Hall Memorials, continues east of the village where Tank fought Tank for the first time, to Adelaide Cemetery and ends at the Australian National Memorial and CWGC Cemetery at Fouilloy.

• **Extra Visit:** Australian Memorials at le Hamel
• **Total time:** 5 hours 30 minutes
• **Total distance:** 66 miles
• **Distance from Calais to start point** via A26-E27 Motorway: 105 miles
  Motorway Tolls
• **Base towns:** St Quentin, Amiens
• **Maps:** *Major & Mrs Holt's Battlefield Map of the Somme*, Maps 1 and 3
      Michelin 302 Local 1:150,000
      Exit from the A26 motorway at the St Quentin Exit No 10. Continue in the direction of St Quentin on the N29

• *St Quentin*

It must be said that St Quentin town centre is extremely difficult to negotiate and to park in. If you nevertheless wish to visit this interesting town,
      Follow signs to Centre Ville and then 'i' for Tourist information to the Tourist Office on rue Victor Basch.
There you can pick up a town plan and leaflets about restaurants, hotels and other attractions. They also produce an interesting booklet in English *Saint Quentin and The Great War*, which lists the sites in the city with connections to the Great War. The most important '14-'18 Memorial is found by crossing the ornate bridge over the St Quentin Canal, built between 1927 and 1929, to the Place aux Monuments aux Morts/Square de Souvenir Français. It was designed by Paul Bigot in the shape of a triumphal portico whose ten pillars bear the names of the missing. At either end two *bas-reliefs* designed by Landowski (qv) and Bouchard recall the heroic defence of the town which was for many years the frontier between the French and Austrians. On the right the siege of 1557 and on the left the siege of 1870 are represented whilst in the centre the Great War struggles of the city are vividly depicted.

At first occupied by the British (who had their HQ in the Grammar School, Place du Lycée Henri Martin, which was used as a hospital for the wounded from Le Cateau, the town was also the HQ of the RFC from 25 August 1914) St Quentin was attacked by the Germans on 28 August 1914 and the next few days saw bitter combat in the outskirts as the French 1st Army Corps counter-attacked. They were rebuffed, however, and from September 1914 to February 1917 the town was under German occupation. On 15 February the Kaiser visited St Quentin as part of his grand inspection of the German lines to celebrate his fifty-sixth birthday. Many bronze memorials from the Franco-Prussian War were demolished and sent to Germany for melting down to make munitions.

On 28 February the civilians were evacuated as the town became one of the most important bastions of the German reorganisation onto the Hindenburg Line. It was then systematically pillaged and heavily bombarded. From its ruins the German offensive of 21 March was launched. It was finally retaken on 1-2 October 1918 by the French when it was almost completely destroyed. Capt H.A. Taylor in his wonderful

1928 book, *Goodbye to the Battlefields*, revisited the city and remembered that in 1917 and 1918, 'In those days distance lent enchantment. For all its broken roofs and riddled gables, the city was fair to the eyes of the trench-bound soldier. When, ultimately, in the autumn we came this way again, and St Quentin fell, the city was a sorry picture of ruin and desolation, and one wondered how many decades must elapse before it could recover its former neatness. On my last visit to St Quentin I was astonished at the progress that had been made. There are streets and boulevards in which one might walk observantly without guessing that war had devastated this city so recently... On the whole the rebuilding of St Quentin has been done tastefully.'

After the war St Quentin was adopted by Lyon and the long reconstruction began. Many of the main buildings were rebuilt in the popular *Art Deco* style (notably the main post office in rue Vesoul) and today it is an elegant and interesting town.

The famous Basilica received its first damage on 1 July 1916 when some of the precious SGWs were blown in by the explosion of a munitions train in St Quentin station. German wounded from the Somme battle were treated here until it was deemed too dangerous as more windows collapsed. On 4 April 1917 the French Gen Humbert ordered French troops to try to avoid the Basilica when shelling the city but on 17 August it caught fire and the vaulting caved in. After the war there was a notice in the Basilica, 'Visitors, do not forget that before they left the city in October 1918 the Germans drilled ninety holes for explosives in the pillars and structural elements of the Basilica. This was clearly intended to blow up the building, which would have been completely destroyed if the French had not arrived twenty-four hours earlier than expected by the enemy'. In 1941 the Germans ordered the holes to be filled in.

It was not until October 1956 that the rebuilt Basilica was inaugurated and the belfry was not completed until 1976. Today guided tours can be arranged from the tourist office (qv).

In the **St Quentin Northern Communal Cemetery** in the St Jean Quarter (see City Map G2) is a small plot of WW1 and WW2 CWGC graves. It contains the graves of **Rifleman J. Hughes**, 2nd RIR, age 20 and **Pte Thomas Hands**, 1st King's Own R Lancasters, age 21. Both were shot by the Germans on 8 March 1915 when they were captured wearing civilian clothes and thus automatically deemed to be spies and subject to the death penalty. Their story is similar to that of Robert Digby (qv) and his companions, also sheltered by local people and shot when discovered in Le Catelet. The formers' case is well-documented from minutes of the St Quentin Town Council, copies of which are held in the *Historial*. They reached St Quentin during the Retreat at the end of August and couldn't get out before the Germans arrived to occupy the town. They were looked after by townspeople but were eventually arrested, Rifleman Hands after he was imprudent enough to go out after the 1900 curfew, and Hughes after being denounced. They were tried by a military tribunal on 11 February 1915 when their attitude was described as 'dignified'. Their death sentence was declared the very day of their execution, 8 March. Hughes asked to see Madame Preux who had sheltered him and who treated him like one of her children. This was refused. They were taken to the barracks and shot by a firing party of six. The Germans refused them burial in the newly-created St Martin German Cemetery (qv) where other Allied soldiers were buried. 'You can put Frenchmen in our cemetery', said Lt Hauss of the German Command, 'but not Englishmen. They are scum'. They were therefore buried in the St Jean cemetery and their graves were soon covered in flowers by the local people.

Gustave Preux, the weaver who had hidden Hughes, was condemned to fifteen years of forced labour in Germany and returned after the war, his health broken. At the same time eleven British soldiers and the miller who had taken them to hospital were shot in nearby Guise (qv). On 14 April a letter arrived at the *Mairie* saying that the Commandant of the 2nd Army was punishing the town of St Quentin with a fine of 50,000 francs because two Englishmen had recently been found in the town and because after their execution insulting notices to the Command were still being posted around the town. Count Bernstorff, the Commandant, also posted a notice around the town proclaiming the execution of the two English soldiers.

Continue direction St Quentin on the N29 to the first roundabout. Turn left and then immediately right and stop in the small parking area for the French Military Cemetery. **Set your mileometer to zero.**

Christian Cross backed by a Muslim Stone, French Nécropole Nationale, St Quentin.

• *Nécropole Nationale de St Quentin/0 miles/ 10 minutes/Map 9C/1*

This vast French cemetery contains 4,947 WW1 French burials, 1,319 of which are in two ossuaries, plus two Rumanians and 117 Russians. There are also 207 French burials from the '39-'45 War. It was started in 1923 with burials from the 1914-1918 Aisne battlefield. It was enlarged in 1934-5 with exhumations from cemeteries around St Quentin and the Aisne. In 1954 the WW2 burials were brought in from the Aisne. At the entrance there are **Information Panels**, one describing the Battle of Guise, 1914.

Return to the roundabout and continue towards St Quentin to the next roundabout. Go left signed to Cambrai on the N44 and continue over two sets of traffic lights following signs to Cambrai to the left.

N.B. At 2.4 miles on the left is a well-maintained WW2 Memorial to twenty-seven patriots killed by the Nazis on 8 April 1944, with a plaque to commemorate the fiftieth Aniversary.

Continue to a left turn signed to Fayet on the C4. Turn left and continue towards power lines on the top of the plateau. Stop below them. You have now reached the area of the German front line trench and to your front is No Man's Land.

• *German Trenches, Fayet/2.9 miles/20 minutes/Map 9C/2*

The German jump-off trench lines here in the wood to the right ran almost due south for about 2,000 yards and at this point were barely 100 yards from the British trenches. The attack was made in the direction you are driving. The British force between here and the northern edge of St Quentin (the cathedral should be visible to your left) was the 2nd/8th Worcesters, part of 182nd Brigade of 61st Division of the 5th Army. These were Forward Zone positions. The battalion put two companies forward, A and B, each covering a front of about a mile with their company HQs in Fayet village (B Coy) and

Memorial at Francilly-Selency to Manchester Hill and to the 2nd and 16th Manchesters.

The Oxford Water Tank, with its ornate façade, Fayet.

Fayet Memorials with Plaque to French Forces and 6th BR Division on left and Evacuation/ Destruction Memorial on the right.

1,500 yards south of it (A Coy). D Company was nominated as a counter-attack force and centred on Fayet village, while C Company and battalion HQ occupied a central redoubt about a mile behind the lines, i.e. in front of you.

The *Regimental History* described the defences as 'for the most part merely shallow ditches not more than waist deep. Neither labour nor materials had been available to improve the defences. There was but scanty wire protection save around the actual defensive posts.'

What happened here is described now in selected extracts from the *Regimental History*. On the night of 20 March a raiding party went into the German trenches. 'The raiders brought back prisoners from three different German regiments. Those prisoners stated that the German army would attack the next day. The Corps Commander decided to put into force the pre-arranged dispositions for meeting an attack. The order to man the battle stations reached HQ 61st Division at 0435 and at that very minute all along the line the German artillery opened fire... For several hours the platoons of the 2nd/8th Worcesters endured the bombardment. The mist, torn only by the blaze of the shell bursts and then thickened by their smoke, hid everything from the eyes of the crouching sentries. Gas shells added their fumes to those of the high explosives and the survivors groped in the trenches, half-blinded by their gas masks. On every side parties of the enemy's infantry came looming through the mist... instead of advancing in regular waves they worked in *groups*. The forward posts were overwhelmed one by one.'

All of the Worcesters' companies were decimated, small bands of survivors struggling back to battalion HQ: 'A ring of small defensive posts connected by a trench... from 1020 attack after attack beat against the defences. The enemy closed in from every side... two-thirds of the defenders had been killed or wounded... ammunition ran out... the German infantry charged in with the bayonet and the remnants of the defenders were compelled to surrender.' It was 1730 hours. What the gallant Worcesters did not know was that Holnon, the village a mile or more behind them, had been taken and passed by the enemy seven hours earlier. Altogether the battalion lost nineteen officers and 560 men on that day, almost exactly the same total as the Tyneside Scottish lost at la Boiselle on the first day of the Somme.

To your right about 100 yards away across the fields, is an arc of wood. In that wood original German jump-off trenches still remain and, crops permitting – be very careful not to damage anything that may be growing – it is possible to walk to them across the field. You can therefore stand exactly where the Kaiser's Battle began.

Continue over the crossroads into the village of Fayet.

It is a *'Village Fleuri'* and if you visit it during the spring or summer you will be overwhelmed by the colourful glory of the flowers throughout the village.

Continue to a ruined archway on the right and stop on the left at an ornate structure at the corner of the Chemin Vert.

• *Water Tank, Fayet/3.6 miles/5 minutes/Map 9C/3*

The elaborately carved structure contains a water tank, donated to Fayet by the town of Oxford after the war. The ruined archway over the road is all that remains of the *Ecole Apostolique*.

Continue to the T junction, turn left and immediately stop at the beautifully tended memorial park beside the Mairie.

• *Fayet Memorials/3.7 miles/10 minutes/Map 9C/4*

In the centre is the main village obelisk Memorial. To the left are Memorials to the fighting of 28 August-16 September 1914 and to the trench warfare along the Hindenburg Line from March 1917-March 1918. It celebrates the retaking of Fayet on 30 September 1918 by the 46th and 47th French Divisions and the 6th English [sic] Division. On the right is a Memorial to the evacuation of the villagers to Marpent on 15 and Noyon on 22 February 1917, the total destruction of the village by fire or mines in March 1917 and the felling of all trees from April 1916-March 1917.

> *Turn round and go downhill past the church then turn left at the bottom of the hill on the rue Quentin de la Tour signed Francilly. Immediately after the road crosses the motorway there is what appears to be a rectangular wooded area about 100 yards off the road to your right with a track leading to it. Stop and walk to the redoubt.*

• *Enghien Redoubt/4.5 miles/10 minutes/Map 9C/5*

The area enclosed by trees is in the precise form and position of a British redoubt called Enghien (presumably based upon an earlier French fortification, since Enghien was the name of the Marshal of France who gave Vauban his opportunity to become France's greatest fortifications exponent). The northern boundary of 2nd/8th Worcesters was the road along which you are driving. One thousand yards due south of here was Ellis Redoubt where the Worcesters had battalion HQ. Redoubts were meant to be mutually supporting and the ground between them covered by machine-gun fire. The mist prevented that. This redoubt was held by the 2nd/4th Oxs and Bucks, who, with a few Worcester stragglers, survived until 1630 on 21 March.

> *Continue to the T junction and turn right, then take the next left signed to Francilly-Selency on the D683 and continue to the church on the right and the memorials in front of it.*

• *2nd & 16th Manchesters/Manchester Hill & French Memorials, Francilly-Selency/5.6 miles/5 minutes/Map 9C/6*

Headed 'Manchester Hill', the British Memorial commemorates the actions of the 2nd Manchesters on 2 April 1917 and the 16th Bn on 21 March 1918. It was erected by the King's Regt on 30 June 1998. Beside it are the village WW1 Memorial and Memorials to the Battle of 18-19 January 1871 (during the Franco-Prussian War) and to Lionel Lefèvre, 1902-1974 and Cdr de la Légion d'Honneur Joseph Loiseau, chief of the Aisne Resistance, deported by the Nazis in 1943 to Camp Dora the V2 Weapons site near Nordhausen – there is a museum there today.

> *Continue through the village and over the motorway to the T junction and turn left on the D68 towards St Quentin into Maison Rouge. Stop just beyond the last house on the left beside which is a gateway.*

• *Manchester Hill/7.2 miles/Map 9C/7*

To the right of the gate is all that remains of the scene of the heroic defence of the Redoubt at Manchester Hill on 21 March 1918 – a small wooded mound known to the Germans as *Margarine Hohe*. Today it is fenced around and the traces of the concrete and steel artillery post on top are hard to find – and remember it is on private ground. Behind the mound are the remains of the quarry that existed in 1918. In his 1934 book,

The gateway to the remains of 'Manchester Hill'.

The Memorial, with its empty plinths, German Cemetery, St Quentin.

Memorial to racing drivers, Guy Ouint and Louis Trintingant near Brie.

The Bridge at Pargny.

The March Retreat, Gen Sir Hubert Gough wrote, 'The defence of Manchester Hill in the Forward Zone is another instance of the heroic behaviour of our troops. This hill – opposite St Quentin on the front of the 30th Division – was held by the 16th Manchester Regiment, under Lt Col Elstob. On taking over the defence of this position, he had already impressed on his battalion that, "there is only one degree of resistance and that is to the last round, and to the last man". This injunction was heroically carried out to the letter. At about 11 a.m. Col Elstob reported to his brigade that the Germans were swarming round his redoubt. At about 2 p.m. he said that most of his men were killed or wounded, that he himself was wounded, that they were all nearly dead-beat, that the Germans had got into the redoubt, and hand-to-hand fighting was going on. He was still quite cheery. At 3.30 p.m. he answered a call on the telephone and said that very few were left and the end was nearly come. After that, communication ceased. Wounded three times, using his revolver, throwing bombs himself, and firing a rifle, he was last seen on the fire-step, and when called on to surrender by Germans within thirty yards, replied "Never!" upon which he was shot dead.'

For this act of heroism, **Lt Col Wilfrith Elstob** was awarded the **VC**. His name is recorded on the Pozières Memorial (qv).

Continue under the motorway, keeping left at the water tower at the next junction and continue downhill. At the bottom turn sharp left signed Vermand and continue straight onto a tree-lined avenue to the German Cemetery on the left.

• *St Quentin German Cemetery/10.1 miles/10 minutes/Map 9C/8*

Over 6,000 named burials marked by small black crosses, some irregularly placed, with up to four soldiers in a grave, are gathered here, originally known as St Martin, many

from the 1918 Offensive. They are interspersed with Jewish Stars of David which bear the legend 'With the help of God' in Hebrew. The cemetery was actually inaugurated by the Kaiser on 18 October 1915 and there is a record of the cordial meeting he had – in perfect French – with the *Maire* of St Quentin to discuss the setting up of the cemetery. Inside the entrance on the left-hand border of the cemetery is an impressive Memorial in the classical style carrying the names of almost 2,000 missing with no known grave. The Kaiser was particularly concerned with the site of the monument so that it would receive the best possible light. A short flight of steps was flanked by two larger-than-life Graeco-Roman soldiers by the Berlin academician Wilhelm Wandschneider which were pejoratively described locally in 1917 as 'gross idols of an abject Munich-style of art'. The statues were, however, of a very high artistic quality and because of their bronze content very valuable.

The untended graves area, St Quentin German Cemetery.

Fearing that they would become the targets of art collectors or vandals, the *Deutsche Kriegsgräberfürsorge* have taken them to their local headquarters at Chaulnes where they will be renovated while a decision is made as to how to display them safely. The steps lead to a central panel with laurel wreath and sword, headed by the words '*Resquiescat in pace*' – Rest in peace.

In June 2004 the cemetery, in which there are some beautiful beech trees, had a neglected air, with litter lying around.

Turn right opposite the cemetery on rue A. Parmentier and continue to the T junction. Turn left, still on rue A. Parmentier. Continue to a dead end and turn right on rue C. Naudin. Turn left at the roundabout with the French Cemetery on the right, direction Amiens on the N29. Continue through Holnon.

In the village is the delightful Pot d'Etain restaurant (qv) on the right.

Continue through Vermand and past Poeuilly to the junction with the small road to the right to Vraignes.

N.B. Just before the junction is a well-maintained **Monument to the '10 Victims of the barbarous Nazis, 29 August 1944'** from the Commune of Vraignes.

As you make your way towards Amiens following the line of the retreat, two literary personal accounts will considerably add to your understanding of what it was like to have taken part in this momentous and often terrifying event. First there is Col Rowland Feilding's moving *Letters to a Wife*. In 1918 this sensitive and popular Regimental officer was commanding the 1st Civil Service Rifles. His account of the Battalion's withdrawal from Ronssoy to Bray is dramatic and realistic, describing the casualties, the pitiful refugees who fled before the armies and his own wounding and treatment. Second, there is Sir Herbert Read's *In Retreat*, published in 1925. Read was a Captain in the Yorkshire Regiment, and served with distinction, winning the DSO and the MC. *In Retreat* is both coolly factual and vivid. It describes men as 'dazed', 'haggard'; the fighting as 'bloody', 'hellish', 'ghastly'. We share the light relief of his battle-weary group when a forager brings (no questions asked about its provenance) 'French bread, butter, honey and hot, milky coffee in a champagne bottle! We cried out with wonder: we almost wept. We shared the precious stuff out, eating and drinking with inexpressible zest.' Of such contrasts are battles made.

Continue to the crossroads with the D937 (24 miles).

N.B. On the right is a fine Memorial to two motor racing drivers, **Guy Comte Bouriat Ouint and Louis-Aimé Trintingant,** who were killed in trials for the Grand Prix de Picardie on 20 May 1933. Trintingant's nephew, Jean-Louis, was a famous actor and movie star (he played a racing driver in *Un Homme et une Femme*, 1966) and his brother Maurice twice won the Monaco Grand Prix and the Le Mans 24 Hours race.

Continue into Brie, passing a sign to Brie Brit Cemetery to the left. Immediately after crossing the Somme and the Canal du Nord (or Canal de la Somme – the two merge above Péronne) turn left on to the D62 and continue through St Christ-Briost and Cizancourt, under the A29 motorway and through Epénancourt.

As one drives from Brie to Pargny the line of the Canal de la Somme, with the River beyond it, is to the left. These waterways formed a barrier to the Germans' advance and for them an intact bridge was vital – hence the importance of the one at Pargny.

Continue into Pargny village. As the road enters the village, it runs abruptly left as the buildings begin. Pause.

• Site of Maj Roberts' VC, Pargny Village & Bridge/31.8 miles/15 minutes/Map 9B/1

When the German attack opened, the 1st Battalion of the Worcesters was at Moringhem six miles east of St Omer. Next morning they and the whole of 24th Brigade marched to St Omer and entrained at midday, reaching Amiens that night. After a short delay the train continued to Nesle some five miles south of here where the troops got out at 0230 hours on 23 March in darkness. The Worcesters marched north and took up positions on the west bank of the Somme covering Pargny. Their task was to hold the river line and to cover the retreat of the Fifth Army. Very early in the morning the route across the Somme, through the village, became congested with refugees and by 1400 hours battalions of the Fifth Army began to stream back, closely followed by the Germans. That evening, about 2000 hours, Germans began to cross the Somme by the bridge at Pargny, which had been incompletely blown. Maj (acting Lt Col.) F. C. Roberts of the Battalion, seeing what was happening, gathered about forty-five men, where you now are, determined to drive the enemy back across the Somme. At 2100 hours **Maj Roberts'** party set off from here towards the bridge in an action that was to win him the **VC**.

Drive through the village, bearing left past the church, to the bridge and stop.

You can now read the story in Maj Roberts' own words, 'We started off with fixed bayonets and magazines loaded. For the first hundred yards or so we went in two parties in single file on each side of the main road at the walk and as quietly as possible. The first sign I had of the enemy was some shouting from houses we were passing and then both machine-gun and rifle fire from windows and doors, with small parties dashing into the streets and clearing off in the direction of the bridge. Once this started we all went hell-for-leather up the street firing at anything we saw and using the bayonet in many cases. Every man screamed and cheered as hard as he could and, by the time we reached the church, the village was in an uproar – Bosches legging it hard for the bridge or else chucking their hands up. In the churchyard itself the hardest fighting took place – tombstones being used as if in a game of hide and seek. After clearing it we had a few moments rest and went smack through to the bridge where a crowd of Bosches were trying to scramble across. Some did and some did not. That more or less ended it – we actually captured six light machine guns, fifteen to twenty prisoners and killed about eighty. Our own losses were heavy.' Maj Roberts later became a Maj-Gen and on 25 June 2005 a plaque in his honour was unveiled at St Laurence College, Ramsgate, his old school.

Turn round, return past the church and turn left to Nesle, still on the D62. Then follow signs to the right to Pargny Brit Cem on the D103. When you stop at the cemetery on the left it is advisable to leave your hazard lights on.

• Pargny British Military CWGC Cemetery/33.2 miles/10 minutes/ Map 9B/2

The beautiful cemetery, sloping up the hillside, was made after the Armistice by concentrations from the surrounding battlefields. Fragrant box shrubs shaped like pyramids line the central path that leads to the Cross. The majority of the men here are of the 61st (S Midland) and 8th Divisions whose resistance at the Somme crossings of 24 March materially helped to delay the German advance. There are sixty-one soldiers and airmen from the UK, six Canadians of the Motorised Machine Gun Service and Special Memorials on the left as one enters, to sixteen UK soldiers and two RAF officers,

Cross to Robert Westphal and Eugen Holtz, Béthencourt German Cemetery.

Monument to Col Rabier and the 55th Inf Bde, Foucaucourt.

The pollarded avenue of trees, Heath CWGC Cemetery.

Pargny Brit Mil CWGC Cemetery.

Lt C.H. Roberts and 2nd Lt J.H. Davies, 98 Sqn, RAF, 19 August 1918. Between their graves is a headstone describing how they were originally buried in Pertain Mil Cemetery which was destroyed in later battles.

Three quarters of the 619 burials are Unknown. Buried here is **Rfn Berry**, 2nd Bn Rifle Bde, 23 March 1918. A message in the Visitor's Book recorded that Berry won the MM for defending the Bridge at Pargny, but the decoration is not inscribed on his headstone.

Continue uphill and down to the crossroads with the D15. Turn left to Béthencourt. Enter the village and turn left before the bridge on the D62, signed to the German Cemetery. Continue to the cemetery on the left. It is by the exit sign of the village before the local cemetery and is not signed at that point. The entrance is up a path to the left.

• *Béthencourt German Cemetery/35.7 miles/10 minutes/Map 9B/3*

In stark contrast to the neglected German Cemetery at St Quentin this is immaculately maintained although devoid of any colour. A fine beech hedge surrounds the cemetery in which there are some great oak trees. In the centre is a large black cross around which are the small black crosses and two Jewish headstones that mark the 1,242 burials. The majority are from 1916, but there are some from 1917 and others from the March attack of 1918. The Cemetery Report was missing when last visited.

The Canal runs beside and just over the road from the Cemetery.

Continue through Fontaine-les-Pargny back into Pargny. Return to the N29 Amiens road by retracing your steps to Brie. Turn left and continue towards Amiens through Estrées and Mons (not to be confused with the Mons in Belgium!). Continue to the junction with the N17. Stop at the French cemetery on the right.

• *French National Cemetery/Chinese Graves, Villers Carbonnel/43.2 miles/10 minutes/Map 9/1*

The cemetery contains 2,285 burials, of which 1,295 are in two mass graves. There are fifty-nine named men in Ossuary 1 and thirty-five in Ossuary 2. Inside the cemetery is the local WW1 Memorial. In 1941 eighteen French bodies from WW2 were exhumed and reburied here. In the adjoining local cemetery there is a plot hidden in trees at the back containing three Chinese CWGC graves from October 1918. The concrete frames of the graves are inscribed '*Concession à perpétuité*'. Normally French graves have a limited concessionary period and signs offering graves for reburials are often seen in

French cemeteries. It is pleasing to know that the remains of these obscure Chinese Labourers, who came so far to give their lives, will always be preserved here.

Continue over the A1 motorway into Estrées Deniécourt.

N.B. On the right is a memorial to **Lt Col Puntous and the French 329th Division**, 4 July 1916 (46.5 miles) **(Map 9/2)**.

Continue to the junction with the D164.

N.B. To the right is signed the site of the **destroyed village of Fay**, the ruins of which are now defined by the CGS/H with **Information Panels (Map 9/3)**.

Continue through Foucaucourt to a small, easy-to-miss cross on the right as the road bends sharply to the left.

N.B. This **monument is to Col Rabier and the French 55th Inf Bde,** 24 September 1914 (50.2 miles) **(Map 9/4)**.

Continue to the CWGC Cemetery on the left.

• *Heath CWGC Cemetery/53.5 miles/15 minutes/Map 9/5*

The cemetery is so named from the wide expanse of country on which it stands. It has an attractive, somewhat pagoda-shaped shelter with a dramatic avenue of pollarded trees leading to it.

Not made until after the Armistice, the Cemetery stands on the site of a French military cemetery, started in August 1914, that contained 431 French and 1,063 German graves which were all removed. After the war, 1,813 bodies were buried here from the Bray-Harbonnières battlefields and it now contains 958 Australian soldiers and airmen, 839 UK, nine Canadian, six New Zealand, two South African, 369 unknown and twenty-four Australian and nineteen UK Special Memorials. Among the large Australian contingent lie **Pte Robert Matthew Beatham, VC** of 8th Bn Aust Inf, killed 11 August 1918, age 24 and **Lt Alfred Edward Gaby, VC** of 28th Bn Aust Inf, killed the same day, age 26. Beatham attacked four German machine guns, killing ten and capturing ten men and was killed while bombing a further machine gun. Gaby captured four machine guns and fifty prisoners at Villers Bretonneux on 8 August. Unfortunately the headstones are very worn in this cemetery.

Continue through Lamotte-Warfusée (with its distinctive 'fret-work' Art Deco church spire), and over the traffic lights. On leaving the village a wood can be seen approximately 1 mile to the right. Pause.

• *Site of Carey's Force Action, Warfusée-Abancourt/57.3 miles (Map 9)*

The German advance towards Amiens was so rapid that, fearful for the safety of the city, Gen Gough decided to occupy an old French defensive position, the 'Amiens Defence Line', which had been constructed in 1915. It was eight miles long and ran across the St Quentin-Amiens road immediately west of this village. On the night of 25 March an ad hoc force about 3,000 strong was gathered to occupy the position under the command of Maj Gen C.G.S. Carey and it became known as 'Carey's Force'. Among the patchwork of small units involved were two companies of American 6th Regiment Engineers from the US 3rd Division, totalling some 500 men. The Americans occupied the line from the road to the wood about one mile to your right (north) along the D122 and came into action on the night of 27 March. They were probably the first Americans to fight in the line. The Prime Minister, Lloyd George, referred disparagingly to the rapid withdrawal of Gough's 5th Army and gave undue importance to the action of Carey's Force by saying that 'it closed the gap to Amiens for about 6 days' and that it had been formed on the initiative of Gen Carey. In fact it and other similar forces had been formed by Gough – Carey's Force had been created while Carey was on leave in England!

Continue to the first turn to the right, the junction with the C201, signed to Le Hamel.

Extra Visit to Australian Corps Memorial Park (Map 9A/1), and RB, le Hamel (Map 9A/2).
Round trip: 5.4 miles Approximate time: 30 minutes

Turn right on the C201 and continue following signs to le Hamel into the village.
Turn right following green signs uphill to Monument Australien National Park.

N.B. Along the route green numbered signs with a brown Australian sunburst will be passed. These refer to a detailed Australian battlefield tour described in a booklet obtainable at the Villers Bretonneux Museum (visited later).

N.B. Motorised access to the memorial is now limited to the hours of 0900-1800 1 April-31 October and 0900-1600 1 November-31 March, after which time a barrier is lowered. For information contact the Mayor on + (0)3 22 96 88 06.

The Australian Corps Memorial Park/OP. Stand with the sign 'Bus car parking' to your right and look over the Valley of the Somme. At 12 o'clock on the skyline is the Australian 3rd Division Memorial, at 11 o' clock is the chimney of the 1918 Richthofen crash site brickworks, at 10 o' clock are the twin towers of Corbie church. The direction of the Australian attack was from Corbie church.

On 4 July 1918 this was a German position known as the *Wolfsberg* and was on the final objective line for the assault. Apart from being a great success a novel aspect of the attack was that the Australians were resupplied by parachute. The choice of 4 July for the attack had been influenced by the hoped for participation of the recently arrived American 131st and 132nd Regiments, but Pershing ruled this out though four companies did take part with 100 casualties. It was from these positions that the Australians set out on 8 August in the Allied offensive that marked the beginning of the end for the Kaiser, a day that Ludendorff called *Der Schwarze Tag*.

The land for this memorial was donated to the Australians on the 80th anniversary of the Battle of le Hamel. The park contains picnic, toilet and drinking facilities in the edifice in the car park (that can be seen for miles around) and **Information Panels** which give a very positive Australian view of the Somme battles.

A path (from which, as it turns to the left, the tip of the Australian National Memorial can be seen on the horizon beyond the village church) then leads towards the main memorial, telescope, orientation tables and more **Information Panels** (e.g. re the **VCs** of **Driver 'Harry' Dalziel** (qv) and **L/Cpl Tom Axford**, the knighting of Gen Monash in the field). There is a recreated trench system and, in front of the main Memorial, walls surmounted by the divisional and unit badges of the AIF. On the black marble Memorial, which stands out boldly from the surrounding gentle countryside, is a huge engraved sunburst, a quotation from C.E.W. Bean and a portrait of Lt Gen Sir John Monash.

The Australian Memorial, le Hamel.

Trenchline below the Memorial.

Ross Bastiaan Plaque, le Hamel.

Extra visit continued

Return to le Hamel, turn left and then right and stop by the church on the left.
In front of the church is a fine **Ross Bastiaan commemorative bronze Plaque** about the Battle of le Hamel, sponsored by Hugh and Marcus Bastiaan, John and Hazelle Laffin and Carbone-Lorraine.
On a wall to the right of the Church is a **May-June 1945 Plaque with an Anchor to the Senegalese** who had a medical facility nearby. This is rue du Général John Monash.
Turn round and at the first crossroads turn right on the C202 then 204 signed to Villers Bretonneux. Return to the N29 and turn right. As you return to the main itinerary a short distance along the N29 from where you left it, taking this Extra Visit will slightly alter your continuous mileage.

Continue towards Villers Bretonneux. Just before you enter the village, stop on the left just beyond the Demarcation Stone.

• Villers Bretonneux Demarcation Stone/Local Cemetery Allied Graves/60.3 miles/5 minutes/Map 9A/3

After the war the Touring Clubs of France and Belgium planned to erect 240 marker stones along a line agreed by Maréchal Pétain's General Staff to be the limit of the German advance along the Western Front from Dixmuide to the Swiss frontier. 'Here the Invader was brought to a standstill, 1918', is the inscription. The authors, knowing that the Germans had actually penetrated as far as the other side of the village, asked the local *Souvenir Français* organisation why the stone had not been placed there. 'They were there for less than 24 hours', was the reply. Local historians now wish to move the stone to what they consider to be the correct site. The stones were paid for by public subscription and were erected between 1921 and 1927. In the end 118 were erected of which eight were paid for by the Americans. Full details of the stones and much more can be obtained from Rik Scherpenberg www.wra.be

Some 300 metres further on, on the left, is the **Local Cemetery**. Just inside the wall is a **CWGC Plot** containing six graves from 1918, four of them Australian.

Continue to the crossroads in the village.

The Villers Bretonneux Demarcation Stone.

> **N.B.** At this stage a diversion could be made by turning left down the rue Maurice Seigneurgens, D23 (signed to Crucifix Corner CWGC Cemetery) and D935 following Itinerary Five of *Major & Mrs Holt's Battlefield Guide to the Somme* which covers the 1918 actions of the Americans, the British, the Canadians and the French from Villers Bretonneux to Montdidier, via Demuin, Morisel, Sauvillers Mongival, Grivesnes and Cantigny.

Continue to the next left turn on rue de la République. Continue to the large Town Hall on the left in Place Charles de Gaulle.

• *Villers Bretonneux Town Hall/RB/60.8 miles/5 minutes/Map 9A/4*

The main Château in the centre of the town was also destroyed and it has been replaced by the Town Hall and adjoining memorial garden. In front of it is an **RB bronze Plaque** unveiled on 30 August 1993 by the Governor General of Australia, the Hon Bill Hayden. Inside the Town Hall is a room devoted to the various connections between the village and Australia – Villers Bretonneux is twinned with Robinvale in Australia and there are still many joint activities.

Robinvale was named after **Lt Robin Cuttle from Ultima**, Victoria, Australia. In 1914 Robin volunteered but was inexplicably rejected. Not to be deterred he went to England and applied to join the RFC. Again he was rejected – because of his size: he was 6ft 8ins tall. So he joined the RFA in July 1916 and served as a Lieutenant throughout the Somme battles. Whilst attached to the 9th Scots Guards at the Butte de Warlencourt in November 1916 he was awarded the MC when he assisted in capturing many German guns. In 1917 he reapplied to join the RFC and by early 1918 was flying over France with C Flight of 49th Squadron as an observer. Whilst returning from a reconnaissance and bombing mission on 9 May 1918 his plane was shot down. His body was never found and in 1923 members of his family came to France to try and find where he was buried. With the help of members of his squadron and local people they found bomb pieces similar to those carried by Robin's plane, as well as aircraft wreckage, by a crater at Caix near Villers Bretonneux. Back in Australia in October 1924 the expanding railway reached Ultima and a name was needed for the new station. Robin's mother, Margaret, hung a sign over the station which said 'Robin Vale' ('farewell Robin' in Latin). The mother's tribute to her dead son was eventually accepted as the name for the new township which, after initial hardships, prospered. In 1977 Alan Wood, the local MP, visited Villers Bretonneux and the links between the two townships were formed. Cuttle is commemorated on the Arras Flying Services Memorial.

To the left of the car park is the beautifully maintained **Local War Memorial** with a stone **Memorial to the Australians** in front and a sunburst gate.

Continue on the rue de Melbourne and turn right at the crossroads on to rue Victoria and continue to the school on the left.

• *Villers Bretonneux School & Franco-Australian Museum/61.0 miles/20 minutes/WC/Map 9A/5/6*

A plaque on the school wall records that the building was 'the gift of the children of Victoria, Australia, to the children of Villers Bretonneux as a proof of their love and good will towards France': 1,200 of their fathers, uncles and brothers gave their lives in the recapture of the village on 24 April 1918. Inside the school is a permanent exhibition of photographs of Australia.

The Memorial obelisk in front of the school records the story of the school building project, from the visit by the President of the Australian Council on 25 April 1921, to its inauguration on 25 May 1927. The left wing of the school is marked 'Salle Victoria'. This hall is panelled in wood, surmounted by carvings by an Australian artist of Australian fauna, individually illuminated. A plaque by the entrance records the dedication of the museum – which is on the top floor – and which was founded by Marcel Pillon in 1975. It has since been taken over by the council and completely refurbished. It is run by M Jean-Pierre Thierry, for many years the Research Officer at the *Historial*, December 2004 recipient of the *Médaille d'Argent du Tourisme pour la Somme*, and has a documentation centre with an audio-visual presentation and a small book stall. The collection now includes some superb photographs, personal items, ephemera, artefacts, a bronze of the original 2nd Division Memorial at St Quentin which was destroyed by the Germans and the flag used to drape the coffin of the Australian Unknown Soldier during rehearsals for the ceremony of removing it to Australia. The family of kangaroos once housed in the Town Hall have taken up residence at the entrance here. **Open:** Wed-Sat 1000-1200 and 1400-1800. Tues 1400-1800. Closed on public holidays (except 11 November). Tel: + (0)3 22 96 80 79. Entrance fee payable. Well worth a visit.

Continue on the D168 downhill in the direction of Cachy, under the railway and stop at the small memorial, which is easily missed, at the bottom of a dip on the right.

• *First Tank versus Tank Battle Monument, Cachy/62.0 miles/5 minutes/ Map 9A/7*

The historic tank versus tank action took place in the fields to your left and to your right on the slope up towards Villers Bretonneux behind you on the morning of 24 April 1918. At 0345 hours German artillery began an HE and gas shell barrage on British positions in the town and on the feature on which the Australian National Memorial now sits. The attack began at 0600 hours and, led by thirteen A7V tanks (only twenty were ever made), the Germans inflicted heavy casualties on the East Lancashires of 8th Division in the area around the railway station. By 0930 four A7Vs were coming across the fields towards you. Earlier that morning three British Mark IV tanks, lagered in the wood to the right ahead of you, were ordered to move to this area forward of Cachy. They too were coming this way at about 0930. Commanding one of the British tanks was Lt Frank Mitchell and in his book, *Tank Warfare*, he told what happened:

'Opening a loophole I looked out. There, some three hundred yards away, a round squat-looking monster was advancing, behind it came waves of infantry, and farther away to the left and right crawled two more of these armed tortoises. So we had met our rivals at last. Suddenly a hurricane of hail pattered against our steel wall, filling the interior with myriads of sparks and flying splinters... the Jerry tank had treated us to a broadside of armour-piercing bullets. Then came our first casualty... the rear Lewis gunner was wounded in both legs by an armour-piercing bullet which tore through our steel plate. The roar of our engine, the nerve-wracking rat-tat-tat of our machine guns blazing at the Bosche infantry and the thunderous boom of the six-pounders all bottled

Headstone to the removed Unknown Australian Soldier, Adelaide CWGC Cemetery.

The Australian National Memorial and CWGC Cemetery, Villers Bretonneux.

Interior of the Franco-Australian Museum.

Plaque on the wall of Villers Bretonneux School.

Tank v Tank Memorial, Cachy.

up in that narrow space filled our ears with tumult while the fumes of petrol and cordite half stifled us.'

Mitchell's tank attempted two shots at one of the A7Vs. Both hit but seemed ineffective, then the gunner tried again, 'with great deliberation and hit for the third time. Through a loophole I saw the tank heel over to one side then a door opened and out ran the crew. We had knocked the monster out.'

When the war was over, Mitchell, tongue in cheek, recalling that the tanks were called 'landships', and that naval crews are entitled to prize money for sinking enemy ships, applied for prize money for himself and his crew for having knocked out an enemy 'landship'. The War Office descended into a puzzled silence and then turned the application down.

Before the day was over, seven of the new British Whippet tanks charged into the German infantry and the advance stopped. The Germans, however, were now poised on the high ground. If Amiens were to be saved they had to be moved.

Just after dawn on 25 April two Australian brigades attacked astride the N29 road from Amiens and met on the other side of the town, taking almost 1,000 prisoners. It was ANZAC Day and Amiens was safe. After the action the Australians recovered one of two German tanks that had broken down and shipped it to Brisbane (Mephisto), where it remains today. The village was obliterated by the fighting and so great was the destruction that a sign was put up in the ruins proclaiming, 'This was Villers-Bretonneux'.

The small **Memorial to the Tank Action** on the right with a caption in three languages, English, French and German, states that 'Here on 24 April 1918 the first ever tank battle took place between German and British armour.'

Continue towards Cachy and at the crossroads turn right on the D523 signed Fouilloy/Corbie. [Do not cross the motorway to the left.] Continue to the crossroads with the N29.

• *The Nearest Point to Amiens/63.4 miles/Map 9A/8/OP*

The German attack on 21 March 1918 forced the British and French Armies into a hurried retreat, troops pouring towards you on their way back to Amiens. To your right on the crest is Villers Bretonneux and it was not until 28 March that the German advance (which had begun some 50km away at St Quentin) was stopped 3km east of the village – i.e. the other side to where you are now – mainly due to the efforts of the 1st Cavalry Division. Short of troops, and with Amiens in great danger, Haig looked 100km north to Flanders and ordered down the Australians. Thirty-six hours after the German onslaught began again at dawn on 4 April it seemed as if Villers Bretonneux would be taken, but Lt Col H. Goddard, commanding the 9th (Australian) Brigade, newly based in the town, ordered the 36th Battalion forward in a bayonet charge. The advancing Germans broke and withdrew and, before they could attack again, one of their aerial heroes, the 'Red Baron' (qv) was killed.

By 10 April, Haig knew the situation was critical and he begged Foch to take over some portion – any portion – of the front held by British and Commonwealth forces, stretched to the point of exhaustion. Foch agreed to move up a large French force towards Amiens. The next day (12 April), still waiting for them to arrive, a worried Haig issued his famous 'Order of the Day' (qv).

In the dawn mist of 24 April the German 4th (Guards) Division and the 228th Division, supported by thirteen tanks, tried again. It was one of the first actions in which the Germans had used tanks and the first action in which tank fought tank.

This time the enemy got into and through the village, despite determined resistance by 2nd West Yorkshire Regiment at the railway station, so that by 2000 hours that evening the front line ran at right angles to the N29 along the D523 (where you now are). It was the nearest point to Amiens that the Germans reached. That evening at 2200 hours the Australian 13th Brigade counter-attacked in the area on the right of the N29 but were caught in fierce fire by German machine guns of 4th (Guards) Division set up in the wood – Abbey Wood. In a remarkable action which won him the **VC, Lt C.W.K. Sadlier** led a small party into the wood and destroyed six machine-gun positions, thus allowing the attack to continue. An hour later the Australian 15th Brigade, in the light of flames from the burning Château in the village, attacked in a pincer movement through the area beyond the railway line to your front.

Turn right on the N29 and continue to the CWGC Cemetery on the left.

• *Adelaide Cemetery/63.9 miles/15 minutes/Map 9A/9*

The cemetery, which has the most delightful and varied array of plants, was started in early June 1918 and used by 2nd and 3rd Australian Divisions. By the Armistice it contained ninety graves and then 864 other graves were concentrated here. There are now over 500 Australians, 365 soldiers and airmen from the UK, including **Lt Col S. G.**

Latham, DSO, MC and Bar, age 46, killed on 24 April while commanding the 2nd Battalion the Northampton Regiment, and twenty-two Canadians. The 113th Australian Infantry Brigade, the 49th, 50th, 51st and 52nd Australian Infantry Battalions and the 22nd DLI all at one time erected wooden crosses here to commemorate their dead in the actions of Villers Bretonneux. In Plot III, Row M, Grave 13 is a most unusual headstone. It records the fact that 'The remains of an **Unknown Soldier** lay in this grave for seventy-five years. On 2 November 1993 they were exhumed and now rest in the Tomb of the Unknown Australian Soldier at the Australian War Memorial in Canberra.'

Continue, crossing the railway. On the left is
Memorial to the Villers Bretonneux Déportés of WW2.
It is next to the site of the **Villers Bretonneux Château** whose flames lit up the attack of the Australian 15th Brigade on the night of 24 April. After the War it was used as the HQ of the Australian Graves Registration Unit. Until November 2004 the ruins of the Château (owned by the Commune) served as a visible reminder of the War but it was then demolished as it was deemed dangerous. There are plans to erect a hotel/restaurant or supermarket on the site.

Continue to the crossroads in Villers Bretonneux and turn left on the D23 signed to the Australian Memorial. Stop by the memorial.

• *Australian National Memorial & Fouilloy Military CWGC Cemetery, Villers Bretonneux/RB/65.9 miles/30 minutes/Map 9A/10/11/OP*

Outside the cemetery is a **CGS/H Information Panel** (with the reproduction of a photo from the Museum of an archetypal 'Digger'.

It was an extraordinary coincidence that the two Australian brigades which encircled Villers Bretonneux should meet in the early hours of 25 April 1918 because three years earlier on that morning, then a Sunday, the Australian Imperial Forces had landed at Gallipoli. What happened on that terrible day lives on in the nation's memory, and every year young Australians make their way down to the Gallipoli Peninsula to commemorate what came to be known as ANZAC Day (see *Major and Mrs Holt's Battlefield Guide to Gallipoli*). It is remembered at Villers Bretonneux too, for here is the Australian National Memorial which commemorates 10,797 Australians who gave their lives on the Somme and other sectors of the Western Front and have no known grave. Until the end of the 1980s Australian veterans regularly visited the village at this time. In the cemetery, known as Fouilloy Cemetery, lie 1,085 UK, 770 Australian, 263 Canadian, four South Africans and two New Zealand burials. There are some memorable private inscriptions on the Australian graves, which merit careful reading, e.g. **Pte C.J. Bruton**, 34th AIF, age 22, 31 March 1918 [II.C.5/7], 'He died an Australian hero, the greatest death of all'; **Pte A.L. Flower**, 5th AIF, 29 July 1918 [III.B.6.], 'Also **Trooper J.H. Flower**, wounded at Gallipoli, buried at sea 05.5.1915.' In VI.AB.20 lies **Jean Brilliant, VC, MC**, 22nd Bn French-Canadian, age 22, 10 August 1918. His headstone, engraved in French, records that he volunteered in Quebec and 'Fell gloriously on the soil of his ancestors. Good blood never lies.' His wonderful citation is in the Cemetery Report. There is a hospital named after Brilliant in Quebec. On the right as one walks towards the memorial are several poignant graves from 11 November 1918.

Within the left-hand hedge at the edge of the lawn before the main memorial, there is an **RB bronze Plaque**, unveiled on 30 August 1993 by the Governor General of Australia. From this point the heights on the left can be seen, with the tall chimney of the Colette brickworks near which the Red Baron was shot down.

Unveiled by King George VI on 22 July 1938, the impressive main **Memorial** consists of a wall carrying the names of the Missing and a 100ft-high central tower which can be climbed with due caution. If the gate to the tower is locked the key maybe obtained from the Gendarmerie on the N29 at Villers Bretonneux. If you intend to go up, allow an extra twenty minutes. The memorial was designed by Sir Edwin Lutyens and, due to delays occasioned by lack of funds, it was the last of the Dominion Memorials to be inaugurated. The original plan for the Memorial had included a 90ft-high archway but this was omitted, presumably for financial reasons. It bears the scars of World War II bullets (deliberately retained as an historical reminder) and the top of the tower was struck by lightning on 2 June 1978 and extensively renovated. By facing directly away from the memorial, the cathedral and the Perret Tower in Amiens can be seen on a clear day. How near the Germans came!

The war correspondent Philip Gibbs described how, 'The Germans came as near to Amiens as Villers-Bretonneux on the low hills outside. Their guns had smashed the railway station of Longueau, which to Amiens is like Clapham Junction to Waterloo. Across the road was a tangle of telephone wires, shot down from their posts. For one night nothing – or next to nothing – barred the way, and Amiens could have been entered by a few armoured cars. Only small groups of tired men, the remnants of strong battalions, were able to stand on their feet, and hardly that.'

Later he reported: 'Foch said, "I guarantee Amiens". French cavalry, hard pressed, had come up the northern part of our line. I saw them riding by, squadron after squadron, their horses wet with sweat. To some I shouted out, '*Vivent les Poilus*', emotionally, but they turned and gave me ugly looks. They were cursing the English, I was told afterwards, for the German break-through. '*Ces sacrés Anglais!*' Why couldn't they hold their lines?'

Gibbs acknowledges that: 'Amiens was saved by the counterattacks of the Australians, and especially by the brilliant surprise attack at night on Villers-Bretonneux under the generalship of Monash.'

In one of the strange coincidences of war, Gibbs was relieved to bump, quite accidentally, into his 'kid' brother Arthur who had become lost from his unit and was bringing up his field guns towards Amiens. 'I had never expected to see him alive again, but there he was looking as fresh as if he had just had a holiday in Brighton.'

• *End of Kaiser's Offensive Battlefield Tour.*
OR Go to Amiens or Albert for RWC

THE SECOND BATTLE OF THE MARNE

(The Ourcq, Château Thierry, Belleau Wood)

JULY – AUGUST 1918

'The British Army, entirely disorganised by the events of March and April,
is still far from being re-established'
Field Marshal Haig
(The reaction of the British Commander-in-Chief to Joffre's Memorandum
of 24 July 1918 setting out his plans for exploiting the German
defeats with a series of energetic attacks.)

'The French Army, after four years of war and the severest trials,
is at present worn out, bled white, anaemic.'
General Pétain

'The American Army asks nothing better than to fight, but it has not yet been formed.'
General Pershing

As a result of the brilliant conduct of the 4th Brigade of the 2nd US Division
who have taken in a noble fight Bouresches and the important support point
of Belleau Wood, bloodily defended by a numerous adversary, the General
commanding the VIth Army has decided that from now on in all official
communications Belleau Wood shall carry the name *Bois de la Brigade de Marine.*
General Degoutte

SUMMARY OF THE BATTLE

On 15 July 1918 Ludendorff opened an attack towards Reims designed both to capture the city and also to be part of a feint for a planned major offensive in Flanders. It did not work. Three days later the Allies, including the newly arrived Americans, struck back and by 6 August the front lines were back on the River Vesle from Soissons to Reims. Casualty figures are difficult to substantiate as nations use not only different criteria but also different time periods. Broadly the Germans lost over 150,000, the French almost 100,000, the British 13,000 and the Americans 12,000.

OPENING MOVES

On 27 May 1918 the German 7th Army under Blücher drove a deep wedge across the Chemin des Dames to the west of Reims into the heart of the French 6th Army. By 30 May its left flank bordered the Marne past Dormans and as far south as Château Thierry. The salient, less than ten miles short of Villers Cotterêts and La Ferté, pointed straight towards

Meaux some fifteen miles away and twenty-five miles beyond there to Paris (see Map 10). The Allies were caught by surprise, the sector having been a quiet one which included three 'resting' British divisions of IX Corps in the front line – the 50th, the 8th and the 21st. Neither the British nor French higher commands had thought an attack to be likely though intelligence sources in the AEF had warned of a possible assault in the area. By midday the Germans had crossed the Aisne and by the end of the day had penetrated to Fismes on the Vesle, which they crossed. Two days later they renewed their attacks, reaching Fère-en-Tardenois and taking Soissons. But as they had advanced their front had gradually narrowed. It was now restricted to the east by Reims and to the south by the Marne and so they shifted their attention down the land corridor between the rivers **Ourcq** and **Marne** towards Paris. Just as they had done in 1914, during the first battle of the Marne, the Germans created a salient into the allied lines in the direction of Paris. The success of their offensive had taken the Germans, as well as the Allies, by surprise and this success caused them to continue with the attacks beyond what was needed for the planned diversionary feint to such an extent that the scheduled Flanders attack never took place. Thus, as June opened, the German attacks continued but now without rapid territorial success, the French adopting a defence-in-depth policy which sapped the enemy's momentum. Nevertheless the salient crept forward reaching out towards **Château Thierry** and **Belleau Wood**. At Château Thierry on 1 June the American 3rd Division blew the main bridge over the River Marne just as the Germans were arriving and so their emphasis switched northwards, to the very tip of their salient at Belleau Wood. There once again they were stopped by the Americans in dramatic fighting that has become legendary in the history of the United States Marine Corps. There was now a pause while both sides recovered breath and planned their next moves. Ludendorff with his eyes upon Paris and Joffre, now flushed with the arriving Americans, some 250,000 of whom would be temporarily 'lent' to the French to help to stem the German tide.

On 15 July the German attack opened aiming to push the bulge towards the French capital and the Paris-Verdun railway. The 7th Army headed towards Dormans and Château Thierry west of Reims, and the 1st and 3rd Armies towards Châlons to the east.

WHAT HAPPENED

Along a fifty mile front on 15 July the German attack began between 0415 and 0530. The new French policy of elastic defence, in which the defender gave way cautiously, sapped the strength of the already tired Germans and to the east of Reims the attack failed. The idea has been generally described as the 'Gouraud Manoeuvre' but in truth it owes it origin to Pétain's method of defence in depth – thinly held positions in front and more strongly held positions in the rear. In addition prisoners taken on the evening of 14 July told that an attack was planned for the morrow, even giving the time of the opening barrage so that the French artillery opened their fire on the German positions as the attacking troops prepared to assault.

To the west, between Reims and Paris, the Germans had some success against the French 5th and 6th Armies including the II Italian Corps, and on the 17th the 7th Army crossed the Marne on either side of Dormans and moving behind Reims threatened to cut it off. But by concentrating their artillery fire on the Marne crossings the French disrupted the German supply chain and by repeated counter-attacks broke up the German advance into disconnected local actions. By the end of the 17th the German offensive was over and in that pause Pétain gathered himself for the great counter-offensive which was aimed at the German bulge between Soissons and Reims.

At 0435 on 18 July after a night of heavy storms, the allied artillery bombarded German positions from the Marne to the Aisne and sixteen Divisions supported by tanks and aircraft advanced against the western side of the bulge taking the Germans completely by surprise. Mangin's 10th Army (see page 32) east of Soissons followed a rolling barrage without local preliminary preparation and quickly advanced to the plateau north-east of Villers Cotterêts while enemy concentrations at Fère-en-Tardenois and Oulchy-le-Château were attacked from the air. It is estimated that on the first day the Germans lost some 12,000 men as prisoners and 250 guns.

Two days later the southern tip of the bulge protruding south of the Marne below Dormans (see Map 10) was attacked by the French 9th Army supported by the British 51st and 62nd Divisions. The southern bank of the Marne was reached that day, the Germans having withdrawn, but it was two more days before the French took Château Thierry and the American 3rd Division crossed the river to the east. German resistance continued, particularly over the heights dominating the Ourcq River where the American 42nd Division was involved in furious fighting and the German lines held between Fère-en-Tardenois and Ville-en-Tardenois as they sought to extract their forces from the bulge – or the 'Marne Sack' as they called it.

By the end of July both sides were tired. Pétain moved more American Divisions into the line – the 4th, 28th, 32nd and 42nd, resting the 3rd and 26th – and urged his 6th and 10th Armies into further attacks, but at dawn on 2 August the Germans had gone. They had withdrawn to the Vesle River. Soissons was reoccupied unopposed that evening and over the next two days the Allied forces gathered along the banks of the Vesle, the American 42nd Division taking Fismes. The Second Battle of the Marne was over.

THE BATTLEFIELD TOUR

• **The Route:** The tour proper begins at Fismes (with an alternative of Reims) where it crosses the US 28th Div Memorial Bridge. It then visits the French 109th RI Memorial at Fismette; the US 4th Div Mem at Bazoches; the French and German Cemeteries at Loupeigne; the American Oise-Aisne Cemetery; Monuments at Meurcy Farm on the Ourcq River; Seringes Memorial Church; Roosevelt Memorials; Landowski's *Fantômes*, Butte de Chalmont; Belleau – Stricker Grave, Belleau Cemetery; Pennsylvania Fountain, Demarcation Stone and Belleau US 26th Division Memorial Church; the American Aisne-Marne Cemetery; Belleau Wood and Memorials; German Cemetery; US 2nd Division Boulders; Château Thierry – American Aisne-Marne Monument, American 3rd Division Monument, US 3rd Division and French Memorials, MAFA & Roosevelt Memorial, American Methodist Church.
• **Extra Visit:** CWGC Cemetery, Jonchéry-sur-Vesle
• **Total time:** 6 hours 30 minutes
• **Total distance:** 72 miles
• **Distance from Calais to start point:** 198 miles.   Motorway Tolls
• **Map:** Michelin Regional 513: Ile-de-France
• **Base towns:** Reims, Château Thierry

MAP 10 : THE SECOND BATTLE OF THE MARNE: JULY – AUGUST 1918 (The Ourcq, Château Thierry, Belleau Wood)

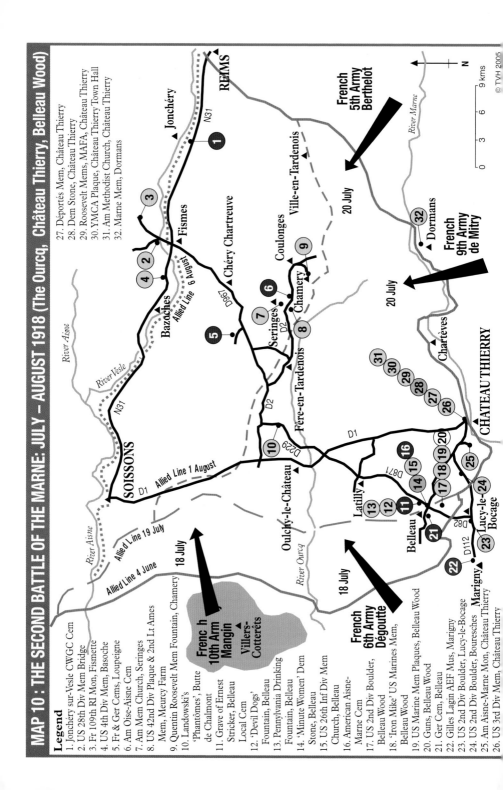

© TVH 2005

Legend

1. Jonchéry sur-Vesle CWGC Cem
2. US 28th Div Mem Bridge
3. Fr 109th RI Mon, Fismette
4. US 4th Div Mem, Basoche
5. Fr & Ger Cems, Loupeigne
6. Am Oise-Aisne Cem
7. Am Mem Church, Seringes
8. US 42nd Div Plaque & 2nd Lt Ames Mem, Meurcy Farm
9. Quentin Roosevelt Mem Fountain, Chamery
10. Landowski's 'Phantômes', Butte de Chalmont
11. Grave of Ernest Stricker, Belleau Local Cem
12. 'Devil Dogs', Fountain, Belleau
13. Pennylvania Drinking Fountain, Belleau
14. 'Minute Women' Dem Stone, Belleau
15. US 26th Inf Div Mem Church, Belleau
16. American Aisne-Marne Cem
17. US 2nd Div Boulder, Belleau Wood
18. 'Iron Mike' US Marines Mem, Belleau Wood
19. US Marine Mem Plaques, Belleau Wood
20. Guns, Belleau Wood
21. Ger Cem, Belleau
22. Gilles Lagin AEF Mus, Marigny
23. US 2nd Div Boulder, Lucy-le-Bocage
24. US 2nd Div Boulder, Bouresches
25. Am Aisne-Marne Mon, Château Thierry
26. US 3rd Div Mem, Château Thierry
27. Déportés Mem, Château Thierry
28. Dem Stone, Château Thierry
29. Roosevelt Mems, MAFA, Château Thierry
30. YMCA Plaque, Château Thierry Town Hall
31. Am Methodist Church, Château Thierry
32. Marne Mem, Dormans

From Calais take the A26/E17 and leave it at Exit 13 Laon, then the N2 direction Soissons and the D967 via Bruyères to Fismes. Continue to the bridge over the Vesle at Fismette and stop.

OR you may wish to take this tour as a continuation to the Champagne or Meuse-Argonne tours in which case you could start from Reims and take the following **Extra Visit** en route.

Extra Visit to Fismes from Reims via Jonchéry-sur-Vesle CWGC Cemetery (Map 10/1).
One-way mileage: 15.6 miles. Approximate time: 45 minutes

From the A4 take Exit 22 Tinqueux and then the N31 direction Rouen/Fismes. Continue to a right turn into Jonchéry-sur Vesle.

It was here that Gen Franchet d'Espérey had his 5th French Army HQ. It was also over this village that the French claim their first aerial combat when on 5 October 1914 the French Voisin biplane, No V89 of Squadron V.24 piloted by Sgt Aviator Frantz and Mechanic Quénault, gave chase to a German biplane over Reims and hit it with their machine-gun fire. [The first British aerial combat casualties were Lt C.G.G. Bayly and 2nd Lt V. Waterfall, brought down over Mons on 22 August 1914.]

In the spring of 1918 the Americans had an ammunition depot here.

Drive straight through the village on the Route Nationale to a large junction and turn right following green CWGC signs. Stop at the cemetery on the left.

Jonchéry-sur-Vesle CWGC Cemetery (8.5 miles). The cemetery was created after the Armistice from isolated graves and cemeteries on the battlefields of May-August 1918 in the area. It contains 360 UK, one Canadian and five Special Memorials. Buried here in this peaceful spot is **Capt John Harmon Massey, MC, MiD**, *Croix de Guerre* **& Palms** [sic], 45th Bde, RFA, died of wounds 27 May 1918, BA Cantab, born New Zealand, Mentioned, as was his Battery, in Gen Berthelot's Ordre Gen No 351 of 16 July 1918.

On 27 August 2003 the remains of an **Unknown Soldier**, found during the excavations for the new railway line at Bonleuse, were re-interred here. It is thought that he was killed in the fighting of May-June 1918.

Turn round, continue straight over the crossroads to the N31 and continue into Fismes. Follow signs for town centre and turn right on the D386 direction Laon, past the superb Hôtel de Ville that was virtually destroyed, as was much of Fismes, in the war, over the railway bridge to the bridge over the Vesle at Fismette. Stop just short of the bridge.

Headstone of Capt J.H. Massey, MC, MiD, Croix de Guerre + Palmes, Jonchéry-sur-Vesle CWGC Cemetery.

Set your mileometer to zero.

• US 28th Division Memorial Bridge over the Vesle/0 miles/5 minutes/ Map 10/2

The bridge, built in 1927, was designed by architects T. Atherton and **P. Cret** (qv). On it is the golden inscription, 'This bridge is dedicated to the 28th (Pennsylvania National Guard) Division of the American Army and was raised by the State of Pennsylvania in memory of those who gave their lives for the liberation of Fismes.' The monumental pillars support statues of Peace and Agriculture and carry the seal of the USA and of Pennsylvania. There are small heads of Doughboys at the corners of the pillars. A new Plaque donated by Meadsville, PA. was erected on 4 September 1994 on the 50th Anniversary of the WW2 Liberation of Fismes in reaffirmation of Franco-American friendship.

From the Fismette side of the bridge take the D386 direction Baslieux and continue to the monument on the crest.

• Monument to 109th RI/0.6 miles/5 minutes/Map 10/3

This polished red marble obelisk was dedicated by the veterans of the 109th RI to their 800 comrades who fell on 27 and 28 May 1918, when they tried to deny the passage of the Vesle to three German divisions. From it there is a superb view over the Valley of the Vesle and the line of the River due south.

On 7 August 1918 the US 28th Division launched an unsuccessful attack on Fismette, but the following day two attacks with heavy artillery preparations succeeded in taking part of the village and it was completely taken on 10 August. The Germans, however, mounted fierce counter-attacks and in the fighting that day **Sgt James I. Mestrovitch** of the 28th was awarded the **MoH** for crawling out under enemy fire to his wounded company commander. He took his officer on his back to safety where his wound was treated. On 27 August the Germans, using flamethrowers, encircled the village and killed or captured all Americans remaining in it. In this fighting and up to 6 September when they reached the Aisne in pursuit of the Germans, the 28th lost about 5,300 men and the 77th Division nearly 4,800.

Turn round (you may have to drive slightly further on to do this safely) and return to the River bridge. Cross over the bridge and the railway and immediately turn right, right again at the T junction and left at the next T junction. Continue over the roundabout on the N31 signed Soissons and continue to an obelisk on the right.

• US 4th Division Memorial, Bazoches/3.3 miles/5 minutes/Map 10/4

The Monument, which is well-maintained, simply bears the words '4th Division US Army 1918'. The Division advanced from the south early in August 1918, taking the high ground beyond the road (to your left) on 4 August and reaching here two days later. Strong German counter-attacks forced the Americans back to the line of the railway in the valley on 8 August. Heavy artillery fire prevented the building of bridges for a sustained river crossing and even men attempting to swim over were unable to do so. Between 7-9 August 1918 the Division launched several attacks on Bazoches, the village just up ahead, but was unable to take it and by 12 August it had lost approximately 3,500 men. Eventually after intermittent struggles the Germans withdrew from Bazoches on the night of 1 September and the American 77th Div occupied it the next day.

Turn round with care (there is fast-moving traffic) and return towards Fismes, turning left towards Reims on the N31 then sharp right to Château Thierry on the D967 signed American Monument and German Cemetery. Continue to the crossroads with the D79 in Mareuil-en-Dôle through lovely countryside with sweeping valleys and woods to each side. The town was captured by the 42nd on 2 August and here were the Headquarters of the 4th and then the 77th US Divisions during the fighting for Bazoches in August. *Turn right signed French and German Cemeteries. Continue to the cemeteries on the right.*

• French and German Cemeteries, Loupeigne/13.3 miles/10 minutes/ Map 10/5

These sadly unloved and somewhat colourless cemeteries – the French to the left with 598 burials of which 118 are in an ossuary and the German to the right with 478 burials – have a unique layout. Crumbling steps lead up to a small Chapel in the centre. It is dedicated to **the Officers of Artillery and Infantry who fell in 1917-1918.** The *Tricolore* is flying but the French Register is missing. The cemetery was created in 1919 from the battlefields of the Aisne.

Turn round (you will probably have to drive a way up the road to do so), return to the D967 and turn right. Continue towards Fère-en-Tardenois.

On the left at 16 miles you will pass the 4-star Château de Fère Hotel, Tel: + (0)3 23 82 21 13. Here, by the ancient ruins of the Castle, the US 77th Division had their HQ at the beginning of September 1918.

Continue into Fère-en-Tardenois (17.7 miles).

Fère-en-Tardenois is an attractive small town which has a charming main square and an historical and ancient grain market in the centre. It served as a military hospital during the war. There is a variety of restaurants for your lunch break. The US I Corps had its HQ here from 5-13 August after the Germans had been driven back from the Ourcq.

Turn left at the traffic lights in the centre on the D2 and continue following signs to Seringes et Nesles and the American Cemetery. Stop in the parking area on the right by the Visitor's Room.

• American Oise-Aisne Cemetery/19.5 miles/30 minutes/Map 10/6

The cemetery, the second largest American cemetery in Europe, is set in thirty-six acres of beautifully landscaped park, stately trees and shrubs, which surround the lawn in which 6,012 US military dead lie, most of whom were killed in this area in 1918. The lines of headstones, laid out in four plots lined by trees and rose beds, rise in a gentle slope from the entrance to the Memorial at the far end. At the intersection is a circular plaza and the flagpole present in all US cemeteries. The rose-coloured sandstone Memorial is in the form of a curving colonnade, with a stone sarcophagus somewhat like the CWGC War Stone in the centre, flanked by a chapel at one end and a map-room at the other. On one of the beautiful coloured marble pillars is a Plains Indian head, the insignia of US 2nd Division. The soldiers' magazine *Stars and Stripes* reported in May 1919 that the Germans were fearful of the idea of facing American Indians in battle and an American officer, captured by the Germans in the St Mihiel Salient, was surprised to be interrogated not on the movements of his division and its objectives but on 'how many Indians there were in units opposing them in that sector'.

Paul Cret's elegant 28th US Division Memorial Bridge over the Vesle at Fismes.

American 4th Division Memorial, Bazoches.

THIS BRIDGE HAS BEEN ERECTED BY THE STATE OF PENNSYLVANIA AS A TRIBUTE TO THE HEROIC SERVICE AND NOTABLE ACHIEVEMENT OF THE 28 TH DIVISION AMERICAN EXPEDITIONARY FORCES 1927

Plaque and Doughboy's Head.

Colonnade, Oise-Aisne American Cemetery.

On the colonnade are *bas-reliefs* showing warriors through the ages. The chapel contains an altar of carved stone and the map room contains an engraved coloured wall map portraying the military operations in the region in 1918. The architects of the cemetery were Cramm & Ferguson of Boston with landscape architect George Gibbs Jr, under **Paul Cret**, Consulting Architect for the ABMC. Cret was born in Lyons and trained in Lyons and Paris before being offered an assistant professorship at the University of Pennsylvania. When WW1 broke out he was in France and reported for duty with the Chasseurs Alpins. In 1919 Mrs Theodore Roosevelt asked Cret to design a memorial for her son, Quentin, in Chamery (visited later). Cret designed the Monuments at Varennes, Fismes, Château Thierry, Bellicourt and Flanders Field Cemetery, Waregem. He died in 1945.

To the right is a plaque commemorating the inauguration on 31 May 1998 of the Carillon here presented by the Robert R. McCormick Tribune Foundation (qv).

Here the poet **Joyce Kilmer**, 165th Inf, 42nd Div, age 31, journalist and author (for example of the famous poem, *Trees*, published in 1914, is buried (in Plot B Row 9, Grave 15) with many other of the 42nd Rainbow Division men killed during the Battles of the Ourcq and the Marne. Kilmer was killed on 30 July 1918 (see below) and was awarded the *Croix de Guerre.*

Trees
I think that I shall never see
A poem lovely as a tree
A tree whose hungry mouth is pressed
Against the earth's sweet flowing breast.
A tree that looks at God all day,
And lifts her leafy arms to pray,
A tree that may in summer wear,
A nest of robins in her hair,
Upon whose bosom snow has lain,
Who intimately lives with rain,
Poems are made by fools like me,
But only God can make a tree.

Grave marker of black soldier, Pte Lewis A. Holley.

Kilmer also wrote a poem *On the Death of Rupert Brooke.*

Also in Plot B is **Nurse Kathryne Green**, Base Hospital 8 A.N.C., 22 October 1918.

Between 1921-23 extensive efforts were made to trace the relatives of the American dead as it was their choice to repatriate their loved ones or to let them be buried in an American Cemetery in Europe, but some families were impossible to trace. Over sixty per cent of the bodies were eventually sent home, but for those who were buried in Europe a '**Gold Star Mothers**' programme was started whereby mothers and occasionally unremarried widows (but fathers were not eligible) were given a return ticket, with all expenses paid, to visit their son's grave. One of the most poignant visitors under the scheme was the widow of **Pte Lewis A. Holley,** Coy B, 542nd Engineer Corps, eligible because his mother had died. Her request to bring her little daughter with her was refused. Holley was a black African American, a non-combattant who died of pneumonia in October 1917 in the Naval Base Hospital at Brest. Originally he was buried in the US Cemetery at Lambezellac under a cross wrongly inscribed 'Paul Schuur', then the Graves Registration Service moved his body to another site in the same cemetery and finally on 15 October 1921 he was moved here to the Oise-Aisne Cemetery (when his own identification tag was discovered) in Plot D, Row 20, Grave 17. On 14 August 1930 his widow Katherine, a schoolteacher from Hegesville W Virginia, left her home and travelled by train to New York where she boarded the SS *American Merchant*, landed in France, went by train to Paris and then to the cemetery.

There was no distinction made between Protestants, Catholics or Jews, rich or poor, but black mothers and widows were certainly treated as second class, travelling (as did Katherine) on merchant ships in contrast to the luxury liners which transported the white women. Seven African American women declined to travel because of this segregation.

Many women travelled under the scheme in 1930, 3,653 between 16 May and 22 September alone. By 31 October 1933, when the project ended, 6,693 women had made the pilgrimage of the more than 17,000 who qualified. Their average age was between 61 and 65. The full story is told by Constance Potter on the US Archives website.

Turn round and then take the first right on the D795 to Seringes et Nesles. Continue bearing left through the village and stop at the church on the left.

• *Seringes American Memorial Church/20.4 miles/15 minutes/Map 10/7*

To visit this fascinating little church walk back to the large farm on the left belonging to the Mayor, M. Alvoet, who has the key and will be pleased to open up for you. The dog is friendly. To phone in advance: Tel: + (0)3 23 82 20 34.

On the right wall inside the church the names of the more than 400 men who fell in taking the village (including **Joyce Kilmer**) are inscribed, listed under 'buried in the Oise-Aisne Cemetery' and those 'buried elsewhere'. To the left is a stone *Piéta* in *bas-relief* 'in memory of the glorious soldiers of the USA buried here at Seringes who died with the Allied Nations to give all people definitive Peace and Liberty'. Above the altar is a beautiful SGW to the memory of US **Lt William F...?** of Coy M, 307th Regt, 77th Div, 28 August 1918. Sadly the pane of glass with his surname is missing, but our researches have discovered that it was **Cahill** and he is buried in the Oise-Aisne American Cemetery in Plot A, Row 15, **Grave 12**, with the date 29 August. His name is also on the wall here. The village was taken by the 42nd Division on 2 August.

Continue downhill towards the Ourcq and rejoin the D2. Turn left and then right at the small sign to Meurcy. Drive up the track and stop just after the house on the right by a large willow tree at the side of the small river.

This small stream joins the Ourcq itself about one mile south-west of here. The bells of the American Cemetery carillon ring out hauntingly over the stream, occasionally playing hymns.

• *Private Memorial to 2nd Lt Ames & US 42nd Rainbow Division Memorial, Meurcy Farm/21.2 miles/15 minutes/Map 10/8*

Walk some 300m along the near side (or the far side if it looks easier) of the stream to the small iron bridge. Just short of it is

A red granite stone with the inscription 'In loving memory of **2nd Lt Oliver Ames II**, **DSC**, 165th Inf, kia at Meurcy Farm July 29 1918.' Ames is buried in the Oise-Aisne Cemetery in Plot A Row 3 Grave 7. He was killed at this spot where the day afterwards the poet Joyce Kilmer (who, although officially acting on the Regiment's Intelligence staff as an Observer, had, following the death of Ames, attached himself as Adjutant to Maj William Donovan commanding the 1st Bn) was killed by a sniper. The two were originally buried together here. Kilmer, who had enlisted as a Private soldier in 1917, was described by Lt H.E. Allen, the 165th Intelligence Officer under whom he worked, as 'Probably the best non-commissioned intelligence officer in the 42nd Division.' Just beyond the stream on 28 July, Sgt Frank Gardella Jr of the 42nd Div shot down one of two German aeroplanes which fell in flames onto the second one and they both crashed. He was awarded the DSC. The farm was taken by the 42nd Div on 31 July and the Germans withdrew some ten miles to the River Vesle during the night of 1 August and the following day the Division advanced across the area now occupied by the US Cemetery.

Return to the tree and walk into the beautifully tended garden of the Farm (remember that you are on private property, so do ask permission if anyone is around) *to the plaque on the wall of the open barn ahead.*

The flags of the USA and of France flank this fine bronze **Plaque** with the coloured insignia of the **42nd (Rainbow) Division** which was unveiled on 27 May 2001 in an impressive Franco-American ceremony. It was the inspiration of Rainbow Div veteran, Bill Shurtleff, who researched the 1918 exploits of his Division and who met the Maire of Seringes et Nesles. He then persuaded the 42nd Memorial Foundation to allocate the funds for the Memorial and himself drafted the words. It commemorates the exploits of the Division and its attached units who suffered 6,459 killed and wounded with an additional 983 casualties in attached units. His account states that they formed up on a 3,000 yard front just south of the river and under constant enemy machine-gun and artillery fire crossed the river on 28 July. Then followed six days of hand-to-hand combat before the key positions at Hill 212, Sergy, Meurcy Farm, Bois Colas and Seringes et Nesles were finally captured.

The caption ends with the verse,

'Comrades true, born anew, peace to you!
Your souls shall be where heroes are
And your memory shine like the morning star.
Brave and dear, Shield us here, Farewell'

To the right is a well-preserved **mortar.**

Gen Douglas MacArthur recalled, 'We took Meurcy Farm in a hand-to-hand fight but the center at Nesles still held. Their artillery was concentrated; their machine guns east and west of the town raked us fore and aft; but nothing could stop the impetus of that mad charge. We forded the river; we ascended the slopes; we killed the garrison in the town to a man. At dusk on July 29 we were in sole possession.'

In the bitter fighting round the farm a **Medal of Honour was won by Sgt Richard W. O'Neill** of the 42nd Div. He advanced ahead of the assaulting line and attacked an enemy force of about twenty-five men. He continued to fight in command of his detachment although he had sustained several pistol wounds and was suffering from loss of blood until, wounded again, he was forced to be evacuated, where he insisted on being taken to the battalion commander to tell him valuable information about the enemy positions.

Return to the main road, turn right, drive on past the cemetery and continue through Nesles on the D2 to Chamery. Turn right on the D14 signed Souvenir Roosevelt and

SGW to Lt William Cahill, Seringes Church.

Private Memorial to 2nd Lt Ames, Meurcy Farm.

Plaque to the US 42nd (Rainbow) Division, Meurcy Farm.

Meurcy Farm Mortar.

Memorial Fountain to Quentin Roosevelt, Chamery.

continue to the drinking fountain on the left.

• *Quentin Roosevelt Memorial Fountain and Memorials, Chamery/ 25.1 miles/5 minutes/Map 10/9/OP*

The large stone fountain, designed by Paul Cret (qv), with the water emerging from a lion's head bears the seal of the USA on the left and the arms of France on the right. It commemorates 'Lt Quentin Roosevelt, aetat XX (age 20), Air Service USA who fell in battle at Chamery on 14 July 1918'. "Only those are fit to live who are not afraid to die" (quoted by Gen MacArthur at Rainbow Div Reunion, 14 July 1935).

There are **Memorials on the site of Roosevelt's crash and of his nearby original grave** in the fields just above the village. In 2004 the track leading to them was non-navigable but the Commune has plans to resurface it in the future.

Stand to the right of the monument, a monument's width away, and look at 11 o' clock to a solitary tree in the middle foreground.

Quentin, the youngest son of ex-US President Theodore Roosevelt, served in the 95th American Aero Sqn, 1st Pursuit Group. His Nieuport 28 was said at the time to have been shot down by a more experienced adversary – Sgt Johannes Thom, a German Ace with twenty-four victories – but research by historian Gilles Lagan (qv) appears to prove that he was actually brought down by an undistinguished pilot, Sgt Carl Emil Gräper, attd Jasta 50, and crashed by the woods beyond the tree. It was just three days after he won the *Croix de Guerre* for a daring feat when finding himself in the rear of six German planes he opened up with his machine gun, shot one of them down, then pursued by the

Quentin Roosevelt's Original Grave.

remaining five he managed to get back to his own lines. The Germans buried him (it was always believed with full military honours), placed a crude cross fashioned from the two wheels and propellor of his plane over his grave and also dropped a note about the young aviator's death and his flying boots over the American lines. However a photograph in Lagin's possession shows a group of jubilant Germans (including Gräper) standing by the completely burnt out wreck of a plane and the decomposing body of Roosevelt – obviously several days after the crash. When the Allies retook the area four weeks later the American 32nd Division made an elaborate concrete frame to the grave and added a large cross. The grave became a place of pilgrimage to French and Americans alike.

'Teddy' Roosevelt, whose Mexican War Rough Rider exploits had made him a legend in France, had warned President Wilson about America's unpreparedness for war and had been ready to raise his own division and go to France himself. Wilson refused his offer and Roosevelt had to content himself with sending his four sons. **Archie** served as a 1st Lt with the 16th Regt, 1st US Div, and was then attached to the 26th Regt and was wounded in March 1918 in Alsace being awarded the *Croix de Guerre*. In WW2, thanks to the intercession of his cousin Franklin, he served in the Pacific as a Lt Col commanding the 162nd Inf Regt and was awarded the Bronze Star, two Silver Stars and the Purple Heart – the only US soldier to have been 100 per cent disabled in two world wars. He died in 1979. **Kermit** served with the British M-G Corps in September, in France and Mesopatamia, winning the MC. He was then attd 'C' Battery, 7th US Fld Arty in the Meuse-Argonne. After the war he became an author and committed suicide in Alaska on 4 June 1943.

Theodore Jr served as a Major commanding the 1st Bn, 26th US Inf Division. He was wounded in May 1918 at Cantigny and again at Soissons in July. Promoted to Lt Col in September he commanded the 26th Regt and was awarded the DSC, the *Légion d'Honneur* and *Croix de Guerre*. In WW2 he served with conspicuous gallantry, reaching the rank of Brig Gen and being awarded the Medal of Honour. He died on 12 July 1944 soon after the landing at Utah Beach and is buried in the American Cemetery at St Laurent in Normandy. In 1955 the body of his youngest brother, Quentin, who had died nearly twenty-six years to the day earlier, was then moved to lie beside him.

It is said that Teddy Roosevelt never recovered from Quentin's death and he died six months later from an embolism in the coronary artery. The author Edith Wharton wrote a poetical lament for him entitled, *With the Tide*.

Some supposed remains of Quentin's plane are to be seen in the MAFA building in Château Thierry, to be visited later in the tour.

Return past the American Cemetery to Fère-en-Tardenois (30.5 miles) and in the Market Square continue on the D2 signed to Oulchy-le-Château and Saponay and at Beugneux turn left on the D22, signed to Mon National de la 2ième Victoire de la Marne and then left on the D229. Stop at the monument on the right.

• Landowski's Fantômes, Butte de Chalmont/40.2 miles/20 minutes/ Map 10/10

This moving and impressive National Monument to the 2nd Battle of the Marne consists of three parts. In the foreground is a 5m high Statue of France 1918, holding a shield, then four groups of three steps representing the four years of the war, then the *Fantômes* sculpted by Paul Landowski. The eight 8m high granite statues are the ghosts rising from the battlefield: **1.** A young Recruit; **2.** A Sapper; **3.** A Machine-gunner; **4.** A Grenadier; **5.** A Colonial; **6.** An Infantry soldier; **7.** An Aviator. With their bodies they protect the naked figure of a young martyr escaping from his shroud. Their eyes are closed yet they seem to be searching for their dead comrades. Begun in 1919 the Monument was not unveiled (by Pres Albert Lebrun) until 1935. Gen de Gaulle came here to celebrate the 50th Anniverary of the Victory of 2nd Marne. The Butte de Chalmont stands above the Plain from which, from 15 July to the beginning of August 1918, thousands of Allied soldiers launched their attacks on the crest which dominates the northern bank of the Ourcq (from 15 July to the beginning of August 1918). The site for the Monument was chosen by Veterans and from it there is a panoramic view over the battlefield towards the Ourcq (roughly due south) and Fère-en-Tardenois (roughly due east). The entrance is flanked by large stones listing the ORBAT in the 15 July-4 August 1918 Battles and describing the progression of the ultimately victorious Second Battle of the Marne. During the offensive which involved American, British, French and Italian forces, the Butte de Chalmont was taken, Soissons was retaken, the Paris-Chalons road was re-established – thus lifting the threat to the capital – and 30,000 prisoners and a considerable quantity of materiel were also taken.

On the outbreak of war Landowski (1875-1961) (qv) joined the 35th RI. After the war he completed more than eighty war memorials – in Algeria, in Casablanca as well as in Paris (including the Tomb of Marshal Foch) and other parts of France. The neo-classical Fantômes, with their hint of the *avant-garde*, are acknowledged to be his masterpiece.

Continue on the D229 to Wallée and turn right on the D473. Continue round a sharp right hand bend and then turn sharp left to Armentières on the D80. Cross the River Ourcq and the railway, pass the ruined Château on the right, continue through Armientières on the D79 to the D1. Turn left direction Château Thierry, continue through Rocourt St Martin. At the T junction turn left on the D973 and then right to Le Charme on the 'C' road. Continue through Le Tartre, turn sharp left direction Château Thierry and at the T junction right on the D1390 through Givry to Belleau. Some 200m before the small bridge, stop on the right and walk to the entrance to Belleau Local Cemetery on the right.

• *Grave of Ernest Stricker, Belleau Local Cemetery/57.2 miles/ 10 minutes/Map 10/11*

At the top is the grave of Ernest Stricker, from Clayton, Wisconsin who claimed to have fought in Belleau Wood and who returned to visit the temporary US Cemetery on 2 April 1928. His body was found beside the 2nd Infantry Division Monument at 1600 hours and next to him was a high calibre revolver. In his pocket was his suicide note addressed to the American Legion in Paris explaining that he could not bear to be still alive when so many of his comrades had been killed. He committed suicide so that he could lie with them but the ABMC denied him the right to be buried in the American cemetery and his lonely grave under a white Roman Cross remains here. Stricker is generally described as being a US Marine and his grave is honoured by visiting Marines each Memorial Day (qv). However, no trace of an Ernest Stricker can be found in official Marine records.

[**N.B.** By continuing past the cemetery in the direction of Monthiers to the top of the hill and then parking by a small path that leads to the right – which can be driven with care

218 • Major & Mrs Holt's Battlefield Guide to The Western Front – South

if dry – you can park, walk up the path and then turn right at the junction to the grey stone **Memorial to Lt Jean Peyroche** of the 174th RI who was killed here with twenty of his men on 20 July 1918. On the reverse is a message from the Commandant of the Regiment and the dedication of the Memorial. In the small wood beside the Memorial German trenches can still be seen.]

Cross the iron railing bridge over the small stream. Some 200m further on to the right in the Place Gen Pershing is the Château de Belleau de Beaucaron.

Inside the grounds of the Château on the right, on the wall beyond a large plane tree, is the **'Bulldog' Fountain** (Map 10/12) which is a focal point of USMC ceremonies. When an important contingent visits Belleau each Memorial Day (qv) for impressive ceremonies, complete with Marine Senior Officers, local dignitaries, Marine and French Army bands, they come here. The Germans gave the Marines the nickname 'The Devil Dogs' – hence the memorial fountain – from which visiting Marines drink on their ceremonial visits. Legend has it that drinking from the fountain gives a Marine an extra twenty years of life. In 2000 the water stopped running but fourteen Marines serving in Europe, who were visiting Belleau, fixed it with some plastic pipe. Note that it is on the private property of the local Countess. Oddly, if one is strictly accurate, although the US Marines did indeed take Belleau Wood they did not take Belleau village. It was taken by the 26th (Yankee) Division, a National Guard formation raised in New England. Don't tell that to the Marines!

Fork left and continue uphill to just before house No 9, a few metres short of the Major Road Ahead sign. To the left is

• *Pennsylvania Drinking Fountain, Belleau/57.6 miles/5 minutes/ Map 10/13*

A marble **Plaque** bears the legend that this was presented to the Commune of Belleau by the 'Belleau Wood Association' in memory of the soldiers of the State of Pennsylvania who fell at Belleau Wood.

Continue to the junction. Ahead is

• *'Minute Women' Demarcation Stone/US 26th Inf Division Church, Belleau/57.8 miles/10 minutes/Map 10/14/15*

The **Marker** is one of the standard Demarcation Stones designed by sculptor Moreau-Vauthier that indicate the nearest point that the Germans reached along various axis roads to major towns. As with the one near Villers Bretonneux on the Somme the historically accurate siting of this stone is disputed in *American Armies and Battlefields in Europe*, 'the Germans having been in possession of all Belleau Wood'. Thus the marker should have been placed on the southern, Lucy-le-Bocage, side of the wood. It was sponsored by '**The Minute Women**' of America.

To the left is the

26th Infantry Church. The village church was originally situated by the Château but was destroyed during the war. In the early 1920s there was a desire, led by Ralph Eastman, President of the Veterans' Association in Boston, to commemorate the achievements and sacrifice of the 26th. After much discussion the decision to build a Memorial Church in Belleau opposite the American Cemetery was made – it is said

Grave of the suicide, Ernest Stricker, Belleau Local Cemetery.

Landowski's dramatic Fantômes.

Ceremonial drinking from the 'Devil Dogs' Fountain, Château de Belleau.

Memorial Day Decorations, Aisne-Marne American Cemetery.

rather to the annoyance of the then-Chairman of the ABMC, Gen Pershing. The site is actually where 2nd Div trenches were dug following the capture of the wood on 25 July. Fund-raising was slow but eventually, with the help of all men of the current Division donating a day's pay, suffcient money was raised to build the church and the cornerstone was laid by the Bishop of Soissons on 23 December 1928. (The 'donation' of a day's pay reminds one of the authors about a similar donation made while in the army – it was 'voluntary' and if one did not want to donate, then all one had to do was to write one's name on a notice board for everyone else to see!). As much of the old church as could be salvaged (stones and window casings etc) was used in the rebuilding. The glorious SGWs were designed by Wilber H. Burnham of Boston and depict among others Washington and Lafayette, a WW1 Doughboy and a *Poilu*. Stone Memorial Tablets are engraved with the names of the 2,700 dead of the Division. There are many plaques, including to Maj Gen Clarence P. Edwards, Commanding the '26th Yankees' 1917-1918, to the YMCA and to the 26th Div, 12th October 1996. There is an eagle lectern from the original church. At one time the tower of the church could be climbed and direction arrows at the windows pointed to various points of the battlefield. In recent years the church has fallen into disrepair and two 26th WW2 Veterans, Albert Megna and Vincent Seconne, have campaigned vigorously to raise money for repairs. It is an ongoing task and donations may be sent to Mr A. Megna, 117 Butler Road, Quincy MA 02169 2237, USA.

Drive into the Cemetery entrance ahead and park behind the Visitors' Building.

• *American Aisne-Marne Cemetery/58 miles/30 minutes/Map 10/16/OP*

The cemetery occupies forty-two acres in a sweeping curve at the foot of the Belleau Wood hill and is on the site of a WW1 temporary cemetery, AEF Cemetery No 1764 Belleau Wood. It contains 2,289 American dead (251 of whom are Unknown), laid out in the form of a 'T', mostly from the battles in the vicinity and the Marne Valley in the summer of 1918. They include **MoH recipient Lt Jr Grade Weedon Osborne**, USN Dental Corps, Attd US Marines, born 13 November 1892 in Chicago. During the hottest fighting during the attack on Bouresches at the edge of Belleau Wood on 6 June, Osborne, 'threw himself zealously into the work of rescuing the wounded and was killed while carrying a wounded officer to safety' [Plot A Row 3 Grave 39]. Also buried here is **Cpl Allison M. Page**, *Croix de Guerre*, 47th Coy, 5th USMC, 25 June 1918, nephew of Walter Hines Page, US Ambassador to London.

Doughboy detail Memorial Chapel, Aisne-Marne Cemetery.

The Memorial Chapel stands on the hillside and is decorated with sculptured heads of Allied combattants – a French *Poilu*, a French Nurse, an American Aviator, a Scottish Soldier, a Russian Soldier, a Portuguese Soldier, a Canadian Aviator and a British Women's Army Corps Driver. There are **SGWs** with details of wartime equipment, insignia and personnel and a magnificent carved and gilded altar of Italian marble. The names of **1,060 Missing** are inscribed on the walls. There is an observation platform in the tower which gives excellent views over the battlefield. The architects were Cram & Ferguson of Boston and the 'embellishments' in the Chapel were designed by William F. Ross & Co of East Cambridge, Mass and executed by Alfred Bottiau of Paris. It was dedicted on Memorial Day (May 30) 1937. During WW2 it was slightly damaged by a shell.
Cemetery Open: 0900-1700. Superintendent's Tel: + (0)3 23 70 70 90. There is a well-furnished apartment originally built to accommodate the Gold Star Mothers (qv) near the Superintendent's Office.

Drive out of the Cemetery and turn right and right again following signs to Belleau Wood. On the right is

• US 2nd Division Boulder, Belleau/58.6 miles/5 minutes/Map 10/17

This is a typical 2nd Div Boulder, with remnants of its painted Indian Head insignia, and more are visited later in the tour. The Division began placing them soon after the armistice. Rik Scherpenberg (qv) on his *Ribbon of Stone* DVD lists twenty-two sites where the boulders were placed and is currently trying to raise funds to preserve those which are in need of repair. The Division was actually raised in France in 1917 and included one brigade of Marines (see below).

Enter the wood.

• Belleau Wood, USMC Memorials and Guns/59.1 miles/30 minute/ Map 10/18/19/20

The wood was officially named '*Bois de la Brigade de Marine*' by the French in honour of the unit mainly responsible for its capture. The 200-acre boulder-strewn wood, which has been replanted with a variety of trees, including oaks, still bears many traces of the battle – shell holes, trenchlines etc – is intersected with paths and is full of atmosphere. It is maintained by the ABMC. The road leads to the flagpole in the centre intersection of the wood where there is a monument known as '**Iron Mike**', to the 4th US Marine Bde of 2nd Div. It is in black granite with a *bas-relief* bronze statue by Felix de Weldon of New York, of a Marine, naked to the waist, attacking with rifle and bayonet. The bronze plaque below the statue records how the General commanding the French 6th Army renamed the wood on 30 June 1918 in recognition of the courageous action of the Marine Bde in the seizure of this wood in the face of determined German resistance. On 27 May 1918 the Germans launched a major surprise offensive which crossed the Chemin des Dames and captured Soissons. By 31 May their armies were advancing rapidly down the Marne Valley towards Paris, i.e. the direction of their attack at this point would be roughly from the north-east. The 2nd US Div, of which the 4th Marine Bde (the 5th and 6th Regiments) commanded by General James Harbord formed a part, was rushed into the deepest point of the penetration to assist the French Forces in stopping the advance of the enemy. Rapidly occupying defensive positions south and

US Marines Ceremony at 'Iron Mike', Belleau Wood.

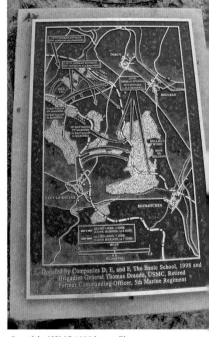

One of the USMC 1998 bronze Plaques.

Artillery piece with split barrel.

Germany Cemetery, Belleau.

View in Lagin Museum, Marigny, of 'Devil Dog' Poster.

west of Belleau Wood (the American Cemetery which you have just visited is at the northern end of the wood) just north of Lucy-le-Bocage which you visit later, the Division stood firm under unremitting enemy attacks from 1 to 4 June. The Germans set out to inflict maximum damage upon the Americans in an attempt to show that their presence was not of military significance, but on 6 June the Marines began a series of attacks which culminated on 25 June with the capture of the entire Belleau Wood area and the defeat of the German offensive in this sector. 'May the gallant Marines who gave their lives for Corps and Country rest in peace.'

The wood rewards some careful exploration with several remnants of German fortifications. Around the statue are **captured artillery pieces**, some of them further into the wood, including one whose barrel was split by a premature round. Off the path to the left (facing Iron Mike) is a semi-circle of **bronze Plaques placed in 1998** by the Marines Basic School and former commanding officers. The first one bears an accurate *bas relief* map of the area with battle lines. Others chart the story from 6-23 June 1918 of the actions in the vicinity and the bravery of the **men who were awarded the MoH** for their gallant actions: **Coy Sgt Maj C.A. Jansen USMC; Lt JG W.E. Osborne, US Navy** [spelt 'Osbourne' in the English text]; **Lt O.H. Petty USNRF; Coy Sgt F.W. Stockham USMC.** On 11 June following the pre-dawn attack fighting was down to platoons, then squads and finally to individuals one by one by bayonet and hand-to-hand combat. A probably apocryphal story concerns a Marine Sgt Dan Daley who in a particularly intense period of fighting is said to have rallied his troops by shouting, 'Come on you sons of bitches, do you want to live forever?'.

The achievements of the Marines in Belleau Wood – their 'Holy Grail' – have become the stuff of legend and without in any way diminishing their achievements (on 6 June

1918 they lost more in one day than in all their previous history) it has to be said that the reason so much prominence was given to their exploits, rather than those of the equally committed other units of the 2nd Division, was that Pershing forbade the US Army to talk to the Press. He made no such prohibition for the Marines and therefore the Press concentrated their reports on them. In fact the story of the Marines at Belleau Wood became common knowledge in America because Floyd Gibbons, a war correspondent, had sent a dispatch about their actions to Paris for censorship just before he was shot in the left eye on 6 June. However, the rumour spread that he had been killed and the Paris censor, who was a friend of Gibbons, decided that the dispatch could go uncensored in memory of his 'dead' friend and America learned that it was the Marines that were winning the war.

Belleau Wood was bought by the Americans for $16,000 in 1923, when there were many American visitors, and a Museum was built. This was destroyed in WW2.

Fighting around Château Thierry and in Belleau Wood with the French, to whom Gen Pershing had loaned them, was the 369th all-black American Regiment (the 15th New York), who were not actually permitted to fight with a white unit. They had been raised in New York but were forbidden to take part in the farewell parade in December 1917 with the Rainbow Division, as 'black is not a colour of the Rainbow'. They were among the first regiments to arrive in France where they became known as 'The Harlem Hellraisers' and went on to become amongst the most decorated formations (with 171 individual medals and a *Croix de Guerre* for the Unit), spending a record 191 days in combat under their proud CO, Col Hayward, who maintained, 'My men never retire, they go forward or die'. Serving in the regiment was the famous jazz musician James Reese Europe and in February 1919 he led it up 5th Avenue on a victory parade. The 369th have a Memorial at Sechault in the Champagne region.

The most famous son of the Regiment was **Henry Johnson**, who together with **Needham Roberts**, was awarded the French *Croix de Guerre* for their heroic action on 14 May 1918. The two, serving with the French 116th RI, were on sentry duty guarding a recently captured bridge at Outpost 29 in the Maffrécourt Sector near Sainte Menéhould (qv) when the Germans counter-attacked. Johnson was wounded, their small supply of ammunition ran out and Roberts was captured. Johnson then single-handedly took on the Germans in a bloody combat with his bolo knife, killing twenty and recapturing Roberts, though he himself was severely wounded with many bayonet cuts. Though Johnson's *Croix de Guerre* also had the Golden Palm, indubitably because of his colour he received no recognition from his own country, not even a Purple Heart (which was not awarded to him until seventy-eight years after his wounding) or disability allowance, and after a long stay in hospital was discharged in February 1919, then a Sergeant. His fame gradually became known, mainly through articles that described 'The Battle of Henry Johnson', and he was used to promote the sale of Liberty Bonds. Theodore Roosevelt described him as 'one of the nine bravest Americans' but because of his serious injuries he was never able to work and gradually fell out of the public eye (except that in 1976 the Army used him in a Bicentennial recruiting poster). He died in poverty at Walter Reed Army Hospital in Washington and was buried in Arlington Cemetery on 2 July 1929 but his grave, in a segregated area near the slaves section, became worn and forgotten until 2002 when his son, himself a Major in the US

Army, laid a wreath on it. In 2001 New York State Governor Pataki, after a long campaign by the Johnson family, Senator Schumer and Congressman McNulty, succeeded in raising awareness for Johnson's unsung bravery and a State Fair Exhibition highlighted Johnson's accomplishments. A move to get him awarded a well-deserved Medal of Honour then began but although the Clinton administration recommended the award the following Bush administration refused to endorse it. However in February 2003 Johnson's Distinguished Service Cross was finally presented to his family and in September 2004 the Congressional Black Caucus again raised the subject in the Senate.

Return to the cemetery entrance and continue on the D9 to the German Cemetery on the left.

• German Cemetery, Belleau/61.4 miles/5 minutes/Map 10/21

Established in 1922 it contains 4,307 individual burials under grey stone markers and 4,322 in a mass grave at the rear. It is thought that some seventy of the burials are from the First Battle of the Marne and that the majority are from the Second and the fighting with the Americans. In the centre is a large black cross. The entrance shelters are constructed of red stone.

N.B. From here a visit may be made to the interesting **Museum of the AEF of Gilles Lagin (Map 10/22)** by continuing over the crossroads and turning left on the C1 into Marigny, past the local cemetery on the left with a CWGC sign (which contains the pilot of a WW2 Lancaster shot down near the village and located by Gilles), turning right at the T junction and stopping on the left opposite the beautiful seventeenth century Market building at No 24 Place de la Halle, 02810 Marigny-en-Orxois. Gilles has become the ultimate expert on the battlefields around Château Thierry and Belleau Wood, helping countless American families to trace where their ancestors fought. He has worked tirelessly in his impeccable researches and also in constructing, with his own funds, and by his own efforts, a Museum to house a fascinating collection of artefacts found on the battlefields. On display are WW1 ephemera, arms and uniforms in the large barn behind his house. Gilles also runs superb battlefield tours for groups or individuals for which there is a fee.

N.B. It is essential to contact Gilles in advance for a tour or a visit to the Museum. Tel & Fax: + (0)3 23 70 46 54. E-mail: Gilles.Lagin@wanadoo.fr

---

Continue to the crossroads and turn left on the D82 to Lucy-le-Bocage. Enter the village, continue past the church and on the right is

• US 2nd Division Boulder, Lucy-le-Bocage/63.8 miles/5 minutes/ Map 10/23

This is a beautiful little village with immaculate and colourful flowers everywhere. Under a chestnut tree in its own well-tended garden is another 2nd Div Boulder with their Indian Head insignia and star commemorating June 1918 on a bronze plaque.

Continue downhill to the left to Bouresches on the C4, keeping to the left of the Coupru sign. Enter the village and go left at the church on the rue de Lt Osborne (qv – a MoH winner) and at the junction with a sign to the American Cemetery on the left is

• US 2nd Division Boulder, Bouresches/65.5 miles/5 minutes/Map 10/24

This Boulder has its plaque missing.

> Continue straight on the D1390 (when the southern edge Belleau Wood and the American Cemetery may be seen to the left across the valley as you drive, this having been part of the initial line adopted by the 2nd Div) to the junction with the D9 and turn right towards Château Thierry. At the junction with the N3 go straight over signed to the American Monument. Take care. This is a very difficult crossing with fast-moving traffic. Drive up the roadway to the monument.

• American Aisne-Marne Monument, Château-Thierry/69.5 miles/15 minutes/Map 10/25/OP

The Monument stands on Cote 204 and two stone pylons mark the entrance from the N3. It consists of an impressive double colonnade rising above a long terrace. On the west façade are heroic sculptured figures representing the USA and France. On the east façade is a map designed by **Paul Cret** (qv), of the American military operations in the

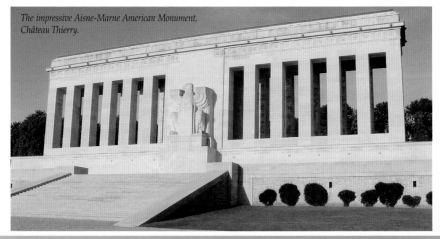

The impressive Aisne-Marne American Monument, Château Thierry.

US 3rd Division Memorial, Château Thierry.

Quentin Roosevelt Memorial, MAFA Building, Château Thierry.

SGW, showing Lafayette and French Generals greeting Gen Pershing, American Methodist Church, Château Thierry.

Beautifully tended US 2nd Division Boulder, Lucy-le-Bocage.

region showing the ground gained by US forces from 18 July 1918 There is also an orientation table below a huge stone American Eagle. Marble tablets are inscribed with a brief resumé of the fighting. There are superb views over the Marne Valley.

Drive back down to the N3 and turn right to Château Thierry. Go straight over the first roundabout signed Centre Ville and over the traffic lights with the River Marne on the right. Continue to the parking area just before the Post Office and stop.

• US 3rd Division and Déportés Memorials, Demarcation Stone, Château-Thierry/71.9 miles/15 minutes/Map 10/26/27/28

Château-Thierry got its name from the castle on a hill on the north bank of the Marne which, according to legend, was built by the Charles Martel for the King of the Franks, Thierry IV. On 9 September 1914 the British I Corps under Haig crossed the Marne here and moved forward to Fère-en-Tardenois. The town then remained behind the lines until the German Offensive of 27 May 1918 (see OPENING MOVES above) when the German tide swept southwards towards the Marne. Foch pleaded with Pershing for help and despite his intent to maintain a wholly American command, Pershing released five divisions to help along the Marne. General Joseph Dickman's 3rd Division was sent to Château Thierry where on 31 May the 7th Machine Gun Battalion, arriving first, took up positions along the south bank of the river. Two guns under Lt John T Bissell were sent over the river via the main bridge. In their move to the town, and as they took up their positions, the Americans met hundreds of *Poilus* streaming southwards some shouting, *'la guerre est finie'*. At 1000 the following morning, as the Germans arrived, the bridge was blown up in front of them isolating Bissell and his guns. They got back that night using the railway bridge. The Germans had been stopped and Pétain talked of the Division's 'incomparable glory' but in America, much to the Division's annoyance, it was the Marines who once again got the applause. 'Germans stopped at Château Thierry with the Help of God and Few Marines', cried the headlines. The division dug in being responsible for the defence of the river from Château Thierry to Chartèves, five miles to the east (see Map 10). The sector now became quiet but on 15 July the great German Offensive opened and six regiments of the 7th Army attacked along the 3rd Division front using small boats and pontoons to cross the river. Although some did make it across they were eventually forced back and two days later the German attack was spent. The performance of the 38th Infantry of the 3rd Division earned it the name 'Rock of the Marne'. Twenty four hours after that the Allied counter-attack began and on the night of 19 July the German High Command ordered a withdrawal from this part of the front. On 21-22 July the Division once more regained the north bank using footbridges and empty petrol cans as floats. The Germans were on the run.

Beside the park is the impressive **US 3rd Infantry Division Memorial** to their heroic deeds in WW1 and WW2 with distinctive blue lettering. In the centre is a Crusader's Sword and at each side the insignia of the Marne Division. Over the road is a black Memorial in the shape of a **'V' to Jean Moulin**, hero of the Resistance and on the corner a **Demarcation Stone**. Beyond the Post Office is a dramatic **Monument to Déportés** and the 'Camps of Slow Death' It lists the Concentration Camps under a stark *bas-relief* head. Raised by public subscription it also remembers the clandestine Resistance.

Continue and take the first left (note the main bridge over the river to your right on the site of that blown in 1918) to the Place de l'Hôtel de Ville and park. Walk back along the road you have driven up to No 2 Place des Etats Unis.

• Roosevelt Memorials, MAFA Building/72.4 miles/10 minutes/ Map 10/29

The rebuilt *Maison d'Amitié Franco-Americain*, once the old Hotel de l'Eléphant, was donated to the town in 1930 by the American Church and contained an important American exhibition. Now very run-down it contains in the courtyard, through the entrance and to the right, what is described as **the Engine and part of the Propellor of Quentin Roosevelt's plane** and a bronze **Plaque** which reads, 'In memory of the American and Allied Forces whose struggle in the Western Front 1914-1918 so greatly affected the course of the 20th Century', Great War Society, Stanford Ca, 1991. In fact the engine is from a Samson and Roosevelt flew a Nieuport 28. There are photos of the original Roosevelt grave and memorial – all sadly tatty – and a marble **Plaque to Jean Douguet**, 25 RI, 10.6.1940.

Return to the Place de l'Hôtel de Ville.

• YMCA Plaque, Town Hall and American Methodist Church/72.4 miles/ 15 minutes/Map 10/30/31

In the Square there are splendid Theatre and Market buildings. In the Town Hall there is a **Plaque** upstairs in commemoration of the heroic days of the Great War when the Sons of France and the Sons of America side by side gave their lives for Liberty. It was placed by the **YMCA** (known to the Americans as 'The Y') as the town was one of the many centres from which the YMCA served the Forces of the Allies.

The **Church**, which is quite beautiful, was founded in 1919 by The Methodist Episcopal Church of America. During the war the Church raised funds to build soldiers' homes and with the surplus decided to build this Memorial in the style of current American Methodist Churches designed by architect M. Chauquet. As memorials to individuals or to express solidarity with the French, American families financed all the furniture, the organ and the superb **SGWs**. They depict Gen Pershing and Lafayette with Gens Foch, Joffre, Pétain and Nivelle as well as important figures in the Reformation movement (such as Calvin). The bell, founded in England, was donated by the Mereensburg Academy and the great Bible by Mrs Theodore Roosevelt. There is a Memorial Tablet to all members of the American Protestant Church killed 1917-18. Inside the porch is a Plaque from the 'Boys of Mercersburg Academy'. Above the entrance in *bas-relief* a winged figure crowns the heads of a Doughboy and a *Poilu* with laurel leaves.

Open: Fri 1000-1200 or **Contact:** Edmond Andrianavony. Tel: + (0)3 23 83 02 88. Note that Friday is market day. It is a very large and bustling market and it will not be possible to park in the square.

At the corner of the Square is the
Tourist Office: 1 rue Vallée. Tel: + (0) 3 23 83 10 14.

• End of Second Battle of the Marne Tour
OR If the Monument to the Victory of the Marne at Dormans (qv) hasn't already been visited, it may be visited now by continuing on the N3 direction Epernay.

CHAMPAGNE

JULY – OCTOBER 1918

'Signal the attack and the enemy advance. Delay him by all means necessary.
Hold the position cost what may unto death. If he succeeds, the highest
recompense will be awarded to the officer commanding the position.
If he fails, it will be reported in the War Council.'
Letter to Lt Gouin defending Tahure marked
'Only to be opened in the event of an attack.'

'During the 15 July you have broken the effort of 15 German Divisions supported
by 10 others. According to their orders they should have reached the Marne
that evening. You stopped them exactly where we wished to win the battle.
It is a hard blow for the enemy. It is a beautiful day for France'.
General Gouraud commanding the 4th Army

'To be able to say when this war is finished, "I belonged to the 2nd Division,
I fought with it at the Battle of Blanc Mont Ridge"
will be the highest honour that can come to any man.'
Maj-Gen John A. Lejeune, USMC

THE CHAMPAGNE BATTLES – AN EXPLANATION

The area known as Champagne is broadly centred upon Reims. It extends roughly forty
miles from there towards Verdun to the east, 100 miles south to Burgundy, fifteen miles
west to Picardy and fifty miles north to the Belgium border. Fighting took place in
Champagne throughout the war. Different authorities name varying fighting periods as
a '**Battle of Champagne**' and not all agree on dates and times. There is broad
agreement that the French attack of 20 December 1914 was the start of the **First Battle
of Champagne** (it was part of a general attack along the whole of the Western Front
which had started on the 14th) and the fighting continued until 20 March 1915. The
British attack at Neuve Chapelle was part of the offensive. A generally accepted **Second
Battle** is the fighting between 25 September and 6 November 1915, a major assault
planned by Joffre in Champagne and Artois of which the British Loos battle formed the
northern element.

The Nivelle offensive of 16–20 April 1917 may be referred to as the **Third Battle of
Champagne** but more frequently is described as the Second Battle of the Aisne (qv). In
the last year of the war the German attack of 15-19 July is known as the **Champagne-
Marne Offensive** or sometimes as the first part of the **Second Battle of the Marne** (qv).
Other contenders are the French 4th Army advance from 26 September to 27 October
and the American Meuse-Argonne actions in October.

Perhaps one way of looking at the confusion is to consider a symphony which is

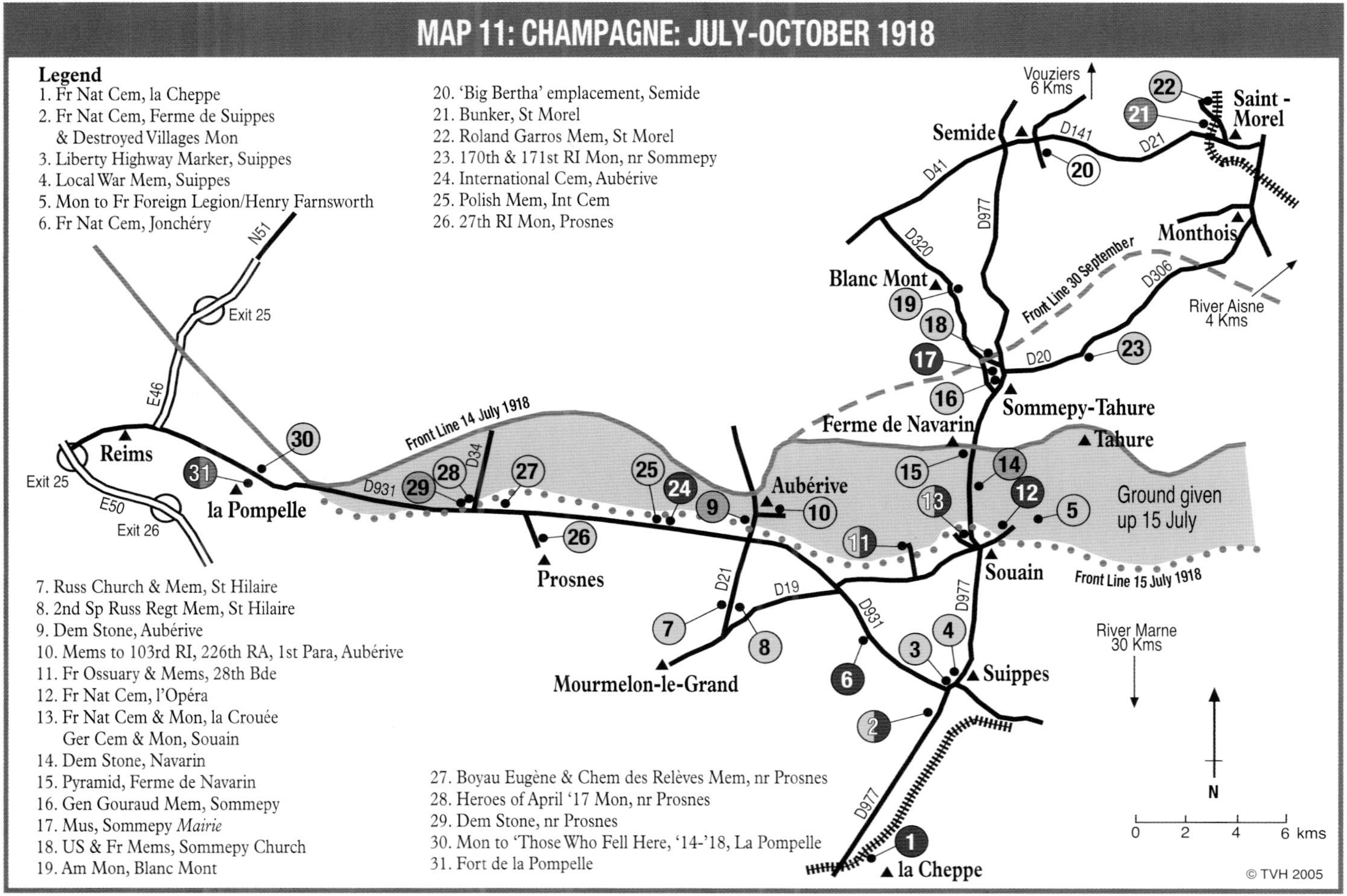
MAP 11: CHAMPAGNE: JULY-OCTOBER 1918
Legend
1. Fr Nat Cem, la Cheppe
2. Fr Nat Cem, Ferme de Suippes & Destroyed Villages Mon
3. Liberty Highway Marker, Suippes
4. Local War Mem, Suippes
5. Mon to Fr Foreign Legion/Henry Farnsworth
6. Fr Nat Cem, Jonchéry
7. Russ Church & Mem, St Hilaire
8. 2nd Sp Russ Regt Mem, St Hilaire
9. Dem Stone, Aubérive
10. Mems to 103rd RI, 226th RA, 1st Para, Aubérive
11. Fr Ossuary & Mems, 28th Bde
12. Fr Nat Cem, l'Opéra
13. Fr Nat Cem & Mon, la Crouée Ger Cem & Mon, Souain
14. Dem Stone, Navarin
15. Pyramid, Ferme de Navarin
16. Gen Gouraud Mem, Sommepy
17. Mus, Sommepy *Mairie*
18. US & Fr Mems, Sommepy Church
19. Am Mon, Blanc Mont
20. 'Big Bertha' emplacement, Semide
21. Bunker, St Morel
22. Roland Garros Mem, St Morel
23. 170th & 171st RI Mon, nr Sommepy
24. International Cem, Aubérive
25. Polish Mem, Int Cem
26. 27th RI Mon, Prosnes
27. Boyau Eugène & Chem des Relèves Mem, nr Prosnes
28. Heroes of April '17 Mon, nr Prosnes
29. Dem Stone, nr Prosnes
30. Mon to 'Those Who Fell Here, '14-'18, La Pompelle
31. Fort de la Pompelle
Vouziers 6 Kms
Semide
Saint - Morel
Monthois
River Aisne 4 Kms
Blanc Mont
Front Line 30 September
Sommepy-Tahure
Ferme de Navarin
Tahure
Ground given up 15 July
Front Line 15 July 1918
Front Line 14 July 1918
Reims
la Pompelle
Prosnes
Aubérive
Souain
Suippes
Mourmelon-le-Grand
la Cheppe
River Marne 30 Kms
N
0 2 4 6 kms
Exit 25
Exit 26
N51
E46
E50
D931
D34
D21
D19
D977
D41
D320
D141
D20
D306
© TVH 2005

composed of contributions from all sections of the orchestra. One can examine the woodwinds alone, which gives neither a complete picture of the symphony nor information about the other parts of the orchestra, such as the strings, but it does allow a valid and concise, if partial, examination of a constituent part of the whole – all are contributing to the same symphony. We have taken the **fighting in the Champagne area east of Reims** to be the symphony and have chosen in the main one constituent part to examine – the ground, and what there is to see there, because that is what makes up a battlefield tour. Other elements of the symphony are examined elsewhere in this book and in our companion volume, *Western Front – North*. Thus we have named this section as simply 'Champagne' and concentrate upon July and September 1918 though the percussion and brass sections may intrude from time to time.

SUMMARY OF THE BATTLES

On 15 July 1918 the Germans opened Operation FRIEDENSTURM (The Peace Offensive) whose aim was to take the defended area of Reims and then to threaten Paris as part of a feint for a planned offensive in Flanders. The attack headed both east (part of von Mudra's 1st Army plus von Einem's 3rd) and west (7th Army under Blücher) of Reims along a front of almost sixty miles from Château Thierry to Massiges. The attack to the west became the struggle known as the Second Battle of the Marne, involving French, American and Italian forces, while that to the east was stopped by Gouraud's French 4th Army helped by the US 42nd Division. If it is possible to name a turning point in the war then the defeat of the Germans here must be a strong contender for the title. Not only had their attack here in Champagne been stopped but on 18 July General Mangin's offensive opened against the Marne Salient west of Reims (see Map 10). Ludendorff's dream of victory was gone and the morale of the German troops was shattered.

On 26 September the French 4th Army began an attack astride Suippes (Map 11) that aimed to reach the River Aisne and then stretch beyond to the Meuse between Sedan and Mesières. With help from the American 2nd, 36th and 93rd Divisions the drive reached the Aisne on 12 October where the liberation of Vouziers (twenty miles north of Suippes) signalled the end of the battles of Champagne.

OPENING MOVES

On 27 May 1918 Ludendorff opened a German offensive along the Chemin des Dames (sometimes known as the Third Battle of the Aisne). By mid-day he had crossed the Aisne and by the evening the Germans were crossing the Vesle west of Fismes. On 30 May they reached the Marne. Two days earlier the first 'American' offensive of the war had taken place at Cantigny where the 1st Division took and held the village against fierce counter-attacks. Further evidence of the fighting prowess of the newly-arrived American Armies was given at Château Thierry (qv) and later at Belleau Wood (qv) – some 300,000 more Americans were arriving each month. It was clear to Ludendorff that the Americans were now a major and growing factor in the war and that no time should be lost in making the final full-out attack that he believed would decide the outcome of the war. Nevertheless, when he stopped the offensive on 4 June, Ludendorff's men had made a thirty miles wide, twenty miles deep dent in the Allied lines (see Map 10) and he planned to exploit it before he made his treasured war-winning stroke in Flanders.

The stumbling block in his plan was the fortified area and city of Reims and he proposed to surround and take it by a two-pronged attack. It is said that the Kaiser himself came to Sommepy to watch the opening of the battle. Meanwhile, however, Foch, who had been appointed Supreme Commander on 3 April, was himself planning a major attack and the question now was, 'who would strike first?'

WHAT HAPPENED

Here, as explained above, we deal with the actions to the east of Reims (see Map 11). On 14 July German prisoners, captured that day by the French 366th RI, told of an imminent attack whose bombardment would begin at 0010 hours the following day and that the German infantry would climb out of their trenches at 0415.

One hour before the German barrage was due to begin Gouraud's 4th Army artillery rained down fire from almost 800 batteries upon communication trenches, troop concentrations, supply dumps and artillery positions. The Germans held their fire until 0010 but even then their fire was ineffective. Gouraud had planned his defence so that he had what was called the 'Sacrifice Line' right at the front, only thinly manned by troops inevitably known as 'sacrifice' troops (one wonders what their feelings were when they were 'selected' – some were volunteers). The main French forces were held back out of the immediate field of German fire. Just after dawn as the German infantry advanced the French soldiers in the Sacrifice Line withdrew some 3kms to prepared positions in their Intermediate Line and allowed the enemy to come on as Gouraud had planned (see Map 11). The French artillery fell in massive blows upon the German soldiers and their advance was brought to a complete stop.

On 16 July the Germans launched a series of fierce attacks, particularly in the areas of Prosnes and Suippes, but the French stood firm on the Intermediate Line and held, thanks to effective support from artillery working closely with air observation. The Germans would get no further. Two days later to the west of Reims the Second Battle of the Marne began and by 4 August the River Vesle was reached. Reims was safe.

On 26 September, after an artillery bombardment of six hours, the 4th Army attacked from Suippes to the Aisne in concert with the American assault to the east that same day that is known as 'The Meuse-Argonne' (see page 294). The Germans attempted to use the same tactics that had worked for the 4th Army by giving way before the attack, but the French used a rolling barrage in close cooperation with tanks and machine guns that earned gains of between two and five kms before mid-day on the first day. The 22nd (Breton) Division recaptured the Ferme de Navarin, XXI Corps took Souain and IX Corps took the high ground at Tahure after it had changed hands three times. By the end of the day more than 7,000 prisoners had been taken. Two days later the Germans brought up ten more divisions in an attempt to stem the French progress but to no avail, the penetration in the German lines moving steadily towards Monthois despite fierce resistance. By the evening of 30 September some 8,300 prisoners and 300 artillery pieces had been captured.

On 2 October in the centre just above Sommepy (Somme Py), roughly northwards along the line of the D977 road, the American 2nd Division took over operations astride the road and captured the area of Blanc Mont where the American Memorial now stands and then in turn handed over to the American 36th Division on 9 October, which, with French forces on either side, took the advance to the River Aisne. The battles of Champagne had ended.

THE BATTLEFIELD TOUR

• **The Route:** The tour proper is preceded by a visit to Reims, then moves up the Champagne battlefield visiting the French Cemetery at La Cheppe; the French Cemetery & Monument, Ferme de Suippes; the French Cemetery at Jonchéry-sur-Suippe; The Russian Church, Cemetery and Memorial, St Hilaire-le-Grand; the Ossuary of 28th Bde, Souain; French National Cemetery, L'Opéra; French National Cemetery, La Crouée; German Cemetery, Souain; Pyramid of the Ferme de Navarin & Ossuary; Sommepy US & French Memorials; Blanc Mont US 2nd, 36th & 93rd Monument; 'International' Cemetery, Aubérive; Monuments to 27th RI, Boyau Eugène & Chemin des Relèves, Heroes of April 1917 & Demarcation Stone, D34. It ends with a visit to the Monument 'To Those who Fell Here' and Fort de la Pompelle.

• **Extra Visits to:** Demarcation Stone and Memorials, Aubérive; Foreign Legion/Henry Farnsworth Monument, Camp de Suippes; 'Big Bertha' gun emplacement, Semide; Roland Garros Memorial, St Morel and 170th & 174th Memorial near Sommepy.

• **Total distance:** 72 miles

• **Total time:** 6 hours 15 minutes

• **Distance from Calais to start point:** 197 miles. Motorway Tolls

• **Base town:** Reims

• **Maps:** IGN Carte de Promenade No 10: Reims Verdun

From Calais take the A26 to Reims. To visit Reims at the beginning of the tour take Exit 24, Reims Cathedral and follow signs to Centre/Cathedral. Park as near the Cathedral as possible (car parks are well-signed) and go to the Tourist Office to the left of the Cathedral and beyond the statue of Jeanne d'Arc.

• *Reims Tourist Office/City Tour*

Pick up a city plan from the Tourist Office to visit the sites which interest you.

After the First Battle of the Marne (qv), the Germans were pushed back, Paris was saved and life almost returned to normal in the Marne Department. But to the north-west of Reims German heavy batteries shelled the city. On 19 September 1914 the Cathedral, despite the fact that it was being used as a hospital, became the target. Fire raged around the historic building and important archival collections were lost. The Allied world greeted this as as a cultural outrage. The American writers Henry James and Edith Wharton, who travelled extensively together in France, had both visited the Cathedral before the war. When it was set on fire James wrote to Wharton declaring that it was 'the most hideous crime ever perpetuated' on humanity. Edith Wharton then spent most of the war years organising charities for war relief in both France and Belgium and was awarded, among many other decorations for her humanitarian work, the *Légion d'Honneur*.

Gradually the Germans advanced on the ancient city and bitter fighting took place, notably in the Fort de la Pompelle, visited later. The German lines were only 3 or 4 kilometres from the city and massive German artillery pieces were threatening from the surrounding hills. Nevertheless some 15,000 citizens remained in their homes, sometimes sheltering in the Champagne caves where schools carried on teaching.

Political differences were submerged in the '*Union sacrée*', firemen were on constant duty and for their devotion their standard would receive the *Légion d'Honneur* in 1917. In the vineyards of Champagne the harvest took place under shellfire. The year 1917 was particulary cruel for Reims. On 6 April 20,000 shells fell on the city, destroying the Hôtel de Ville, the theatre, the Palais de Justice and many other important buildings. Finally the citizens were evacuated on 10 April.

In February 1918 the civil authorities left the city, now a mass of ruins, yet still the objective of fierce German attacks from May to July. Reims became a sort of Salient, or perhaps more of an island, bravely defended on the west by the 1st Colonial Army Corps who held on despite being ordered to abandon the city if pushed to it by the enemy. Gen Gouraud and his 4th Army (qv) held firm and on 18 July launched a huge counter-offensive in concert with Mangin's offensive to the west of the city known as the Second Battle of the Marne. The threat to Reims receded. On 26 September, reinforced by Gen Pershing's fresh Americans, Gouraud retook the ground lost in July and on 4 October the very last shell fell on Reims and the Germans abandoned the heights around the city.

Many ruined areas of the city were rebuilt in the fashionable *Art Deco* style, notably the Carnegie Library, the Villa Douce and the Church of Saint Nicaise. The glorious Cathedral of Notre-Dame, known as 'the Cathedral of the Angels' because of its many angel statues and where twenty-five French monarchs were crowned, most famously the Dauphin, crowned Charles VII with the aid of Jeanne d'Arc, was reopened in 1938. Three of the damaged SGWs were replaced with modern designs by Marc Chagall.

Near the old Parc Pommery on Bvd Henry-Vasnier (just off Place Gen Gouraud) is the Hotel-Restaurant Les Crayères (qv). Beside it is a **Plaque to commemorate the Colonial Forces** who were credited with saving Reims on 15 July 1918. It replaces a splendid Monument to the Colonial troops which was erected after the war in Reims in the form of a fine bronze group of statues of African soldiers. It was taken for melting down by the Germans on 10 September 1940 and was replaced by this simple *stèle*. Two copies of the original monument were made and the other still stands in Niger, the old French West African province, from where many of the Colonial forces came.

Salle de la Reddition. On 7 May 1945 the defeated Germans, represented by Gen Jodl, capitulated to the Allies in a hall on the first floor of the Technical College of Reims where Gen Eisenhower had established his headquarters. Today the room is preserved exactly as it was on that historic day.

12 rue Franklin Roosevelt. **Open:** 1000-1200 and 1400-1800 April-November, Closed Tues, 1 January, 1 May, 14 July and 11 November. Tel: + (0) 3 26 47 84 19. In winter apply to the Musée des Beaux Arts. Tel: (0) 3 26 47 28 44.

Rejoin the A26 and then take the A4 Autoroute de l'Est and take Exit 28, St Etienne.
It is highly recommended to fill up with petrol and buy the makings of a picnic at a motorway stop before you exit. Shops, restaurants and petrol stations are few and far between on this route.

Set your mileometer to zero at the Péage. *Take the D977 direction Suippes. Continue over the railway and take the right turn on the D366 signed la Cheppe. Just by the huge France Luzerne building turn left before the railway along a rough track and stop at the cemetery on the left.*

• French National Cemetery, la Cheppe/3.4 miles/10 minutes/Map 11/1

The famous Flight 67 *'Escadron de Chasse'*, formed in Lyons on 17 September 1915, arrived at the airport at la Cheppe later in the month before moving on to the Verdun sector where it covered itself in glory and decorations. In December 1917 the 124th Lafayette *Escadrille* was based here, living in rough and draughty wooden huts with a line of sausage balloons flying above.

The cemetery was created in 1915 to take the dead from the adjacent medical facility of Mont Frenet and enlarged between 1916 and 1918 and again in 1929-30 when bodies were exhumed from surrounding military cemeteries. It was completely relandscaped in 1985-6. There are **Information Panels** near the entrance and it contains an interesting mix of nationalities: 2,282 French, twelve British, three Czech and one American, also nine French from WW2. The British graves, under a standard CWGC headstone, include **Driver B.V. Green** of the French Red Cross, 6 March 1917 and **Driver F.P. Lewis**, of the British Red Cross, age 22, who is buried next to **Brig Emile Chevalier** of the 175th RA. They were both killed on 31 October 1918.

A large, non-standard cross surmounts the grave of American **Stanley Hill**, 1896-1918, Ambulance Service attd French Army who was mortally wounded at midnight on 15 July 1918 at Avenay and died on 14 August at La Veuve. He was awarded the *Médaille Militaire* and *Croix de Guerre + Palme*.

The only colour in the cemetery comes from a few shrubs in the corners.

Memorial Cross to American Stanley Hill, Ambulance Service.

Return to the D977 and turn right. The vast Military Camp of Mourmelon is now to the left. Continue to the cemetery on the left and stop in the parking by the second gate, which leads to the WW1 section.

• French National Cemetery, La Ferme de Suippes & Monument/8.2 miles/10 minutes/Map 11/2

The cemetery contains 7,425 WW1 French burials, 528 in two ossuaries, one Belgian and three Russian, and 1,932 French from WW2. There are **Information Panels** near the entries of both the WW1 and WW2 sections. Beside it is a **Monument erected by the Touring Club of France** to the five destroyed villages in the Military Camp de Suippes (to the right).

The terrain round the villages was so mangled by war that they were never rebuilt and the area was given over to the military as an artillery range and therefore not visitable. Every two years in September the Commandant of the Camp organises a 'Day of the Destroyed Villages' so that descendants of the villagers can come and remember.

Continue on the D977 towards Suippes

Extra Visit to Suippes War Memorial, Foreign Legion/Henry Farnsworth Monument, Camp de Suippes/Map 11/5
Round trip: 15 miles. Approximate time: 45 minutes

N.B. At this stage if you wish to visit the Monument to the Foreign Legion and American Henry Farnsworth which is in the firing range area of the military camp, you will have to have contacted well in advance the Officier de Tir du Camp de Suippes. Tel: + (0)3 26 67 81 02/Fax: + (0)3 26 67 81 61. Alternatively the Superintendent at the American Cemetry at Romagne may be able to set up the visit for you. Tel: + (0)3 29 85 14 18.

Continue into the town

As the road takes a sweep to the right there is a splendidly painted **Liberty Highway Marker (Map 11/3)** ahead. A little further on on the wall of the Hôtel de Ville on the left is the local **War Memorial (Map 11/4).** It depicts a particularly poignant scene of a young girl who has interrupted her harvesting to visit the tomb of her fiancé whose headstone bears his helmet. She carries a sheaf of corn and has placed another one on his grave. It was sculpted by Félix Desruelles and inaugurated in 1930 – the ruined village itself had to be rebuilt before the memorial could be considered.

It was here in Suippes that the infamous *Affaire des 4 Corporaux de Suippes* took place. In March 1915 the fiery Divisional Commander of the 336th RI, Gen Reveilhac, ordered repeated attacks on the heavily defended German lines at Perthes-les-Hurlus. They were all unsuccessful but costly. On 9 March he sent in the 21st Coy who had suffered grievously two days previously and could see their dead companions hanging on the German wire. When their commanding officer blew his whistle and clambered up the scaling ladder from their trench he was only followed by another officer and handful of NCOs. They were met by murderous fire and had to fall back. A furious Reveilhac then ordered the Divisional Artillery Officer, Col Bérube, to fire on the 21st Coy's trenches. This Bérube respectfully refused to do. Reveilhac then ordered four corporals and sixteen men to be sent out in broad daylight to cut the German wire. They were immediately raked with machine-gun fire in this suicidal mission and understandably cowered in shell-holes or scrambled back to their trench. Reveilhac then convened a court martial at Suippes on 16 March but surprisingly exonerated the privates as 'they had not heard any orders to advance'. The corporals were sentenced to death the following day. The shaken firing squad killed two of them but only wounded the other two. The firing squad commander had to finish them off with his pistol – just as an order arrived from the unpredictable Reveilhac to postpone the execution. The 336th now teetered on the edge of a genuine mutiny.

Opposite the Hôtel de Ville is the Hôtel de Champagne and Restaurant. Tel: + (0)3 26 69 81 16.

Continue past the Hôtel de Champagne on the D931 signed Verdun. Continue to the easily missed entrance to the Military Camp de Suippes to the left signed to Cabinet Medical de Garnison with a large red Terrain Militaire beyond, ignoring all signs to the Camp to the right. Continue following signs to Securité and PC [Command Post] Camp. Park behind the PC building.

Foreign Legion/Farnsworth Monument and Ossuary complex, Camp de Suippes.

Henri Vaumarin, 4th Zouaves, who lost his leg after fighting in the Bois Sabot.

Brilliantly painted Liberty Highway Marker at the entrance to Suippes.

Suippes War Memorial.

In front of the building are two Liberty Highway Markers, a **Demarcation Stone** and various memorials and pieces of military equipment. The entrance to the Officier de Tir's office is to the left of the building. Report there according to your appointment. From there you will be escorted to the Monument, passing several signs to the five Destroyed Villages of Perthes-les-Hurlus, Hurlus, le Mesnil-les-Hurlus, Ripont and Tahure in the camp area along the way. Also in the Camp are a **Monument to the 64th & 65th RIs, the Ripont Monument aux Morts, a German Bunker** and the remains of a **German Cemetery.**

The **Memorial to the Foreign Legion** was erected by the family of one of their members, the **American Henry Farnsworth** who fell in September 1915, age 24, with the 2nd Bn, 1st Foreign Legion. Farnsworth was a Harvard graduate and spent the summer of 1912 in Europe and reported on the Balkan War. When war broke out he went to England and tried in vain to become a War Correspondent. He then joined the Foreign Legion on 5 January 1915 and was one of 128 Legionnaires to die on 28 September 1915. He was posthumously awarded the Military Medal. As well as erecting the memorial here, Farnsworth's parents funded a research room at Harvard University. It was dedicated on 5 December 1916 thus becoming the first memorial to an American WW1 casualty. Farnsworth is also commemorated on the **Monument to American Volunteers in the Place des Etats-Unis at Paris.**

Extra visit continued

At the approach to the Monument is an **Information Panel.** The Monument here, which is also a cemetery containing 130 Foreign Legionnaires in two ossuaries – the names are on panels on the side walls, was dedicated in the presence of Farnsworth's parents and his sister in 1920. The Farnsworth Monument is the wall ahead as you approach the complex. To build such an ambitious (17 x 22 metres) monument in the moonscape that was the Champagne battlefield was a difficult feat: trenchlines, barbed wire, unexploded shells, all represented danger to the workmen. There were no houses, railway or decent roads; water had to be transported in tankers from Souain and the stone from the quarry in Souppes (from which the Arc de Triomphe had also been constructed); the marble plaques came from Namur in Belgium; fertile soil for the surrounding fir trees had to be brought from Seine et Marne, and yet it was completed in six months. One of the plaques records how in September 1915 a great number of the Foreign Legion of many races were killed nearby attacking the German blockhouse in the Bois Sabot. Among them was Farnsworth who was struck in the throat and the back by machine-gun fire. The Bois Sabot was approx 1,300 yards to the south-east of the Monument, still within the Camp area.

Also gravely wounded in the Bois Sabot was Soldier **Henri Vaumarin** of the 4th Zouaves who were brought up to the front on 15 September. At midnight on 1 October Gen Mangin ordered them into the trenches at le Bois Sabot and at 0600 on 6 October their Sgt Maj gave the order, '*En avant les enfants, c'est pour la France*'. Scrambling over the top the twenty-two-year-old ran two metres only before being cut down by machine-gun fire in both legs and managed to roll back into the trench clutching only his water bottle (which contained a potent mixture of rum and ether). Zouave stretcher bearers carried him to the nearby field hospital (probably at l'Opéra). From there, near to death, he was taken to la Pitié Hospital in Paris where a Dr Arrou amputated his gangrenous left leg. The family received a telegram '*Fils gravement blessé. Venez vite*'. (Son seriously wounded. Come quickly.) Only fourteen from his company of 130 had survived the attack. Henri Vaumarin eventually made a full recovery and went on to be awarded the *Légion d'Honneur*, the *Médaille Militaire* and the *Croix de Guerre avec Palme*. For many years he communicated with the doctor who had saved his life. He died after a successful career in insurance in 1985 aged ninety-two and blind, and was the father of Ghislaine Kitson, a friend of the authors.

On your return to the PC Building you may get permission to visit the small but interesting **Museum** on the first floor which contains battlefield artefacts recovered from within the confines of the camp and gives details of the five destroyed villages.

Return to Suippes and pick up the main itinerary.

Just before entering the town turn left on the D931 signed to Jonchéry-sur-Suippe. Continue along the D931. There are good condition Liberty Highway Markers along this road. Continue to the cemetery on the left.

• *French National Cemetery, Jonchéry-sur-Suippe/12 miles/5 minutes/ Map 11/6*

At the entrance is a Monument bearing the *Croix de Guerre*. The double (back to back) rows of stone crosses in the cemetery are bare of any flowers and in 2003 a notice in the Register box behind the monument apologised for its appearance – wild animals had caused considerable damage. In it are buried 7,906 French soldiers, 3,009 in the four ossuaries at the top. There are also four Czech graves.

Continue on the D931.

Just before entering the village of Jonchéry is a stone memorial on the left with its inscription sadly unreadable.

Continue towards St Hilaire-le-Grand and turn left just before the village on the D19E signed to Mourmelon and continue on the D19 to the junction with the D21. Turn sharp right signed to Cimetière Russe and continue to the church on the left.

• *Russian Church/Cemetery and Memorial, St Hilaire-le-Grand/ 17.4 miles/10 minutes/ Map 11/7/8*

It is an extraordinary sight to see this **Russian Orthodox Church** with traditional golden onion dome and the adjoining **Russian Cemetery**, deep in the heart of France. In 1916, following the rules of the military reciprocity convention of the Franco-Russia Alliance, the Tsar provided an Expeditionary Force of four brigades. Two brigades went to Salonica and two, the 1st and 3rd, to Champagne, arriving in April and September 1916 respectively. In July in the Fort de la Pompelle (qv) area the 1st Brigade withstood determined German attacks and held their ground until relieved by their sister brigade in October. However, following the Workers' Revolution in March when Russia effectively left the war, the French Government demobilised the brigades re-forming them as labour companies. The Russians became angry and the *Poilus* saw them as traitors. Prompted by the French mutinies following the April 1917 Nivelle offensive, the 1st Brigade itself mutinied in May while the 3rd Brigade remained loyal. Unable to settle their differences, the French armed the 3rd Brigade and ordered them to shell the 1st Brigade camp. The rebels surrendered. Some of their leaders were imprisoned in France and some in Algeria. In October the Russian Legion was formed under General Lokhvitsky the former commander of the 1st Brigade and on 10 December the formation was formally recognised by the French government, going on to become accepted as a formidable fighting force. There were four battalions and in January 1918 they joined the 4th Moroccan Infantry. The Legion went on to fight at Villers Bretonneux in April, the Chemin des Dames in May (so distinguishing themselves that they were named as a '*Legion d'Honneur*') and at Château Thierry in July. Their losses between 1916-18 were 4,000 killed, some 1,000 of whom lie here. In 1934 the Russian War Association of Survivors bought the land to build this traditional church, designed by architect Benois in fifteenth century style. Each Whitsun there is a commemorative pilgrimage by Russians to this site.

Beside the church is a cemetery, with an **Information Panel** at the entrance, containing 915 Russians under white crosses and 426 who lie in the two ossuaries. There is one WW2 burial. In the centre of the cemetery is a **Memorial.**

In the clearing opposite is a **Monument to the Dead of the 2nd Special Russian**

The unusual Russian Memorial Church, St Hilaire-le-Grand.

Russian Memorial opposite the Church.

Memorial in the Russian Cemetery.

Regiment (part of the original 1st Brigade) which bears the legend, 'Children of France, when the enemy is vanquished and you can freely gather flowers on these fields, remember us, your Russian friends, and bring us some flowers.' The battalion received the *Croix de Guerre* and two Army Citations. A Plaque commemorates their links with the 34th Regt d'Aviation.

On the roadside is a large **Information Panel** showing the campaigns of the Army of Champagne.

Continue to the crossroads with the D931.

Extra Visit to Demarcation Stone (Map 11/9) and Monuments (Map 11/10), Aubérive.

Round trip: .8 mile Approximate time: 10 minutes

Continue on the D21 to the marker on the left.
This is one of the traditional **Demarcation Stones** erected by the Touring Club of France.

Continue to a track to the right just before the silo and turn along it.
It leads to a series of well-tended Memorials. The first is to the **103rd RI**, Sept-Oct 1915. It mentions l'Abbé Vittrant, Aumonier of the 7th DI, and several junior officers. Beside it is a small obelisk to **4 soldiers of 3rd Pièce, 24th Bty, 226th RA** killed by a German shell on 12 April 1917. The next memorial is to a **soldier who fell on 25 September 1915** and who was reinterred in Jupilles Arthe on 8 October 1921. Finally there is a polished grey memorial is to **Lt Charles Raymond Cahusac**, the first military parachutist of France who was killed in aerial service on 19 October 1937 at Aubérive. It was erected by the National Association of Military Parachutists.

Return to the crossroads and pick up the main itinerary.

Turn right signed St Hilaire on the D931.
There are Liberty Highway Markers along this road in very good condition.

In St Hilaire turn left on the D19 by the church. Continue to just past the line of pylons to a sign which is only readable if coming in the opposite direction! It points to the Ossuary of the 28th Brigade. Turn left up a very rough track (the Ferme de Navarin Monument can be seen on the horizon to the right at 2 o' clock as you drive) and drive the 1.5km to to the monuments on the crest.

• Ossuary & Monuments of 28th Brigade/25.5 miles/10 minutes/Map 11/11

This unusual Cemetery/group of Monuments was the inspiration of the Brigade's Padre (Aumonier) R.P. Doncoeur so that the young generations should remember the sacrifice of their elders. The *Tricolore* flies before the large main cross, to the left of which is a Monument to the 44th RI killed between 25 and 29 September 1915 and to the right a Monument to the 60th RI for the same dates. Large stone crosses commemorating individuals and regiments surround the cross in two large circles. There is an **Information Panel** here. In 2003 it was in a bad state of repair but when visited again in 2004 some elementary repairs had been carried out.

Return to the main road and continue along the D19.

Here you will pass the vast Ferme des Wacques complex on the right (the scene of bitter fighting in September 1915). The D19 between St Hilaire and Souain along which you are driving was the intermediate line of front that the US 42nd Division (attached to the French XXI Corps) was responsible for prior to the German attack of 15 July 1918. The forward line ran parallel to this road, roughly through the area of the Memorial just visited, and the rear ran about one mile to your right. The front lines ran some four miles to your left just short of the Navarin Memorial. The 42nd's instructions were to prepare for defence and to hold at all costs. This they did, falling back to the intermediate line (see Map 11) in accordance with the overall plan but losing some 1,600 casualties.

Continue to Souain Perthes-les-Hurlus when the church is straight ahead. Drive left round the church and left again at the junction following signs to the French Cemetery L'Opéra.

You will be driving along rue Henry Farnsworth. The road was inaugurated by Farnsworth's sister, Mrs Loomis, in September 1965, the 50th Anniversary of the Champagne Battles. Beyond the cemetery is the Foreign Legion / American Monument. **Do not be fooled by local signing into thinking that you can drive directly to the Foreign Legion Memorial. See the instructions above at Suippes. You can, however, drive to the cemetery.**

Follow the signs to the cemetery on the left.

• French National Cemetery, l'Opéra/28.5 miles/10 minutes/Map 11/12

This is a most unusual cemetery. A large stone marker, near the usual **Information Panel**, in the grassy area in front of it says 'The soldiers who lie here gave their lives for France'. The graves area is enclosed by a stone wall and there are several individual graves surrounded by small walls and other graves containing several burials. There is one large pink granite cross to **Lt Louis Damez**, 23rd RI, Civil Engineer of Mines, 25 August 1887-4 October 1915. There is a high proportion of junior officers, one of whom is of the 2nd Foreign Legion. There was a military hospital on this site in 1915.

Frustratingly the flag that flies over the Foreign Legion Monument (qv) can be seen within the sealed off military area ahead but there is no direct route from here.

Return to the main road and turn right on the D977 and some 100m later turn left following signs to the German Cemetery along a small road.

N.B. On the left is passed the local cemetery with a green CWGC sign at the gate. In it in a small plot is the crew of an RAF plane of 15 Sqn, 18 November 1943: **Air Gunner Sgt Gilbert Lesley Gard**, 29; **Flight Sgt D. Curry**, 25; **Pilot Officer J. S. Calder**, RNAF, 25; **Flight Sgt J.W. Childs**, 33; **Wireless Operator/Air Gunner Sgt J. M. Bliss**, 20, whose inscription is the Brooke quotation, 'There is some corner of a foreign field which is forever England'; **Air Gunner Sgt R.S. Bowers**, 19 and **Flying Officer/Air Bomber P.L. Bowden**, 20.

Continue to the Cemetery on the right.

• French National Cemetery & Monument, la Crouée/30.2 miles/10 minutes/Map 11/13

The cemetery contains 30,732 burials, of which 21,688 are in eight ossuaries (the known names are listed on tall monuments) and two burials from WW2. In it there is a **Monument to the Dead of the 1915 Offensives**. Like most of the cemeteries in the area the grey crosses are unrelieved by any colour. There is an **Information Panel** here.

Beside the cemetery is

• *German Cemetery & Monument, Souain/ 30.3 miles/10 minutes/Map 11/13*

The entrance gate is flanked by two large red stones with interesting white strata marks. It contains 2,463 individual burials and 11,320 in a mass grave. In it is a large stone **Monument to the Thüringians** with an inscription bearing some verses by the German poet **Walter Flex** who was killed on the Island of Ösel on 16 October 1917 serving with the 50th RI. They translate as:

> God created you in grey armies
> And made you guardians of time
> Near the limpid source of honours
> And near the sombre wells of pain.

Buried here is the twenty-seven years old German painter, **August Macke**. One of his last paintings was titled *'Farewell'*. His work is much collected today. Overlooking the French cemetery are the ossuaries with a big red granite cross and the names inscribed on bronze panels.

Return to the D977 and turn left. Continue some 1.8 miles.

On the right is a **Demarcation Stone (Map 11/14).**

Continue to the parking on the right for the large monument on the left.

• *Pyramid of the Ferme de Navarin & Ossuary/33.2 miles/20 minutes/ Map 11/15*

The Monument is on the site of a farm originally called Rougemont – the colour of the soil before the war churned up the white chalk to the surface. It was an inn serving travellers between the Marne and the Ardennes and it is said that the present-day name of Navarin came from the landlord's patois declaration that he had nothing to offer today – *'Anhue ava rin'*!

This impressive memorial was raised by subscriptions, many of them small amounts from widows and children together with pathetic letters about their loved ones. It stands on the area of some of the most bloody fighting of July 1918, the German trenches having crossed the road at right angles here from September 1915 to July 1918. It is surmounted by a group of three statues, the central figure being Gen Gouraud, Commander of the 4th Army, who inspired the Monument to commemorate the Dead of the Battles in Champagne. The other two figures represent one of the sculptor's brothers (on the left) who fell on the Chemin des Dames and (on the right) Quentin Roosevelt (qv) son of the American President. It was inaugurated on 28 September 1924 in the presence of Gen Gouraud, Marshal Joffre, the *Chargés d'Affaires* of the USA and Czeckoslovakia and other dignitaries. It was sculpted by Real del Sarte and the base bears the names of the divisions who fought in Champagne during the war: 93 French Infantry and 8 Cavalry, an Air Division, 4 American Divisions, the 1st Polish Regiment, 2 Russian Brigades and 1 Czech. At the rear of the reception room is a beautiful SGW with a *Poilu's* head in the centre. In the crypt is a Chapel and the Ossuary where 10,000 soldiers, mostly unknown, lie in huge sarcophagi and there are many commemorative plaques on the walls, some very interesting **Information Panels** and contemporary photographs.

One of the **Plaques is to the four sons of Pres Paul Doumer**, *'Morts pour la France'*. Lt André commanded the 22nd Bty, 8th RI. He was mortally wounded near Nancy on 24 September 1914: Capt René received the *Légion d'Honneur* after being wounded in 1914.

Ossuary and Monuments of the 28th Brigade, Souain.

Monument to the Thuringians with verses by Walter Flex, Souain German Cemetery.

Non-standard grave of Lt Louis Damez, French Cemetery L'Opéra.

On his recovery he transferred to the Air Service and commanded Escadrille Spad 76 – an ace with seven victories he was killed in aerial combat by Erich Hahn of Jasta 19 on 26 April 1917: Capt Marcel commanded Escadrille Spad 88 and was also killed in aerial combat in the Forest of Villers Cotterêts on 9 June 1918. The fourth brother, Armand, a Medic, died on 5 August 1922 from the effects of gas during the war. Doumer, the 13th President of the Republic, was shot by Russian emigré Paul Gorguloff and died the following day, 6 May, 1932. Gorguloff was sentenced to the guillotine.

At his request **Gen Gouraud** was himself buried here in an imposing ceremony on 26 September 1948. This legendary soldier fought in the Sudan, and on the outbreak of the war in August 1914 commanded the Moroccan troops. In September he returned to France and became the youngest general of a French Division. In January 1915 he was wounded in the Argonne and then took command of the Colonial Army in Champagne in March. He then was posted to the Dardanelles and on 30 June he was seriously injured and lost his right arm. Six months later he returned to Champagne and took command of the 4th Army by whom he was idolised. He was awarded the *Grand-Croix de la Légion d'Honneur,* was given the honour of being the first to enter Strasbourg – returned to France after its loss in the Franco-Prussian War of 1870. In 1919 he was appointed Commander in Chief in Syria and in 1923 Military Governor of Paris, a post which he held for fourteen years during which he was venerated by the citizens of the city. In 1945 he returned to Paris after the Liberation, where he lived until his death in 1948.

To the right of the Tomb is a **Plaque** is to the US 42nd (Rainbow) Division.

There are commemorative ceremonies here, normally on the third Sunday in July. The 80th Anniversary of the 1918 battles was celebrated in style in the presence of President Jacques Chirac. Restoration of the whole complex was begun in 1994. An orientation table beneath the group of figures, which can be reached by steps, indicates points on the surrounding battlefield and there are vestiges of the war in the ground around, together with some isolated memorials. Battles raged around the farm from September 1914, during the winter of '14-'15, during the offensive of 25 September

The Pyramid Memorial of the Ferme de Navarin to the Dead of the 4th Army.

Close-up of the figures of sculptor Real de Satre's brother, General Gouraud and Quentin Roosevelt surmounting the Pyramid.

1915, the offensive of April-May 1917, the voluntary retreat of 15 July 1918 and the offensive of 25 September 1918. The current Gen Gouraud is the President of the Association for the Memory of the Armies of Champagne.

Open: mid-March-end September, Fri, Sat 1400-1800, Sun 1000-1200 and 1400-1800. 1 & 11 Nov 1000-1200 and 1400-1600. Other days by appointment: Tel: + (0)3 26 66 82 32. There is a helpful guardian, Jacques Baur, and a small selection of books and postcards on sale. The visit is free, but there is a box for contributions to the work of the *Association du Souvenir aux Morts des Armées de Champagne*.

Continue on the D977 towards Sommepy-Tahure and fork left on the D20E9, signed Sommepy and American Monument.

On the right as you enter the village is the Logis de France Hotel and Restaurant, La Source du Py. Tel: (0)3 26 68 21 64. This is a 'gourmet' restaurant with exquisite food – no omelettes and chips here!

On the left is

• Memorial to the 4th Army of Gen Gouraud/35.5 miles/5 minutes/ Map 11/16

This small Monument also commemorates Gen Spirele and the 22nd DI, the 19th RI de Bred and Lt Col Vassal who liberated Sommepy on 28 September 1918.

Continue to the church, turn left before it and stop by the grassy bank on the right.

• US & French Memorials/Franco-American Museum, Sommepy/35.6 miles/15 minutes/Map 11/17/18

In the bank is an **American 2nd Division Boulder** with a large star on which are three small stars. To the left of it but difficult to spot because of the vegetation is a marble **Plaque to the American 2nd Division Marine Bde** of Gen J. Lejeune, 1914-1918, with a badge showing a hand holding a lighted torch. Further round the bank are poignant **Markers to all the ruined villages in the area.** Sommepy added the name of one of them, 'Tahure', to its own in memory of a nearby destroyed village. There are also the remains of a German bunker with a shell beside it. The bunker was used by 2nd Division HQ from 6–10 October 1918.

Continue round the bank and take the first right, then right again at the junction, past the Mairie to the church car park and stop.

The German advance reached the village on 2 September 1914 and most of the population fled, the remainder being forcibly evacuated by train to Rethel. For the next four years its situation just behind the German front line made it a constant target. It was liberated on 28 September 1918 and enemy forces were finally expelled on 3 October by the 2nd US Division. By this time the village was entirely destroyed. Lt André Huiller, who was born here, was despatched to the United States to appeal for help in the rebuilding and the 'Sommepy Fund' was founded. On 19 September 1925 the new *Mairie* and 'Franco-American Memorial Hall' were built beyond the church. They were inaugurated in the presence of the United States Ambassador, Myron Herrick. A room in the *Mairie* has now been

US 2nd Div Boulder Memorial, Somme, Church bank.

transformed into a **Museum** which has a fine collection of photographs, arms, uniforms and original paintings by an American artist etc. Visits by appointment. **Contact:** Tel: + (0)3 26 66 80 04.

In the church is a fine **SGW** on the right to **Aviators Jacques Lasseur and Henri Thamin**, C61 Squadron, who fell at Sommepy on 11 October 1915. A small aeroplane surmounts the group on the right.

Turn right past the church and drive downhill. At the bottom fork left on the D320 signed to American Memorial.

On the Calvary between trees is a **Plaque to commemorate the French and Allied soldiers** who fell here 1914-1918. This road is the boundary between the Marine Brigade (left) and the Infantry of 2nd Division (right) as they attacked, in the direction you are travelling, on 2-3 October 1918.

Continue following signs to the American Memorial and stop in the parking area. Walk to the Memorial.

• *Blanc Mont Monument to US 2nd, 36th, 42nd and 93rd Divisions 38.4 miles/15 minutes/Map 11/19/OP/WC*

This imposing high yellow limestone tower is dedicated to the American and French Armies united in the offensives of 1918. It stands on the Blanc Mont Ridge and is surrounded by vestiges of the war – trenches, dugouts, gun emplacements etc. There is a viewing platform on the top with superb views over the battlefield. Inside the entrance an inscription relates the American operations in the vicinity when 70,000 troops took the site. The assault from the Souain direction began at 0530 on 3 October supported by French tanks and air. By 1130 the 2nd Division controlled the crest, clearing it completely by the end of the next day. Furious German counter-attacks prevented further advance until the 36th (Texas) Division took over on 10 October and drove the enemy back to the Aisne. During the fighting near here of 3 October **Cpl John Pruitt, Pfc Frank J. Bart and Pte John Joseph Kelly won the MoH**. Pruitt (of the Marine Bde) single-handedly attacked two machine guns, killed two enemy and captured forty. He was killed soon afterwards by shellfire. Bart (of the Inf Bde) was a company runner when the advance was held up by machine-gun fire. He voluntarily picked up an automatic rifle, ran out ahead of the line and silenced a German machine-gun nest, killing the gunners. The advance was then able to continue and when it was again held up Bart repeated his gallant action on the second machine gun. Kelly (of the Marine Bde) ran 100 yards through the American barrage in advance of the front line, attacked an enemy machine-gun nest, killing the gunner, shooting another crew member with his pistol and returning through the barrage with eight prisoners.

Another **MoH winner** involved in the battle was the exceptional **USMC Lt Henry Lewis Hulbert**. Born in the UK he entered the Colonial Service, served in Malaysia until a scandal forced him to flee to the Klondike and in 1898 enlisted in the Marine Corps. He was awarded his MoH in the Philippines in 1899 for 'extraordinary heroism'. In 1917, now aged fifty and a Sergeant Major, the first to qualify in the new grade of Marine Gunner, he insisted in being sent to France. There he resisted the offered non-combat roles and became a platoon leader with the 66th Coy, 1st Bn, 5th Marines. Wounded in the Regiment's first major engagement in Belleau Wood on 6 June 1918 he was twice cited for acts of bravery. After a third act of heroism he became one of the first Marines to be decorated with the DSC. He was again wounded at Soissons, gained another citation and was commissioned as a 1st Lieutenant.

In October his promotion to Captain was approved but Henry never lived to receive it. On 4 October he was killed by machine-gun fire. He was posthumously awarded the Navy Cross and a fourth citation and the French honoured him with the *Croix de Guerre*. The fifty-one-year-old hero is buried in Arlington Cemetery and was further honoured by the naming of the destroyer USS *Henry L. Hulbert* which served until its decommission in 1946.

Near the tower is a small Visitor Centre with a Visitor's Book to sign and wonderfully clean toilets.

Extra Visits to 'Big Bertha' Gun Emplacement (Map 11/20) Semide, Bunker & Roland Garros Memorials (Map 11/21/22) St Morel and 170th & 174th RIs Memorial near Sommepy (Map 11/23).
Mileage: 25 miles. Approximate time: 1 hour 45 minutes.

Rejoin the D977 (you may do this by continuing along the chalk road which runs past the monument site, which becomes very lumpy and bumpy but is only some 1.2 miles, or by returning to Sommepy) and turn left. Continue to the D41 and turn right to Semide. Turn right after the Mairie and continue some .6 mile to a track to the left just before the start of the trees.

The track is very rough but although this would be easier tackled by 4-wheel drive it can be driven with care by car if dry.

Continue to the small group of trees on the left.

You will have to walk the last few yards, being careful not to disturb any crops. There is also a DANGER sign at the edge which should be heeded.

Remains of Large German Gun Pit. There is an old faded **Information Panel** here which tells how at the end of 1917 villagers noticed a mysterious occurrence. The village had been occupied since 1916, and during the year the Germans built a railway past the village in the direction of Les Valottes (the secret location of this pit). Then one morning two wagons were seen carrying a 380mm gun but its destination remained a secret. At the beginning of 1918 the Germans covered the

'Big Bertha' Gun Pit, Semide.

Roland Garros Memorial, St Morel.

The dignified American Monument at Blanc Mont.

Monument to the 170th & 174th RIs near Sommepy.

*Monument to the Boyau Eugène
and Chemin des Relèves.*

Extra Visits continued

valley with a thick smoke screen and the piece fired seventeen shells at seven-minute intervals – and that was that. Several days later the gun passed through the village on the railway again and never returned The local consensus was that the target for the shells was Châlons-sur-Marne but that they fell short. Perhaps the gun became unusable. The gun is similar to the ones that bombarded Paris (qv).

Return to the Mairie and continue to the right turn on the D141. Turn right and continue through Mont St Martin and continue on the D21 to the church at St Morel.

In front of the church in Place Roland Garros is a grey stone **Memorial to Roland Garros** in the form of a small bust between two large wings. It has no inscription.

Turn sharp left by the church following signs to Stèle Roland Garros to the right and then to the left. Continue over the railway.

There is a big **Bunker** on the left just after the railway line.

Continue to the memorial.

Roland Garros Memorial. This beautiful polished grey granite memorial is lovingly tended. According to the season it has a bed of bright flowers in front, two trees behind and the *Tricolore* proudly flying. It is maintained by the *Association Roland Garros de l'Aviation au Tennis* in St Morel and bears an inscription which describes how, 'at this place on 5 October 1918 Garros's plane of 26 Sqn was brought down after several dogfights. He was an Officer of the *Légion d'Honneur*, conqueror of the Mediterranean in 1913 who volunteered in 1914. In 1915 he had shot down three enemy planes, was taken prisoner, escaped three years later and demanded to return to the front where he met the glorious death which crowned his brilliant career.' Garros is buried in the National Cemetery at Vouziers and his name now lives on in the Tennis Stadium in Paris where the French Open Championship is held each year.

The Association organises commemorative ceremonies on various Garros anniversaries (of his birth, of his death etc.) and puts on temporary exhibitions from time to time.

*Return to the church, noting another **Bunker** on the left before the railway line. Continue on the D21 to the D982 and turn right direction Monthois. On entering the village there is a sign to the left to the German Cemetery, Monthois. At the end of the village turn right on the D306 direction Sommepy-Tahure, through Aure and continue on the D6/D20 to the large cross to the left.*

Monument to the 170th, 174th RIs, 1914-1918

The large stone cross commemorates the Dead of the 170th and 174th RIs. A plaque describes how on 28 September 1918 at this site, under enemy machine-gun fire, the 170th and 174th from Epinal in the Vosges took heavily fortified positions and followed through. It was refurbished on 8 April 1982 by soldiers of the 170th and to the left is a **Cross** which commemorates the Commandant of the 170th, **Col Joseph Carle**t, killed here on 28 September 1918. Behind the memorial is the **Tomb of Georges Emile Estival**, 333 Coy des Chars d'Assaut, 28 September 1918 and behind the tomb a large **Bunker.**

Continue to Sommepy and pick up the main itinerary.

Return via Sommepy and Souain to St Hilaire and there take the D931 direction Reims.
The road is called *Voie de la Liberté* and Liberty Highway markers lead all the way to Reims.
It was in the area some 2.5 miles to the right of the road that the prisoners who revealed
the impending German assault of 15 July were taken on the morning of 14 July 1818.
Continue to the cemetery on the right.

• 'International' Cemetery, Polish Memorial, Aubérive/60 miles/10 minutes/Map 11/24/25

Here is Aubérive-sur-Suippe **French National Cemetery** with 6,424 graves, 2,908 of which
are in three ossuaries with a **German Cemetery** behind containing 5,359 graves. To the left
is the interesting **Polish Cemetery** le Bois du Puits. To the right of the entrance is a **Memorial
to the Polish Soldiers** who died for the communal cause, 1914-18 on French ground. It was
erected on 8 July 1928 by *L'Association Polonaise de Conservation des Tombes des Héros.* The
graves bear French-style crosses. In the centre is a large cross with the Polish Coat of Arms.
It was renovated in 1991 by Polish Veterans in France. There are 129 soldiers of the Marne
from WW1 and 266 soldiers from WW2. The Polish Army was formed in France in 1917. The
Polish 1st Division received its standards on 22 June 1918 at Sept Saulx and it fought with
the French 4th CA (Colonial Army) in the 15 July Battle of Prunay between here and Reims.
*Continue to the small crossroads to the right of which is a large wooden cross. Turn left
and continue to the monument to the left.*

• Monument to the 27th RI, Prosnes/64.1 miles/5 minutes/Map 11/26

This commemorates the battle of Prosnes 31 January 1917 and bears the Territorial
Regiment's battle honours – Artois, Somme, Verdun, Champagne. As is evident from
Map 11 the D931 which you are following was the fall-back position adopted at the end
of 15 July and the towns along it saw furious fighting in the struggles that followed.
Return to the main road and continue to the small memorial on the right.

• Monument to the Boyau Eugène & Chemin des Relèves/64.9 miles/5 minutes/Map 11/27

A small stone marks the Boyau (Trench) Eugène and the Chemin des Relèves (Supply
Road) along which thousands of French soldiers perished.
Continue to the next crossroads with the D34. On the right is

• Heroes of April 1917/Demarcation Stone/65.8 miles/5 minutes/Map 11/28/29

This striking red granite monument was erected in 1957 by the *Comité du Souvenir du
VIII Corps* and '*Ceux de Verdun*'. On the front above the caption '*Aux Héros et Martyrs des
Offensives d'Avril 1917*' is a powerful ceramic death's head *Poilu* and on the reverse a
poignant picture of a *Poilu* caught on the barbed wire. They are by the ceramist Guy
Perron 'after' the artist André Lagrange. On concrete posts around it are the numbers
of the regiments involved: the 1st & 37th RAC, 27th, 85th & 95th RI. On the steps that
lead up to the monument are the years 1914, 1915, 1916, 1917 and 1918. On the side of
the road is a **Demarcation Stone.**
*Continue and follow signs to the Fort de la Pompelle. Stop in the parking area. Up a small
path to left is*

• *Monument to Those who Fell Here, Aug 1914-October 1918/72 miles/ 10 minutes/Map 11/30*

Beside the large Memorial Cross to some of the 172 Regiments who fell gloriously in this area flies the *Tricolore*. There are many small plaques around it, including one to fifty-eight-year-old architect, Lt Max Doumic who was Head of Architecture at the Montreal Polytechnic and returned to France to enlist in the 1st Foreign Legion. He was killed 11 Nov 1914.

Walk back to the parking area. From here there is a pedestrian tunnel which leads to

Dramatic ceramic plaque on Memorial to Heroes of April 1917.

• *Fort de la Pompelle/72 miles/30 minutes/Map 11/31*

The fort, designed by the engineering genius, Séré de Rivières (qv), was constructed between 1880 and 1883 to complete the circle of fortifications around Reims after the Franco-Prussian War of 1870. It was unarmed in 1913 and was occupied, with a struggle, by German troops on 4 September 1914. After the Victory of the Marne it was reconquered after a fierce battle by the 138th RI on 24 September. From then on it became the key to the defence of this sector of the Reims battlefield and was subjected to four years of German bombardments and attacks by mine, gas, artillery and tanks. Some 180 French Regiments served in the fort during the war as well as two Russian Special Brigades in 1916/1917.

After WW2 the ruined Fort was abandoned and then sold in 1956 to the André Maginot National Federation, then to the City of Reims and the Conseil Général de la Marne. Now the impressive museum houses an outstanding collection of German helmets, sections devoted to the Crapouillots (qv), the Russian Expeditionary Force, the French Ace René Dorme (credited with twenty-three victories and who was killed near the Fort on 15 May 1917) as well as examples of the famous '75's.

Regular ceremonies of commemoration of the '14-'18 war are held here.

Open: 1 November-31 March: 1000-1700; 1 April-31 October: 1000-1900.
Closed: Tuesdays. Annual closure from 24 December-6 January. Tel: + (0)3 26 49 11 85.

• *End of Champagne Tour*
OR Return to Reims for R/WC

Fort de la Pompelle.

Monument to those who fell near La Pompelle, Aug '14-Oct '18.

ST MIHIEL SALIENT: THE RECAPTURE

12-16 SEPTEMBER 1918

'Marshal Pétain sent down to the First Army, two days after the battle, about 800 French officers and NCOs to see for themselves how the American troops had succeeded in crossing this hitherto considered impassable obstacle [barbed wire]. A French officer told me afterwards that the evidence on the ground convinced him that our infantry had walked over the wire, but he thought perhaps they were assisted in this remarkable performance by the size of their feet.'
George C. Marshall, *Memoirs.*

'When the word finally went back to the United States that I had been wounded it said I had been hit in the Toul sector. I had to be sure everyone realised this was a section of France, not my anatomy.'
Mark Clark.

'Now you probably realise that Saint Mihiel was a rather well executed movement. Everything seemed to run smoothly. For the first mile or so we faced some artillery and had to knock out a Maxim but after that it was mainly pushing forward and taking prisoners. We had one sergeant who captured thirty by just walking into a dugout armed only with a pistol.'
1st Lt John C. Madden, 89th Div quoted in *Make the Kaiser Dance* by Henry Berry.

SUMMARY OF THE BATTLE

On 12 September 1918 the American First Army under Gen 'Black Jack' Pershing carried out its first offensive. More than half a million Americans supported by some 110,000 French attacked and within thirty-six hours reduced the German St Mihiel Salient. American losses were about 7,000, German 20,000.

OPENING MOVES

America declared war against Germany on 6 April 1917 and on 26 May 1917 Maj Gen John J. Pershing, who got his nickname 'Blackjack' from having commanded negro troops in the Spanish-American War, became C.-in-C. of the American Expeditionary Force (AEF). In response to urgent appeals from the French and the British, the Americans gathered together Regular units to form the 1st Division and sent it to France. The main body arrived at St Nazaire on 26 June 1917, two weeks after Pershing and his staff landed at Boulogne.

In October 1917, preliminary training over, one battalion from each regiment in the 1st Division was sent into the line with the French for ten days' experience. The sector chosen, Toul, had been a quiet one for three years and on 23 October 1917 a battery of the 6th Field Artillery fired the first American Army round of the war. There were by now four American Divisions in France – all opposite the St Mihiel Salient in Lorraine, each about 28,000 strong. There was the 1st Regular, the 2nd (mostly Marine), the 26th, a National Guard force mainly from Massachusetts and the 42nd 'Rainbow', with men from every state in the Union. Its Chief of Staff was Douglas MacArthur.

Pershing made clear to the Allies that he did not want his troops to go into battle until they were fully trained, and that they would remain under American command and fight as such. It was a policy he may have inherited from the King of France when he sent troops to help George Washington to fight the British at Yorktown in 1781. Pershing was a hard taskmaster and he emphasised to staff and soldiers alike that they were training for open warfare and not for life in the trenches. By the end of the year there were about 180,000 American troops in France but they had not yet fought together in large groups. On 20 April 1918 the first 'American' contest took place. It may well have been provoked by the Germans to try to undermine the confidence of the untried Americans. Early in the morning behind a divisional barrage some 2,000 Germans emerged from their positions around **Montsec** (see Map 12) and headed towards the Doughboys of the 26th (Yankee) Division. The fighting centred around the village of **Seicheprey** five miles east of Apremont. The Germans took it that day. The Yankees took it back the day after. They had proved that they could fight, although they lost many men as prisoners. All the Doughboys (who probably got their name from their days in the Mexican Wars, when their uniforms got covered with white adobe dust) needed was more experience.

A month later on 28 May, the 28th Infantry Regiment of the 1st Division attacked German positions at **Cantigny**, twenty miles south of Amiens. They took the village in less than an hour and with the help of the 18th Infantry held on to it through forty-eight hours of German counter-attacks. It was a clear victory for the Americans in France. Those Doughboys who fought at Seicheprey and Cantigny saw themselves as an elite – just as did the 'out-since-Mons' Tommy.

However, Pershing's 'All American Force' concept was not holding firm and, with the breakthrough of German forces at the Chemin des Dames on 27 May in Operation Blücher, part of the Kaiser's Offensive, he was persuaded to allow his five divisions to be used as supports in the Marne area. Cooperation between the Allies was the name of the game and Pershing allowed his troops to cement the tired bricks of French divisions. On 31 May the US 3rd Division stopped the Germans at **Château Thierry**. On 4 June the US 2nd Division halted the enemy at **Belleau Wood** and recaptured it on 25 June. Pershing, though, wanted his men back. He had had in mind, since the entry of America into the war, that the first offensive by the American Army should be against the St Mihiel Salient. By July 1918 there were one million Doughboys in France and their C.-in-C. wanted to bring them all under his control. At an Allied Commanders' conference on 24 July his proposal to reduce the Salient in order to cut the Metz-Maubeuge railway was agreed as a 'local attack', On 10 August Foch, the Allied Supreme Commander since Doullens on 26 March, finally gave in to Pershing's frequent and forceful demands that there should be an American 1st Army. It was a supreme, dreamed-for moment for Pershing. Five days later he upgraded the St Mihiel plan to a 15-division assault designed to 'strike the heaviest blow possible and secure the maximum results'.

On 30 August Foch tried to scale down the American attack and he and Pershing had a head-on disagreement. Foch wanted to split the Americans in two, putting one half with the French in the Argonne and the other in Champagne. Pershing flatly refused. He would agree to fight in the Argonne, he said, but as an American Army under American control. Even so, before that his Army would have its first battle, and that would be a 'limited' offensive at St Mihiel to pinch out the German salient. Foch had no alternative but to agree, and he did so formally on 2 September. The Doughboys had ten days to get ready for their first fight in an all-American operation.

WHAT HAPPENED

The Americans were spread from the Channel to Switzerland. Six divisions were with the French on the Aisne, two with the BEF at Ypres and others just arriving or training behind the lines. Pershing set about assembling them.

The German-occupied salient, triangular in shape, lay about twenty miles south-east of Verdun. Its base was roughly twenty-five miles between Pont à Mousson and Verdun and it pointed about 13 miles into Allied territory to the little town of St Mihiel (see Map 12). Since their arrival in 1914 the Germans had constructed considerable trench, wire and bunker defences. The staff planning for the American attack was done by Col George C. Marshall and the idea was to hit both flanks of the triangle with overwhelming force. The plan called for the main assault by the American I and IV Corps to be against the southern face and three hours later a second diversionary attack on the western side by the US V Corps together with the French 15th Colonial Division.

At 0100 hours on 12 September 3,000 guns opened fire with HE, following up as the light improved, with smoke. At 0500 the main assault went in led by French Renault tanks and low flying aircraft. So intense was the bombardment that the German Crown Prince said that, 'it exceeded anything we had known at Verdun and on the Somme'. The American advance through the wire was extraordinarily rapid. Just after dawn the following day elements of 26th Division from the western assault made contact at Vigneulles-les-Hattonchâtel (see Map 12) with men of the 1st Division from the southern assault. The Salient had been pinched off and the 1st Army had taken some 16,000 prisoners and over 440 guns.

THE BATTLEFIELD TOUR

(This also includes the 'St Mihiel Salient: The Formation' tour as it was fought over much of the same ground. Because it includes the two campaigns it is a long tour that is crammed with interesting features and would be best spread over two days. If only one is available, then careful reading of the itinerary is advised so that you can select the points of greatest interest to you. Note that the workings for the High Speed Train line across the battlefield may cause deviations.)

• **The Route:** The tour begins at Pont à Mousson (at the south-eastern corner of the Salient) and the American Field Ambulance Fountain, visits the French National Cemetery at Montauville; Fey – the SGWs in the Church, the Monument to the destroyed village, the Croix des Carmes; the destroyed village of Regniéville with

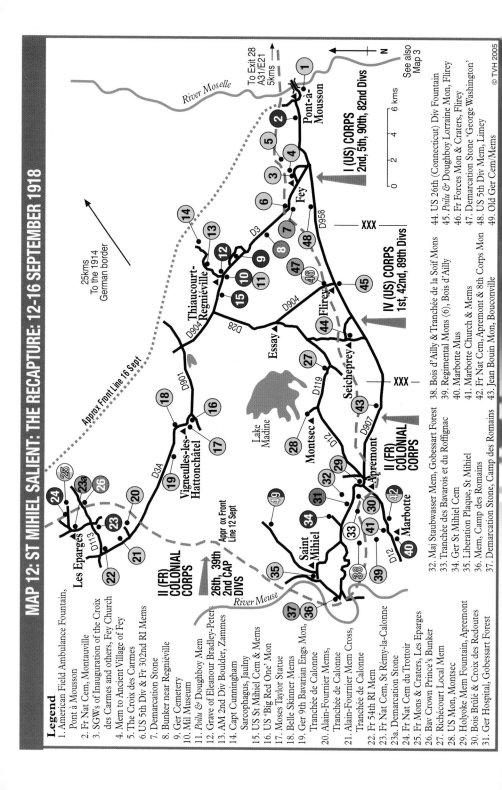

MAP 12: ST MIHIEL SALIENT: THE RECAPTURE: 12-16 SEPTEMBER 1918

© TVH 2005

See also Map 3

N

River Moselle

To Exit 28 A31/E21 5kms

Pont-à-Mousson

I (US) CORPS
2nd, 5th, 90th, 82nd Divs

0 2 4 6 kms

25kms To the 1914 German border

Approx Front Line 16 Sept

Fey

Thiaucourt-Regniéville

D3

D958

XXX

IV (US) CORPS
1st, 42nd, 89th Divs

D904

Flirey

D28

Essay

D904

Seicheprey

D901

XXX

Vigneulles-les-Hattonchâtel

Lake Madine

Montsec

D119

D12

Apremont

D907

II (FR) COLONIAL CORPS

D3A

Marbotte

Les Éparges

D113

Saint Mihiel

II (FR) COLONIAL CORPS

26th, 39th 2nd CAP DIVS

Approx Front Line 12 Sept

River Meuse

Legend

1. American Field Ambulance Fountain, Pont à Mousson
2. Fr Nat Cem, Montauville
3. SGWs of Inauguration of the Croix des Carmes and others, Fey Church
4. Mem to Ancient Village of Fey
5. The Croix des Carmes
6. US 5th Div & Fr 302nd RI Mems
7. Demarcation Stone
8. Bunker near Regniéville
9. Ger Cemetery
10. Mil Museum
11. *Poilu* & Doughboy Mem
12. Grave of Eleanour Bradley-Peters
13. AM 2nd Div Boulder, Zammes
14. Capt Cunningham Sarcophagus, Jaulny
15. US St Mihiel Cem & Mems
16. US 'Big Red One' Mon
17. Moses Taylor Statue
18. Belle Skinner Mems
19. Ger 9th Bavarian Div Mon, Tranchée de Calonne
20. Alain-Fournier Mems, Tranchée de Calonne
21. Alain-Fournier Mem Cross, Tranchée de Calonne
22. Fr 54th RI Mem
23. Fr Nat Cem, St Rémy-la-Calonne
23a. Demarcation Stone
24. Fr Nat Cem du Trottoir
25. Fr Mons & Craters, Les Éparges
26. Bav Crown Prince's Bunker
27. Richécourt Local Mem
28. US Mon, Montsec
29. Holyoke Mem Fountain, Apremont
30. Bois Brûlé & Croix des Redoutes
31. Ger Hospital, Gobessart Forest
32. Maj Staubwasser Mem, Gobessart Forest
33. Tranchée des Bavarois et du Roffignac
34. Ger St Mihiel Cem
35. Liberation Plaque, St Mihiel
36. Mem, Camp des Romains
37. Demarcation Stone, Camp des Romains
38. Bois d'Ailly & Tranchée de la Soif Mons
39. Regimental Mons (6), Bois d'Ailly
40. Marbotte Mus
41. Marbotte Church & Mems
42. Fr Nat Cem, Apremont & 8th Corps Mon
43. Jean Bouin Mon, Bouconville
44. US 26th (Connecticut) Div Fountain
45. *Poilu* & Doughboy Lorraine Mon, Flirey
46. Fr Forces Mon & Craters, Flirey
47. Demarcation Stone 'George Washington'
48. US 5th Div Mem, Limey
49. Old Ger Cem/Mems

Memorials to the French 302nd RI, US 5th Division and Demarcation Stone; Thiaucourt German and American Cemeteries, passing the Museum and Memorials; the American Memorial at Montsec; the Holyoke Fountain in Apremont; Croix des Redoutes, Bois Brûlé; Gobessart Forest – the German Hospital, Monument to Maj Staubwasser, Tranchées des Bavarois et de Roffignac and the German St Mihiel Cemetery; St Mihiel – Liberation Plaque, Camp des Romains Memorials & Demarcation Stone; Bois d'Ailly German trench lines and *Tranchée de la Soif* Memorials, Regimental Memorials; Marbotte – Museum, Memorial Church and Apremont-la-Fôret French National Cemetery & VIII Corps Monument; the Jean Bouin Monument in Bouconville; the US Fountain and Plaque at Seicheprey; the Lorraine Franco-American Memorials in Flirey and ends at the US 5th Division Obelisk in Limey.

- **Extra Visits:** US 2nd Division and Capt Cunningham Monument, Jaulny; US Ist Division Monument and Moses Jones Statue, Vigneulles; Hattonchâtel and Belle Skinner Memorials; Alain-Fournier Memorials & Grave, Tranchée de Calonne, St Rémy Cemetery; Le Trottoir French National Cemetery, Historic Site & Memorials, Les Eparges; French Memorial, Demarcation Stone, Mine Craters & Sgt Rochas Cross, Flirey.
- **Total distance:** 80.9 miles
- **Total time:** 9 hours 30 minutes
- **Distance from Calais to start point:** Approx 310 miles (varies according to exit taken from A4).
  There are Motorway Tolls on the Calais-Reims and Reims-Metz sections.
- **Base towns:** Reims, Pont à Mousson, Verdun, St Mihiel, Metz
- **Map:** Michelin 307 Local, Meurthe-et-Moselle, Meuse, Moselle. 1:175,000
  From Calais take the A26 to Reims, then the A4 direction Metz and either take Exit 32 at Fresnes-en-Woevre, following well-signed road to Pont à Mousson via the D980/904/D3/D958 [OR if staying at Metz, Exit 35, then the A31 and take Exit 28 to Pont à Mousson].

N.B. There is a conveniently placed Campanile Hotel near the Exit 28.
Tel: + (0)3 83 81 00 42. Fax: + (0)3 83 81 10 31.
Continue to Pont-à-Mousson on the D910 and cross the river.

N.B. There is a superb *Art Deco* French War Memorial Pillar on the right by the bridge.
Continue following signs to Centre into the central square. Stop.
Set your mileometer to zero.

• American Field Ambulance Fountain, Pont à Mousson/0 miles/ 10 minutes/Map 12/1

Almost central in the square, Place Duroc, (which is surrounded by picturesque arcades, with a Tourist Office and a variety of restaurants and cafés) is a **Memorial Fountain** in Renaissance style. It is a reconstruction of the original fountain, damaged during the war, and was erected by the American Field Service after the war as a memorial to its dead. The Field Service was a group of volunteer ambulance sections that joined the French Forces in 1915 (c.f. Ernest Hemingway's *Farewell to Arms*) later reinforced by vehicle sections after America entered the war. Drivers were recruited from universities and colleges and ambulance sections often comprised men from a particular university, e.g. Yale or Harvard etc. When the AEF reached Europe the strength of the Field Service was about 2,000. At the end of 1917 most personnel were enlisted or commissioned into the American Army but the Service itself did not serve with US forces. On the Western Front it remained with the French until the end of the war. There is also a Memorial Plaque to nurses of the Field Service in St. George's Memorial Church in Ypres in Belgium.

The town was taken by the Germans in 1914 but quickly recaptured by the French and held until the end of the war despite regular shelling by German artillery.

Take the D958 west out of Pont à Mousson on the Avénue Patton following signs to Verdun and continue to the Church at Montauville (1.8 miles).

N.B. There is a sign to the right here on the D105 to the French Military Cemetery, Le Pétant and Bois le Prêtre. **Do not take this road.**

Continue on the D958 to the road to the right which leads to the cemetery car park and drive to it.

• French National Cemetery, Montauville ('Le Pétant') & Memorials/ 2.3 miles/20 minutes/Map 12/2

There are 5,199 French WW1 burials in this vast cemetery which stretches all the way up the hillside to the Bois le Prêtre behind it, including 1,014 in an Ossuary, one Serbian, and 8,199 French WW2, including 4,438 in three Ossuaries, 105 Soviets, twelve Poles and one Yugoslav. To the left on entering is a large plot of Muslim headstones. There is a Monument to the Dead of the Bois le Prêtre, 1914-1918 and a dramatic statue entitled 'The Road to Exile, 1939-1945'.

The cemetery was started in 1920 and gradually increased by concentrations from other small cemeteries in the region, many from the bloody battle in the Bois le Prêtre. When the German Army was stopped on the Marne in September 1914 the German 5th and 6th Armies mounted a vigorous offensive between Verdun and Nancy, reaching St Mihiel and making a huge salient in the French lines. They heavily fortified the 372m high Bois le Prêtre position and the French 73rd RI was charged to take it. Bitter fighting continued until they managed to retake it on 8 June 1915, by which time they had lost 64,000 men in the area. The 73rd became known as *Les Loups du Bois le Prêtre* (The Wolves of the Prêtre Wood). In August 1918 the Americans took over the sector and between 1948 and 1951 the bodies of French POWs were repatriated from Germany and Austria and in 1968 bodies were reinterred here from the Meurthe-et-Moselle districts. In 1971 the bodies of POWs from the concentration camp of Rawa-Ruska in the Ukraine were reburied here.

At the entrance is an **Information Panel** describing the fighting in the Bois le Prêtre *Continue.*

On the left is the Bois de Pluche where more fierce fighting took place.

Turn right on the D3 signed to Thiaucourt and Regniéville to a right turn to Fey-en-Haye. Continue into the village, turn left just before the church and stop.

• Stained Glass Windows, Croix-de-Carmes Church, Fey-en-Haye/ 5.5 miles/10 minutes/Map 12/3

N.B. If the church is locked, apply to M. Jean-Pierre David in No 3 rue de la 73ième Division, opposite, for the key.

On the façade of the church to the right is the most spectacular War Memorial. It occupies the whole wall, culminating with a figure on the pinnacle. Forming part of the huge cross at its centre are two **SGWs** which show the inauguration of the controversial Croix des Carmes (qv). In 1915 a simple cross was raised in one of the bloodiest parts of the Bois le Prêtre (qv) which became an emotive symbol to the French troops fighting in the area. In 1919 the cross was transferred to the Le Pétant French Cemetery (qv). This provoked the formation of two rival memorial associations – one maintaining that the cross should be returned to its original site, the other that it should stay in the cemetery. The somewhat vituperative argument was solved in 1923 by the erection on the original site of a 7m high granite cross upon which are carved two soldiers who uphold the 'true Croix des Carmes' which is stone faced with blue tiles. The inauguration on 23 September was an important affair and the SGW shows President Poincaré in mid-speech surrounded by various national and local dignitaries and a large crowd of spectators. Beneath is the insignia of the *Croix de Guerre*, and the citation of Louis Barthon when it was conferred on 9 April 1921. The rival faction was satisfied when in 1935 the pyramid bearing a Cross of Lorraine was erected in the Le Pétant Cemetery (qv) with the simple inscription,' To the heroes of the Bois le Prêtre'.

From inside the lovely church, rebuilt in neo-Gothic style in 1924 and christened 'The Church of the Croix-des-Carmes', the SGWs glow with extraordinary colour and there is a further beautiful window showing medics treating a wounded soldier. Around the church, which was skilfully restored in 2003-4, are several other regimental and personal memorials. There are plans to install the originally intended SGWs of various crosses.

Continue on a road that narrows, past the local cemetery on the left and turn right at the T junction. Continue and on the right is

• *Memorial to Ancient Village of Fey-en-Haye/6.0 miles/5 minutes/ Map 12/4*
On an undulating mound with the remains of an elegant arch and other rubble is a monument to 'Our ancestors whose tombs were destroyed during the 1914-18 war' with **Information Panels** which describe how some of the old cultivated flowers of the village still continue to bloom here and what happened to the village during the war.

Drive straight over the junction following signs to the Croix des Carmes and Le Père Hilarion. Continue along the track, which is negotiable by car with care if dry, to the large stone monument to the right.

• *Croix des Carmes/Trenchline/7.4 miles/15 minutes/Map 12/5*
In the centre of this impressive Monument is the original wooden Croix des Carmes (qv) and a plaque states that it is the property of the Viard Family. The cross, raised by public subscription, designed by sculptors and architects Prouve, Charbonnier and Bachelet, inaugurated by Pres Poincaré on 23 September 1923 and last renovated in 1989, is framed by a stone cross flanked by two *Poilus* figures. On the rear is the ORBAT of forces which fought in the area in 1915 and some *bas-reliefs*.

Behind the monument is a small stone marking the original site of the Cross and **Information Panels** about the fighting around it. A well-cleared trail leads round

American Field Ambulance Fountain with Town Hall behind, Pont à Mousson.

The Croix des Carmes Monument.

Two of the extraordinary SGWs of Fey Church recording the inauguration of the Croix des Carmes.

impressive trenchlines, shell craters, remains of dugouts and barbed wire, with more **Information Panels** about saps en route.

N.B. The track continues a further 1km or so to the site of the lone house of Father Hilarion which stood in No Man's Land in the Bois le Prêtre beside which was a fountain to which both French and Germans came for water at a set time, during which no shots were fired.

Return to the Ancient Village, passing en route several informative signs placed by the Automobile Club Lorrain. Turn left and then right until you have completed the circuit back to the church, return to the D3 and turn right. Continue to a sign to the Destroyed Village of Regniéville and stop in the car park on the right at the crossroads.

• *Ancient Village of Regniéville, US 5th Div & French 302nd RI Memorials/Demarcation Stone/11.4 miles/10 minutes/Map 12/6/7*

The village no longer exists. It was one of a considerable number that were so utterly destroyed during the war that they were never rebuilt.

By the parking area is a **Monument to the US 5th Inf Div**, 12 September 1918 and their 700 mile drive from the Normandy Beaches in September-October 1944. It bears their Red Diamond insignia. Unlike the US 2nd Div who have concentrated upon the preservation of WW2 memorials, the 5th Division Association funded half of the costs of refurbishing fifteen of their WW1 monuments during the 1990s. *Souvenir Français* provided the other fifty per cent.

Walk back along the road you have driven to the memorial on the left. This Memorial, in somewhat sorry condition, is to the **French 302nd RI** who defended this position from 1 July 1915-20 May 1916 and who won the *Croix de Guerre*.

Cross over the road and walk back to the junction. In the corner on the left is

A **Demarcation Stone** surmounted by a French helmet. This is one of three sponsored by Mr Guérard of Seattle, Washington (qv). To the left is signed the Destroyed Village of Remenauville.

The crossroads going left and right run over or beside the line of the American I Corps forward trenches. Your direction of travel is the direction of attack towards the German lines barely 400 yards up the road. The 5th Division led off here on 12 September 1918 and despite fierce machine-gun fire from the woods, broke through the barbed wire, crossed the enemy

US 5th Div Obelisk, WW1 and WW2, Regniéville.

trenches and by nightfall had moved three miles up the road towards Thiaucourt.

Continue, passing on the right

Cross on site of destroyed Cemetery of Regniéville (11.6 miles).

Continue and on the left is

A large **Bunker** (13.3 miles) **Map 12/8.**

Continue downhill on the D3 and watch out for a small turning to the left after a long right bend. Follow it to the cemetery on the right.

• *Thiaucourt German Cemetery/15.1 miles/15 minutes/Map 12/9*

Facing across the road and away from the cemetery it may be possible to see the prominent hill of Montsec in the distance about nine miles away. The white American Memorial surmounting it continues to be a good orientation marker for the rest of the tour.

The cemetery was extensively renovated during the 1980s and most of the grave markers are black crosses. Here and there between the crosses headstones mark the resting place of Jewish soldiers. More than 8,700 named soldiers are buried with a further 2,970 in a mass grave. At the bottom left of the cemetery some isolated old stones mark the graves of soldiers from the 1870 conflict, beyond them is a row of individual 1914-18 headstones and opposite them a plinth upon which a German eagle once stood. The villagers here, having been invaded in 1870, 1914 and 1940, were not prepared to be overlooked by this symbol of German might and destroyed it.

Continue downhill into the village, under the railway bridge and over the Rupt de Mad River.

Ahead the church spire looks extraordinarily like a German Pickelhaube.

Continue uphill to the first turning to the left (Rue Neuve). At the corner is

• *Thiaucourt Military Museum/15.8 miles/15 minutes/Map 12/10*

This private WW1 museum covers the period 1900-1950 and has many uniforms and artefacts pertaining to the two World Wars, but concentrates on the St Mihiel Salient, 1914-1918. Theoretically it is **open** on Sundays and Public Holidays from 1 April-11 November 1400-1830. Otherwise by appointment. Tel: + (0)3 83 81 98 36.

Continue uphill and stop opposite the memorial in front of the church.

• *Thiaucourt Poilu-Doughboy Memorial/Capt Cunningham Plaque/ 15.9 miles/5 minutes/Map 12/11*

The French *Poilu* and the American Doughboy figures are shaking hands. It is a most photogenic Memorial, its small surrounding garden always immaculately tended. On the sides are *bas-reliefs* showing the Americans crossing the river and the plight of the inhabitants. The 2nd Division entered the village on the afternoon of the first day of the battle. The village was an important link in the German railway supply system and one of the main objectives of the US I Corps, which captured eleven field guns loaded on railway flats here.

To the right of the church door is a **Plaque to Capt Oliver Baty Cunningham**, 15th Fld Arty, 2 Div AEF, born in Chicago, 17 September 1894, killed on the battlefield near Jaulny (qv) 17 September 1918. The three bells in the church were dedicated to Capt Cunningham on Memorial Day (30 May) 1920. For his brave actions in combat Cunningham was awarded the DSC and the Silver Star Medal (posthumously). He was the only officer of the 15th Fld Arty to be kia during WW1. Cunningham was of the Yale Class of '17 and a Foundation Scholarship was set up in his name.

Continue uphill to the right turn to Jaulny on the D28.

Extra Visit to US 2nd Div Monument (Map 12/13) and Capt Cunningham Monument (Map 12/14), Jaulny. Round trip: 5.2 miles. Approximate time: 45 minutes

N.B. A sharp right turn leads to the local cemetery in which, to the right of the entrance, is the lonely grave (under a marker shaped liked an official American cross) of Eleanor Bradley-Peters, 6 July 1865-1 November 1941 (Map 12/12). She is the mother of Capt Cunningham (qv) who came to live in Thiaucourt after the war and funded the rebuilding of the Church and the Town Hall.

To the left is a single CWGC headstone to Guardsman T.J. Kite, Grenadier Guards, 8 December 1918, age 24.

Continue along the D28, over the TGV rail line and after a sharp right bend in the bank on the right is
US 2nd Div Monument. This white-painted boulder bears the grey star of the US 2nd Division.

Continue into the village of Jaulny (in the centre of which is the fascinating Antiquités de Jaulny shop with helpful proprietor who can direct you to the Cunningham monument) *and through it to the local cemetery on the right. Take the track to the left of the cemetery.*
There is then a fairly demanding 500m or so walk up a steep stony path which is rewarded by seeing a moving and little-visited memorial in beautiful woods. Of course if you have a 4-wheel drive you can drive a long way up the track.

Continue into the wood and take the second track to the right and then to a clearing, to the left of which is
Monument to Capt Cunningham. This is a significant stone sarcophagus in a large rectangular enclosure to Capt Oliver Badly [sic] Cunningham. The inscription (and 1996 plaque erected by the ALHIMIC) records how this young American officer received the DSC for repeated acts of heroism at Villemontagne, Château Thierry from 21 July-17 September 1918 when he took no account of his own safety and was exposed many times to enemy fire. On 17 September, his twenty-fourth birthday, acting as Forward Observer he was killed by an enemy shell whilst leading his men.

N.B. By continuing along the track one would reach the dramatic statue of WW2 pilot Capt Astier and it would be possible to complete the circuit by returning to the village on rue Capt Astier.

Return to the village and back to Thiaucourt to rejoin the main itinerary.

Continue out of the village to the American Military cemetery on the left. Stop.

• American St Mihiel Cemetery, Thiaucourt/16.5 miles/30 minutes/ Map 12/15

Like all American cemeteries in Europe this one has a resident English-speaking Superintendent who has an office in the cemetery and there is a comfortable visitors' room, with leaflets about the cemetery, the cemetery registers, visitors' book and toilets.

Poilu and Doughboy Memorial, Thiaucourt.

Boulder Monument of the US 2nd Division, Zammes.

Personal Tribute on Headstone, German Cemetery, Thiaucourt.

Monument to Capt Cunningham in the woods near Jaulny.

Across the road is the Superintendent's house which was the official summer residence of Gen Pershing when he was President of the ABMC.

Each one of the 4,153 soldiers buried here has a white Italian marble headstone – either a Latin cross or a Jewish Star of David. Among them, picked out in gold, is the **Medal of Honour** winner, **2nd Lt Wickersham J. Hunter** of the 353rd Inf, 89th Div. On 12 September 1918 near Limey (qv) Hunter was severely wounded in four places by the burst of an HE shell as he advanced with his platoon. Before receiving any aid himself he dressed the wounds of his orderly and then, although weakened from loss of blood and with his right arm disabled, led a further advance and continued firing his revolver with his left hand until he fell and died from his wounds. Also buried here is **Capt Oliver Cunningham** (qv).

In the centre of the cemetery is a large sundial in the form of an eagle. At the end of the north-west axis from the eagle is a sculpture by Paul Manship showing a typical young American officer in field uniform. This was funded by Capt Cunningham's mother (qv). The main architectural feature of the cemetery, designed by Thomas H. Ellet, of New York, is the Memorial building marked by two flags at the far end of the main avenue. On the left within the peristyle is a chapel with altar and beautiful mosaic walls featuring the national colours of America and France and the Angel of Victory, with Doves of Peace. To the right, through bronze doors with striking 'Doughboy's head' handles, is a Chapel with a magnificent coloured marble wall map illustrating the St Mihiel campaign. The scale of the map is 1:100,000. The cemetery is marked upon it and you can readily follow the route you have driven and also the route you have yet to drive. On the end walls, carved in black marble panels are the names of those soldiers missing with no known grave. Beyond the building, Montsec is visible on a clear day. **Open:** 0900-1700. Tel: + (0)3 83 80 01 01.

Continue past the cemetery to the left junction in Beney-en-Woevre.
This area was captured by the 89th Division on the first day.

Doughboy's head handle on the chapel.

The great Seal, gateway to US St Mihiel Cemetery.

*Long Extra Visits to Memorial to 'Big Red 1' (Map 12/16) &
Statue to Moses Taylor, Vigneulles (Map 12/17); Hattonchâtel –
Belle Skinner Memorials & Château (Map 12/18); 9th Bav Mon
(Map 12/19); Alain-Fournier Memorials & Grave, Tranchée de
Calonne (Map 12/20/21), 54th RI Mem (Map 12/22); St Rémy
Cemetery (Map 12/23); Le Trottoir French National Cemetery
(Map 12/24); Historic Site & Memorials, Les Eparges (Map 12/25);
Kronprinz Bunker (Map 12/26).*
*Round trip: 42.5 miles. Approximate time: 2 hours (add up to 2
hours if you follow the walking paths at Les Eparges).*

> *Continue straight on to the crossroads at St Benoit-en-Woevre. Turn left signed
> Bar le Duc/St Mihiel on the D901. Continue to the next roundabout. Cross the
> roundabout and on the far side is the monument. Pull in on the right beside it.*

Memorial to the US 1st Division ('Big Red 1') which is similar to those at Cantigny
on the Somme and at St Juvin – all were sculpted by Jo Davidson of Paris in 1919. It
bears the names of the kia of the St Mihiel Sector and the mia of the Battle of St Mihiel
of 12-13 September 1918 when attacking from Seicheprey. The 1st Division entered
Vigneulles early on the morning of 13 September, joining the 26th Division and
cutting off the Salient. They suffered ninety-eight killed, 489 wounded and missing.
It bears the message, 'The Commander in Chief has noted in this Division a special
pride of service and a high state of morale never broken by hardship nor battle'.

> *Turn round and turn left at the roundabout. Continue on the D908 into
> Vigneulles-les-Hattonchâtel and stop opposite the Town Hall by the local War
> Memorial.*

On the rear of the impressive Memorial is the **Statue of a Doughboy** with the
inscription '*A la mémoire d'un jeune américain mort pour la France*' (In memory of a
young American who died for France). A Plaque below records that he was **Moses
Taylor Jr**, 9th Inf, 2nd Div, born 8 June 1897, died from wounds received in action
24 March 1918. Lt Taylor is buried in the Meuse-Argonne American Cemetery
(qv). The Plaque bears the star insignia of the Division. Moses's father, together
with a Miss Bishop, paid for the Monument to his son, killed near Vigneulles. It
was unveiled after the celebratory events at Hattonchâtel (qv), when the entire
distinguished assembly trooped down the hill and the new bell rang out the peals
of the Angelus. In the square around it the number of trees corresponds with the
number of local men killed in the war. The village was liberated by the 26th
Division and amongst its prisoners was an entire regimental band.

> *Continue 100m and turn right, signed Hattonchâtel on the D179. Drive to the
> village at the top.*

In springtime the hill is covered with delicate white blossom and is an absolute
picture.

> *Stop by the Mairie and School on the right.*

Mairie and School/Belle Skinner Memorials/Château/Fountain.
Hattonchâtel is a charming village, with a timeless medieval feeling to it. Its name
came from Hatton, the ninth century Bishop of Verdun who built the castle here.

Long Extra Visit continued

The church contained the earliest work attributed to Ligier Richier (qv) – a magnificent altar screen. This was removed by the Germans during their occupation but later restored. For centuries the *château-fort* dominated the Valley of the Woevre. Several of the old buildings that survived the war, such as the fifteenth century *Maison des Arcades*, are listed *Monuments Historiques*. The *Mairie* and School were destroyed and the American benefactor, Miss Belle Skinner of Holyoke, Mass, paid for their rebuilding, including a library and a cinema, in an attractive, arcaded style.

Belle was born to a wealthy family of English extraction in Skinnerville, Mass, USA. A lively, well-educated woman (unusually for a girl of her generation she was educated at Vassar where today there is a Concert Hall named after her) she espoused the feminine cause, becoming Director of the International Federation of University Women, was the author of many books and travelled extensively in Europe before the war, visiting Hattonchâtel which made a lasting impression on her. In 1918 she travelled again to her beloved France and looked at the ruins of Hattonchâtel, then in its fourth year in German hands, through field glasses from the safety of the French lines. The Curé had led his flock to safety as the enemy approached in September 1914, leaving behind their homes and all their possessions. In September 1918 Miss Skinner's compatriots drove the Germans out of the St Mihiel Salient, several citizens of Holyoke (the town to which her father moved the family and in which today the old family home is a museum) being killed in the assault. She immediately offered her assistance to the French Government to help the scattered French population return to their devastated homes and begin to rebuild them. She was appointed President of the Committee for *Villages Libérés*. In 1919 she returned to Hattonchâtel and, appalled by the wreckage, decided to 'adopt' and help to rebuild it. As well as the school/townhall complex, Miss Skinner built a dispensary at the foot of the hill with a visiting French nurse. It was later incorporated into the English Hospital and Miss Skinner funded a complete wing. Modern farm machinery was acquired and new stock brought in from Normandy so that agriculture was soon thriving again.

Under the archway to the left is a Plaque to Miss Skinner and the inscription describes how the building was inaugurated in the presence of President Raymond Poincaré and the representative of the American Ambassador on 13 September 1923, the anniversary of the village's liberation in 1918 by French and American troops. Another Plaque refers to Miss Skinner as 'the sweet godmother' and is in gratitude to her magnificent generosity (in 1919 she had been awarded the Gold Medal of *Reconnaissance Française* and in 1920 the *Légion d'Honneur*). On the right is a bronze *bas-relief* of Belle Skinner, also dated 13 September 1923. It was a joyous day for the village and a new bell, christened 'Sarah Isabelle' rang out to replace the old one stolen by the Germans for its bronze.

Note that the school section of the building is now a private house and in the rear is a permanent exhibition of the paintings of the talented artist, Louise Cotton, whose family donated her works. At the rear of the building is a terrace which on a clear day gives superb views to Montsec and the Lac de Madine.

Wiggle round the main street of the village to the Château.

Monument to the 'Big Red 1' near Vigneulles.

Statue of Moses Taylor, 9th Inf, 2nd US Div, Vigneulles.

German Monument to 9th Bav Engineers, Tranchée de la Calonne.

Belle Skinner Plaque, Hattonchâtel.

Long Extra Visit continued

Château de Hattonchâtel

After the war Belle Skinner bought the ruins of the ancient Château and then made it her home. On the right of the entrance grille is a Plaque to Miss Skinner who died in Paris on 8 April 1928. Her brother William gave the Château to the Ecclesiastic Syndicate of Verdun on 7 September 1933. It is now privately owned but guided visits are available on Saturdays and Sundays, 1030-1130 and 1430-1730. Fee payable. Apply to the guardian at the Guard House.

Return following the one-way system and take the DSt 3i signed to Les Eparges out of the village.

On the right is the old **Fountain with a Plaque to Miss Skinner**, inaugurated on 13 September 1920. The installation of a complete water system was one of her most practical actions. On returning to their ruined homes the women of the village had to carry their washing down to the little pond at the foot of the hill and toil back up with it. Once the fountain was installed an American petrol engine hoisted water from a purified spring into a new reservoir and the women were once again able to use the historic Gothic lavoir in the centre of the village to do their washing.

Belle Skinner's water fountain.

Continue to the junction with the DSt3A.

On the left is a **German Memorial**. The difficult to decipher worn insciption appears to be to Josef Ahor?, Karl Kreichauf and Georg Kreichauf of the 9th Bav Engineers, 21 September 1914, Vieville.

Carry straight on on what is now the DSt3A signed to Verdun.

The road then becomes the famous **Tranchée de Calonne**. The name actually came from a road dug out from the hill which enabled M. de Calonne, Louis XVI's Minister of Finance, to reach his Château at the foot of the Meuse heights, which was destroyed during the Revolution. He planted rosebushes all along the

Long Extra Visit continued

road and during WW1, when the road did indeed become a 'trench', wild roses bloomed along its length. The woods to right and left were riddled with French and German trenches, command and observation posts, shelters and dugouts, ambulance stations and barbed wire. Their remains can still be seen today.

Continue over the D101 and the D154 to the sign to Fosse d'Alain-Fournier to the right and stop in the parking area. Follow the signs into the woods on the right.

It is an approx 1km round trip walk to the Memorial through beautiful woods, carpeted with celandine in springtime.

Continue to the clearing in the woods.

Memorials to Alain-Fournier and Companions. In the centre of the glade is a large glass pyramid under which is an artificial flower wreath and twenty-one named stones, including one to Alain-Fournier. It was unveiled on 27 September 1993. To the left is a stone memorial with a stylised flame beneath which is a *képi* and a stone effigy of Fournier's famous book, *Le Grand Meaulnes.* Around the memorials are **Information Panels** (including extracts from the book *Les Grandes Enigmes* and local newspaper articles) telling the story of Alain-Fournier and his twenty companions of the 288th RI who disappeared on 22 September 1914.

Henri-Alban Fournier ('Alain' was his pen name) was an accomplished poet and author. Born in 1886 he joined the army in 1907 and left as a Lieutenant in 1908. The following year he tutored T.S. Eliot in French and later becames friends with Péguy (qv). In 1913 his novel *Le Grand Meaulnes* was published and became an immediate success. Today it is a cult work in France; for instance when the new French Minister of Education, François Fillon, was appointed in 2004 he chose to be interviewed by *Le Figaro* in the school which was the setting for *Le Grand Meaulnes,* and there is an Association des Amis d'Alain-Fournier. Tel: +(0)2 48 63 03 07. When the country mobilised on 1 August 1914 he immediately rejoined his regiment, the 288th RI, seeing action around Verdun. On 22 September 1914 while fighting in the Tranchée de Calonne Fournier and some of his men disappeared. Jacques Rivier, his brother-in-law, spent many years searching for his body but it was not until the 1990s, following research in German archives, that a shallow ditch containing his and other bodies was found. There were three officers including Fournier, and fifteen soldiers. All have been re-interred in St Rémy cemetery, visited later. There have been suggestions that in the fighting Fournier and his men fired upon a German ambulance and that when captured they were shot as reprisals.

Return to the main road and turn right. Continue to the next crossroads with the C5. On the right is

Memorial Cross to Alain-Fournier and his men who disappeared in this sector on 22 September 1914. A plaque records that they were found on 2 May 1991, one kilometre from this Monument.

Continue straight on to the next crossroads. On the right is

A stone **Memorial to the 54th RI,** 22 Sept 1914-2 Aug 1915.

Turn right on the D113 signed to St Rémy and Tombes d'Alain-Fournier/Site des Eparges and follow the winding road down into the valley. At the cross roads at St Rémy-la-Calonne turn right following Fournier signs and right again to the

Long Extra Visit continued

French National Cemetery.
French National Cemetery of St Rémy-la-Calonne. This simple but beautiful cemetery on the hillside now contains the bodies of Alain-Fournier and the twenty other men of 288th RI, reburied here after they were found in 1991 (qv). They lie under new white crosses to the right, the three officers at the end of the row with Capt Boubée de Gramont on the extreme right. An **Information Panel** tells the story and gives information about the Cemetery. In the centre is a large stone and **Plaque to Cpl Rene Worms** of the 54th RI. At the top, below the proudly flying *Tricolore*, is an ossuary containing 166 bodies from several infantry regiments, including Moroccan and Senegalese.
Continue to the small church.
This will probably be locked but even from the exterior a SGW to Lucien Hube of the 67th RI can be seen (the first on the right hand wall). During the war a concrete German shelter stood on the ruins of the church in which was a heavy gun which fired on Les Eparges.
Below St Rémy is the village of Dommartin-la-Montagne. Between the two villages is the Bois de Bouchot. In March 1915 the battlefront crossed the Calonne Trench and through this wood when both sides bombarded the other and there were constant attacks and counter-attacks. The French Marines brought up their 5.5in naval guns with a range of 13,000 yards and hammered the German lines over the hill of Les Eparges. On 20 April the Germans launched a massive attack gaining ground until 26 April when two battalions of Chasseurs arrived to reinforce the Marines. The Germans reformed and attacked again on 5 May but the Moroccan Bde joined the fray and all the ground lost to the Germans on 24 April was retaken.
Turn round and return to the crossroads. Continue straight over on the D154.
On the right is
A **Demarcation Stone** in very good condition marking the front line of 18 July 1918.
Continue into the village of Les Eparges.
The ancient village of Les Eparges, which traces its history back to the early Middle Ages, had a population of some 320 in 1914. On 9 September 1914 it was occupied by the Germans as their invading tide swept over the Plain of Woevres. On 21 September they were forced to evacuate the valley but clung on to their vantage points on the hill of Les Eparges. There followed the desperate struggle for domination of the heights, culminating in the battles of April 1915.
Turn right at the junction on the D203 signed Site des Eparges. Continue uphill to the National Cemetery.
French National Cemetery du Trottoir. This contains 2,960 burials and eighty-five Unknown in the Ossuary. There is an **Information Panel**.
N.B. The visit to the important site of Les Eparges can be completed in forty-five minutes if you confine yourself to driving to the three main memorials just off the metalled road. Throughout the area are green signs to other sites of interest, with their distance in metres so that you can gauge the time it will take to complete them. The well-defined walking paths that lead to them are marked by a large

Memorials to the writer Alain-Fournier and his companions of the 223rd/288th RI, who disappeared here on 22 September 1914.

Dramatic Monument to the 106th and 132nd RIs, Les Eparges.

Long Extra Visit continued

green spot. It could be very dangerous to deviate from the marked paths which lead to some remarkable sites through well-preserved German trenches, interspersed with the remains of concrete emplacements and the most enormous mine craters. It is highly recommended to take at least one of them. The effort is rewarded by seeing some extraordinary original WW1 vestiges. The full range of the walking paths may be obtained from the Tourist Office at Verdun (qv) where you can also book a guide for a detailed visit.

The area is completely wooded. After WW1, as part of the Germans' reparation, Bavarian fir trees were planted to cover the ravages of war in what was declared a *Zone Rouge* – deemed too dangerous to clear. They thrived in the thick clay and can still be seen strongly growing today. After WW2 a different type of fir was planted which was not suited to the soil and which has recently fallen prey to a particularly vicious grub which has killed many of them. The great storm of 1999 also ravaged the weaker trees and in 2004 the area adjoining the central road resembled a recent battlefield, with (in the winter and spring) shell holes filled with water and broken trees lying all around. Deeper into the woods the healthy fir trees are interspersed with gloriously flowering wild cherry trees, the ground carpeted with celandine, cowslips and violets. On a fine day walking through them is an unexpectedly delightful, as well as a sad, experience when one contemplates the terrible loss of life that took place here.

Continue uphill to the large parking area and picnic site on the right. Ahead are steep steps leading to

Monument to the 106th and 132nd RI, September 1914 – April 1915. This powerful and disquieting Memorial shows a death mask looking heavenwards on a rough pyramid on which there are skeletal beseeching hands and skulls and the words, *JE CROIS* (I BELIEVE). It was designed by Real del Sarte (qv) and Georges Ricome in 1935. Below it is a *bas-relief* group of a dead soldier cradled by a helmeted female figure, in the style of a Piéta. Beside it are signs to various sites and monuments via walking trails.

Continue to the left on the D230A to the large monument on the left.

Engineers' Monument. The seven pillars which form the Monument represent the seven branches of the Corps whose work was so important and whose losses were so heavy at Les Eparges.

At this point the French (behind the Memorial) and the German (in front of it) trenches were only fifty metres apart. In July 1914 the crest of the hill was occupied by crack French forces who were quickly withdrawn to defend Paris in the first anxious days of the First Battle of the Marne, thus leaving the top virtually undefended. The Germans took it on 21 September and dug in in force, reinforcing their trenchlines, dugouts and command posts with incredible speed and efficiency with thousands of tons of concrete. One of their main concrete factories was in the Camp Maguerre, near Loison (fourteen miles to the north-east of Verdun) of which there are still some remains to be seen. The experimental works tested different types of moulds in the shape of planks, logs and sheet metal. Narrow-gauge rail lines led to and from the factory. Each blockhouse was

Long Extra Visit continued

constructed differently to test for resistance against explosives. An inscription on one of them reads *ERBAUT VON DER BERAUNTER LEITUNG D. HAUPTM MARGUERRE* – Built by the concrete factory under the direction of Capt Marguerre, a member of the Prussian Royal Engineers. Marguerre became a spy in WW2, reputedly working for Admiral Canaris and then for the Russians.

N.B. By walking to the first turning to the right and following the walking path signs to *Monument du Coq* a marvellous tour covering many unique vestiges of the war can be taken. Allow a good hour if you do. At the top of the steps a huge **mine crater** is reached. Beyond it is the large **Monument** surmounted by a **French Cockerel**, sculpted by Lefebvre-Klein, with German shells, fenced by a chain of grenades. It lists the French and American Divisions which fought in the area, and reminds one of the 11,000 unknown French casualties who fell in a ten mile radius from here. On one side is inscribed Order No 68 of the General of the Army Corps which translates: 'During 5 months with a courage and tenacity the likes of which no previous war had furnished an example, the troops of the 12th Inf Div pursued the

The Cockerel Monument to 12th Division, Les Eparges.

siege of the formidable fortress that our enemies established on the heights of Les Eparges, in spite of shells, machine-gun fire and bombs. These heroic troops, each day liberating a few metres of soil which they paid for with their blood, have engraved, step by step the steep slopes of the height. Supported by an admirable artillery whose vigilance was constant they repelled 18 counter-attacks, inflicting on the enemy such bloody losses that they had to be completely withdrawn. Yesterday, at last, definitive success crowned their efforts. Battling at Les Eparges you have written a glorious page in history. France thanks you.'

The conditions here were horrendous. The scene in a field dressing station was described by Paul Voivenel, a French medic, 'Wounded men were everywhere. The ground was covered with sticky red pieces of clothing. The smell of blood was sickening... Our poverty-stricken, mud soaked clientele poured in, crowded around us. There was scarcely room for the stretchers to pass. We trod on a reddish-brown mixture of saliva, water, blood and cotton wool thrown to the ground.'

By turning right along the path behind the Monument another huge **crater** is reached, on the side of which are the remains of a **German OP**, subject to years of vandalism, as are so many of the fortified German positions, mainly for their metal reinforcements. There are the incredible number of thirty-four craters from French mining activity on the site.

From the Cockerel Monument the path leads downhill through the woods via a series of steps, to each side of which are many traces of trenchlines, shell-holes and fortified positions, to a great bunker on three floors. This was a **German Medical Facility** or CCS where elemental first aid was administered – serious cases were sent on to the large German Hospital over the valley on the opposite spur of the hill. It was constructed during the winter of 1914-1915 with a metal roof and access to the first or third floors above and below this level. It went deep in the hillside and contained many bunks. The metal doors and windows were removed after the war for their scrap value. Like all the deep bunkers and tunnels on the hillside entrances to dangerous rooms and tunnels have long been filled in by the French Army.

Standing with one's back to the bunker the village ahead is Combres-sous-les-Côtes and there is a superb view over the pleasant valley of the Woevre, planted with fruit trees and vines (the area is famous for its sparkling wine as the Germans quickly found in 1914). In the far distance was the 1914 German border over which the enemy poured in September 1914.

The path then skirts the valley, past a welcome seat and a fortified position that was the **German Telephone Post** and descends to a wide foresters' track, turns left and passes a large concrete structure. This was the entrance to the mile-long tunnel that ran thirty metres down and in which there was a narrow gauge railway. This has been filled in by the Army for safety. By turning round and continuing to a sharp turn to the right uphill, the extremely steep path eventually comes out behind the Point X Memorial.

Long Extra Visit continued

Continue along the D203A to a large crater on the right and another on the left.
On the left is a board with a sketch map showing the French and German trenches and mine craters, September-October 1915.

Continue, passing more craters, to the parking area. Stop and walk to the memorial ahead.
You will be walking along the Avénue de la Comtesse de Cugnac. The Comtesse's fiancé was killed at les Eparges and she donated the money to plant a commemorative avenue of trees here to him. Again to right (German) and left (French) there are craters, trench lines and concreted shelters. The shallow and fragile French lines were quickly over-run by the Germans in September 1914 and fortified by them. They were then blown by French mines.

To the left of the main monument is a **Memorial** to the **302nd RI,** 20 September 1914-21 March 1915. The large monument is at the site known as **Point X** (the French used the end of the alphabet to identify particular sites, e.g. Points W, Y and Z). Beside it is an **Information Panel** with photocopies of the trenchlines and craters. The **Monument is dedicated to Les Eparges 1914-1918** and bears several individual plaques. It is maintained by *Souvenir Français*. On the rear is a fine *bas-relief* of a young officer leading his men into battle. Note that they had no

*German Medical Facility,
Les Eparges.*

*US Monument,
Montsec.*

*Monument to the
Fallen, Point X, Les
Eparges.*

Long Extra Visit continued

protective steel helmets or heavy boots. In 1957 a *table d'orientation* was erected behind the monument. It overlooks the Woevre Plain towards Fresnes-en-Woevre and its distinctive large silo. On the far horizon is the River Meuse.

Drive back past the Demarcation Stone on the D154 and continue towards St Rémy, turn left on the D113 towards Combres and cross the Longueau again.

On the right you will pass a **WW2 Memorial**.

Continue past the picnic site and stop on the left just past the large bunker to the left.

Abri du Kronprinz

The façade visible today, which contains the guard room, fronted a huge complex that went far into the hillside. The numerous rooms contained command posts and stores and connected with communication tunnels. There was a narrow gauge railway leading into the complex and the roof was reinforced with steel. It is said that the ceiling from the Ligier Richier House in St Mihiel (qv) was taken to embellish the officers' quarters here. *Les Amis du Saillant de St Mihiel et de la Région* have cleaned up the long-neglected bunker, opening up some of the entrances and reinforcing them. Several large command bunkers in the area bear the name 'Kronprinz of Bavaria' (not to be confused with the Crown Prince of Germany, the son of Kaiser Wilhelm and the heir to the throne) without much concrete evidence that he actually occupied them for any length of time. He did technically command the German forces that attacked Gen Sarrail's 3rd Army on the Heights of the Meuse on 7 September 1914.

Walk up the steps beside the bunker. They lead to

Communication/Control Bunker.

The path beside the bunker leads on up to the Monument du Coq (qv) and eventually to the Point X Monument (qv).

Return to the junction in Beney-en-Woevre.

Turn left on to the D904, follow signs into Essey and turn right into the square.

Essey Village. Off the main square to the right is a road named after Col Driant (qv). The village is in the centre of what was the area for the 42nd (Rainbow) Division. One of the Division's two brigades, the 84th, was commanded by Brig Gen Douglas MacArthur. He went over the top with his men and in or around this village he met Maj George Patton. Both remained upright as if daring the other to acknowledge the danger of German artillery fire and MacArthur later claimed that Patton did flinch briefly and that he said to him, 'Don't worry Major, you never hear the one that gets you.' MacArthur's front line leadership here earned him his fifth silver star for gallantry in action.

Continue on to the D28, rue du 12 Septembre, signed to Montsec. Turn right on the D119 and continue to Richécourt (25.5 miles).

Richécourt has a magnificent **Local War Memorial** (Map 12/27) with the Cross of Lorraine, wounded *Poilu* in *bas-relief* and the victims year by year.

Continue on the D119, over the Rupert de Mad stream and in the village of Montsec follow signs to the left to Butte de Montsec on the D12. Continue uphill to the parking area.

• *Montsec American Memorial/28.9 miles/20 minutes/Map 12/28*

This hill offers visibility over much of the Salient and observers on it directed German artillery fire. The American fire plan included a great deal of smoke around Montsec in order to blind the enemy. The hill was honeycombed with tunnels and protected by belts of barbed wire. Traces of the trench systems still remain around the Memorial.

The Monument, which commemorates the capture of the St Mihiel Salient and other American operations, is a circular colonnade – a classical design like the Jefferson Memorial in Washington and similar to the smaller WW1 Memorial in Atlantic City. It was inaugurated in September 1931, when many relatives travelled from the United States. Within the circle, set on a stone plinth, is a bronze relief map laid out to match the ground and three small Sèvres porcelain illustrative plates. It is possible, on a clear day, to match the map to the view, and set into the floor below the columns are the points of the compass. Carved in and around the Memorial are the names of the French and American units that took part in the operation, the names of villages liberated by the Americans, battle honours and notices in French and English, including one that explains how the Memorial was damaged (by American Artillery) on 2 September 1944.

In good visibility the American Cemetery that you visited earlier may be seen across the large Lac de Madine to the north-east, though, because of the trees on the hill, you may need to stand in the car park to see it. The Lake was merely a small pool during the war and did not impede the American advance. It was enlarged after the war to supply water to Metz and as a pleasure lake. In the far distance to the south and swinging westwards are the heights of the Meuse. St. Mihiel is due west of here. The attack of 12 September 1918 came broadly from the south, i.e. the opposite direction to Lake Madine whose bulk is to the north.

George Patton commanded the American-manned tanks used in the operation and twenty-six years later (but for nine days) as Commander of the liberating 3rd Army in 1944, he came back. As always he was chafing at what he saw as delays in advancing.

'Montsec has a huge monument to our dead,' he wrote. 'I could not help but think that our delay in pushing forward would probably result in the erection of many other such monuments'. There was little delay in 1918. The Americans had a precise task at St Mihiel. Their next offensive (the Meuse-Argonne) was almost upon them and they had precious little time to prepare for it.

Drive back to the bottom of Montsec and turn sharp right onto the D12.

Watch out for a large **Bunker** on the right in the middle of a field (30.7 miles).

Continue via Loupmont to Apremont on the D12.

• *Apremont Holyoke Memorial Fountain/34.2 miles/10 minutes/Map 12/29*

Just short of the church on the right is a Memorial Fountain, housed in a large red brick building, to those Americans who fell here, donated by Holyoke, Massachusetts.

Continue past the church.

The road to the right is rue Belle Skinner (qv).

Continue uphill on the D907 in the direction of St Mihiel.

About 0.5km from Apremont, in a quarry after a bend on the left, the Germans carved out a huge village with rooms furnished from local houses, complete with carved woodwork and carpets, an Officers' Mess and beer shop. There were terraces and flowering plants and a concrete staircase leading to a concrete trench which dominated the position in the infamous Bois Brûlé (qv) at the edge of the Forest of Apremont and overlooking the village. Remnants of this sophisticated structure can still be made out on the hillside.

Continue some half a mile through the woods, which in springtime are carpeted with white celandine, to a sign to the left to Croix des Redoutes and Bois Brûlé. Turn and follow the path to a large parking area with a picnic area nearby and stop.

• Croix des Redoutes, Bois Brûlé/35.3 miles/45 minutes/Map 12/30

This is **'Plate-forme No 3'** on the ANSM (qv) route. In the car park are **Information Panels** (in English, French and German) with photos and sketch maps which describe 'The Beginnings of the Salient', 'The action in the Bois Brûlé and round the Croix des Redoutes', the *Sentiers de Découverte* (short walking routes round each 'Plate-forme', marked with a green logo and white signs) and *Sentiers de Randonné* (walking paths which link all four 'Plate-formes' signed with a yellow and orange logo with barbed wire). A sign post bears the logos of the Dumez Construction Coy, who helped with the refurbishment of the site, and of *Souvenir Français*, both inspired by M Norbert Kugel (qv), President of the *Association Nationale le Saillant de St Mihiel* (ANSM).

Walk up the steps to the right.

Here there is a splendid coloured Panorama/Table d'Orientation (made by the National Forestry Office) overlooking the valley of the Meuse to the Heights beyond, ranging from the Tranchée de la Soif to Toul on the Moselle at the left extremity.

Walk along the path to the right following Sentier de Découverte signs which will bring you back to the car park.

N.B. You are strongly advised to keep to the marked *sentiers*. The uncleared woods and trench lines are full of unexploded *matériel*, crumbling saps, rusty barbed wire and other dangers. You will be walking through the most amazing system of first line German fortified trenches, shelters with multiple entrances, saps, firesteps and ammunition store holes constructed by the Germans from 1914 onwards. The trench line leads to the Croix des Redoutes. The first construction you encounter is a firing post (which would originally have been covered) over which a sturdy wooden viewing bridge and railings have been erected. The underground shelters were some seven to eight metres deep.

Opposite, just a few metres away, the ANSM has dug out a section of the **French front line trench** recreated complete with fascines and wooden gabions. Around it are remains of barbed wire gathered round their pickets – of the type the French call '*queues de cochon*' (pig tails) which can be silently screwed into the ground like a corkscrew. Note the different construction method and concept of the French and German trenches, the former originally hastily dug, the latter deep and highly reinforced.

Continue a few metres along the path to a small Memorial on the left.

This is to **Sgt Eugène Vintousky** (qv) of the 27th RI, killed 21 December 1914, erected by his family. The fighting for the *Redoutes* (Redoubts) here began in September 1914. The Germans occupied St Mihiel and their supplies came along the road from Apremont that you have just driven. They therefore tried to drive out the French from here. In three months of fighting the Germans advanced 300 metres and 15,000 French and German soldiers died.

The Holyoke Fountain, Apremont.

Memorial to Mayor Otto Staubwasser, Forest of Gobessart.

Panorama of the Heights of the Meuse, Bois Brûlé.

German Command Post, Tranchées des Bavarois.

Continue to the large Memorial Cross in the clearing.

This is the famous **Croix des Redoutes**, recently renovated by the ANSM, erected by surviving veterans, in affectionate memory of their martyr comrades, commemorating the appalling carnage that took place in the area, known as the *'Patte d'Oie'* (goose foot) in January – April 1915. When the veterans, led by l'Abbé Marquet, decided to erect it in 1925 they had to force their way through the broken tree stumps, the barbed wire and the almost impenetrable thicket that had grown up to find the site of their front line. It was then necessary to go 700 metres distant, to Hill 360, to find enough wood to make it, so devastating was the destruction of the forest. The *'Redoutes'* of the name were two small forts or bastions constructed long before the war and which offered little resistance to the assaulting Germans. By November 1914 they had been totally reduced by enemy shells. An officer of the 27th RI wrote that 'there were corpses everywhere, wounded French and Germans lie on the barbed wire for days without us being able to release them, so atrocious are the combats. The fierce German artillery bombardment comes from two great vantage points – Montsec and the Fort of the Camp des Romains and will soon oblige us to abandon this abominable and indefensible sector'. Broadly the viewpoint faces south. Montsec is to the north-east and the Camp des Romains site (visited later) is due west. On 14 December one battalion lost two-thirds of its strength in a matter of minutes. Participants blamed the carnage on poor intelligence as to the strength of the enemy and the insistence on the 'cursed' policy of *'attaque à l'outrance'* (all-out attack).

Below the cross is a **Plaque** to the legendary Adjutant (a French warrant officer rank) **Jacques Pericard** of the 95th RI whose immortal rallying cry **Debout les Morts!** has gone into French history. It was shouted to his dead, dying and wounded companions on 8 April 1915 in the midst of a violent enemy attack. Pericard, who was a journalist before he joined up, went on to be promoted Lieutenant and in 1942 was arrested at Lyons by the Germans. Trying to escape by bicycle he was shot twice in the back. The **Plaque** is also to **Cpl Joseph Berthelon**, 7 April 1915, age 32.

The cross was recently renovated by the Dumetz company and members of the ANSM. The 95th continued to fight in the sector despite their dreadful losses and on 24 May the news that Italy had declared war on Austria was greeted with a hearty rendition of *La Marseillaise!*

Follow the Sentier de Découverte signs back to the car park, return to the main road and turn left and continue to a Memorial on the right.

It is inscribed **17 June 1940** and the casualty lists of the 155th RI, 4th Mitrailleurs, 146th RI and some Unknowns.

Turn right here into the Fôret de Gobessart along a metalled road following signs to Hôpital Allemand (German Hospital). The next sign, some 0.3 miles along pointing to the right, is easy to miss. Park by the sign and walk into the woods.

• German Hospital, Fôret de Gobessart/36.5 miles/15 minutes/Map 12/31

N.B. The German Hospital, the Maj Staubwasser Monument and the German Cemetery visited later form **ANSM Plate-forme No 5.**

The path leads to an incredible **Bunker**, surrounded by a clearly defined trench system. This was the German Hospital and an **Information Panel** describes how this masonry 'Collecting Station', capable of withstanding shells, was 35m long with one large ward and three smaller rooms. A narrow gauge railway led to it but the wagons that took the wounded to the rear were drawn by horses to minimise the sound. There was an Ambulance Station in the school at Woinville and a Collecting Station in Vigneulles. After the battles of St Mihiel and Bois d'Ailly (where there were Field Hospitals) the casualties were taken to St Mihiel where there were twelve 'Lazarettes' (dressing stations) and thence by train to Germany.

Continue to the next crossroads and turn right. Continue to the next crossroads and park and walk following two signs to Stèle Allemande into the wood.

• *Memorial to Mayor Otto Staubwasser/37.2 miles/15 minutes/Map 12/32*

The Memorial to Maj Staubwasser, Commanding Officer of the 1st Bn, 7th Bavarian Infantry Regiment, who fell leading his battalion in the Bois Jurat, is in the shape of a shell. Staubwasser had just been promoted to Major but his promotion had not become effective before he was killed. His grave in the German Cemetery, visited later, still bears the rank of '*Hauptman*' (Captain). Around this, his original grave, are deep earthworks, trenchlines and shell holes.

Return to the main road and drive straight across following signs to Tranchées des Bavarois et de Roffignac along a metalled road and stop in the large parking area with a nearby picnic area.

•*Tranchées des Bavarois et de Roffignac/38.5 miles/45 minutes/Map 12/33*

This is **ANSM Plate-forme 4** and has the same series of **Information Panels** as Plate-forme No 3 above, including one on Trench Artillery. It is advisable to walk back a short distance and go into the woods following the white *Sentier de Découverte* sign to the German trench system. This includes an impressive German command post bunker with the inscription *In Treue Fest* (In True Solidarity) and *Bay PKomp* (Bavarian Pioneer Company: Pioneer = Engineer).

The French front line trenches here are called 'de Roffignac' as the name was found on a French trench map in the Liouville Fort. The Comte de Roffignac, Capt in the 85th RI, was killed on 5 December 1914 in the Bois de la Louvière, Marbotte. He is buried in the cemetery at Vignot, some eight miles due south of St Mihiel.

Return to the main road and turn left. Continue to the sign to the right to the German Cemetery and turn along the metalled road into the forest to the car park in front of the cemetery.

• *German St Mihiel Cemetery/40.2 miles/15 minutes/Map 12/34*

This interesting cemetery contains a large plot of the familiar stark black crosses but at the top there is a fine nude male statue, *Pickelhaube* under one arm, rifle in the other. This was originally in the German cemetery at Woinville. To the right and left are mass graves containing 2,096 soldiers and beyond them at each side glades with ornately carved stone headstones (probably regimental markers erected during the war) including two Iron Cross winners. In the left-hand glade is a Monument to the Sanitäts KP3, Bayr III AK, 1915 and in the right-hand one a Monument to the fallen heroes of the Maas-Mosel-Wacht. There is a total of 6,046 burials in the cemetery in which the only colour is provided by the tiny flowers in the ground cover which replaces grass. The original headstone of soldiers Goldhan and Junghans was recently found in the forest and transferred to the cemetery. They are actually buried in Block 2, Grave 362.

Return to the main road and turn right. After some 0.2 miles there is
A large **Bunker** by a white post on the left. This is followed on the right by a large Moto-Cross course.

Continue on the D907, past signs to Bois d'Ailly/Tranchée de la Soif to the left, into St Mihiel.

N.B. After entering the town by taking the D901 direction Metz and driving through the forest you will come to a sign to the right to *Monuments Allemands*. It points to two rare **German Memorials,** (Map 12/49) one a battered statue of a lion, the other a large cross with a tombstone behind with difficult to decipher inscriptions to the 3rd Bty 36th Fussart Regt and the 13th Bav Regt, 23 Sept 1915. They are all that remain from what was once a considerable German Cemetery in Mouton Wood which at one time was littered with German graves and shelters. The ANSM has plans to refurbish the lion.

By continuing on the D901 and taking the left turn on the D162 to Lavignéville, then continuing through Lamorville to just before the large silo on the right there is a **Demarcation Stone** on the left.

By continuing to Lacroix-sur-Meuse and taking the D964 direction Verdun the Séré de Rivières **Fort de Troyon** is passed on the right (see Map 3). The fort played a vital role in the First Battle of the Marne and in the formation of the St Mihiel Salient and from 8-14 September 1914 it received 2,800 shells, its 450 defenders, commanded by Capt Heym, repulsing an assault by 10,000 of the enemy, thus blocking the passage to the Meuse and the outflanking of Verdun. At the entrance to the fort is a **Memorial Pyramid** and a small **Memorial to the Defenders of Fort Troyon**.
Open: Easter-30 November pm or by appointment. **Contact:** Assoc Ceux de Troyon, 6 rue de la Mairie, 55300 Troyon. Tel President: + (0)3 29 90 13 06/Office: + (0)3 29 85 89 29. The Association has done much work to rescue the fort from being completely overgrown by vegetation and organises events in it.

Drive into the centre through the large archway in the vast Town Hall complex and stop immediately in the parking area to the right.

• St Mihiel: Liberation Plaque/44.4 miles/5 minutes/Map12/35/RWC

St Mihiel is an historic town full of fascinating ancient buildings, notably the House of Ligier Richier, St Mihiel's most famous son. Born in 1500 he was regarded as one of France's greatest Renaissance sculptors. Examples of his work can still be seen in the St-Etienne and Saint-Michel Churches in St Mihiel and in many other churches in the area. It is said that the coffered ceiling of the house (now privately owned) was taken by the Crown Prince of Bavaria to embellish his huge bunker at Les Eparges (qv) but was later re-installed. Also of interest is the picturesque turn of the century covered market. A curiosity is the row of seven huge coralline rocks known as the Ladies of the Meuse on the approaches to the town on the D964 Verdun road. Three of them feature on the town's coat of arms.

Cross the road to the Tourist Office.
The **Tourist Office** is adjacent to the fine Benedictine Library which holds some 9,000 well-preserved works including some rare sixteenth and seventeenth century editions.

The office has leaflets on the battlefields and walking paths, information about accommodation etc and on request will show a ten minute video made by local school children about the life of the '14-'18 *Poilu* and the vestiges of war in the sector.

Walk back through the archway and into the main entrance to the Town Hall. Note that it will close for lunch.

St Mihiel was captured by the Germans on 24 September 1914 but it was not attacked during the offensives in 1918. The Germans abandoned it and Gen Pershing gave the honour of entering it to the French 26th Division (amongst them the Prime Minister's son, Capt Michel Clemenceau) under Gen de Belenet on 13 September. That evening Generals Pershing and Pétain entered the newly-liberated town after its four years of occupation. Seventy years later on 11 November 1988 a grey marble **70th Anniversary Plaque** was unveiled in the entrance to the Town Hall by the American Ambassador. It reads, 'On 12 Sept 1918 Gen Pershing and his American and French troops undertook the capture of the Salient of St Mihiel'.

Return to your car or make St Mihiel your lunch stop and enjoy some of its historic buildings. Continue and at the cross roads turn left on the D964 signed Neuf Château. Continue uphill to the crest and turn right signed to Bislée on the D171. Stop by the memorials on the left.

• Camp des Romains Memorial & Demarcation Stone/45.7 miles/10 minutes/Map 12/36/37

The Memorial here was removed in 2001 by *Souvenir Français* from within the camp itself, where it had been vandalised, to this more visible site. It describes how the 166th RI and a Battery of the 5th RAP strongly resisted violent bombardments and the assaults of the Bavarian 6th Division but were overwhelmed by the number of their assailants on 23-25 September 1914. Beside it are two explanatory 'lecterns' with photos describing the Fort here and other Séré de Rivières Forts. The Camp des Romains was one of the two forts built on old Roman remains that protected St Mihiel. When the

German Army of Metz crossed the Meuse on 24 September 1914 and occupied St Mihiel, the camp was isolated, with no troops on the plain to defend it. The Germans therefore left it, only bombarding it when entrenched round the town, when they quickly reduced the fort's guns and turrets. The small garrison who resisted heroically was eventually smoked out, the Germans presenting arms to them as a mark of admiration and permitting the officers to keep their swords. The Germans then built their habitual concrete blockhouses around the fort.

The **Demarcation Stone** here is of particular significance as it marks the actual tip of the St Mihiel Salient.

Monument to 166th RI & 5th RAP and Demarcation Stone, Camp des Romains.

Deer in the Bois d'Ailly.

Fortified German dugouts in the Tranchée de la Soif.

Trench of Thirst
Monument.

Turn round, return to the crossroads and turn right on the D964 signed to Neufchâteau, descending the winding road. At the tip of the second hairpin bend turn left on the D171B to Ailly with the meandering branch of the Meuse on the right. Drive to Ailly and take the first left uphill on the Route du Bois d'Ailly. At the junction at the top turn right following signs to Bois d'Ailly and Tranchée de la Soif. Stop in the car park.

• *Bois d'Ailly Memorials and Trench of Thirst/49.2 miles/40 minutes/ Map 12/38*

This is **ANSM Plate-forme No 1.** By looking back from where you have come you can see the river and it was from there that the French 26th Division atttacked the German positions here on 12 September 1918 as part of the American offensive. The Division was part of the II Colonial Corps whose front extended from les Eparges to Seicheprey (see Map 12).

The trench system here is one of the most comprehensive 'real-state' complexes to be found anywhere on the Western front. It was constructed by the Germans (who called it 'the Hell of Ailly Wood') and the detailed earthworks of front-line support and communication trenches are locked together by concrete shelters and command posts and the whole wooded area is peppered by shell holes. In recent times the walk along the trench and bunker line has been made much easier and safer to negotiate and helpful **Information Panels** give the history of this fascinating area. At the beginning of the walk is an **Obelisk** commemorating the achievement of the **French VIII Corps** in taking this position, with a symbolic cemetery in front of it. Some 60,000 French soldiers were lost in the woods of Ailly, of Apremont and le Prêtre in the year of 1915 alone. They were known as 'The Tomb of the 8th Army Corps'. **Information Panels** list a number of walking trails (*Sentiers de Découvertes*) in the area with suggested timings.

'*Maudit soit qui ne maudit pas la guerre*' is the quotation here from Paul Cazin of the 29th RI, Bois d'Ailly 1915 (Cursed be he who does not curse the war). President Poincaré called the action here an, 'extraordinary exploit of a battalion of the 172nd'.
Follow the well-preserved and fascinating trenchline to the monument at the other end. You can then walk back to the car park – allow thirty minutes for the round trip. [Alternatively if you prefer, you can drive directly to the monument.] From the car park drive along the road and turn left. Continue to the monument.

• *Tranchée de la Soif Monument/49.6 miles/5 minutes/Map 12/38*

At the end of the trenchline is another **Memorial to the 172nd and 372nd RI** commemorating the bravery of the small number of French soldiers of the 2nd Bn of the 172nd RI under Chef de Bataillon d'André who on 19 May 1915 were cut off here for three days without food or water and short of ammunition, resisting all enemy attacks [by the Prussians of the 48th RI of von Stülpnagel], and who gave the area its name, 'Trench of Thirst'.
Return to the T junction, turn left and continue down the rough track ahead, navigable by car with care.
Driving down the hill you will now pass a series of monuments (Map 12/39). All have been renovated by *Souvenir Français*. Watch out for deer on this track, especially at dusk. Note in the woods to either side the remains of trenches and shell holes.
After .5 mile from the car park you will pass on the right

Crater from 7 July 1915. (50.1 miles)
The only crater in this sector it was blown under the 10th RI.
Continue and at the junction go straight on to a stone cross on the left.

The following Memorials on the path between the *Tranchée de la Soif* and Marbotte were renovated by *Souvenir Français:*
Monument to the 134th RI. (50.9 miles)
Continue to a large wooden cross on the left

Cross to the 134th RI. (51.0 miles)
This is the Croix St Jean and the wood around is known as the Bois de la Croix St Jean.
Continue to the wooden cross on the left.

Cross to the 171st RI. (51.1 miles)
Continue to the stone monument on the left

Memorial to the 10th and 210th RIs, '14-'18. (51.2 miles)
Raised by subscription by their comrades to those who fell in the Forest of Apremont 1914, 1915, 1916.
Continue to the monument up steps to the right

Memorial to 171st RI 1914-1915. (51.5 miles)
Continue to the stone monument on the left
Memorial to 27th RI 1914, 1915, 1916. (51.6 miles)
From the survivors: this marks the spot where their comrades, who fell in the Forest of Apremont, were first buried.
Continue to the T junction.

N.B. To the right along the road to Mécrin is a **Memorial to the 13th RI** on the left and in Mécrin a **Monument to the 56th RI.**

Ahead is

• *Marbotte Mairie Museum and Documentation Centre/Fort de Liouville/51.8 miles/20 minutes/Map 12/40*

Turn left and park by the Mairie/Museum.
N.B. The time and mileage above refers to a visit to the Museum only. A visit to the Fort would add about ninety minutes or so, depending if there is a military event there. The Museum, Church and Cemetery at Marbotte and the Liouville Fort form **ANSM Plate-forme No 2.**

In the Museum you will find details about the **Fort de Liouville**, a gothic style ogival fort constructed between 1876 and 1878 and directions to it (it is signed from the Museum). Its 700-man garrison had been put on alert on 3 August when war was declared and the fort came under heavy bombardment in the initial German offensive of September 1914. The fort's guns replied with vigour until they were destroyed. The garrison was withdrawn as they had no means of defending themselves. At the beginning of 1915 it was used by observers who operated under enemy fire and the fort retained its strategic importance as an OP over the Woevre Plain and control over the battles of the St Mihiel Salient until the town's liberation in September 1918. After the war it gradually fell into overgrown disuse until recently when enthusiastic volunteers of the ASFL, created in 1989, cleared the site and now hold occasional interesting events there. Of particular interest is its metal Galopin cupola for a 75mm gun, constructed in 1905. The renovation of the fort, which is ongoing, was mainly due to an extraordinary man, Jacky Bruneteau, known as *le Poilu d'Apremont*. Dressed in '14-'18 Horizon Blue he lived rough around the area, finally in the Forts de Paroches and de Liouville and did much to raise awareness of the bitter conditions of the life of the *Poilu* and many of the neglected sites where they fought. For many years he was alone in trying to maintain the forgotten monuments and memorials and sections of the Tranchée de la Soif.
The Museum is quite fascinating and well worth a visit. On two floors, it has a section devoted to Jacky Bruneteau, changing displays of photographs and documents, collections of arms, trench art and other items of the daily life of the *Poilu* and of his commanding officers. Up the stairs is a brilliant display of original regimental standards (reproductions hang in the church visited later) and on the landing some fine modern portraits of *Poilus*.
Liouville Fort: Open: 3rd Sunday of the month April-September 1400-1800.
Museum: Open every day May-October, except Tuesday, 1400-1800 or by appointment.
Contact for both: + (0)3 29 90 70 84. Note that if the Museum is closed you may find M. Bastien, the Mayor and Curator, in the house opposite.
Continue to the church on the left.

Wooden cross to Sgt Rochas, Bois de Mort.

Doughboy and Poilu Lorraine Memorial, Flirey.

SGW Marbotte Church depicting the
immortal cry, Debout les Morts!

102nd Inf. Fountain, Seicheprey.

• *Marbotte Memorial Church/51.9 miles/15 minutes/Map 12/41*

The church, unusually in the area, is always open. Like the *Souvenir Français* Chapel at Rancourt (qv) and St George's Memorial Church in Ypres its walls are covered by personal memorial plaques (one in the porch is to **Sgt Eugène Vintousky** (qv) of the 27th RI, who also has a small Memorial in the Bois Brûlé) and beautifully made reproductions of the standards that hang in the Museum. The **SGWs** here are absolutely glorious. The two each side of the altar were made by Graff and Adam of Bar le Duc. To the left is the *Sacré Coeur*, with a vision of the wounded *Poilu* below. To the right is the Virgin above the scene of the first visit to the grave of a father and a husband. Down the side are windows by the glass maker J. Benoit of Nancy. They depict the stories of Adjutant Pericard's immortal exhortation, *Debout le Morts!* in the Bois Brûlé, of Commandant d'André and his beleagured men at *La Tranchée de la Soif* and of the dead who lay in the church, impregnating the paving stones with their blood, with a plea to pray for their souls. The high altar and the fine Piéta are also dedicated to the 30,000 victims of the fighting in the Bois d'Ailly and the Forest of Apremont. The church is now in perfect condition, thanks to *Souvenir Français* and local benefactor, Dr Jean Cretin, who was recently married in it. During the work forty-eight marble plaques and fifteen monuments were restored.

During the war the eighteenth century church was the only building left standing in Marbotte and it served as a CCS and shelter for the wounded and, increasingly, as a mortuary. On 24 October 1914 the Abbé Bringuer recorded that during his mass the bodies were so tightly packed in the nave that to reach the choir stalls he would have had to climb over the pews. A wounded soldier remembered being frozen with horror at the sight of the blood flowing through the length of the church. It remains the sacred centre of remembrance for those who gave their lives in the sector and a visit to it with some quiet reflection is virtually essential to all pilgrims.

Continue to the cemetery on the right.

• *Apremont-la-Forêt French National Cemetery & VIII Corps Monument, Marbotte/52.0 miles/15 minutes/Map 12/42*

The cemetery contains 2,652 French burials, of which 388 are in the Ossuary. There are four Russian graves. It was created in 1922 with the burials from the battles in the Bois d'Ailly from 1914-1918. Later bodies were exhumed and brought here from other military cemeteries in the area and from the Heights of the Meuse. At the top of the cemetery is the impressive 11m high Monument to the VIII Corps whose base forms an altar on which the commemorative Mass is performed in August of each year. The 1.9m high *Croix de Guerre* weighs five tons. The column bears the names of the surrounding sectors. The Monument was inaugurated on 23 August 1931. Along the Meuse from here to Verdun are ten National Cemeteries and there are nine more within ten kms east of the river.

Continue to Apremont on the D12.

To a first approximation your route now follows the front line of September 1918 with the attack going right to left. From here to Seicheprey the attack was made by the French 39th Division.

Take the D907 to the church in Bouconville (59 miles).

N.B. In front of the church is a **Memorial** (Map 12/43) with a *bas-relief* bust and letters picked out in gold. It is to **Jean Bouin** of the 163rd RI who was killed in Bouconville on 29 September 1914, one of France's most prestigious athletes who competed in the 1912 Olympic Games, when he set the world record for the 10,000m. His French national record for the 5,000m was not beaten until 1948. The monument was erected on 23 April

1966 by athletes from Marseilles where Bouin was born and in whose stadium is a poem in his honour, written in 1923. A Stadium in Paris is named after him.

Continue over the railway and turn left on the D958 through Rambucourt and then Beaumont. Just after the village turn left on the D28E (with a superb view of Montsec to the left) into Seicheprey and stop by the church.

• Fountain to 102nd Inf, 26 US Div & Plaque, Seicheprey/63.8 miles/ 10 minutes/Map 12/44

It was here at Seicheprey that the first real German/American contest took place. Early on the foggy morning of 20 April 1918 over 1,000 Germans launched a major trench raid from the direction of Montsec with the aim of taking a large number of American prisoners and then using them for propaganda purposes. They quickly over-ran the 500 or so Connecticut men of the 26th (Yankee) Division despite stubborn resistance in a hand-to-hand struggle, even the 102nd's cook getting involved with his meat cleaver. However, when the Germans withdrew later in the day, assisted by the activities of small groups of Americans, they left more than 150 dead behind. The 26th lost 1 officer and eighty others killed, three officers and 211 gassed and five officers and 182 others missing.

Some reports claim that the Germans took around 130 prisoners, photographed them with their hands up and dropped the pictures behind French and British lines with the caption, 'Are these the men who are going to save the war for you?' The action was also used for propaganda by the Americans. Back in the USA it was promoted as a first American victory and did much to increase the sales of Liberty Bonds but it was clear that while the Yankees had more than sufficient fighting spirit they were yet lacking in professional fighting skills.

The inscription on the **Fountain** reads, 'To the commune of Seicheprey to commemorate the service of the 102nd Inf, 26 Div recruited from Connecticut. Defenders of Seicheprey April 20 1918 in the firm belief that the friendship of Frenchmen and Americans sealed in this place in battle shall serve the cause of peace among all nations. Presented by the men and women of Connecticut.' It is a message which could well have served as a model in the strained relations between the two nations following the Second Gulf War of 2003. In September the village was in the area of the American 1st Division and the rest of your route is in the American sector.

In the church porch is a **Plaque to commemorate the US troops January-November 1918**. On the village War Memorial are **Plaques to Lucien Petit,** 11 September 1914 and to the **French and American soldiers.**

Return to the main road and turn left. Continue to the crossroads in Flirey.

• Doughboy/Poilu Lorraine Memorial, Flirey/67.8 miles/5 minutes/ Map 12/45

Before entering the village you passed the remnants of railway embankments and it was in these that the American 89th Division had its headquarters. The village was just behind the assault line, the attack going from your right to left. The American 1st Army's achievement was quite remarkable and came from the offensive attitude encouraged by Pershing, the energy and enthusiasm of the soldiers, the thorough and professional staff work and the intricate co-operation of infantry, tanks and aircraft. Some 2,000 Allied aircraft under 'Billy' Mitchell, who was to become well known in the Second World War, provided air support. That Ludendorff had ordered the gradual evacuation of the Salient on 8 September and that some of the heavier German weapons had been withdrawn is, however, relevant. Doubtless the attitude of the German defender was less stubborn since he knew that withdrawal was imminent but as the Memorial, erected by the people of Lorraine shows, the French were in no doubt about the capabilities of their American allies. The Germans also knew that the game was almost over. In their first all-American battle the Doughboys had 'walked over the wire'. By the end of the following day, 13 September, the Americans had pinched off the Salient. Pershing's faith in an all-American army was vindicated. It was his fifty-eighth birthday.

The **Lorraine to the United States Memorial** has statues of French and American soldiers and commemorates the first offensive of the US Army commanded by Gen Pershing and their liberation of numberless communes in Lorraine. On the side of the memorial are listed the American Divisions that fought in the area.

Over the road is the **Memorial to the 163rd RI**, raised by *Anciens Combattants*. A plaque on the *Mairie* proudly, and perhaps defiantly, records that the reconstruction of the village was undertaken without the gifts of foreigners!

Extra Visit to Monument to French Forces, Mine Craters and Cross to Sgt Rochas (Map 12/46); Demarcation Stone (Map 12/47). Round trip: 1.7 miles. Approximate time: 30 minutes.
Turn left and continue to the large memorial on the right.
This large monument (in a fairly poor state of preservation) records the units of the many French forces who during four years of defending La Patrie struggled, held on, suffered and died in this sector in preparation for victory.

A few metres further along the road on the right, beyond a turning into a car park is a well-preserved **Demarcation Stone**. This is another of the three Markers sponsored by Mr Guérard (qv) of Seattle, Washington State in March 1926 and bears the name 'George Washington'. The third, known as the 'Lafayette Marker', was at Pont à Mousson.
Turn into the parking area and stop.
In it are **Information Panels** about the mine warfare in the Flirey Sector.
Walk along the path into the woods.
This leads to an impressive and well-defined Mine Crater.
Continue bearing right to the edge of the wood.
Here there is a large modern wooden **Cross** and **Information Panel** describing how Sgt Joseph Léon Rochas, Volunteer in the 275th RI, MM, was killed on 11 April 1915 leading a charge brandishing his pistol. It was erected in 1997.
Return to the crossroads in Flirey.

Continue on the D958 through Limey to the small obelisk on the left.

• *US 5th Division Obelisk, Limey/71.9 miles/5 minutes/Map 21/48*
The **Memorial** (missing its plaque but bearing the Division's Red Diamond insignia) commemorates their actions in this area.

• *End of St Mihiel Battlefield Tour*
OR *Return to Pont à Mousson for RWC*

THE AMERICAN MEUSE-
ARGONNE OFFENSIVE

26 SEPTEMBER – 20 OCTOBER 1918

'There is a general opinion that the Americans went into the Argonne
and ended the war. This is simply not true.
From September 26 until November 1 the AEF had a very rough time,'
Henry Berry, *Make the Kaiser Dance*

'The only way to begin is to commence.'
George C. Marshall, *Memoirs*

SUMMARY OF THE BATTLE

On 26 September 1918 under the overall strategic direction of Marshal Foch the
Allies began a coordinated pincer attack against the Germans on the Western
Front between Ypres and Verdun. The American 1st Army as the southern pincer
fought along the heights of the Meuse and into the Forest of the Argonne. It was a
bloody affair. By the time of the Armistice the Americans had lost some 117,000 men,
almost 20 per cent more than the Germans.

OPENING MOVES

On 24 June 1918 Pershing, Pétain and Haig met Marshal Foch and he outlined his ideas
for a grand September offensive along the front from Ypres to Verdun. The Americans
were to be in the south around Verdun, the French in the middle and the British opposite
and south of Ypres. Meanwhile, while the great affair was being organised, a number of
smaller offensives were to be launched. One opened on the Somme on 8 August when
the British 4th Army (containing Australians and Canadians) and the French 1st Army
came out of the early morning fog on to von der Marwitz's 2nd Army. By the end of the
day advances of up to eight miles had been made and the Germans had lost some 27,000
men. The official German account described the day as 'the greatest defeat which the
German army has suffered since the beginning of the war'. Ludendorff wrote later,
'August 8th was the blackest day of the German Army in the history of this war.'
    Another of the 'smaller' offensives was the American action at St Mihiel. Foch had
wanted to dissolve the Americans into his master plan but Pershing refused. Foch
backed down but Pershing had to compromise too by agreeing that his 1st Army would
not push on past the base of the Salient and that his objectives would be limited so that
it could then take part in the master plan.
    Meanwhile, following the 'black day', Ludendorff offered the Kaiser his resignation.
It was refused. However, communist agitation and strikes were causing major
difficulties in Germany and by the middle of August the Kaiser and Ludendorff were

MAP 13: THE AMERICAN MEUSE-ARGONNE OFFENSIVE: 26 SEPT-1 OCT 1918

Legend

1. Ste Menéhould Mus
2. Fr Nat Cem, les Islettes
3. CWGC Graves, Lachalade Churchyard
4. Garibaldians Mon, Lachalade
5. 87th RI Mon, Lachalade
6. Crew of 622 Sqn RAF Mem, Haute Chevauchée
7. Fr Nat Cem de la Forestière
8. Argonne Mon, Ossuary, Craters, la Haute Chevauchée
9. Kaiser Tunnel, la Haute Chevauchée
10. Dem Stone, le Four de Paris
11. Abri du Kronprinz
12. Henri Collignon Mon & 'K' Coy Plaque, Butte de Vauquois
13. Vauquois Mus
14. Tunnels, Vauquois
15. Vauquois Mon & Craters
16. Fr Nat Cem, Vauquois
17. Varennes Mus
18. Pennsylvania State Mem, Varennes
19. Missouri State Mem, Cheppy
20. Ger Cem, Cheppy

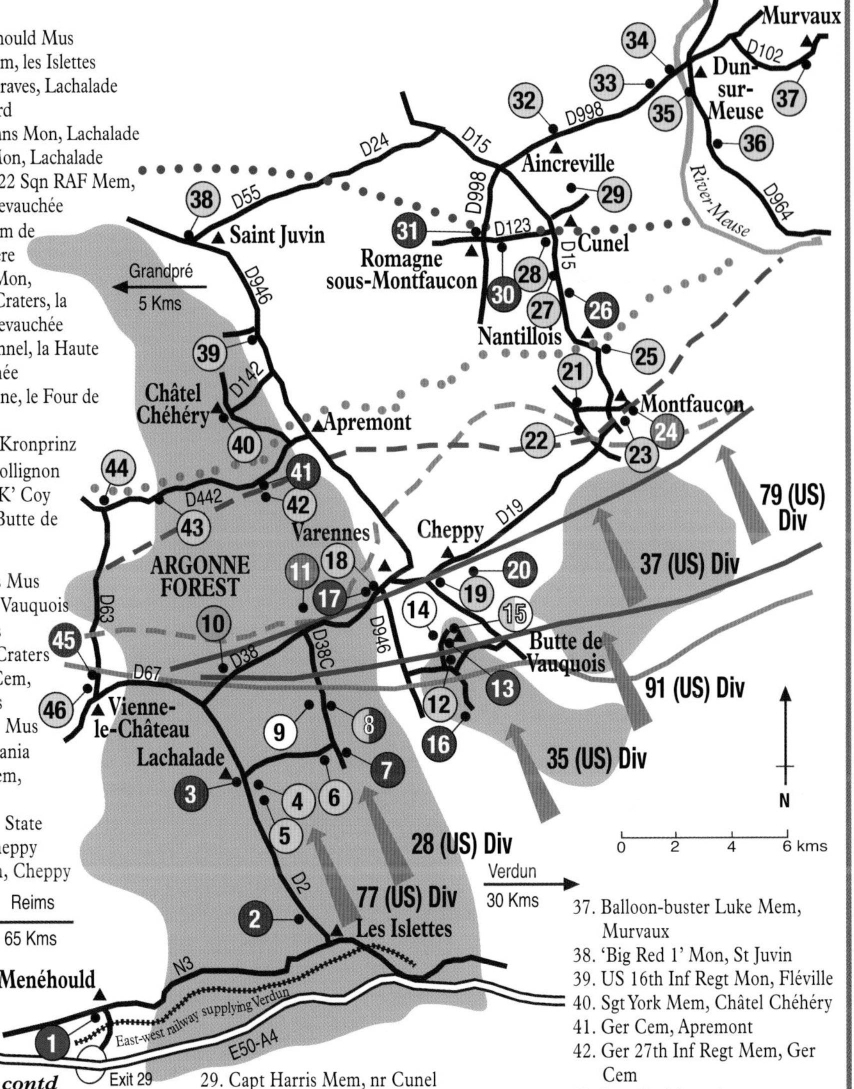

Legend contd

21. 'Sammies' Mem, Montfaucon
22. US 37th Div Almshouse, Montfaucon
23. Montfaucon US Mem
24. Bunkers, Trenches behind Mem
25. Pennsylvania Mem Fountain, Nantillois
26. Ger Cem, Nantillois
27. US 5th Div Obelisk, nr Nantillois
28. Boston Mem Fountain, Cunel
29. Capt Harris Mem, nr Cunel
30. Am Meuse-Argonne Cem
31. Ger Cem, Romagne
32. Capt Harris inscription, Aincreville
33. US 5th Div Obelisk, Doulcon
34. US 5th Div Plaques, Dun Bridge
35. US 5th Div Obelisk, Dun-sur-Meuse
36. US 5th Div Obelisk nr Dun-sur-Meuse
37. Balloon-buster Luke Mem, Murvaux
38. 'Big Red 1' Mon, St Juvin
39. US 16th Inf Regt Mon, Fléville
40. Sgt York Mem, Châtel Chéhéry
41. Ger Cem, Apremont
42. Ger 27th Inf Regt Mem, Ger Cem
43. Lost Bn Mem, Apremont
44. Fr 9th Cuirassier Mem, Binarville
45. Fr Nat Cem, St Thomas-en-Argonne & la Gruerie Ossuary
46. Tulip Tree Plaque, Vienne-le-Château

Murvaux
Dun-sur-Meuse
River Meuse
Aincreville
Saint Juvin
Romagne sous-Montfaucon
Cunel
Nantillois
Grandpré
5 Kms
Châtel Chéhéry
Apremont
Montfaucon
Varennes
Cheppy
ARGONNE FOREST
Butte de Vauquois
Vienne-le-Château
Lachalade
Sainte Menéhould
Reims
65 Kms
Verdun
30 Kms
Exit 29
East-west railway supplying Verdun

79 (US) Div
37 (US) Div
91 (US) Div
35 (US) Div
28 (US) Div
77 (US) Div
Les Islettes

N
0   2   4   6 kms

Approx Lines of German defence
—— First
— — Second – Giselher Stellung
• • • • Third – Kriemhilde Stellung

———— Approx US Line 0530 26 Sept
– – – Approx US Line 2359 26 Sept
• • • • Approx US Line 1 Oct

© TVH 2005

speaking of the need to sue for peace. Yet Ludendorff managed to withdraw his forces away from the constant allied attacks without letting the Allies break through. It was a trying time. By the first week in September the Germans had lost all the territory that they had won in the March offensive and Ludendorff began to show signs of strain, swinging wildly from optimism to pessimism. His stepson Erich, a flyer, had been killed on 21 March and Ludendorff had had to identify the exhumed body. Personal and national tensions were testing him to breaking point.

Foch's master plan was almost a mirror image of the German March Offensive, with massive blows planned to take place at different times and different places along the Western Front. Four were planned altogether to be launched on consecutive days. The first would be a joint Franco-American affair on 26 September 1918 which the Doughboys would call 'The Mews Argonne', but the Americans had to move a long way from St Mihiel. It would be no easy task to move them, let alone launch the offensive. Four days before the battle of St Mihiel began the 1st Army Operations Officer, Lt. Col George C. Marshall, was told to prepare the movement order to have the Army moved away from St Mihiel and in position for an attack on 25 September south of the Argonne forest. He had never prepared such an order before.

WHAT HAPPENED

George Marshall later wrote, 'About 10 minutes consideration made it apparent that to reach the new front in time to deploy for a battle on 25 September would require many of these troops to get under way on the evening of the first day of the St Mihiel battle. This appalling proposition rather disturbed my equilibrium and I went out on the canal to have a walk while thinking it over. After half an hour of meditation [I] returned to the office still without any solution. I called a stenographer and started the dictation of the preliminary order. I started with the proposition that the only way to begin is to commence. In less than an hour I had completed the order.'

Marshall's order worked. By midday on the second day of St Mihiel troop movements to the Meuse-Argonne were under way. There were only three usable roads over which to move half a million men, 2,000 guns and more than 900,000 tons of supplies and ammunition. Yet it was done, and almost entirely by night. Three army corps, each with three divisions in line and one in reserve were in position and ready to go. The fire support was to be provided by 2,700 guns and some 190 small French tanks, 140 manned by Americans, would accompany the infantry.

At 0230 hours on 26 September the opening bombardment began. Three hours later the 1st Army went over the top in dense fog. This was no repeat of St Mihiel. Three of the divisions had never been in combat before, five had not completed their training. Like Marshall with his movement order, they had not done anything like it before. The ground over which they had to advance was churned as if by a giant's plough from bombardments as far back as Verdun. Thick belts of wire and tangled woods made almost impassable by fallen trees contributed to a growing confusion. The energy and enthusiasm of the troops took them through the first German positions but their lack of experience prevented them from fully exploiting their gains. Over the next two days the Americans continued to move forward but German resistance was stiffening. Casualties were heavy and communications broke down. Ludendorff might have had his doubts about victory, but the German soldier was fighting well. On 29 September the Americans went on the defensive in order to reorganise. The French 4th Army, which had attacked with the US 1st Army, did little better.

By 1 October the advance stopped between seven and ten miles into the German lines. Altogether the French and the Americans had taken 18,000 prisoners but Foch was disappointed and tried to reinforce the Argonne offensive with another French army. Pershing would not agree. The Americans began attacking again on 4 October and while they made gains Foch commented that they were 'inferior to what it was permissible to expect'. In mid-October Prime Minister Clemenceau wrote to Foch about what he called the Americans, 'marking time' and Pershing's 'invincible obstinacy' and canvassed Foch's opinion on whether he should, 'tell President Wilson the truth and the whole truth concerning the situation of the American troops.' Foch did not agree with Clemenceau, having, as he said, 'a more comprehensive knowledge of the difficulties encountered by the American Army.' In a written reply Foch kept to the bare essentials and ended his letter, 'There is no denying the magnitude of the effort made by the American Army. After attacking at St Mihiel on 12 September 12th, it attacked in the Argonne on the 26th. From September 26th to October 20th its losses in battle were 5,158 men – in exchange for small gains on a narrow front, it is true, but over particularly difficult country and in the face of serious resistance by the enemy.'

THE BATTLEFIELD TOUR

N.B. There are some fascinating sites to see on this tour which are only open occasionally or by appointment. Please read it carefully before leaving and make advance bookings if necessary. It will be well worth the effort.

• **The Route:** The tour begins at Ste Menéhould, continues to the French National Cemetery, les Islettes; Lachalade CWGC, WW2 graves & Italian Memorials; La Haute Chevauchée Memorial to Crew of 622 Sqn, Lachalade French National Cemetery, Ossuary, Argonne Memorial & Craters; Kaiser Tunnel; Abris du Kronprinz; Butte de Vauquois Memorials, Tunnels, Craters & US Plaque, Chapel; Varennes Museum & Pennsylvania Memorial; Cheppy Missouri Memorial and German Cemetery; Montfaucon Village Sammy Memorial and 37th Division Plaque; American Memorial, Montfaucon; Nantillois Pennsylvania Monument & German Cemetery; Cunel Boston Memorial Fountain; the American Meuse-Argonne Cemetery and the German Cemetery at Romagne.

• **Extra Visits to:** Capt Harris Memorial, Cunel; Capt Harris Plaque, Aincreville; US 5th Div Memorials at Doulcon and Dun-sur-Meuse; Memorial to Luke, Balloon-buster, Murvaux; Big Red 1 Monument, St Juvin; US 16th Inf Monument, Fléville; Sgt York Memorial, Châtel Chéhery; German Cemetery, Apremont; Lost Battalion Memorial, Apremont; French 9th Cuirassier Monument, Binarville; French National Cemetery St Thomas–en-Argonne & Ossuary de la Gruerie; Tulip Tree Plaque, Vienne le Château.

• **Total distance**: 44.8 miles

• **Total time**: 6 hours 15 minutes

• **Distance from Calais to start point:** 231.8 miles. Motorway Tolls

• **Base Towns:** Reims, Verdun

• **Maps:** IGN Série Bleue Thiaucourt-Regniéville 33314 O and Apremont-la-Fôret 3214 E. Michelin 306 Local Aisne, Ardennes, Marne

From Calais take the A26 to Reims and then the A4-E50 direction Metz. Continue on the A4 and take the Ste. Menéhould Exit 29.

Set your mileometer to zero at the Péage.
Continue to the T junction and turn left signed Toutes Directions/American Cemetery.
Continue on the D982E into Ste Menéhould Centre and park in front of the Mairie in the
main square, Place du Géneral Leclerc.

• *Ste Menéhould Tourist Office/Museum/1.8 miles/20 minutes/Map 13/1*

Ste Menéhould was extraordinarily fortunate in having avoided much of the destruction suffered by neighbouring towns in the area during WW1, so its elegant main square retains much of its eighteenth century charm. There are several restaurants/cafés/hostelleries around it, some serving the local delicacy, pigs' trotters. In the public gardens a statue of the famous Dom Perignon, the inventor of Champagne, was erected in 1956. Extraordinarily none of the banks here would exchange Sterling for Euros.

The Tourist Office, 5 Place Gen Leclerc, has some helpful literature about battlefield sites in the area, hotel/restaurant lists etc. **Open** until 1800. Tel: + (0) 3 26 60 85 83. Fax: + (0) 3 26 60 27 22.

The Museum is opposite in a seventeenth century building (next to the library) and has a room dedicated to WW1 with a private collection of equipment, ephemera and postcards. **Open:** Sat, Sun, holidays 15 May-11 November, 1500-1800 or by appointment. Tel: + (0) 3 26 60 84 07.

In the centre of the square is the local **War Memorial,** designed by de Tarnoswky. It depicts a *Poilu* in bronze with all his equipment. Unusually he has his mascot dog with him. His stolid stance, wearing his long overcoat, has been compared to Rodin's massive statue of Balzac.

Continue on the N3 direction les Islettes/Verdun passing en route
A series of 1944 Liberty Highway markers.

Continue into les Islettes. Turn left on the D2 signed to Champs de Bataille and continue
to the cemetery on the left

• *French National Cemetery, les Islettes/7.5 miles/10 minutes/Map 13/2*

The Germans entered the village on 3 September 1914 but were driven out two weeks later. They made continuous efforts to retake les Islettes, which sits on the important east-west railway from Verdun (see Map 13), but failed. It became a major supply and stores centre and was on the French-American Army boundary at the start of the battle. The cemetery was created as a concentration cemetery in the region of la Biesme. It has 2,206 named burials from the Argonne battlefield and covers an area of 1,100 square metres. There is no mass grave. The cemetery was relandscaped and the graves remarked in 1957.

Continue on the D2 into the Argonne Forest.
The road is heading directly towards the German front line. To a first approximation in 1918 the French 4th Army was on the left and the American 1st Army on and to right of the road for about nineteen miles to the east.

Continue to le Claon.
Here, on 6 August 1914, the 4th Regt of the First Foreign Legion, Italian volunteers raised by Riccioti Garibaldi, son of the architect of Italian unity, Guiseppe Garibaldi, first regrouped in the Argonne on 17 December 1914 and stayed here until 24 December. They were under the command of Garibaldi's grandson (also Guiseppe). On Christmas Eve

Monument to the Garibaldians, Lachalade.

Memorial to Crew of 622 Sqn, RAF, la Haute Chevauchée.

The Poilu and his Dog War Memorial, St Menéhould.

Monument to the Battles of the Argonne, la Haute Chevauchée, reminiscent of the Brooding Soldier at Vancouver Corner, Ypres Salient.

they went up into the line and attacked the German trenches in the Bois de Bolante (through which you will drive after the visit to the Garibaldian memorial) crying '*Viva Italia!*', their green tunics unbuttoned to show the famous red shirts. During this attack and those of January 1915 the Garibaldians, as they were known, suffered heavy losses. On 8 January the survivors were sent to reinforce the French forces on the Haute Chevauchée where the situation was critical. Their heroic charge helped to re-establish the situation and to retake part of the line. On 11 January their tiny remnant was sent back to Italy, rejoined Italian regiments and later came back to France to fight on the Marne.

Continue to Lachalade and stop by the church on the left.

• CWGC WW2 Graves, Lachalade Churchyard/11.8 miles/5 minutes/ Map 13/3

At the back of the cemetery are four headstones containing the graves of **Pilot Officer W.J. Morcomber**, RAustAF, age 20, **Flt Sgt R. M. Conroy,** Air Gunner, RAustAF, **Sgt A.A. Ough,** Air Gunner, age 19, RAF, **Flt Sgt H.L.R. Richards,** RNZAF, **Sgt A. Sly,** RAF, **Flt Sgt D.S. Smith**, Navigator, RAF, **Sgt S.A. Thomas**, Wireless Operator, RAF, all died 18 November 1943. A memorial to them will be visited on the Haute Chevauchée.

Walk back to the memorial on the left.

• Monument to the Garibaldians, 87th RI Mon/11.8 miles/10 minutes/ Map 13/4/5

Erected in 1932 by the National Association of Italian Volunteers the monument is to Bruno (26 December 1914) and Constante (5 January 1915) Garibaldi (grandsons of Guiseppe) who with their 500 Legionnaires also served in the heroic vanguard at Vittorio Veneto in N. Italy. It was sculpted by S. Vatteroni of Carrara.

Further back along the road is a Board commemorating **the Ancient Cemetery of the Garibaldians** of the 4th Regt de Marche of the 1st Foreign Legion who fell in Argonne in the combats of the winter of 1914-15. It is believed that the Italian dead were repatriated after the war.

Behind it on the bank and guarded by a statue of the Virgin Mary is a **Monument to Jules Flamant and Vincent Chevalier of the 87th RI, 1914.**

Turn right signed by a board headed 'Mur Michelin' to the Cimetière Militaire de Lachalade, Haute Chevauchée and then right again.

N.B. The road now becomes very narrow and increasingly bumpy and pot-holed as it rises through the dense forest (Bois de Bolante), planted and well-maintained with firs, beech and oak. It must be driven with care (preferably in a 4-wheel drive vehicle and definitely not in a coach.) An alternative route to la Haute Chevauchée but missing Lachalade would be to take the D38c from les Islettes.

Continue to just short of the crossroads in a clearing and stop on the right.

• Memorial to Crew of 622 Sqn RAF, la Haute Chevauchée/14 miles/ 5 minutes/Map 13/6

This truly beautiful monument bears the RAF crest in colours and the names of the men whose graves were visited in Lachalade Churchyard, plus Sgt Robert Harper who managed to escape, was recaptured, deported to Buchenwald and died in 1977.

Over road on the right is

• Lachalade French National Cemetery de la Forestière/14 miles/ 5 minutes/Map 13/7

This is the only French cemetery to be planted with lush hydrangeas. This was done by the Countess of Martinprey (qv), believing her husband to be buried in it. However his body was never identified which led to the decision to build an ossuary on the Haute Chevauchée (qv). The cemetery contains 2,220 burials from the Argonne battles. There is an **Information Panel** at the entrance and a highly polished bronze box containing the register.

Turn left signed to Haute Chevauchée and Kaiser Tunnel on the D38c.

This road along the path of an ancient Roman road was heavily fortified by the Germans in 1915.

Continue past the Carrefour du Mont de Villers to a large parking area on the right with **Information Panels.**

The panels in three languages describe The War in the Trenches in this area and how on 26 September 1918 the attack of the I Corps of the American Army swept aside the forward defences on the Haute Chevauchée and then stalled (making only two kms from 27 September – 3 October). On 4 October the Americans exerted heavier pressure and the exhausted German defence evacuated the Argonne. The final attack of 1 November liberated the entire massif. There is a plan of the mine craters and a panel describing the reconstruction after the tempest of 1999.

A path along an old communication trench leads behind the car park to the monument or you can walk along the road to.

• Argonne Monument, Ossuary, Craters, la Haute-Chevauchée/15.8 miles/15 minutes/Map 13/8

This is the principal French Monument to the Battles of the Argonne and is the focus of commemoration here on the first Sunday of July. Designed by the architect Bolloré and the sculptor Becker on the initiative of the Countess of Martinprey (qv) in memory of her husband Capt Jean de Martinprey and of the 150,000 French combattants it was raised by subscription and inaugurated by President Raymond Poincaré on 30 July 1922. The names of 275 French Regiments, eighteen Italian Regiments, the Czechs and thirty-two American Divisions who took part in the Argonne battles are inscribed on the Monument. In the crypt, inaugurated on 17 June 1923 by Gen Gouraud, are the remains of several thousand unknown soldiers. Behind the monument is a vast **mine crater**. On the far lip is a Memorial Cross and an **Information Panel** about the mine which blew with 52.5 tonnes of ammunition on 12 December 1916, then the biggest German mine in the Argonne. It is 50 metres across and 10.5 deep. A walking trail with numbered stops leads into the wood behind the Monument and just before it there is a marker on the right pointing to the site where **Gen Gouraud**, commanding the 10th DI, was wounded on 13 July 1915 at La Fille Morte and a sign on the left leading to the **Memorial to Cpl Pamart** of the 72nd RI, 13 July 1915. This spot, known as Hill 285, was on the jump-off line for the American 28th (Keystone) Division on 26 September.

This is an incredible site and a thorough exploration of the paths through trench lines and craters would take a good hour.

Continue a few metres on the D38C to Information Panels on the left.

Entrance to Kaiser Tunnel with (inset) detail of inscription.

• **Kaiser Tunnel/15.7 miles/30 minutes (+ 1 hour if you enter the tunnels)/ Map 13/9**

They describe the complicated defences of the German Front Line and a trenchline that is virtually intact on the flank of the crest of Côte 285. The Kaiser Tunnel connected these trench systems.

A walking path then leads down past the remains of a sap through the woods to a modern **Information Centre** built in the shape of the Abris du Kronprinz (qv). A few metres further along the road is a driveable track down to the Centre but this can only be used when the Tunnel is open, otherwise there is a barrier. Although the interesting path that leads round the surface of the tunnel and its entrance and exits can always be seen, the doors are kept locked, so an appointment is vital.

Open: first Sunday of each month and every Sunday in the summer 1400-1800. Otherwise by appointment with the Office de Tourisme du Pays de l'Argonne, Clermont-en-Argonne. Tel: + (0)3 29 88 42 22. Fax: + (0)3 29 88 42 43.

Opposite is the exit from the Kaiser Tunnel, so-called not because the Kaiser is ever thought to have visited it but probably for 'K' for 'Kaiser' in the alphabetical sequence of tunnels. The path then winds through the woods, giving an excellent impression of the difficulty of the terrain for both sides for four bitter years. There are the vestiges of German dugouts (they did not live in the tunnel, it was simply for communication purposes), trench lines and craters and a spring which provided water for the Germans. The path ends at the entrance to the tunnel which has a stone sign, 'Kaiser Tunnel 1915-1916' thought to be original.

This important underground complex was constructed by the 173rd Bavarians. Begun in November 1915 the 350m tunnel led from the Ravine des Meurissons to the front. It was completed in March 1916. An extension tunnel was then built towards the second line to the south, called Battalion Tunnel. This was completed on 29 July 1916 permitting the safe circulation of men and supplies. However the northern flank of the German position was still vulnerable to French artillery fire and a third tunnel ('Ortlieb') was dug at the end of 1916. A sophisticated electrical supply system was installed with water pumps and large shelters. A hospital with an operating theatre was made in the northern end of the Kaiser Tunnel. In 1918 the main fighting had moved to the west and the garrison in the tunnel was reduced. Some of the exits were blocked and the electrical system was destroyed.

This area of horrendous fighting lay for eighty years forgotten, its post-war memorials neglected, then in 1998 began the 'Renaissance' of these tragic monuments to the tenacity of the soldiers who fought so doggedly for their *Patrie*. Monuments were refurbished, signing put in, car parks created and great underground works cleared and made safe to visit. This was due to the enthusiasm of local volunteer historians (mainly inspired by Col Martin and his extraordinarily enthusiastic wife, who saw her father shot by the Germans during WW2), with financial aid from the Region and the State.

Continue to the T junction.

N.B. By turning left here along the D38 a **Demarcation Stone (Map 13/10)** captioned 'Le Four de Paris' can be seen on the right some 600m on.

Turn right on the D38 signed to the Abri du Kronprinz and then left following the sign to a parking area.

The 750m track is rough – another place where 4-wheel drive would be an advantage.

• Abris du Kronprinz/18.3 miles/10 minutes/Map 13/11

This structure with its stylised 'bay window' is said to have been used as an HQ by the German Crown Prince during the battles of the German 5th Army in the Argonne and the first assaults on Verdun in 1916. There are other major bunkers and vestiges of trenches and craters in the complex. They sit at about the limit of the first day's advance by the Americans in 1918 and on the boundary of the 28th and 77th Divisions. They were finally taken on 28 September and subsequently used as 77th Division HQ. The area was also known as 'Champ Mahaut.'

Abris du Kronprinz, Champ Mahaut.

Return to the D38 and continue towards Varennes.

As the road leaves the forest there is dramatic and abrupt evidence of the change in terrain. Many Americans believe that the Doughboy's Meuse-Argonne battle took place in the forest. Most of it did not. The plan was that the French 4th Army would attack northwards along the western edge of the forest and the 1st Army northwards along the eastern edge where you now are. The forest is cut by the valley of the River Aire at Grandpré about eight miles north of here and the idea was that the French and Americans would meet there and in so doing pinch out the Germans in the forest without having to assault them head on. There was fighting in the Argonne, of course, but the main effort was made some five miles further east around Montfaucon. The Americans eventually reached Grandpré on 14 October after many days of fierce and protracted struggle.

Continue into Varennes and turn right on the D946 signed to the Butte de Vauquois. Continue to Boureuilles.

Here there is a splendid War Memorial, *Mairie*, School and Crèche.

Turn left on the D212 signed to Vauquois and continue following signs to the Butte. At the rebuilt village of Vauquois turn left uphill.

• Butte de Vauqois: Museum/Tunnels/Craters/Memorials/US K Coy, 35th Regt Plaque, Chapel/French Cemetery/25.5 miles/30 minutes (but add 1 hour if you enter the tunnels)/Map 13/12/13/14/15

The bitter fighting in this area was described in *Nous Autres à Vauquois* (Those of us at Vauqois) by the author André Pézard who served as a Sous-Lieutenant in the 46th RI. He took part in the attacks at Vauquois in February-March 1915, went on to serve at Bouchavesnes in the Battle of the Somme in 1916 where he was wounded in the knee, and died in 1984. His book was at first regarded as difficult to fathom but is now regarded as one of the French masterpieces of the war. 'It is a filthy and mean disorder', he wrote, 'that the burst of dawn illuminates... But the sky also lights up here, on the butte, this great Corps of Lepers; and the earth shrouded under the terrible stink of old corpses, under the stench of noon, hard and glutinous like a poison...There are huge yellow flies, here great blue flies, engorged by the putrefaction and the sun.'

At the foot of the butte where the staircase, flanked by small cannons, mounts to the summit is a **Monument to Henri Collignon** (qv) on the right. It is possible to walk to the summit but you will probably want to drive up the steep hill.

Continue to the car park and stop.

Ahead there is a section of Decauville track complete with Péchot trucks [named after Artillery Officer, Capt Péchot who, inspired by the Ffestiniog Railway in Wales, developed the locomotive with Bourdon of the Decauville Co in 1888], that were re-used in the Maginot Line and **Information Panels.** To the right is the small but fascinating **Museum**. It has a video presentation, aerial photos, trench maps, water-colours, weapons and artefacts found in the vicinity.

Open: Guided visits on the first Sunday of the month from 1000-1200; the 1 and 8 May from 0900-1800, otherwise by appointment with the Association: 1 rue d'Orléans, 55270 Vauquois. Tel: + (0)3 29 80 73 15. There is no underground access without a guide.

The importance of the site was recognised in 1968 when the *Association des Amis de*

Vauquois was formed. Then a walking route was set in place and the huge and extraordinary underground city of Vauquois was explored. Here the 160 inhabitants of the destroyed village (the original was at the top of the hill) occupied the natural caves. Then the military of both sides carved out more quarters until they could hold 2,000 men. There were 800 French (of whom 150 were Engineers) and 1,200 Germans (of whom 320 were Pioneers) who rotated between here and the rear. More research and renovations were completed between 1977 and 1991 so that the site, comprising 4,575 metres of galleries, 184 large rooms, three observation points, four blockhouses and six communication trenches is now safe for visits.

Climb up to the summit.

First you will pass an enormous German mine crater which was blown on 14 May 1916 with sixty tons of explosive, killing 108 men of the 46th RI. Metal *chevaux de frises* surround the area.

The Monument to the fighters and the dead of Vauquois is in the form of a truncated pyramid on the top of which is a lantern. On the main face is a *bas relief* of a *Poilu* and his dead companion and a realistic scene of trench life in 1915 is carved. It tells the story of a chestnut tree, already badly mutilated, that served as a ranging point for the French artillery. In May 1915 it was destroyed by German machine-gun fire and the site marked the edge of the French position. On 27 February 1917 the area was blown up by a huge German mine and in September 1918 the Americans and the Germans faced each other across the craters. In 1926 when the monument was inaugurated (in the presence of Pres Poincaré, Generals Gouraud, Simon and Cottez and Col Santo Garibaldi) the 5,000 pilgrims found traces of the famous tree. There is also an orientation table showing Verdun, Montfaucon etc.

The *Tricolore,* which will probably be flying, marks the site of the original village of Vauquois (the main street ran between the vast craters) and all around are the craters from the explosions which destroyed it during the years of mine warfare that preceded the attack of 26 September 1918. At that time both American and German front-line trenches crossed the hill and five hours before the assault the Americans evacuated theirs and saturated the heights with HE, gas and smoke artillery fire. The US 35th Div then pushed forward either side of the hill leaving the defenders and mopped them up later that day.

The shell-strewn, cratered rubble of Vauquois was still occupied by the Americans in late 1918 when the inhabitants were impatient to return to the remains of their village. In May 1919, after the land had been partially cleared with the financial aid of some citizens of Kansas, half a dozen inhabitants returned. There was no provision to accommodate them as the area was intended to be a *Zone Rouge* (qv). They obstinately refused to budge and the affair became a scandal as they were threatened by the authorities. Even Clemenceau and the Préfet of Bar-le-Duc became involved. Finally the Americans came to their aid and provided a few wooden huts and German prisoners were put to clearing the ground. More old inhabitants returned but no more huts were forthcoming. The controversy dragged on until finally the town of Orleans (from where many of the soldiers who fought here came) was persuaded to adopt the village and a subscription was opened. In 1920 the village was reborn but today is inhabited by a mere thirty residents.

Return to the bottom of the hill.

In the Chapel (if locked apply to the *Mairie* further along the road) to the right is a marble **Plaque to K Coy of the 138th US Inf Regt, 35th Div** who died here in the battle

Section of Decauville track complete with Péchot trucks, Butte de Vauquois.

Decauville track entering tunnel.

Monument to the Combattants of Vauquois.

of September 1918 when they recaptured the village. It was dedicated in July 1973 by a delegation of survivors of the Coy and names the thirteen dead and the survivors. Above the altar is the top half of the Virgin from the original Chapel of Vauquois on the crest of the Butte. It was taken by the Germans and returned some ten years ago. It is now regarded as a Historical Monument.

> **N.B.** To the right of the Chapel a road leads past the pristine local cemetery on the left to the concentration **French National Cemetery, Vauquois** (Map 13/16) some half a mile away, created in 1922, which covers 14,000 square metres and contains 4,368 burials of which 1970 rest in an ossuary. Unusually it has no surrounding walls. In grave 1396 lies is the distinguished politician **Henri Collignon** (qv) who enlisted at the age of fifty-eight in the 46th RI. He was killed by a shell on 16 March 1915 at the Ferme de la Cigalerie. At the top of the cemetery is a calvary around which are many individual plaques.

Return to Varennes and turn right. On the left is

Trenchline, Butte de Vauquois.

• *Varennes Museum of the Argonne/Pennsylvania State Memorial/ 29.1 miles/10 minutes/Map 13/17/18*

The museum has a WW1 section and also describes the capture here of King Louis XVI in 1791. **Open:** 19 April-30 June and 1-30 September: weekends and holidays 1500-1800 hours; 11 July-31 August: 1030-1200 and 1430-1800. Tel: + (0)3 29 80 71 14.

Around the Monument is a park, at the far end of which is a funeral urn capping a symbolic eternal flame and flanked by two colonnades. Varennes was taken by midday on 26 September by the 35th Division and a number of tanks led by Maj George Patton. The town was on the divisional boundary with the 28th Division who fought on the lower ground overlooked by the memorial and indicated by the orientation markers. Many men from Pennsylvania served in the 28th Division. On the 28th Division side of the hill scramblers can find the remains of bunkers and tunnel entrances, but it is safer to take our word for it.

Continue downhill to the River Aire.

Pennsylvania Memorial, Varennes.

The town is famous as the place where Louis XVI and Marie Antoinette were taken by the French revolutionaries in June 1791. They were spotted in their carriage at Ste Menéhould (where you came off the motorway) by M. Drouet the local postmaster who rode through the Argonne Forest to Varennes to rouse the populace. The fugitives were arrested at the Bras d'Or Inn near the bridge. The inn does not exist today but a Memorial Plaque is on the site of the house on the left on the bridge.

Turn right on the D38 immediately after the bridge. Continue to a sign to the left to the US Memorial, Cheppy and continue following signs to Cheppy to the memorial on the right.

• Missouri State Memorial, Cheppy/30.6 miles/5 minutes/Map 13/19

The Memorial is in the form of an imposing figure of Victory holding a laurel wreath, reminiscent of the British 34th Division statues at la Boiselle and at Mont Noir. It bears the State Seal of Missouri and was erected by the State in honour of her sons who died in the Great War. The village became HQ for the 35th, 1st and 42nd Divisions and eventually for V Corps.

Continue on the D19 to a sign to the right and follow it to the German Cemetery.

• German Cemetery, Cheppy/31.5 miles/10 minutes/Map 13/20

The sad colourless, flowerless cemetery contains 2,341 soldiers under black crosses interspersed with some flat Jewish headstones and a further 3,789 in a mass grave.

Return to the D19, turn right towards Montfaucon.

As you drive along this road the Montfaucon American Memorial dominates the hillside ahead, with the tall red and white radio mast to the right which is visible from the American Monument at Sivry (qv).

Continue to the crossroads with the D15 and turn left signed to American Memorial. Continue into the rebuilt village of Montfaucon and stop by the church on the right.

• Montfaucon Village: Sammies Memorial & 37th US Division Almshouse/36.9 miles/10 minutes/Map 13/21/22

Beyond the church is the Memorial that was erected on the 80th Anniversary in 1998 of the September Battle and is in honour of the 'Sammies' of the Meuse-Argonne. 'Sammies' refers to Uncle Sam and was the French nickname for the Doughboys. The Memorial bears the helmet insignia of the 93rd Division.

The central square (in which there is a fine recumbent *Poilu* statue on the War Memorial) is called Place du Gen Pershing. The Americans funded the almshouse here, which is across the square from the *Mairie* and behind the telephone box is a **Memorial Plaque to the 37th Division** which liberated the village on 28 September, many of whose soldiers came from the State of Ohio.

Continue and turn right on the D15a signed to Montfaucon. Continue following signs to the American Monument and park in front of the steps.

• Montfaucon American Memorial/37.5 miles/20 minutes/Map 13/23/24

This 180ft high Doric column of Italian granite with its figure of 'Liberty' on top is the largest American War Memorial in Europe. The figure faces the jump-off line of the 1st American Army on 26 September and from the viewing platform at the top the flag above Fort Douaumont to the south-east at Verdun can be seen. Much of the Meuse-Argonne battlefield is visible, too, of course, including the American Cemetery to the north at Romagne which is the next stop. Around the wall at the top are direction indicators which help orientation, but if you feel able to climb the 234 steps, do not forget to take your binoculars, map and camera. Even in less than perfect visibility the ruins of Montfaucon (Falcon Hill) village can be seen at the base of the column as a bird's-eye view. Inside the column at the bottom is a vestibule with American and French flags, a coloured wall map showing the Meuse-Argonne offensive and explanations in French and English. The Monument, designed by John Russell Pope, was erected by the US Government and commemorates the forty-seven days of fighting in the Meuse-Argonne between 26 September and 11 November 1918.

In the woods behind the Memorial (approached by a road to the left of it which can be driven) are the ruins of the original village of Montfaucon. An exploration on foot is recommended. There are **trenchlines, German fortifications, concrete bunkers** which had been prepared over four years from 1914, including a large observation tower in the ruins of the old Gothic Church on which is an historical Plaque. The Kronprinz briefly had his command post in the ruins of the Château Leriche.

On 26 September, the first day of the offensive, American troops of the 37th and 79th attacked the hill at about 1800 hours but were unable to take it. The two Divisions attacked through a rainstorm at dawn the following day and by midday Montfaucon was theirs. **Opening hours** for the Memorial are 0900-1200 and 1300-1630 in the summer and 0800-1200 and 1300-1600 in the winter, when it is closed on weekends. Tel: + (0)3 29 851 418.

To the right is a small **Visitors' Centre** with WCs and a small but interesting exhibition of photos of the building of the Memorial and the American Cemetery. In it is a **YMCA Plaque**. Opposite is a '**Liberty Tree**' planted in May 1991.

Turn round and take the first right following signs to Nantillois. Continue to Nantillois on the D15a then D15 to the monument on the right.

• Pennsylvania Memorial Fountain, Nantillois/39.8 miles/5 minutes/ Map 13/25

This fine creamy stone Memorial Fountain bears the State Seal of Pennsylvania and commemorates the 80th (Blue Ridge) Division AIF so named because its soldiers came mostly from Virginia, West Virginia and Pennsylvania. Opposite is the village War Memorial. *The Salle des Fêtes was paid for by the Americans.*

Continue on the D15 towards Cunel.

N.B. To the right is a sign to Nantillois German Cemetery, visible along a track (Map 13/26). It contains 921 graves.

Continue to the monument on the left.

• US 5th Division Obelisk, near Nantillois/42.5 miles/5 minutes/ Map 13/27

This is the traditional 5th Division Obelisk Memorial with the Red Diamond insignia. The tin plaque explains that this was the left flank of the 9th Inf Bde, 5th US Division and marks their jumping off trench on 14 October 1918.

Missouri Memorial, Cheppy.

Pennsylvania Memorial, Nantillois.

5th Division Obelisk, near Nantillois.

Memorial to Capt Harris, Cunel.

The Montfaucon American Memorial, dominating the hillside.

Continue into Cunel. On the left in front of the church is

• *Cunel Boston Memorial Fountain/43.0 miles/5 minutes/Map 13/28*

This impressive stone fountain with the seal of Boston commemorates three men, university friends, from the city: **Ensign Robert Fitzgerald Clark,** b 13 Sept 1898, killed France 21 Aug 1918; **2nd Lt Charles Henry Fiske 3rd**, 28th Inf Div, b Boston 31 Dec 1896, killed France 24 Aug 1918 and **1st Lt Aaron Davis Weld**, 7th Inf Regt, b Boston 21 Sept 1896, killed France 11 Oct 1918. Weld is buried in the nearby Meuse-Argonne cemetery (qv), Fiske is buried in Suresnes US Cemetery near Paris and Clark must have been repatriated.

Next to it is the village War Memorial with a fine *Poilu's* bust.

Extra Visit to Memorial to Capt Harris (Map 13/29).
Round trip: 2.4 miles. Approximate time: 20 minutes.

Take the D15 signed to Buzancy and continue some 200m to a track to the right by a Calvary. The track is very rough but should be negotiable with care by car if dry. Keep left at the fork and continue to the curiously shaped boulder on the left.

On the boulder are bronze Plaques relating how 'in a nearby trench Capt Charles Dashiell Harris, 6th Bde US Army, met his death while heading the attack that drove the Germans from Clairs Chênes Woods on 20 October 1918 aged 21. He was awarded the DSC. His initiatives and bravery were an inspiration to his men. With a small detachment in advance of his Company Capt Harris captured two German machine guns and 3 prisoners in the trench within the enclosure twenty metres to the south of this spot.' [The enclosure no longer exists.] The wood is opposite and 3rd Division captured it on the day of Harris's death and held onto it despite a fierce counter-attack on the 21st.

Return to the village and pick up the main itinerary.

Continue on the D123 following signs to the American Cemetery. Enter the gates follow signs to Reception and park.

• The American Meuse-Argonne Cemetery/44.0 miles/40 minutes/ Map 13/30

The Visitor's Centre contains the Superintendent's office, the cemetery registers, a visitors' book and a comfortable rest room with toilets. **Open:** 0900-1700 daily. Tel: + (0)3 29 85 14 18.

Like all such centres, it displays a picture of the President of the United States and an example and brief history of the George Washington medal, now known as the Purple Heart. Please pick up a leaflet showing the plan of the cemetery here. In the office is a photo of Gen Pershing who stayed here during his visits to France and a Bronze Palm presented by Albert Lebrun, President of the Republique.

This is the largest American military cemetery in Europe, some 14,200 soldiers being buried here, almost 5,000 more than in the well-known WW2 Cemetery overlooking **OMAHA** beach in Normandy.

Most of the burials are of soldiers who fell in the '47 days', the period from 26 September to the Armistice which had involved some 1,200,000 American trooops. In 1922 some were transferred from the Vosges and from occupied Germany. The major works on the cemetery were finished in 1931, the layout being symmetrical about a broad avenue that connects the reception and the chapel that can be seen in the distance at the top of a steep slope. It is possible to drive around the cemetery to the chapel area.

Amongst the white marble crosses and Stars of David there are nine **Medal of Honour** winners, with their names picked out in gold including **2nd Lt Frank Luke**, the famous 'Balloon Buster', DSC, Italian CDIG, 27 Aero Sqn, 29 September 1918, who is buried in Plot A, Row 26, Grave 13. The other eight are **2nd Lt Erwin Bleckley**, 130th Fld Arty, 35th Div, 6 Oct '18; **Capt Marcellus Chiles**, 365th Inf, 89th Div, 5 Nov '18; **Sgt Matej Kocak**, *Croix de Guerre*, USMC, 4 Oct '18 at Blanc Mont, who received his award (for rushing a machine-gun nest near Villers Cotterêts on 18 July and organising twenty-five Colonial soldiers to take another) from the US Navy and US Army as he was a Marine serving under Army command; **Maj Oscar Miller**, It War Cross, 361st Inf, 91st Div, 30 Sept '18; **Cpl Harold Roberts**, *Croix de Guerre* & Fr Mil Med, It War Cross, 244th Bn, Tank Corps, 6 Oct '18; **Sgt William Sawelson**, It War Cross, 312th Inf, 78th Div, 26 Oct '18, one of

Headstone of 'Balloon Buster' Luke, Meuse-Argonne American Cemetery.

only three Jewish MoH winners in WW1 in which 250,000 Jews served, more than 3,500 being killed and more than 12,000 wounded; **Lt-Col Fred Smith**, 308th Inf, 77th Div, 29 Sept '18 and **Cpl Freddie Stowers**, 371st Inf, 93rd Div, 28 Sept '18, the only black American to receive the MoH, awarded to his two surviving sisters by President George H. Bush in April 1991. He had been recommended for the award by his CO at the time of his action on Hill 188 in the Champagne Sector. Stowers took charge of his Coy and crawled forward under fire to an enemy machine-gun nest which he destroyed and continued to urge his comrades on until he died from his mortal wound. The Hill was then captured. Here too is buried **Lt Moses Taylor** whose memorial was visited at Vigneulles (qv).

The chapel has large entrance doors over which *bas-relief* figures represent Grief and Remembrance, and the carved heads of American soldiers are worked into the design of the door's column capitals. Inside is a marble floor at the back of which is an altar within a semi-circle of flags of the Allied nations. Subdued and coloured light comes in through the beautiful SGWs which carry the designs of the **American divisional and higher formations. A bronze Plaque commemorates the Carillon** donated by the Robert McCormick Tribune Foundation (qv) in May 1995 (www.rrmtf.org) who donate the necessary funding to AmVets National Service Foundation (www.amvets.org). On either side of the chapel are loggia carrying the names of nearly 1,000 soldiers missing with no known grave, and in the west loggia is a marble map showing the progress of the Meuse-Argonne campaign and a separate panel carries the names of the missing from the American expedition to Northern Russia. The landscaping of the cemetery, which was approved by Gen Pershing, began in 1929 and the architectural work was done by York and Sawyer of New York.

Leave the cemetery by the opposite gate to the one by which you entered. Continue to the village of Romagne and there follow signs to the 'Deutsche Friedhof'. Stop.

• *Romagne German Cemetery/44.8 miles/10 minutes/Map 13/31*

There is a remarkable visual contrast between this cemetery and the one you have just left – even on a bright day. This one is sad, sombre and dark with few, if any, flowers among the green ground-cover. The central chapel is heavy and squat, as if trying to hide. The overwhelming impression is one of mourning and regret, while at the American Cemetery the message seems to be of pride. It is interesting to reflect upon whether there is a 'right' way to remember and honour the war dead, and whether national characteristics wittingly or unwittingly show through in the chosen designs. French statuary tends to be dramatic, remembering the élan and sacrifice of conflict. British cemeteries strive to remember the individual and his regiment in a pleasing garden setting.

There are 1,412 burials here, one-tenth of the number at the American Meuse-Argonne cemetery that you have just visited.

The village, which was a large German supply depot, was taken by the 32nd Division on the morning of 14 October 1918, and held by them despite a German counter-attack that night following a heavy gas bombardment. It then became the headquarters of the 90th Division and subsequently III Corps until the Armistice.

• *End of Meuse-Argonne Battlefield Tour (44.8 miles) OR*

Long Extra Visit to American Memorials.

This extra tour starts at the Romagne Germany Cemetery, visits the Capt Harris inscription, Aincreville, (Map 13/32), 5th Div Monument, Doulcon (Map 13/33); US 5th Division Plaques at Dun-sur-Meuse (Map 13/34); Memorial to Balloon-buster, Luke (Map 13/37), Murvaux; 'Big Red 1 Monument (Map13/38), St Juvin; US 16th Inf Regt Monument (Map 13/39), Fléville; Sgt York Memorial, Châtel Chéhery (Map 13/40); German Cemetery & 27th Inf Memorial, Apremont (Map 13/41/42); Monument to The Lost Battalion (Map 13/43) near Apremont; Monument to the French 9th Cuirassiers (Map 13/44), Binarville; French National Cemetery St Thomas-en-Argonne and Osssuary de la Gruerie (Map 13/45); Plaque on Japanese Tulip Tree, Maison de l'Argonne (Map 13/46), Vienne-le-Château. Return to Ste Menéhould.

Distance of Route: 53.2 miles. Approximate time: 2 hours 30 minutes

This route takes in the three 'legends' of the Meuse-Argonne: Balloon-buster Luke, Sgt York and the 'Lost Battalion' as well as some other American Memorials. There are literally scores of other American Memorials in the area (in various conditions) a list of which may be obtained from the Superintendent in the Meuse-Argonne US Cemetery. He is aware of over eighty American Memorials and the 5th Division alone has twenty-two markers within twenty miles of the cemetery.

Continue on the D998 from the German Cemetery to Aincreville.

In front of the *Mairie* on the left is the **local War Memorial in Place Capt Harris** on which is an inscription to the **'brave Capt Harris' and the American liberators of Aincreville** (of the 5th Division who captured the village on 30 October 1918). Capt Charles Dashiell Harris (qv), a graduate of West Point, was the son of the Adjutant General of the Army, Peter C Harris. Capt Harris had commanded one of the companies the US 6th Eng Regt which formed part of Carey's Force during the Kaiser's Offensive of March 1918. He was mortally wounded on 20 October and carried to a dressing station near the village where he died.

Continue to Doulcon and the local War Memorial, on the left just before the junction with the D St 13. Behind it is a Calvary and behind that is

US Obelisk. This is in excellent condition, well painted and with its Red Diamond insignia and tin Plaque intact. The Plaque describes how Doulcon was captured on 3 November 1918 by Coy C, 61st US Inf, 5th US Div. It is on the site of the reinforced Ponton [sic] Bridge over the Meuse for Artillery Trains and supplies of 5th US Div and III US Corps constructed by the 7th US Engineers and attached troops, 5-6 November 1918.

Continue to Dun-sur-Meuse.

On the bridge over the Meuse (6.5 miles) are bronze **Plaques** on each side (one in English, one in French) erected by the Veterans of the US 5th Division to commemorate the crossing of the Meuse and the establishment of a bridgehead on the eastern bank.

Over the bridge is a marvellous *Poilu* War Memorial which also pays homage to the Heroes of the 5th Division who fell in the relief of Dun-sur-Meuse, October-November 1918.

At the T junction over the bridge there is the 2-star Hotel/Restaurant, Logis de France Hotel le Commerce. Tel: + (0)3 29 80 90 25. Fax: + (0)3 29 80 87 66).

German Cemetery, Romagne.

N.B. By turning right here and continuing on the D964 two more **5th Division Obelisks** (Map 13/35/36) may be seen. The first is outside the Gendarmerie on the right some .3 miles distant, complete with immaculate grey polished granite descriptive Plaques and Red Diamond. Some 1.3 miles further on, past the sign to the left to Sépulture de Mortemart, is another **US 5th Div Obelisk**, painted white with Red Diamonds but no descriptive Plaques. Some five miles further along this road is Sivry (qv) and the **American 1918 Monument** visited on the Verdun tour.

US 5th Div Plaque on Bridge over Meuse at Dun-sur-Meuse.

Long Extra Visit continued

Turn left and continue to the first junction.

On the left here is the excellent Restaurant Les Colimençarts with a variety of menus and, if necessary, rapid service, Tel: + (0)3 29 80 81 80.

Turn right to Milly on the 'C' road and continue to Murvaux on the D902.

As you approach the village there is an easy to miss standard metal calvary (10.1 miles) on the right between two trees by a new house. On the stone base is a **Plaque in memory of Lt Frank Luke**, balloon-busting ace of WW1 which was replaced and rededicated in an impressive ceremony on 18 November 2000 on the initiative of Stephen Skinner of the Great War Aviation Memorial Committee and the local people. The new plaque repeats all the minor errors of the original (e.g. the site of the crash and Luke's rank of Lt which was posthumous). 'Luke was

Long Extra Visit continued

critically wounded when he landed his SPAD 700 yards to the north and was killed by German small arms fire on 29 September 1918'. In fact Luke 'flamed' three German observation balloons before being hit by anti-aircraft fire over Murvaux and managing to land his SPAD XIII some 400 yards to the west of the village. The fearless dare-devil Luke was revered as 'a golden boy' by his comrades. In the dangerous job of shooting down enemy observation balloons he had an unequalled record of fourteen victories in eight days, with five victories in eight minutes. His death was long a mystery but Capt Merian C. Cooper, who returned from captivity after himself being shot down, set about finding his friend's last resting place. Eventually he discovered the rusting engine, the remains of the fuselage and Luke's grave. The story of his death, shooting it out, cowboy style with his Colt 45 with the German patrol who tried to take him prisoner, then emerged. He is now reburied in the Meuse-Argonne US Cemetery (qv). The last witness to Luke's final moments, Auguste Cuny, died in January 2000.

Return to the German Cemetery at Romagne (22.2 miles) and turn right to Sommerance on the D123 and then the D54 into the village.

Sommerance was taken on 11 October by 82nd Division.

Continue through Sommerance on the D54 towards St Juvin to the junction with the D946. On the corner on the right is

Monument to 'The Big Red 1' (Map 13/38) (28.6 miles). This is identical to the Divisional memorials at Cantigny on the Somme and at Vigneulles-les-Hattonchâtel (qv). It lists the kia of the Meuse-Argonne and describes how the 1st Division attacked from the crest of Baulny on the morning of 4 October 1918. In eight days it forced the German line back 7 kms and assisted the US 1st Army to join the 4th French Army at Grandpré, thus driving the enemy from the Argonne. Their losses were killed 1,790, wounded 7,126. The Division was commended for 'its special pride and service and high state of morale never broken by hardship in battle'.

Turn left on the D946 towards St Juvin, enter Fléville and continue to the Mairie on the right.

Monument to US 16th Inf Regt Map 13/39 (30.3 miles). This handsome monument with a bronze plaque was erected on 11 November 1999 by the 16th Inf Regt Association. It describes how 'the Regiment fought so gallantly during the heavy fighting in the Meuse-Argonne and who on 4 October 1918 liberated the village of Fléville from the Germans. During the battles twenty-seven men of the Regiment received the Distinguished Service Cross, America's second highest award for gallantry in action. It was after the liberation of Fléville that the 16th IR adopted the blue and white shield from the town's coat of arms as the background to its Regimental Crest (this crest is reproduced on the plaque). It has been worn proudly by members of the Regiment for over eighty years and saw service in WW2 (including OMAHA Beach on D-Day), the Cold War, Vietnam, the deserts of Saudi Arabia, Kuwait and in Bosnia. The regiment stands ready to

Long Extra Visit continued

serve again with pride and distinction. Motto: SEMPER PARATUS – ALWAYS PREPARED. The Regiment and the village of Fléville must never forget the heroic actions of those men and their dedication to their country, the ideals of freedom. We must always remember that FREEDOM IS NEVER FREE. In this small French village in 1918 the price of freedom was very high.'

Turn round and take the D4 signed to Cornay to the left. At the fork with the D42 keep left on the D4 through Cornay and enter Châtel Chéhéry.
On the left is the delightful Château. This is a beautifully restored 3 star hotel with three elegantly furnished bedrooms, a heated pool and dinner on reservation. Tel: + (0)3 24 30 78 54. Fax: + (0)3 24 30 25 51. E-mail: jacques.huet9@wanadoo.fr
Continue into the village and stop by the Mairie. In front of it is
Memorial to Sgt York Map 13/40 (33.4 miles). This handsome black marble Memorial bears the legend, 'On 8 October 1918 on what has become known as Mont York located 1km to the west Alvin C. York, a native of Tennessee serving with the US 82nd Div, armed with his rifle and pistol, his courage and skill, silenced a German Bn of thirty-five machine guns, killing twenty-five enemy soldiers and capturing 132. According to Marshall Ferdinand Foch, C-in-C of the Allied Armies "This was the greatest thing accomplished by any soldier of all the armies of Europe". On the occasion of the Centennial of his birth, Tennessee remembers her heroic native son. Erected by the Tennessee History Commission with the generous support of the Rotary Club of Nashville, Tennessee'. The incredible exploits of America's most decorated First World War soldier, Sgt Alvin C. York (the Audie Murphy of his day) took place nearby. A rip-roaring, hell-raiser from Tennessee, York was converted to become a God-fearing, non-smoking teetotaller – almost a conscientious objector. Yet on 8 October York, serving as an Acting Corporal with the 82nd Division, discovered that, as his senior officers and NCOs were progressively killed, he was in charge of his platoon sent to attack the far flank of the German position. York decided to use Tennessee turkey-shooting procedures and started, one by one, to pick off the German machine-gunners opposing them from the rear, killing about fourteen. He then called on the remainder to surrender; eighty men did, and as York marched them in, by the expedient of holding his Colt to the German Major's head and forcing him to order all enemy they passed to surrender, his bag mounted to an astonishing 132. He was awarded the MoH and was much used in fund-raising and recruiting drives in the U.S.A. The Sgt York Patriotic Foundation in concert with Nashville Rotary preserve his home in Pall Mall Tennessee and there is a statue of him in Nashville. Gary Cooper starred in the Howard Hawks 1941 film, *Sergeant York*.

On the local War Memorial opposite is a chronology of local history, including the fact that the pre-1914 population of 503 was reduced to seventeen. It also acknowledges US losses and participation.

Continue to a left turn to Apremont on the D42. Continue to the Mairie and turn right. At the next junction turn right signed to German Cemetery on the D442.

US 16th Inf Regt Memorial, Fléville.

Memorial to Sgt York, Châtel Chéhery.

Memorial to Balloon-buster Lt Frank Luke, Murvaux.

Plaque on the Tulip Tree, Vienne-le-Château.

Memorial to Landwehr Inf Regt 27, Apremont German Cemetery.

Long Extra Visit *continued*

German Cemetery & Memorial, Apremont Map 13/41/42 (36.8 miles). A brick path leads to this unenclosed cemetery (the original chains are now missing), before the entrance to which is a simple stone cross. The cemetery in which 1,111 soldiers are buried contains no colour. The crosses are mostly a stark black with two Jewish stones but the cemetery is surrounded by and insterspersed with the most beautiful trees and has a strangely calm atmosphere of quiet beauty. In it is a **Memorial to the Landwehr Inf Regt 27** and to the right are some original stone grave markers.

Continue through the forest to a small memorial (easy to miss) on the left.
Monument to 'The Lost Battalion' Map 13/43 (39.5 miles). This commemorates

men of 308th Inf Regt; Coy K, 307th Inf Regt; Coys C & D 306th M-G Bn, 77th Div – another American legend of the First World War, the story of 'The Lost Battalion', which in actual fact was neither a battalion, nor lost! According to Maj Gen Robert Alexander, Commander of 77th Division, 'On 3 October a detachment of 550 men under the command of Maj Charles W. Whittlesey (a lawyer before he volunteered for service), were cut off from the remainder of 77th Div (New York's Own) and surrounded by a superior number of the enemy near Charlevaux in the Forest of the Argonne, from the morning of October 3, 1918 to the night of October 7, 1918. Without food for more than 100 hours, harassed continuously by machine-gun, rifle, trench mortar and grenade fire, Maj Whittlesey's command, with undaunted spirit, successfully met and repulsed daily violent attacks by the enemy. They held the position, which had been reached by supreme efforts under orders received for an advance, until communication was re-established with

Monument to the 'Lost Battalion', Apremont.

friendly troops'.

When relief finally came, approximately 194 officers and men were able to walk out of the position near the ruins of Charlevaux Mill. Officers and men killed numbered 107. Although three **MoHs** were awarded for this action – to **Maj George G. Murtry, Capt Nelson M. Holderman** and to **Whittlesey** himself, Whittlesey was never able to overcome his feelings of guilt for the loss of so many of his men and in 1921 he committed suicide.

In 2001 David Gerber made a most realistic and moving feature film, entitled *The Lost Battalion*, which tells the story in accurate detail. It highlights the grit and tenacity of the disparate New Yorkers, many of them immigrants from the Old

Long Extra Visit continued

World, Whittlesey's dedication in the face of seemingly unreasonable orders and compassion for his men and even shows the last pigeon sent out with a desperate message to HQ. She was called Chère Amie, was shot at by the Germans to prevent her carrying information, yet managed to reach home. She was later stuffed and has a place still in the Smithsonian Museum in Washington.

The memorial overlooks a deep ravine, on the opposite side of which the men were isolated.

Continue past the lake in the ravine on the left to the junction with the D63 and turn left towards Binarville. At the junction is

Memorial to the French 9th Cuirassiers Map 13/44 (40.9 miles). This was erected by their comrades, their parents and their friends of the Regiment. In front is a Memorial to Lt A. Brault, S.Lt Malle, Brig Bonnefont, Cavalier Nemoz of the 2nd Coy, 9th CAP who received a Citation for the retaking of Binarville on 30 September 1918.

Continue through Binarville on the D63 towards Vienne-le-Château and stop at the cemetery on the right.

St Thomas-en-Argonne French National Cemetery Map 13/45 (44.6 miles). This contains 8,085 WW1 burials and eighty-eight WW2 burials. There is an **Information Panel** at the entrance. Over the road is the **Ossuaire de la Gruerie** with an imposing large cream stone **Monument with a figure of Liberty.**

Continue into the village of Vienne-le-Château and turn right then fork left signed to

Maison de l'Argonne (45.1 miles). This Tourist Office has useful information about the district and often has interesting temporary exhibitions. Tel: + (0)3 26 60 49 40. Fax: + (0)3 26 60 49 41. E-mail: maison.argonne@wanadoo.fr

Behind it is the extraordinary, huge Japanese Tulip Tree on which is a Plaque which describes how on 1 December 1914 French soldiers of 6th Coy, 128th RI were working under the tree. Suddenly a lone German 105mm shell burst among them, killing or wounding sixty-three men. Fragments of flesh and uniform were projected onto the tree and it was transformed into a shimmering river of blood. From that day it was called '**The Bloody Tree' Map 13/46.**

[See details of the Tulipier Hotel which is a short distance up the fork to the right in **Tourist Information.**]

Return to the main road and turn right to the Church.

The village Church has evidences of bullet holes from WW2.

Continue on the D63 through Vienne la Ville.

To the right, just before the picnic area is a polished red marble **Monument with the Cross of Lorraine to the Resistants of the Argonne**, 1940-45, with a list of casualties (45.7 miles).

Continue to the entrance to the A4 Motorway at Ste Ménehould (53.2 miles).

OR return to Reims *by continuing on the N44 and following signs to centre.*

BREAKING THE HINDENBURG LINE

29 SEPTEMBER 1918

'The British had given us a big half tumbler of rum before the charge and thank God for that. The Americans would never have done that. We didn't actually take the tunnel, the Australians accomplished that, but we'd softened it up for them.'
Sgt M. D. Cutler, *American 27th Division*

'While Hindenburg and Ludendorff, the Kaiser and his statesmen put their heads together seeking for a formula which might save their Armies and the German nation from defeat and ruin, no warriors in all history in the hour of their defeat, fought with greater courage and skill than the German Armies thrown from the impregnable defences of the Hindenburg Line.'
Lt-Col Seton Hutchison in *Warrior*

SUMMARY OF THE BATTLE

At 0555 hours on 29 September the British 46th Division and American 27th and 30th Divisions set off behind a creeping barrage to attack the Hindenburg Line defences along the St Quentin Canal tunnel complex. The 46th Division broke the line by nightfall and the Americans, fighting with the 2nd, 3rd and 5th Australian Divisions, did so on the following day.

OPENING MOVES

Since his appointment at Doullens as Supreme Commander, Gen Foch had been working towards a coordinated joint offensive involving all Allied Forces. Neither the Americans nor the Belgians had been present at Doullens (though the Memorial SGW in the Hôtel de Ville where the historic conference took place suggests an American representative) but they willingly co-operated with Foch's strategic plan. Gen Pershing, however, first insisted upon seeing through his ideas for the St Mihiel Salient attack.

The grand offensive was scheduled to begin over four days and included:

26 Sept. at 0525 hours the French 4th and American 1st Armies would attack in the Argonne

27 Sept. at 0520 hours the British 1st and 3rd Armies would attack towards Cambrai

28 Sept. at 0600 hours King Albert's Belgian Army Group would attack in Flanders

29 Sept. at 0555 hours the British 4th Army would make a direct assault on the Hindenburg Line

On 16 March 1917 the Germans began a major withdrawal along a front of sixty miles from Arras to Soissons. As they moved back into the new defensive positions that they had spent many months preparing, they laid waste to the countryside much as Gen Sherman had done in America almost sixty years earlier. The Germans called their new defences the 'Siegfried Line' but probably through an inaccurate debriefing of a German deserter our intelligence sources took the name to be 'Hindenburg Line', and that stuck. Almost exactly halfway along the new line was the major town of St Quentin and worked into the defences to its immediate north were a canal and tunnel complex stretching from Bellenglise to Vendhuille (see Map 14). To break that complex was the task of the British 4th Army under Rawlinson. It was probably the most formidable part of the whole Hindenburg Line.

WHAT HAPPENED

The Australian Corps of 4th Army was given the task of taking the Hindenburg Line around the tunnel complex. General Monash, commanding the Corps, knew that his men were tired from almost continuous fighting, a fatigue that resulted in one company mutinying when told to go back into the line. There were two other complications. One was that 'Anzac Leave', a two months' holiday in Australia for those who had served in Gallipoli, was weakening his formations. The second was that, in trying to consolidate his available troops by merging battalions together, Monash offended the soldiers' strong loyalty towards their battalions and some men refused to disband. Ultimately Monash agreed to make the attack when offered the 27th and 30th American Divisions as re-inforcements (these two divisions had served with British forces since their arrival in France and have their own memorial at Vierstraat in the Ypres Salient).

Starting around the middle of September the 4th Army began a number of local attacks against the Hindenburg Line in order to establish good positions for the major offensive on 29 September. The American 30th Division, which entered the line on 24 September, immediately came under artillery fire and over the next two days was engaged in fighting to complete the elimination of the German outpost line, a process begun by the British.

The American 27th Division came into the line on 25 September to find that the British had been unable to take the ground from which the 27th was supposed to make its assault on 29 September. The strong points in the German position were The Knoll, Guillemont Farm and Quennemont Farm (see Map 14). On 27 September the 27th attempted to take these positions leading off with tanks and artillery at 0530 hours but by the end of the day, with heavy casualties and small bodies of men left isolated across the battlefield, no significant progress had been made. In the confusion of the battle there were many acts of heroism – one in particular merited the **MoH. Lt. William B. Turner** took charge of one small group of lost men and single-handed, armed only with a pistol, rushed and destroyed a German machine-gun crew that was firing on them. He then led a charge upon another machine gun and when his pistol ammunition ran out he seized a dead soldier's rifle and using the bayonet led his group across four enemy trenches until he was killed. He is buried at Bony American cemetery, which you will visit.

On the day of the main assault all three forward divisions set off at 0555 hours in fog and under heavy rain clouds. The 30th began at great speed but through lack of experience they did not mop up as they went. Once the Americans had passed over them the Germans came out of deep bunkers and attacked them in the rear. The Australian 5th Division who were supposed to have passed through the Americans now had to retake the ground over which the 30th had already advanced. The situation was extremely complicated because with the Americans somewhere ahead of them and

MAP 14: BREAKING THE HINDENBURG LINE: 29 SEPTEMBER 1918

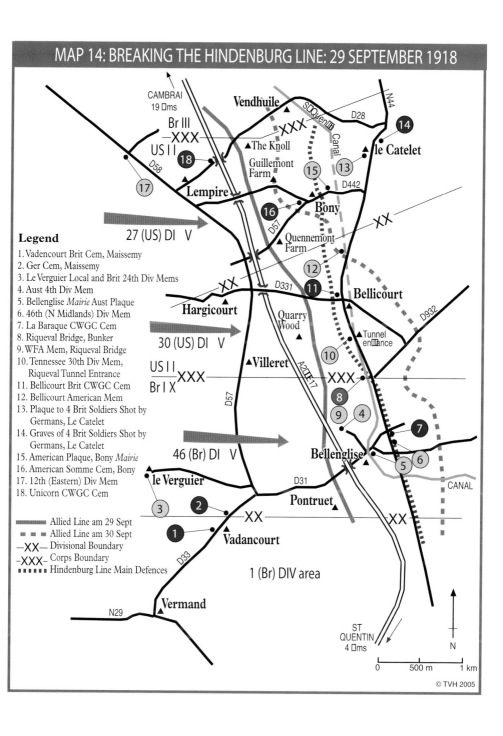

CAMBRAI
19 ☐ms

Vendhuile

S⊡Quentin⊡ Canal

N44

D28

Br III
XXX
US I I

18

17

▲The Knoll

Guillemont
Farm

le Catelet

14

15

13

D442

D58

Lempire

16

Bony

Quennemont
Farm

XX

D57

27 (US) DI V

Legend

1. Vadencourt Brit Cem, Maissemy
2. Ger Cem, Maissemy
3. Le Verguier Local and Brit 24th Div Mems
4. Aust 4th Div Mem
5. Bellenglise *Mairie* Aust Plaque
6. 46th (N Midlands) Div Mem
7. La Baraque CWGC Cem
8. Riqueval Bridge, Bunker
9. WFA Mem, Riqueval Bridge
10. Tennessee 30th Div Mem,
    Riqueval Tunnel Entrance
11. Bellicourt Brit CWGC Cem
12. Bellicourt American Mem
13. Plaque to 4 Brit Soldiers Shot by
    Germans, Le Catelet
14. Graves of 4 Brit Soldiers Shot by
    Germans, Le Catelet
15. American Plaque, Bony *Mairie*
16. American Somme Cem, Bony
17. 12th (Eastern) Div Mem
18. Unicorn CWGC Cem

XX

D331

12

11

Bellicourt

D932

Hargicourt

Quarry
Wood

▲

10

▲Tunnel
entrance

30 (US) DI V

A2⊡E17

▲**Villeret**

US I I
Br I X
XXX

XXX

8

9

4

7

46 (Br) DI V

Bellenglise

5

6

le Verguier

D31

3

2

Pontruet

CANAL

1

Vadancourt

XX

XX

D33

1 (Br) DIV area

——— Allied Line am 29 Sept
■ ■ ■ Allied Line am 30 Sept
—XX— Divisional Boundary
-XXX- Corps Boundary
■■■■■ Hindenburg Line Main Defences

Vermand

N29

ST
QUENTIN
4 ☐ms

N

0   500 m   1 km

© TVH 2005

all mixed up with the Germans, the Australians were unable to make full use of their artillery support. The 27th Division had a particularly hard time to start with because their artillery support, supplied by the British, came down behind, instead of upon, the German strongpoints at The Knoll, and Guillemont and Quennemont Farms, in fear of hitting troops still isolated in the area from the fighting on 27 September. So intense was the German machine-gun fire that the 107th Infantry Regiment had 995 casualties in the day, the heaviest American single day unit loss of the war.

Nevertheless, by noon The Knoll and the area of the present American cemetery and Quennemont Farm had fallen to the Americans and the 3rd Australian Division. Early in the afternoon the Australians began to pass through in order to continue the offensive. The combination of vigour and inexperience which dictated the activities of so many of the Doughboys now led them to join up with the Aussies and some men had still not returned to their units two days later. Sir John Monash who was commanding the Australians spoke highly of the Americans and wrote, 'It was found to be a matter of some difficulty to induce these men to withdraw from the fighting and to rejoin their own units so keen were they to continue their advance.' The 27th Division won more MoHs than any other division. The 46th Division forced a crossing of the canal at Bellenglise making use of the early morning fog. The assault brigade, the 137th, was commanded by **Brigadier J. V. Campbell, VC** who had won his decoration as a Lt Col in 1916. The attack, on a three battalion front, was led with great dash, the quality which had earned Campbell his VC and by 0830 hours the Division was across the canal and established on the east bank. At the end of the day the 4th Army had penetrated the strongest part of the Hindenburg Line to a depth of some 6,000 yards and on a frontage of 10,000 yards. It was the beginning of the end for the Hindenburg Line and for Germany. The Armistice was forty-two days away.

THE BATTLEFIELD TOUR

• **The Route:** The tour begins at Vermand, stops at Vadencourt British CWGC Cemetery and Maissemy German Cemetery, continues to Bellenglise and examines the assault crossing of the St Quentin Canal, visits the 4th Australian Division Memorial, continues through Bellenglise and the Plaque on the *Mairie*, moves to the 46th Division Memorial, the CWGC Cemetery, La Baraque, then to the Riqueval Bridge and WFA Memorial and to the tunnel entrance below the Tennessee Memorial. The next stop is the CWGC Cemetery at Bellicourt and the American Monument, followed by the American National Cemetery at Bony, then the 19th Division Memorial near Epehy and ends at the Unicorn CWGC Cemetery.

• **Extra Visit:** Le Catelet to the graves and plaque to Ptes Digby, Martin, Donohue and Thorpe

• **Total distance:** 27.2 miles

• **Total time:** 4 hours

• **Distance from Calais to start point via the A26-E27 motorway and the N29:** 110 miles. Motorway Tolls

• **Base Town:** St Quentin

• **Map:** Michelin 302 Local 1:15,000

    Exit from the A26 motorway at St Quentin (Exit No 10) and take the N29 direction Amiens. Continue through Holnon.

On the right is the delightful Pot d'Etain, a Logis de France hotel with an excellent restaurant. It has a good choice of varyingly priced menus (even including that rarity in France – a vegetarian menu). Tel: + (0)3 23 09 34 34. Fax: + (0)3 23 09 34 39.

Shortly afterwards **Holnon CWGC Cemetery** is signed to the left.
Continue to Vermand.

N.B. To the left is signed the **Museum of the Vermandois**. Based in an old mill building, the museum includes a section on military uniforms from 1879 to the present day and artefacts from the wars of 1870, '14-'18 and '39-'45.
Opening times are 'occasional'. Tel: + (0)3 23 09 50 51. Fax: + (0)3 23 09 57 07.
Vermand was the ancient capital of the Vermandois district and there are remnants of an ancient city wall still to be discerned today.

Continue to the right turn on the D33 to Bellenglise and US Cem and Mem.
Set your mileometer to zero. *Continue on the D33 to the cemetery on the left.*

• Vadencourt British Cemetery, Maissemy/1.8 miles/10 minutes/Map 14/1

Note that although the cemetery is called 'Vadencourt', the village is spelt 'Vadancourt'. It was begun in August 1917 and operated until March 1918. In October and November 1918 it was used by the 5th, 47th and 61st CCS and Field Ambulances. The original graves are in Plots I-III. It was enlarged after the Armistice with many casualties from the 59th (Northern) Division and now contains 750 burials, 200 of whom are unidentified. They include British, Canadian, Australian, Chinese and Indian, some named on Special Memorials, including five Indians whose bodies were cremated. Their cavalry regiments bear names redolent of a bygone Empire – The Deccan Horse, Gardners Horse, 34th Prince Albert Victor's Own Poona Horse, the 37th Lancers (Baluch Horse)... Some men died of flu in November 1918. The four French, thirty-one Americans and twenty-eight German burials of October 1918 were later removed to their own national cemeteries. In early summer the variety of flowers and shrubs make it heart-rendingly beautiful.

Buried here is **Brig Gen Sir William Algernon Kay, CMG, DSO, KRRC**, 4 October 1918, who had fought in the S. African Campaign, and **Lu Chung Hai,** Labourer, 76th Chinese Labour Corps, 8 November 1918. **Lce Cpl H. Cocker**, Notts & Derby, 4 April 1917, has the inscription, 'If love could have saved him he would not have died. From his loving Mother and Father.' **Pte D. Leather,** 20th Manchesters, died on the last day of the war – 11 November 1918. **Aircraftsman 2nd Class Ernest Wiffen** of the 13th Balloon Flight RAF, died of wounds (gassed) on 23 October 1918, aged 46. **Lt Col John Henry Stephen Dimmer**, KRRC attd 2/4 Berks, 21 March 1918, age 35, won the **MC and the VC** (in Klein Zillebeke on 19 November 1914 for staying by his machine gun although wounded five times). Dimmer, an experienced old soldier who had risen from the ranks, was killed near the cemetery, leading on horseback a counter-attack by his battalion

Headstone of Brig-Gen Sir W.A. Kay, CMG, DSO, Vadencourt Cemetery.

to regain lost ground near Maissemy. Although a gallant gesture it made Dimmer and his mounted groom excellent targets and they were immediately shot as they were silhouetted on the skyline. The attack, in which forty men were killed, failed.

Continue to the cemetery on the left.

• German Cemetery, Maissemy/2.6 miles/10 minutes/Map 14/2

The drab grey stone crosses which bear the names of 15,478 soldiers are separated by a central avenue which leads to the small square stone memorial chapel. The avenue is lined by large slabs which bear the coats of arms of the German home towns and villages of the men buried in the cemetery. In the dark chapel, which is relieved by a coloured mosaic ceiling, is a bronze sarcophagus with angels in *bas-relief*. To each side of the chapel are mass graves containing almost 15,000 more soldiers. A slab in the cemetery records that 30,478 bodies lie within it. It is sobering to reflect that this is forty times as many men as in the British cemetery just visited. This cemetery, unlike others in Northern France, bore no signs of vandalism, the cemetery register was present and gardeners were cutting the grass on our last visit.

Continue uphill to the crossroads and turn left to le Verguier on the D31 and left again at the fork. In the village take the right fork on the D31 signed to Jeancourt. Continue to the church straight ahead with a flamboyant memorial in front of it.

• Le Verguier Local and British 24th Division Memorials/4.7 miles/ 10 minutes/ Map 14/3

Le Verguier was first invaded by the Germans on 27 August 1914, then the village saw conflict as the French cavalry and artillery drove them out temporarily until it was again occupied on 20 September. In April 1917 the British 59th Division liberated the village and in March 1918 the British 24th Division took over and strengthened their line around it. It came under heavy attack again on 21 March which was at first repulsed by the 9th Queens, the 1st Royal Fusiliers and the 3rd Rifle Brigade of 17th Brigade but fell the following day.

After the war links were renewed between the villagers and their liberators and on 3 October 1926 the church bells and clock, donated by the 24th Division, were inaugurated. There is also a plaque in the church porch. The war memorial, with a large coloured figure of a *Poilu*, bears the *Croix de Guerre* and acknowledges the help of the 24th Division. It was inaugurated in the presence of Maj Gen J.E. Capper and refurbished in November 2001.

In the churchyard, to the left of the gateway where a battery was sited, are the graves of three British soldiers from 18 and 19 September 1918.

Turn round and return to the D33, turn left and continue in the direction of Bellenglise under the motorway. Turn left immediately before the Canal de St Quentin, signed to 4th Australian Div Memorial, and stop below the bridge.

• The Bellenglise Crossing/8.6 miles/5 minutes

You are now standing alongside the boundary between the 1st and 46th Divisions (see Map 14) and on the western bank of the canal, the side from which the attack began. The assault crossing by the 46th Division was made across the canal along a line from here northwards to the Riqueval Bridge. The German defences were formidable. On this side of the canal was the outpost line of fire positions, trenches and wire which had to be cleared before the canal itself could be tackled. It ran in a deep cutting between almost perpendicular banks

*Local and British
24th Division
Memorial, le Verguier.*

Graves, German Cemetery, Maissemy.

Sarcophagus in the Chapel.

*The Bellenglise Crossing,
Canal de St Quentin, looking
north.*

30-50ft high over the divisional front from Riqueval to about 500 yards north of here from where it runs virtually at ground level. Where you are now the canal was practically dry but on average between here and Riqueval it ran to a depth of 5-6ft. The bridge crossing points had well-sited concrete emplacements and beyond lay the main Hindenburg Line of deep interconnecting trenches, thick belts of barbed wire and fortified villages.

As a preliminary to the main assault the 138th Brigade made an evening attack on the outpost line on 27 September and occupied the German trenches west of the canal. Once the positions had been consolidated the 137th Brigade relieved the 138th. At 0700 on 28 September a heavy German counter-attack forced the Brigade out of some of the captured positions and the aggressive attentions of red-painted enemy aeroplanes kept heads down during the day. Nevertheless preparations went on for the 29 September action, but not always helped by our own side. Communications forward were mostly by line and this was frequently broken by enemy shell-fire, but one British cavalry unit totally destroyed the communications forward from divisional HQ by cutting out 100 yards of the main cable to use as a picket line for its horses.

The canal was seen as a main obstacle and special mud-mats, collapsible boats, rafts and life-belts from the Boulogne cross-Channel steamers were supplied to the troops and rehearsals in their use took place at Brie Château on the Somme on 28 September. On the night of 28-29 September all of these materials were carried forward by the divisional engineer field companies to as close to the canal as possible. The assault brigade, the 137th (Stafford), was also moved forward to positions along a taped-out forming-up line 200 yards behind the start line for the creeping barrage. The assault was planned on a three battalion front, starting with the 1st/6th Staffords here, then the 1st/5th South Staffords and on the left (farthest north) the 1st/6th North Staffords. Behind them, splitting the divisional area between each other, came the 138th and 139th Brigades as follow-up forces.

As the barrage opened just before 0600 hours the Staffords leapt out of their trenches and poured down the slopes towards the canal through thick mist. They overwhelmed the German defenders and quickly reached the west bank of the canal. Here the 1st/6th South Staffords attacked in four company waves, one behind the other on a one-company front of 400 yards. The canal was almost dry, men and officers wading across shielded from enemy fire by the fog. After a short delay in gaining the far bank they pushed on to their phased objectives – the Blue and Red lines – overcoming enemy resistance in Bellenglise en route. All three battalions advanced to timetable, the centre battalion using all their flotation equipment to cross deep water in the canal and the left battalion taking the bridge at Riqueval. Two and a half hours after they had left their trenches the 137th Brigade had gone through the German outpost line, crossed the St Quentin Canal, broken into the Hindenburg Line and taken over 2,000 prisoners. Its own casualties were 580 officers and men. Quite a day.

Continue past the factory buildings and bear left again signed to the 4th Australian Division Memorial. The muddy and cratered track winds its way uphill towards the obelisk on the horizon. It can be negotiated slowly by car with extreme care if not too wet.

• 4th Australian Division Memorial/9.7 miles/10 minutes/Map 14/4

The Memorial occupies a commanding position with marvellous views over the ground of the attack of the Australian 4th Division which took the high ground in a preparatory assault on 18 September 1918 which came from the other side of the motorway to where you now are. The site, on the German advanced lines, was strongly defended with alternate networks of barbed wire and trenches. Once taken it provided a jumping-off position for the North and South Staffs for their attack of 29 September on the principal German line which ran along the canal.

Return to the road and continue over the bridge into Bellenglise. Continue to the Mairie on the right just before the church.

• *Bellenglise Mairie Plaque to Australia/11.0 miles/5 minutes/Map 14/5*

On the wall is a black marble plaque with the message, 'We do not forget Australia. 1914-1998'. After the war Bellenglise was 'adopted' by Stafford.

Continue past the church and turn right signed Levergies on the D31 on rue du 87ième RI and continue to the junction with the N44. Turn left direction Cambrai and continue to a very easily missed track to the right, just short of the green sign to the Australian 4th Div Memorial (best to reverse up the track a bit). Stop and walk to the obelisk.

• *46th (N Midlands) Division Memorial/11.8 miles/10 minutes/Map 14/6*

This is the area that was known as Bellenglise Mill and the original Memorial to the Division which was erected shortly after the war was a tall wooden cross. The present Memorial was restored in the mid-1980s by East Midlands TAVR Association. The 46th was a Midlands Territorial Division that arrived in France in February 1915 and stood by as a reserve for the battle of Neuve Chapelle. It went on to fight at Hill 60 in the Ypres Salient, at the Quarries during Loos and at Gommecourt in the diversion for the Big Push on the Somme. On 29 September 137th Brigade of the Division took this area, 139th Brigade followed up and by 1730 hours advanced troops of the 32nd Division were passing through to continue the pursuit.

The Memorial, which is again somewhat dilapidated, records that over 4,000 prisoners and over seventy guns were taken on 29 September 1918 between Bellenglise and Riqueval as the Division broke through the Hindenburg Line. There is another memorial at Vermelles.

On the horizon to the left the Australian 4th Division Memorial may be seen.

Continue to a turning to the right signed to La Baraque British and Uplands CWGC Cemeteries. Turn immediately after the turning La Baraque cemetery is on the right.

• *La Baraque CWGC Cemetery/12 miles/10 minutes/Map 14/7*

This beautiful tiny cemetery contains sixty-two headstones, including eight RAMC men, in two rows. All are from 29 September-8 October 1918. In it is buried **Pte James Lawrence Rentoul**, RAMC, age 33, 'Beloved Minister of Ross Trevor Presbyterian Church, Ireland' (to whom a tribute was left in the Cemetery Report box by a Priest from Ross and his son) and **Lt Cairns, MC**, Notts & Derby, 30 September 1918. From the back of the cemetery the 46th Division Obelisk can be seen.

Uplands Cemetery is some distance beyond up the track. It contains forty-three UK burials, many of 32nd Division from September-October 1918, including **Pte S. Larkin MM**, Border Regt, 29 September 1918.

Turn round and return to the N44 and turn right. Continue north on the N44 to the junction with the D932 to Nauray and the Relais du Riqueval on the right. Stop on the left by a brown sign to Pont de Riqueval. There is a small track through the bushes on the left. Walk through it to the bridge.

Australian 4th Division Memorial, Bellenglise.

View of the canal from the Riqueval Bridge.

NOUS N'OUBLIONS PAS
L'AUSTRALIE
1918 - 1998
WE DO NOT FORGET
AUSTRALIA

Plaque to Australia on Bellenglise Mairie.

Detail of WFA Plaque, Riqueval.

The 46th (N Midlands) Division Memorial, near Bellenglise.

1914 1918
REMEMBERING

THE WESTERN FRONT
ASSOCIATION

On September 29 1918 the British 46th (North Midland) Division
attacked the powerful defences of the "Hindenburg Line". A
Company of the 6/North Staffordshire Regiment (137th Brigade)
and a detachment of the Royal Engineers seized the Riqueval
Farm Bridge, the last one left intact across the St Quentin
Canal, an important feature of the German defences. This
greatly assisted the forward flow of supports to complete the
successful storming of the "Seigfried Position", inaugurating
the last phase of the victorious final offensive of the Allies
which ended with the Armistice on November 11.

Le 29 Septembre 1918, la 46ème Division britannique (North Midlands)
attaqua les puissantes défenses de la "Ligne Hindenburg".
Une compagnie du 6ème Bataillon du North
Staffordshire Regiment (137ème Brigade) et un detachement des
Royal Engineers saisirent le pont de la Ferme Riqueval, le
dernier demeurant intact sur le Canal de Saint-Quentin, point
cle des défenses Allemandes. Cette action facilita
l'acheminement des renforts necessaires pour mener à bien
l'assault de la "Position Seigfried", inaugurant ainsi la
derniere phase de l'offensive finale et victorieuse des Allies
qui se termina par l'armistice le 11 Novembre.
Erected on the 75th Anniversary

• *Riqueval Bridge, Bunker & WFA Memorial/13.1 miles/15 minutes/ Map 14/8/9*

The bridge is the boundary between the British IX Corps and the American II Corps. It was in the 46th Division area and was the top end of the 800 yard frontage attacked by the 1st/6th North Staffords. It was known that the bridge was a main supply route for the Germans west of the canal and that on the night of 28 September it was still intact. Therefore it was decided that one company of Staffords under Capt A.H. Charlton should attempt to seize the bridge. On the morning of the attack the visibility was so bad that Charlton had to lead his group forward by compass but as they scrambled down the slope towards the western end they were fired on by a machine gun in a

La Baraque CWGC Cemetery.

trench short of their objective. Charlton took nine men and silenced the machine gun with bayonets and then raced for the bridge. Four Germans, who formed the firing party for the bridge, came out of cover and headed for the demolition charges. Charlton's men won the race, shooting all four Germans and cutting the leads to the charges. The whole company then stormed over the bridge and cleared out enemy posts and trenches on the far side. If you look carefully into the bushes on your way in you will see a **Bunker** on your right.

Beside it is a **Memorial with the WFA insignia**. It records the 29 September 1918 attack of the British 46th (N Midlands) Division which inaugurated the last phase of the victorious final offensive of the Allies ending with the Armistice on 11 November. It was erected on the 75th Anniversary.

One of the most famous photographs of the war was taken here three days later when Brigadier Campbell stood on the bridge and addressed men of his brigade.

Continue on the N44 to a sign saying 'Grand Souterrain de Riqueval' and park on the left near a small memorial column.

• Tennessee 30th Division Memorial, Riqueval Tunnel Entrance/Canal Museum & Tourist Office/13.8 miles/20 minutes/Map 14/10

The small Obelisk was erected in 1923 by the State in memory of the 'Tennessee troops of the 59th and 60th Brigades of the 30th Division who broke the Hindenburg Line on September 29th 1918'. The 30th Division was made up from National Guard units from North and South Carolina and Tennessee and it rejoiced in the nickname 'Old Hickory' after Andrew Jackson who had been born in Carolina.

The American 30th Division, supported by tanks, advanced quickly on 29 September with three regiments forward on a 3,000-yard front and overwhelmed three lines of trenches and barbed wire as well as sealing off this entrance to the tunnel. However, the Germans had constructed many exits through the roof of the tunnel over its four-mile length and once the Americans had passed they came up and attacked from the rear.

Beside the Memorial is a preserved 1910 *'toueur'* and behind it the **Canal Museum of 'Touage' and Office de Tourisme du Vermandois** which describes the history of this fascinating, 5,670 metre underground section of canal, built in Napoleonic times (as a large Plaque to the left bears witness, and a sign to the *Rampe Impériale*). The *'toueur'* is a unique electrical winch boat that tows barges and pleasure boats through the underground canal.

Opening times variable, advertised as all year: Mon-Fri 0930-1230 and 1330-1730. April-September: weekends and holidays 1000-1230 and 1430-1830 . Tel: + (0)3 23 09 50 51. Fax: + (0)3 23 09 57 07. E-mail: pays.du.vermandois@wanadoo.fr There is also **Information Panel No 8** in the *Chemins et Mémoires* series describing the actions here in 1918.

The tunnel entrance is below you and by carefully descending the path and steps it is possible to stand beside the canal and look into the tunnel. This is still a working canal and overhead wires provide electricity for the barges and for lighting. The Germans installed heat, ventilation and light in the tunnel, which was dry, and they added chambers in the walls to use as store-rooms, offices and medical facilities, etc and had closed off the entrances. Barges were used as barracks and ventilation chimneys gave access to machine-gun posts.

It is possible to walk into the tunnel along a small footpath, but discretion is the better part of valour because feelings of disorientation can occur after about twenty-five yards. As you climb up again (and it is very steep) you should be able to spot the remains of German bunkers on the west side that protected roof exits.

Continue to Bellicourt village and turn left at the central crossroads on the D331 signed to Hargicourt and stop at the cemetery on the right.

• *Bellicourt British CWGC Cemetery/14.7 miles/10 minutes/Map 14/11*

The cemetery contains 869 UK, 305 Australian, five S African, one Canadian and three Chinese burials with twenty-one Special Memorials. Stand at the Cross and face the headstones. You are effectively looking at a battalion of men standing in front of you. Many are from September-October 1918. They include **Lt Col Bernard William Vann, VC, MC + Bar**, *Croix de Guerre + Palme*, age 31, Notts & Derby, 3 October 1918. On 29 September Vann led his Battalion across the Canal du Nord through thick fog and under heavy fire. When the attack was held up at Bellenglise he rushed up to the firing line and led the line forward himself, rushing a field gun single-handed and knocking out three of its detachment. He was killed four days later leading another attack. His personal inscription reads, 'A great Priest who in his days pleased God'. The Cemetery Report reveals ten or so MC winners in this cemetery from September and October 1918, notably **Capt R.M. Leake, MC + Bar**, age 24, Loyal N Lancs, 18 September 1918. **Pte William George Boehm**, II Aust M-G Corps, 3 October 1918, served as 'Beams'. Two groups of 14 Special Memorial graves are laid out in rectangles.

Return to the N44, turn left and continue to the large memorial on the left. Stop.

• *Bellicourt American Memorial/15.9 miles/15 minutes/Map 14/12*

This splendid Memorial sits directly over the top of the Bellenglise tunnel and when the foundations were being prepared passages leading to the tunnel and several underground rooms at different levels were found. The tunnel was built by Napoleon between 1802 and 1810 and the low ridge upon which the monument stands was formed by spoil from the original excavations. On the front of the beautiful creamy stone Memorial are the *bas-relief* figures of *'Valor'* and 'Remembrance', executed by L. Bottiau of Paris, flanking an American eagle and below them are the names of battles and the inscription 'Erected by the United States Government in Commemoration of those American units which served with the British Armies in France during the World War.' The designer was **Paul Cret** (qv) of Philadelphia and the Memorial was dedicated on 9 August 1937. A Plaque to the right tells that it is one of eleven monuments erected in Europe for WW1 to commemorate the achievements of the 90,000 American troops who served with the British forces during the war. It describes how on 29 September 1918 after five days of preliminary fighting the attack was launched to breach the Hindenburg Line. The Australian II Corps (with the 27th and 30th US Divisions) had the mission of penetrating the defences immediately to the west of the tunnel. They were supported by British artillery and tanks and only after hard fighting and heavy casualties was the mission successfully accomplished and the enemy driven eastwards.

The other side of the Memorial overlooks the 30th Division area and beyond it to the right, the 27th Division area. By using the map on the rear of the Monument, the

The entrance to the Riqueval Tunnel.

Headstone of Lt Col B.W. Vann, VC, M‑
Bar, Croix de Guerre, Bellicourt Brit‑
CWGC Cemetery.

The elegant American Monument, Bellicourt.

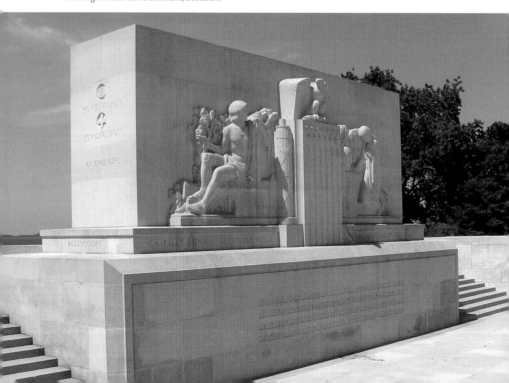

The Tennessee 30th Division Memorial, Riqueval.

ERECTED BY THE STATE
OF TENNESSEE U.S.A.
TO THE TENNESSEE TROOPS
OF THE 59TH
AND 60TH BRIGADES
30TH DIVISION
AMERICAN
EXPEDITIONARY FORCE
WHO BROKE THE
HINDENBURG LINE
ON SEPT 29TH 1918

Plaque to Americans, Bony Mairie

IN MEMORY OF THE AMERICAN SOLDIERS WHO REST IN BONY CEMETERY, AND OF ALL WHO FOUGHT SUFFERED OR DIED ON THE SOMME BATTLE-FRONT IN 1918, THIS BUILDING HAS BEEN ERECTED AND PRESENTED TO FRANCE BY THEIR RELATIVES, THEIR FRIENDS AND THEIR COMRADES.

EN MÉMOIRE DES SOLDATS AMÉRICAINS QUI REPOSENT DANS LE CIMETIÈRE DE BONY, ET DE TOUS CEUX QUI COMBATTIRENT, SOUFFRIRENT, MOURURENT SUR LES CHAMPS DE BATAILLE DE LA SOMME EN 1918, CET ÉDIFICE A ÉTÉ CONSTRUIT ET OFFERT À LA FRANCE PAR LEURS PARENTS, LEURS AMIS ET LEURS FRÈRES D'ARMES.

orientation table beside it and the map in this book, a very good idea can be gained of the progress of the fighting. A little careful searching of the horizon to your right front should reveal an American flag flying just to the right of some trees. This marks the location of the American Cemetery at Bony which is in the 27th Division area and is your next stop. The two American Divisions had more than 7,500 casualties in this area and many lie in the Bony Cemetery.

Continue on the N44 to the next crossroads.

Extra Visit to Plaque (Map 14/13) and Graves (Map 14/14) of 4 British Soldiers Shot by the Germans, Le Catelet. Round trip: 2.2 miles. Approximate time: 20 minutes

Continue towards Le Catelet. Stop on the right in the car park for the Auberge de la Croix d'Or. Walk over the road to the garden to the left of the restaurant.

The Croix d'Or is a charming restaurant specialising in seasonal local produce. Tel: + (0)3 23 66 21 71. It would be courteous to ask the owners Fabienne and Bernard Villemont for permission to visit the Memorial.

On the stone wall is a grey marble **Plaque** with the words '*Ici ont été fusillés en Mai 1916 4 soldats britanniques*' (here in May 1916 four British soldiers were shot) and the names [sic] ROBERT DIGBY, THOMAS DONOHE, MARTIN DAVID, WILLIAM THORBE. They were in fact Pte Robert Digby, Hants Regt, Ptes Thomas Donohoe and David Martin, RIF and William Thorpe, KORL. On the wall behind the Plaque which bears their names there are still supposed to be the bullet marks from the execution squad.

Behind this simple commemorative **Plaque** is one of the most curious stories of the war. It is told in detail in Ben Macintyre's moving tale, *A Foreign Field*.

Briefly, Macintyre, then representing *The Times*, somewhat grudgingly agreed to cover the unveiling of the Plaque in 1999 and after the ceremony was approached by an old lady in a wheelchair who claimed to be Pte Digby's daughter. This led him to research the remarkable story of seven British soldiers who, after the chaos of the Retreat From Mons were separated from their units. After a series of adventures the soldiers arrived in Hargival and were hidden by the aristocratic Jeanne Magniez who, for three months, gave them refuge in a hut in her woods. They were fed and their wounds tended.The Germans, who occupied Le Catelet, with their HQ in the Château and also the Château above Villeret, mounted a determined manhunt for Allied stragglers and local French mayors who sheltered them were faced with the death penalty. Jeanne Magniez despatched the men towards Villeret where they hid in a cabin in the woods until they were split up and hidden by various villagers in their homes. They integrated with the local population and, coached by their hosts, learned to masquerade as villagers. In December the Germans occupied the village and life became even more difficult. But Digby was the most successful in being able to integrate and started a love affair with the pretty Claire Desenne, who became pregnant. Meanwhile there was some collaboration with the occupying

Extra Visit continued

Germans in the region and other hidden Allied soldiers were betrayed and shot. Tensions were running high in Villeret when Claire gave birth to a daughter, Hélène, on 14 November 1915. Some were branding the fugitives as deserters and wondering why they did not make a more determined effort to return to their own lines.

The German population changed as men were sent to the Verdun front and the Uhlans returned in February 1916. The German writer Ernst Jünger was among the new arrivals and vividly described the battered village and its inhabitants. [After the great Somme battle of 1 July, Jünger was wounded in the legs and treated in Villeret's field hospital. He died age 102 in February 1998.]

On 30 March a poster was attached to the Villeret *Mairie* giving a deadline of 30 April for fugitives to give themselves up, after when they would be shot and their benefactors severely punished. Six of Villeret's soldiers hurriedly left, Robert Digby alone remaining. Some were soon captured, others returned. Eventually the four mentioned on the Plaque were reunited and decided to make a run for it and attempt to cross the German lines at Péronne. Within two days they were back, but their presence was reported to the Germans from Le Catelet who stormed into the village at dawn on 16 May. [Macintyre believes he has identified the traitor after much complicated research.] Thorpe, Donohue and Martin were captured as they slept and marched into Le Catelet where they were sentenced to be shot. Several of the villagers were also arrested, tried and were sentenced to hard labour or fined heavily. Meanwhile Digby escaped into the woods where he was beseeched by the father, Emile Marié, of the imprisoned mayor, Parfait, to give himself up, when his life would be spared. On 22 May Digby surrendered to Marié. In Le Catelet he was tried and, despite the assurances, sentenced to death and placed in a cell with his three comrades. In the late afternoon of 27 May 1916 Thorpe, Donohue and Martin were lashed to recently erected execution posts, without blindfolds, and shot. They were then bundled into newly-made coffins (Martin's long legs broken by a German officer to enable him to fit in). They were buried beside the church by the local Curé and the carpenter, their graves later covered with flowers. Later the prisoners from Villeret were transported by train to Germany. Another execution post was erected by the Château wall and on Tuesday, 30 May Digby wrote to his mother and to the Desenne family. After his execution he was buried in the furthest corner of the village cemetery with orders that only one wreath should be placed on his grave.

A complicated network of spies, some working for the Germans, some for the British, existed in the area and speculation was rife as to who had betrayed Villeret's British lodgers.

In 1930 Robert Digby's brother, Thomas, who came across the letter Robert had written to his mother about his little French daughter, travelled to Villeret and officially recognised Hélène 'as his own daughter' and adopted her. She

Extra Visit continued

Plaque to Shot English Soldiers, May 1916, Le Catelet.

Digby's hard to read headstone, Le Catelet Cemetery.

married a man from Le Verguier, Hubert Cornaille, and was still living in 2004. *Continue through the village to the churchyard on the right, just before the L'Escaut River, whose source is a few miles to the right.* In it are buried in a small plot of 3 graves at the front of the cemetery: **Ptes David Martin** and **Thomas Donohue** of the RIF and **William Thorpe** 1st King's Own R Lancs). All are recorded as having died on Saturday, 27 May and then 'buried by the enemy'. **Pte Robert Digby** 1st Hampshires, age 31, whose death is recorded as being on Tuesday, 30 May, but also 'buried by the enemy', is buried at the rear of the cemetery beside another British grave.

Turn round and return to the crossroads to pick up the main itinerary.

N.B. In the local cemetery of the village of **Guise**, some 25kms from St Quentin on the N29-E44, another 11 British soldiers shot by the Germans in the Fort of Guise on 25 February 1915 are buried. They are **Pte D. Buckley, Pte F. Innocent, L/Cpl J. Moffatt, Pte D. Horgan** and **Pte J. Nash** of the Royal Munster Fusiliers; **Pte G. Howard, Pte M. Wilson, Pte T. Murphy, Pte W. Thompson, Pte J. Walsh** of the Connaught Rangers and **L/Cpl J.W. Stent** of the King's Hussars. (Also buried there is **Driver J.W. Yarnell** of the RFA, 25 August 1914.)

Theirs' is an equally fascinating story which starts on 25 August 1914 when 35 British soldiers were isolated from their units. Some managed to escape through Belgium and Holland and eventually return to the front. Eleven of them were found in the village of Iron where they were hidden and fed by the local millers, M and Mme Logez, aided by other villagers, notably the Chalandre family, at great danger to themselves. They were betrayed in a tangled web of love and jealousy. Clovis Chalandre, a 16-year old youth, was obsessed by a married siren who was living with an old man called Bachelet and pestered the couple, whereupon M Bachelet denounced the Chalandre family to the German Commandant of the Citadel at Guise for harbouring the soldiers. They and the Chalandre family were then brutally arrested, the house burned. The 11 soldiers and M Chalandre were shot, Mme Chalandre and her two children were imprisonned. Mme Logez was also imprisoned and her mill was burned. The traitor Bachelet received 10 francs per head for the victims he betrayed. The bodies of the soldiers were exhumed in May 1920 and buried with reverence in the local cemetery.

Turn left and follow signs to the American cemetery through Bony, with its distinctive white church steeple. On the right as you go through the village is the Mairie.

• American Plaque, Bony Mairie/19.8 miles/5 minutes/Map 14/15

On the wall of the *Mairie* is a **Plaque** in memory of the American soldiers who rest in Bony Cemetery and all who fought, suffered and died on the Somme Battlefield front in 1918. The *Mairie* was funded by their relatives, friends and comrades.

Continue to the American Cemetery.

Note the narrow track to the right just before the cemetery wall. It leads to Lempire past Guillemont Farm (qv), the scene of fierce resistance by withering machine-gun fire on 29 September.

Drive through the second entrance to the reception centre.

• The American Somme Cemetery, Bony/20.5 miles/25 minutes/Map 14/16

A temporary cemetery was established here in October 1918 for the burial of those killed in the Hindenburg Line fighting. American policy allows repatriation of their war dead's remains and today some 1,850 burials are left, including some men who fought at Cantigny.

The reception centre houses the normal visitors' room (with registers), toilets and drinking water. From it a path leads to the tall flagpole in the centre of the cemetery, around whose base are four bronze helmets. It is always an inspiring sight to see the Stars and Stripes or the *Tricolore* flying in their respective military cemeteries and many British visitors express regret that our own flag does not fly in our military cemeteries. It is a matter of practicality. We have so many cemeteries, nearly all of them without immediate local supervision, that it would be impossible to administer the provision and maintenance of flags. However, it does fly at the Thiepval Memorial (qv). One official reason for not flying it more generally is that the Union flag does not represent all of the nations commemorated. Indeed the Canadians fly their flag at Vimy and the Australians theirs at Villers Bretonneux, rather than the Union flag. After the American Civil War a day in May was set aside as 'Memorial' or 'Decoration' Day to honour those who died. American War dead are remembered and ceremonies are held and flags placed at all memorials on each grave marker in cemeteries in Europe by the American

340 • Major & Mrs Holt's Battlefield Guide to The Western Front – South

Overseas Memorial Day Association. The Association is based in Paris and was founded in 1930 and is non-profit making. The date of the Memorial Day activities varies slightly, but is as close as possible to the original date of 30 May. In 2000 an organisation called *Les Fleurs de la Mémoire* (The Flowers of Memory) was formed and now numbers several thousand French families. Each family commits to laying a flower on the grave of an American soldier at least once a year and, exceptionally for Independence Day (4 July) in 2003, the 225th anniversary of the treaty of friendship between the two nations, a deep red rose was laid on each of the 60,511 American graves and eleven monuments. This was to counteract the deteriorating Franco-American feelings after the Gulf War of 2003 and to show the gratitude of the French Nation for the American sacrifice in two world wars. The roses were laid diagonally, the head to the right hand corner of each cross to symbolise the American gesture of laying the right arm over the heart when their national anthem is played. In Bony the Mayor and local schoolchildren, as well as some passing WFA members and the authors, took part in this extremely moving ceremony.

There are three **Medal of Honor** winners buried here, their names picked out in gold. They are **1st Lt William B. Turner,** 105th Inf, 27 September 1918, whose bravery you read about earlier. He was also awarded Italian and Portuguese decorations: **Cpl Thomas E. O'Shea**, M-G Coy, 107th Inf, was mortally wounded on 29 September when he left his shellhole to cross fire-swept ground to answer a call for help from an American tank: **Pte Robert L. Blackwell**, Coy K, 119th Inf was killed on 11 October trying to get through heavy shell and machine-gun fire after he had volunteered to take a message asking for reinforcements when his platoon was surrounded. Only 137 of the burials are those of unknown soldiers, although seven of these are in one grave. At the bottom or eastern end of the cemetery is a memorial chapel, inside which the names of 333 soldiers with no known grave are inscribed. Above the bronze doors of the chapel is an American eagle with spread wings and inside are a number of flags beside the altar, all illuminated by the light from coloured SGWs bearing regimental and divisional insignia. On the exterior wall are *bas-reliefs* of a Renault tank, guns and shells. The cemetery architect was George Howe of Philadelphia and the sculptor of the *bas-reliefs* on the chapel, and the two eagles facing the road, was Frenchman Marcel Loyau. On 2 June 1996 two pillars containing a campanile were presented and dedicated by the Robert R. McCormick Tribune Foundation (qv). The carillon plays a 21-gun salute and the bugle call 'Taps' (the American equivalent of 'The Last Post') as the cemetery closes. Every two hours throughout the day marches, anthems and Doughboy songs are played. The sound wafts around the cemetery in a most haunting manner. You can hear 'Taps' by going to http://bensguide.gpo.gov/3-5/symbols/taps.html

The cemetery is **Open from 0900-1700**. Superintendent's tel: + (0)3 23 66 87 20. Fax: + (0)3 23 66 87 27. E-mail: somme.cemetery@abmc-er.org

Continue on the D57, under the motorway to the small crossroads with the D58.

N.B. To the left is the village of Villeret where the **four British soldiers shot in Le Catelet (qv) were hidden**. To the village in October 1916 came pitiful columns of Russian prisoners and an old quarry to the north of the village was converted into a prison camp. Brought in as forced labour to prepare for the German withdrawal to the new Siegfried Line (as the Germans called the Hindenburg Line) they were abysmally treated and many died in the cold winter of 1917. Everything between the old front line and the new fortified line was destroyed to deny it to the Allies – bridges blown, trees felled, buildings burned, land flooded and many booby traps placed. The area became untenable for the remaining inhabitants and they were forcibly evacuated to the Ardennes and other far-off destinations. Châteaux and mansions around Villeret were ransacked and blown to pieces, mines were laid, the church and *Mairie* were packed with explosives and the village was razed to the ground. After the war it was awarded the *Croix de Guerre*.

Turn right on the D332 (which becomes the D58) signed to le Ronssoy. Continue through Lempire to the small crossroads (signed to the right to Malassise Farm) and stop. On the left is

• 12th (Eastern) Division Memorial/25 miles/5 minutes/Map 14/17

This hexagonal cream stone Monument is in memory of the Officers, WOs, NCOs and Men of the Division which arrived in France in May 1915. The first side bears the dates 1914, 1915 and the battle honours Armentières, Loos, The Quarries; the second, 1916, Hohenzollern Redoubt, The Somme, Ovillers; the third, 1917 Arras, Monchy le Preux, Cambrai; the fourth, 1918 Albert, Morlancourt, Nurlu, Epehy, St Quentin Canal, Lens to l'Escaut River; the fifth, the word 'VICTORY' and the sixth the words 'Grant them o Lord eternal rest'. The Ace-of-Spades-shaped divisional insignia is on the base. (Their divisional concert party became famous as 'The Spades'.)

Turn round and return to Lempire. Turn left on the D28, direction Vendhuile.
Just before the Lempire exit sign is the village church and cemetery on which is a green *Tombes de Guerre* sign. In it, right at the bottom, is a small plot of twelve British graves, eight of which are DLI of 20 July 1917.

Continue to the British cemetery on the left just before the motorway.

• Unicorn CWGC Cemetery/27.2 miles/10 minutes/Map 14/18

The cemetery lies just on the American side of the corps boundary between the British III and the American II Corps. Up ahead, just beyond the motorway and to the right of the road, is the area of 'The Knoll', one of the fortified positions that gave the 27th US Division such trouble. Burials began after the Hindenburg battle when men of the 18th Division were buried in what is now the first row of twenty-eight graves on the right. The burials were actually made by the 50th (Northumberland) Division and the cemetery was named from their divisional emblem. After the Armistice the cemetery was extended by bringing in burials from the surrounding area. There are now some 925 British (including one RAF) graves, seventy-eight from Australia, one Canadian, four Indian. The Unknowns number 409. It was designed by Charles Holden, perhaps best known for his designs of London Underground Stations. There is a VC winner buried here and it is perhaps appropriate near the end of this last battlefield tour to include his citation as a tribute to all those who fought. Courage defies absolute definition. In the end, in its finest form, it probably derives from a sense of responsibility towards one's fellow humans. Everyone who served in this war, on whatever side, had to struggle with personal and private fears. Some came through that struggle better than others and rose above the ordinary. A small number of those received our nation's highest honour. Cpl Weathers did. This is his entry in the Cemetery Register:

Headstone of MoH Winner, 1st Lt William B. Turner. The Stars and Stripes fly at half mast in honour of President Ronald Reagan whose death was announced on 6 June 2004.

The immaculate rows of headstones, with the distinctive white tower of Bony Church behind the American Cemetery, Bony.

The 12th (Eastern) Division Memorial near Lempire.

'Weathers, Cpl. Lawrence Carthage, 1153, VC. 43rd Bn Australian Inf. Died of wounds 29th Sept. 1918. Native of North Wairo, New Zealand.' An extract from the *London Gazette*, no. 31082, dated 24 December 1918, records the following: 'For most conspicuous bravery and devotion to duty on the 2 September, 1918, north of Péronne, when with an advanced bombing party. The attack having been held up by a strongly held enemy trench, Cpl Weathers went forward alone under heavy fire and attacked the enemy with bombs. Then, returning to our lines for a further supply of bombs, he again went forward with three comrades and attacked under very heavy fire. Regardless of personal danger, he mounted the enemy parapet and bombed the trench and, with the support of his comrades, captured 180 prisoners and three machine guns. His valour and determination resulted in the successful capture of the final objective, and saved the lives of many of his comrades.'

Please sign the visitors' book.

• End of Breaking the Hindenburg Line Battlefield Tour

Unicorn CWGC Cemetery.

Headstone of
Cpl Weathers, VC.

ALLIED & GERMAN WAR GRAVES & COMMEMORATIVE ASSOCIATIONS

N.B. Please refer to *Major & Mrs Holt's Concise Illustrated Battlefield Guide to the Western Front – North* for more details of organisations with an asterisk (*)

*AMERICAN BATTLE MONUMENTS COMMISSION (ABMC)

As well as the cemeteries the AMBC maintains the impressive WW1 Memorials at Audenarde, Kemmel, Bellicourt, Château-Thierry, Cantigny, Sommepy, Montfaucon, Montsec and Brest (Naval). Outside the Town Hall at Souilly is a bronze tablet marking the site of the HQ of the American 1st Army at the end of WW1 and from where the Meuse-Argonne campaign was conducted.

There are also some 700 Private American Memorials in Europe which are presently being located and listed, often by the Superintendents in the nearest ABMC Cemetery. Many of them are in a neglected state but local authorities are being encouraged to help maintain them and there is now a Private Memorials Administrator at Garche, Lillian A. Pfluke. Tel: + (0)1 47 01 32 50. E-mail: privatemonuments@abmc-er.org

Memorial Day programmes are held on different days near to the actual Memorial Day date at the end of May in each ABMC Cemetery. Then every grave is decorated with the flag of the United States and that of the host nation (who donated the ground for the cemetery), and with speakers, usually including the appropriate American Ambassador, and the laying of wreaths with ceremonies that include military bands and units.

Head Office: Courthouse Plaza II, Suite 500, 2300 Clarendon Boulevard, Arlington, VA22201, USA. Tel: + 703 696 6897. Fax: + 703 696 6666. Website: ww.abmc.gov.
European Office: 68 rue du 19 janvier, 92380 Garches, France.
Tel: + (0)1 47 01 19 76. Fax: +(0)1 47 4119 79.

*COMMONWEALTH WAR GRAVES COMMISSIUON

[Many detailed and different aspects of the origins and work of the CWGC have been covered in other *Major & Mrs Holt's Battlefield Guidebooks*.]

CWGC SERVICES TO THE PUBLIC

The Commission holds records of 1.7 million Commonwealth War dead and its Enquiries Section can provide details of the place of burial or commemoration and where possible, directions to the cemetery or memorial. Enquiries are taken by letter, telephone or e-mail and, increasingly, searches can also be made using the online Debt of Honour Register at www.cwgc.org The facilities of this incredible service are continually growing. A teaching resource, 'Remember me – echoes from the lost generations', with seven units, is now available. Website: www.cwgc.org/education.
Head Office: Commonwealth War Graves Commission, 2 Marlow Road, Maidenhead, Berks SL6 7DX , UK. Tel: + (0) 1628 634221. Fax: + (0) 1628 771208. Website: www.cwgc.org
E-mail: Casualty & Cemetery Enquiries: casualty.enq@cwgc.org.

Area Office in France: rue Angèle Richard, 62217 Beaurains, Tel: + (0)3 21 21 77 00. Fax: (03) 21 21 77 10. **E-mail:** france.area@cwgc.org
Joint Casualty & Compassionate Centre has now taken over from **MOD PS4 the handling of remains of service personnel.
Contact: Sue Raftree, RAF Innsworth, GL3 1HW. Tel: + (0)14522 712612, ext 6303. E-mail: historicso3.jcc@innsworth.afpaa.mod.uk. General MOD Website.

*French Ministère des Anciens Combattants et Victimes de Guerre

Head Office: 37 rue de Bellechasse, 75007 Paris 07 SP. Tel: + (0)1 48 76 11 35.

Volksbund Deutsche Kriegsgräberfürsorge

'War graves memorials are one of the few places where history is made visible.
They truly are memorials of millionfold suffering.
[They] cannot prevent war, but they make us think twice.
And when we stand at these crosses,
we know that it is from here that the best reminder of peace is radiated."
VDKG publication '*Work for Peace*'.

The German War Graves Organisation provides a similar service to that of the ABMC and the CWGC in looking after the German war dead and in assisting relatives to find and, in many cases, visit the graves. One of their main aims now is to further the cause of peace in the world. German cemeteries can be found in almost 100 countries worldwide. They are maintained by the VDKG, founded in 1919 for the 1.9 million German dead of the Great War. The Volksbund stays in contact with soldiers' families, looks after them, gives them information about the cemetery in which their loved one is buried and places flowers on their behalf. In nearly every cemetery young people of many nations have worked together for over fifty years under the banner 'Reconciliation over the graves – working for peace'. A programme for planting trees in memorial sites near cemeteries has begun and over 2,000 have already been planted.

As the Volksbund is a private, not a state, organisation it depends 90% on membership fees and donations, which are appreciated, for the continuation of their work. Boxes are placed at all cemeteries or **Contact:** *Volksbund Deutsche Kriegsgräberfürsorge*, Werner Hilpertstrasse 2, D-34112 Kassel, Germany. Tel: + (0) 1805 7009-99.
French Office: rue de Nesle Prolongée, 80320 Chaulnes. Tel: + (0)3 22 85 27 57.

Parliamentary All-Party War Graves & Heritage Group

Consisting of members from both houses the group exists to support the work of the CWGC, to further educational programmes aimed at increasing knowledge of war heritage and battlefield sites, to support campaigners seeking to conserve and promote heritage sites and to encourage best practice in multi-disciplinary battlefield archaeology. It was formed in 2001 as a result of the threat posed to the Pilckem Ridge in the Ypres Salient by plans to extend the A19 motorway and is now concerned with

The Visitor Centre, American Oise-Aisne Cemetery.

Ayette's Poilu sings 'Victory'.

Visitors' Book and Register,
Consenvoye German
Cemetery.

Memorial Day gathering, American Aisne-Marne
Cemetery.

American Meuse-Argonne Cemetery.

Cross to Ivan Diagueleff, Russian Cemetery, Ste Hilaire.

CWGC Tombes de Guerre sign at the entrance to French National Cemetery, la Cheppe.

battlefield sites in the UK and worldwide (including the threat to the area of the Hohenzollern Redoubt on the Loos Battlefield). **Chairman:** Lord Faulkner of Worcester; **Vice Chairmen:** Nigel Dodds MP, Lord Roper, Lord Burnham and Dr Rudi Vis MP; **Treasurer:** Jeffrey Donaldson MP; **Joint Secretaries:** Peter Barton (e-mail pb@parapet.demon.co.uk , Egbert Road, Faversham, Kent DE13 8SJ) and Peter Doyle (e-mail: doyle.towers@virgin.net) This is a long overdue and much welcomed organisation. **Contact:** Either of the secretaries.

Association Connaissance de la Meuse
Marvellously energetic group of enthusiastic historians who are working hard to restore many of the battlefield sites along the Haute Chevauchée, notably the Kaiser Tunnel, which lay neglected for some eighty years. **Contact:** Madame Martin-Blanchet c/o Office de Tourisme du Pays de l'Argonne, 6 Place de la République, 55120 Clermont en Argonne, France. Tel: + (0)3 29 88 42 22. Fax: + (0)3 29 88 42 43. E-mail: tourisme.argonne@wanadoo.fr

Association National le Saillant de St Mihiel Commission (ANSC)
Group of dedicated local military historians energetically led by Norbert Kugel who are rediscovering, renovating and signing the fascinating battlefield sites in their region. **Contact:** M Norbert Kugel, 71 rue du Dr Vuillaume, 55300 St Mihiel, France. Tel/Fax: + (0)3 29 90 90 07.

*Association des Musées et Sites de la Grande Guerre
Contact: Secretary Jean-Pierre Thierry, O.A.M., c/o Historial, B.P. 63 – 8201 Péronne Cedex. Tel: + (0)3 22 83 14 18. E-mail: df17@Historial.org

Association du Tank de Flesquières
Dedicated to preserving the tank 'Deborah' and the memory of the Cambrai battlefield around Flesquières. **Contact:** 3 Bis rue du Moulin, 59267 Flesquières. Tel: + (0)6 14 30 01 65. E-mail: TankofFlesquiere@aol.com

Association du Souvenir aux Morts des Armées de Champagne
Contact: 4 rue des Condanimes, 78000 Versailles.

Croix de Guerre et Valeur Militaire
Official magazine of French military awards. **Contact:** ANCGVM, Hôtel National des Invalides, 129 rue de Grenelle, 75007 Paris. Tel: + (0)1 44 44 42 38 47

*Durand Group
Contact: Lt Col Mike Dolamore, 5 Wentworth Ave, Temple Herdewyke, Southam, Warks CV7 2VA. E-mail: mike@dolomore.demon.co.uk

Friends of Lochnagar

Organisation to support Founder and Chairman Richard Dunning (qv) in his efforts to preserve the Lochnagar Crater, la Boisselle. Interesting magazine, *The New Chequers*.
Contact: Richard Dunning,
E-mail: Richard.dunning@uwclub.net
website: www.lochnagarcrater.org

*Guild of Battlefield Guides

Aims: to develop and raise the understanding and practice of battlefield guiding.
Contact: Guild Secretary
E-mail: secretary@gbg-international.com
Website: www.gbg-international.com

Les Amis de Vauquois et de sa Région

Another group of dedicated volunteers who have worked indefatigably to clear and make safe the incredible site of the Butte de Vauquois, with its honeycomb of tunnels, stretches of Decauville narrow gauge railway and massive craters.
Contact: 1 rue d'Orléans, 55270 Vauquois, Tel: + (0)3 29 80 73 15.
E-mail: amis.vauquois@wanadoo.fr

*Ross Bastiaan Commemorative Plaques

Contact: Website: www.plaques.satlink.com.au

*Royal British Legion

Pilgrimages, **Contact:** Poppy Travel, RBL, Aylesford, Kent ME20 7NX.
Tel: +(0)1622 716729. www.poppytravel.org.uk

Soissonais '14-'18 Association;

A group of very active volunteers who are charting and progressively clearing and making safe for visit the amazing quarries with their unique sculptures and graffiti along the Chemin des Dames.
Contact: Monsieur Pamart, owner of the Ferme de Confrécourt, leading light in the Association. Ferme de Confrécourt, 02290 Bouvron-Vingré. Tel: + (0)3 23 74 25 90.

Somme Association

Dedicated to coordinating the history of Ireland's part in WW1.
Contact: Somme Heritage Centre, 233 Bangor Road, Newtownards BT23 7PH, Co Down, N Ireland.
Tel: + (0)28 91823202. E-mail: sommassociation@dnet.co.uk
Website: www.irishsoldier.org

Souvenir Français

Head Office: 9 rue de Clichy, 75009, Paris

The coveted and respected Badge of an accredited Guide of the Guild of Battlefield Guides

War Relics Archives

Marvellous research on the Demarcation Stones along the Western Front, on US 2nd Div Memorials and on Belgian War Graves. CD Roms available and recommended. **Contact:** Rik Scherpenberg, St Servaastraat 19/1, B-3700 Tongeren, Belgium. Tel: + (0)475 58 07 83. Website: www.wra.be e-mail: rik.scherpenberg@telenet.be

*Western Front Association (WFA)

Contact: Hon Sec Stephen Oram, Spindleberry, Marlow Road, Bourne End, Bucks SL8 5NL Website: www.westernfrontassociation.com

Norbert Kugel,
President ANSM.

Model of 'Deborah', the tank found at Flesquières.

TOURIST INFORMATION

Beware when driving in France to adhere strictly to the speed limit. Fines for speeding are instant and stringent and speed traps may lurk in the most unexpected places. Here is one in the bushes near the Ferme de Navarin.

PICARDY

This large historic area which comprises The Somme, The Aisne and The Oise is represented in the UK by the Comité Régional du Tourisme de Picardie. Contact: Christine Jolly, UK Marketing & Promotional Representative, French Govt Tourist Office, 178 Piccadilly, London, W1J 9AL. Tel: + (0)20 7399 3542. Fax: + (0)20 7493 6594. E-mail: christine.jolly@france-guide.com. In France: CRT, 80011 Amiens, Cedex 1. Tel: + (0)3 33 22 22 33 66. Fax: + (0)3 33 22 22 33 67. E-mail: contact@picardietourisme.com.

THE SOMME

The Somme is glorious: great rolling agricultural plains give way to the picturesque valleys of the Somme and the Ancre – a paradise for the huntin', shootin', fishin' fraternity. Their summer cabins nestle beside the wooded banks and pools. Local specialities are eels (*anguilles*), duck (*canard*) pâté, guinea fowl (*pintade*) and fresh vegetables from the *hortillonages* (small allotments on the rich mud islands of the Somme at Amiens) are marvellous – when you can track them down – so is the *Ficelle Picarde* (a savoury pancake with ham, mushroom and cream).

Somme Departmental Tourist Office, 21 rue Ernest Cauvin, 80000 Amiens. Tel: + (0)3 22 71 22 71
Fax: + (0)3 22 71 22 69. Tourist information and advice for the whole of the Somme area. Excellent literature. Open normal office hours only.

Amiens makes a good base and has a variety of hotels, from many 1- and 2-star individual hotels, and much-of-a-muchness chains – e.g. Ibis, Balladins, to the 3-star Carlton (which was the historic old Carlton Belfort where Siegfried Sassoon and other notables stayed) in the Station Square and the Mercure by the Cathedral and the Novotel Amiens-Est with outdoor pool in the suburb of Boves, very conveniently placed for the battlefield (Tel: + (0)3 22 50 42 42. Fax: + (0)3 22 50 42 49), with a 2-star Campanile and 1-star Formule 1 nearby. A trip by boat along the Somme from Amiens will help you imagine what it might have been like to have been aboard a hospital barge. *Bateau Le Picardie* Tel: + (0)3 22 92 16 40.

Albert. Tourist Office: 9 rue Gambetta. Tel: + (0)3 22 75 16 42. Fax: + (0)3 22 75 11 72. This is absolutely central for the battlefields. The 2-star Logis de France Hotel de la Paix has refurbished rooms and an excellent restaurant. Patrons are the delightful Isabelle and Frederic Daudigny-Duthoit, 45 rue Victor Hugo, 80300 Albert. Tel: + (0)3 22 75 01 64. Fax: + (0)3 22 75 44 17. The 2-star Hotel de la Basilique is opposite the Golden Madonna. 3-5 rue Gambetta. Tel: + (0)3 22 75 04 71. Fax: + (0)3 22 75 10 47. The 3-star Royal Picardie has twenty-four en-suite bedrooms and restaurant with traditional and regional cuisine. Ave du Gen Leclerc. Tel: + (0)3 22 75 27 00. Fax: + (0)3 22 75 60 19.

Assevillers. Useful motorway stop on Autoroute du Nord, Calais-Paris. Shop, tourist information, cafeteria, fast foods, pleasant restaurant. Next door is the 3-star Mercure Hotel with extra large bedrooms (it was a 4-star hotel originally). It is ideal for the Somme, for Kaiser's Battle, even Hindenburg Line tours. Tel: + (0)3 22 85 78 30. Fax: + (0)3 22 85 78 31. There is also a Formule 1 hotel adjacent.

Péronne. Tourist Office: Place du Château. Tel: + (0)3 22 84 42 38. Now that Péronne has opened the official Museum of the Great War on the Somme, known as *l'Historial de la Grande Guerre* (qv), a visit to this historic and interesting town becomes worthwhile. On the outskirts from the motorway is a Campanile. Tel: + (0)3 22 84 22 22. Fax: + (0)3 22 84 16 86.

Bapaume. Tourist Information: Hôtel de Ville, Place Faidherbe.Tel: + (0)3 21 59 89 84. Leaflets on the history of the town and lists of restaurants/hotels are available here.

This can make a convenient base or lunch break for the Somme. There are two hotels: the 2-star La Paix (a *Logis de France*), Avénue Abel Guidet, with an excellent restaurant, Tel: + (0)3 21 07 11 03. Fax: + (0)3 21 07 43 66 and the 1-star Le Gourmet, rue de la Gare, Tel: + (0)3 21 07 20 00. Fax: + (0)3 21 07 98 81. There are several restaurants, including the Stromboli Pizzeria. Tel: + (0)3 21 59 88 51.

Cambrai. Tourist office: 48 rue de Noyon. Tel: + (0)3 27 78 36 15. They have lists of hotels and restaurants and local attractions. Note that the office is not in the Gran' Place as one would expect but off it down the Avénue de la Victoire, to the right just in front of the Museum with the cathedral to the left. This is another good lunch stop, with a traditional Gran' Place, Town Hall and Belfry Tower and loads of restaurants. Local speciality is the mint sweet known as '*Bétise de Cambrai*'.

There are 2-star Campanile (Tel: + (0)3 27 81 62 00. Fax: + (0)3 27 83 07 87) and Ibis: (Tel: + (0)3 27 82 99 88. Fax: + (0)3 27 82 99 89) hotels on the Route de Bapaume and the more glamorous 3-star Château de la Motte Fenélon, Allée St Roch (Tel: + (0)3 27 83 61 38. Fax: + (0)3 27 83 71 61). The charming 3-star Hotel Béatus, Avénue de Paris. Tel: + (0)3 27 81 45 70, Fax: + (0)3 27 78 00 83, is owned by WW1 tank enthusiast and author Philippe Gorczynski. Attractive décor and gardens.

THE AISNE

Comité du Tourisme de l'Aisne, 36 Avénue Charles de Gaulle, 02007 Laon. Tel: + (0)3 23 27 76 76. Fax: + (0)3 23 27 76 89. In recent years the tourist authority of the Aisne has put much energy into promoting this beautiful and historic area, with many attractive leaflets describing sites of interest in the area and the accommodation possibilities (there are many attractive *Gîtes* and well-equipped camping sites) etc.

In **Laon** are the 2-star Campanile Hotel on the Avénue Gen de Gaulle, Tel: + (0)3 3 23 23 15 05 and the more characterful 3-star Hotel La Bannière de France, 11 rue F. Roosevelt. Tel: + (0)3 23 23 21 44. Fax: + (0)3 23 23 31 56, which has seventeen rooms and an excellent restaurant specialising in regional and fish dishes. Nearby in **Monampteuil**, is the small Logis de France Auberge du Lac, Tel: + (0)3 23 21 63 87. Fax: + (0)3 23 21 60 60 with an excellent restaurant and basic bedrooms. At **Chamouille**, overlooking the Lake of Ailette and golf course is the exceptional Mercure Golf de l'Ailette, Tel: + (0)3 23 24 84 85. Fax: + (0)3 23 24 81 20.

St Quentin. Tourist Office: 27 rue Victor Basch. Tel: + (0)3 23 67 05 00. Fax: + (0)3 23 67 78 71. Lists of hotels, restaurants, attractions in the region, known as the Saint Quentinois. Main sights in the city are the magnificent Basilique and the Hôtel de Ville. There are several modern budget hotels, like the Hotel B&B City, Tel: + (0)3 23 05 81 81 and Hotel Première Classe, Tel: + (0)3 23 64 24 40, both in rue Antoine Parmentier (near the German Cemetery), and the traditional 3-star Grand Hotel, 6 rue Dachery, Tel: + (0)3 23 62 69 77 and 2-star Hotel de la Paix et Albert 1er, Place du 8 Octobre, Tel: + (0)3 23 62 77 62. The latter is near the Canal and the impressive War Memorial. There are the 2-star Ibis, 14 Place de la Basilique, Tel: + (0)3 23 67 40 40, and Campanile, Rue C. Naudin, ZAC de la Vallée, Tel: + (0)3 23 67 91 22. St Quentin has a plethora of restaurants from the 3-star Auberge de l'Ermitage, 331 rue de Paris, Tel: + (0)3 23 62 42 80 to many themed restaurants and fast food outlets.

Ocean Villas Tea Rooms, Auchonvillers.

The attractive pool area at the Novotel Amiens-Est.

Le Tulipier Hotel, Vienne-le-Château.

View from the Mercure, Lac d'Ailette.

Tank enthusiast Philippe Gorczynski's delightful Hotel Béatus, Cambrai.

An excellent way to tour the Chemin des Dames – on your Harley!

The rebuilt Town Hall, Villers Bretonneux.

Floral display, Fayet, Ville Fleurie.

Soissons. Tourist Office: 16 Place F. Marquigny.
Tel: + (0)3 23 53 17 37. Fax: + (0)3 23 59 67 72. Soissons was the first capital of France following Clovis's victory over the last Roman General, Syagrius, and despite the ravages of the '14-'18 War it retains some architectural gems, such as the splendid Gothic Cathedral. Although Soissons was not completely razed to the ground during the war, it was severely damaged and like so many of the main towns in the region, much of its reconstruction was carried out in the then popular *Art Deco* style, notably the Egyptian House at 22 rue du Collège.

CHAMPAGNE/MEUSE-ARGONNE/ VERDUN/ST MIHIEL

Reims. Tourist office: 2 rue Guillaume de Machault.
Tel: + (0)3 26 77 45 25. Fax: + (0)3 26 77 45 27.
This is a lovely place to stay for the above battlefields – a good excuse to see the marvellous Cathedral and indulge in champagne. Hotels in the 3-4 star international standard are plentiful if one is prepared to travel from Reims, e.g. Novotel Reims Tinqueux (Tel: + (0)3 26 08 11 61. Fax: + (0)3 26 08 72 05, outdoor pool, Exit 22 from A4), Mercure Reims Est/Parc des Expositions (Tel: + (0)3 26 05 00 08. Fax: + (0)3 26 85 64 72, Exit 26 from A4). Right in the centre and therefore rather more difficult to access, is the Mercure Cathédrale (Tel: + (0)3 26 84 49 49. Fax: + (0)3 26 84 48 84). There is a host of 2- and 1-star hotels at Tinqueux and in the centre. The 3-star Best Western Hôtel de la Paix, near the Cathedral, has an outdoor pool (Tel: + (0)3 26 40 04 08. Fax: + (0)3 26 47 75 04). On Bvd Henry-Vasnier near the Parc Pommery is the turn of the century 4-star Relais & Château Boyer Les Crayères with gourmet retaurant (Tel: + (0)3 26 82 80 80. Fax: + (0)3 26 82 65 52. www.relaischateaux.com/crayeres
   Well-placed for the Champagne, Meuse-Argonne and even Verdun & St Mihiel tours is the smart, privately owned, modern 3-star hotel, The Tulipier, rue St Jacques, 51800 Vienne le Château, opened in autumn 2003 with thirty-eight rooms, a Conference Centre, indoor pool and small gym. Tel: + (0)3 26 60 69 90. Fax: + (0)3 26 60 69 91.

Ste Menéhould. Tourist Office: 5 Place du Gen Leclerc.
Tel: + (0)3 26 60 85 83. Fax: + (0)3 26 60 27 22.

Metz. Tourist Office: 1 Place de la Comédie.
Tel: + (0)3 87 55 53 76. Fax: + (0)3 87 36 59 43. This is a good alternative base – another glorious Cathedral and the usual range of hotels, e.g. Novotel Centre (Tel: + (0)3 87 37 38 39. Fax: + (0)3 87 36 10 00, outdoor pool, near the Cathedral), Novotel Hauconcourt (Tel: + (0)3 87 80 18 18, Fax: + (0)3 87 80 36 00 outdoor pool, Exit 36 from the A4), Mercure Metz Centre, near the railway station (Tel: + (0)3 87 38 50 50. Fax: + (0)3 87 75 48 18). Mercure Metz Nord (Tel: + (0)3 87 34 20 00. Fax: + (0)3 87 32 73 11, Exit 34 from the A31). Campanile Metz Centre (Tel: 0825 003 003.) Also Ibis, Formule 1 in the Centre. For more atmospheric hotels contact the Tourist Office.

Verdun. Tourist Office: Place de la Nation, 551000 Verdun.
Tel: + (0)3 29 86 14 18. Fax: + (0)3 29 84 22 42. E-mail: verduntourisme@wanadoo.fr
Open: The opening times of the Verdun museums and the Tourist Office itself are incredibly complex, varying from month to month. Although current opening times are given it would be wise to double check with the Tourist Office itself. Basically they all close from 1200-1400 for the all important lunch and open earlier and close later during the summer months! The Office has literature/maps/suggested routes for the battlefields, hotel and restaurant lists. Just off the Quai de Londres is the 3-star Coq Hardi, with excellent cuisine, Tel: + (0)3 29 86 36 36. Fax: + (0)3 29 86 09 21, 8 Avénue de la Victoire. Round the corner in the rue des Rouers are two good regional restaurants – the excellent value and tasty Table d'Alsace and the interesting Breton crêperie Pile ou Face (which more less means 'over lightly or sunnyside-up'). There is a basic Formule 1 Hotel, 50 Avénue de Metz, Tel: + (0)3 91 70 54 23. Fax: + (0)3 29 83 78 75. The 2-star Hotel Les Orchidées is conveniently situated on the Route d'Etain on the way to the right bank battlefields. It has an outdoor swimming pool. Tel: + (0)3 29 86 46 46. Fax: + (0)3 29 86 10 20. E-mail: hotel-orchidees@net-up.com

If you want a treat, try the luxurious 4-star nineteenth century Château des Monthairons set in thirty-five acres on the banks of the Meuse at Dieue, some twelve kms from Verdun, with its finely furnished bedrooms and renowned restaurant. Tel: + (0)3 29 87 78 55, but beware, the restaurant and all but the bedrooms close on Tuesdays!

St Mihiel. Tourist Office: Palais Abbatial. Tel: +(0)3 29 89 06 47.
E-mail: otsi.saint-mihiel@wanadoo.fr Enthusiastic staff, on request showing of short film about the Salient. Hotels in this attractive old town include the 2-star Rive Gauche, Place de l'Ancienne Gare, Tel: + (0)3 29 89 15 83. Fax: + (0)3 29 89 15 35.
E-mail: stephane@rive-gauche.fr Also the 2-star Le Trianon, 38 rue Basse des Fosses. Tel: + (0)3 29 90 90 09. Fax: + (0)3 29 90 96 11. E-mail: letrianon@wanadoo.fr The Domaine de Marsoupe, an old stud farm in the middle of the forest, offers simple accommodation in glorious scenery. Tel: + (0)3 29 89 02 70. There is a good selection of restaurants from pizzerias to kebab houses.

THE MARNE

Château-Thierry. Tourist Office: 16 Place de l'Hôtel de Ville.
Tel: + (0)3 23 84 86 86. Fax: + (0)3 23 84 86 99. Pleasant English-speaking staff and later than normal opening hours. The usual lists of hotels and restaurants and historical and local attractions information. Château-Thierry was the birthplace of the fable-writer Jean de la Fontaine and there is a museum dedicated to his life and works. The city lies on the Marne on the edge of the Champagne-producing area, has a long history and many ancient buildings of note. The remains of the old Château, the ramparts and the ancient gates to the city are worth a visit.

Hotels include the pleasantly-styled 2-star Ibis, 60 Avénue du Gen de Gaulle, Tel: + (0)3 23 83 10 10, Fax: + (0)3 23 83 45 23 and on the Route de Soissons the imposing 3-

star Hotel Restaurant Ile de France, Tel: + (0)3 23 69 10 12. Fax: + (0)3 23 83 49 70. This has a superb restaurant and in 2005 will have a large new wing with Conference Centre and Leisure Facilities.

Compiègne. Tourist Office: Place de l'Hôtel de Ville.
Tel: + (0)3 44 40 01 00. Fax: + (0)3 44 40 23 28. E-mail: otsi@mairie.compiegne.fr
Open: 1 April-30 October – Mon-Sat 0915-1215 and 1345-1815; 1 October-31 March closed Mon mornings and closes 1715. From Easter-31 October also open on Sun and public holidays 1000-1300 and 1430-1700.

Information about hotels, restaurants and other attractions in the area, including the fairytale castle of Pierrefonds (restored by Viollet-le-Duc for Napoleon III and well worth a detour); the Imperial Château, the residence of Emperor Napoleon III, and well restored (it includes the National Museum of the motor car created by the Touring Club of France in 1927); the Historic Figurines Museum, next to the Hôtel de Ville which contains 100,000 hand-painted miniature figures from Napoleonic to WW1. Of the chains there is a pleasant 3-star Mercure Compiègne-Sud, just off the A1 autoroute. Tel: + (0)3 44 30 30 30. Fax: + (0)3 44 30 30 44. E-mail: H1623@accor-hotels.com There are 2-star Campanile, 70 avénue de Huy, Tel: + (0)3 44 20 412 35 and Ibis, rue Eduard Branley, Tel: + (0)3 44 23 16 27 and basic Etap, 1 rue Pierre Sauvage, Tel: + (0)3 44 86 00 66., a 3-star Best Western, the Hotel les Beaux Arts, 33 Cours Guynemer, Tel: + (0)3 44 92 26 26 and a host of more individual choices from Auberges to Châteaux on the outskirts.

Poppies for Remembrance. Kaiser's Battlefield.

There are traditional and speciality restaurants to suit all tastes and pockets (84 are claimed) including a handy Courte Paille, rue Sébastien Masson, but beware, though appearing to be on the main road it has to be approached from the rear!

Fère-en-Tardenois. Tourist Office: 18 rue Etienne Moreau-Nélaton.
Tel: + (0)3 23 82 31 57. Fax: + (0)3 23 82 28 19. E-mail: fere-en-tardenois@com02.com
Useful for lunchbreak on 2nd Marne tour. Charming main square with several historical buildings in the vicinity. English tourist information about history, restaurants and hotels available.

Fismes. Tourist Office: 28 rue René Letilly.
Tel: + (0)3 26 48 81 28. Fax: + (0)3 26 48 12 09. This is off the main square along the Epernay road. Basic information, but has lists of local accommodation including the Logis de France La Boule d'Or, 11 rue Hildever Lefevre (near the bridge). Tel: + (0)3 26 48 11 24.

Meaux. Tourist Office: 1 Place Doumer. Tel: + (0)1 64 33 02 26. Fax: + (0)1 64 33 24 86. 'Town of Art and History', through which flow the River Marne and the Ourcq Canal, the city centre was formerly enclosed by a Gallo-Roman rampart, remains of which can still be seen. Home of Bossuet, Bishop and writer, and famous for its Brie cheese. Lists of hotels and restaurants including 3-star hotels Le Gonfalon, 2 rue de l'Eglise, Tel: + (0)1 64 33 16 05, and Auberge du Cheval Blanc, 55 rue Victor Clairet, Tel: (0)1 64 33 18 03 and 2-star hotels Campanile, 1 rue de la Cave aux Héros, Tel: + (0)1 60 23 41 41 and Balladins, 1 Place de Beauval, Tel: + (0)1 60 32 21 21.

Villers-Cotterêts. Tourist Office: 6 Place Aristide Briand.
Tel: + (0)3 23 96 55 10. Fax: + (0)3 23 96 49 13. E-mail: ot.villerscotterets@wanadoo.fr
A variety of eating places from fast food, pizzas and speciality restaurants. 3-star Hotel Le Régent, 26 rue du Gen Mangin, Tel: + (0)3 23 96 01 46. Fax: + (0)3 23 96 37 57. 2-star Ibis, route de Vivières, Tel: + (0)3 23 96 26 80. Fax: + (0)3 23 96 05 31.

Remember that the Western Front can be very wet and muddy.

ACKNOWLEDGEMENTS

During the long 'recce and research' phase of this book we renewed many old friendships and made even more new ones: so many people who were generous with their knowledge and their time. We have many heartfelt 'thank-yous' to say.

As always we express our admiration for the dedicated work of the **CWGC** and for the assistance we have had from staff at both Maidenhead, notably Mike Johnson, David Parker and Peter Francis, and at Beaurains, in particular, Tim Reeves, Roy Hemington and Colette Vandeville. From the **ABMC** we wish to thank our old friend, Phil Rivers, then at the **Meuse-Argonne** Cemetery and his assistant Dominique Didiot for some exceptional support, the helpful Bobby O. Bell, then at the **Somme** Cemetery at Bony and the secretaries at the **St Mihiel** and the **Oise-Aisne** Cemeteries who furnished us with a list of memorials in their areas. At the **Aisne-Marne** Cemetery then Superintendent David Atkinson was generous with his time. In **Belleau** Gilles Lagin historian and guide extraordinaire to the American battlefields gave us valuable time and information.

On the Somme the indefatigable historian and researcher, Jean-Pierre Thierry, has continued – as he has for more years than we would care to mention – to do 'above and beyond' in his capacity of Sherlock Holmes on our behalf. In **Cambrai** tank expert Philippe Gorczynski made great personal sacrifices to help us. On the **Aisne** and along the **Chemin des Dames** we received an exceptional welcome and outstanding assistance – first from Stephen Kreppel and Marie-Stella Ray of The Hat Factory in the UK then from Stéphane Rouziou, director of the Aisne Tourist Board; Jean Francois Héry, Director of the Caverne du Dragon and his team, Bettina Plichard, the outstanding guide and author Yves Fohlen (who has solved many 'mysteries' for us) the dedicated Monsieur Pamart, owner of the Ferme de Confrécourt. Thanks, too, to Mike Weston, photographer, Ferme de Confrécourt. Isabelle Geffrin of the **Blérancourt Franco-American Museum**. Our dear friend Tony Spagnoly provided us with the story of the Pilgrimage of Lt Col Christopher Buckle's mother. In the **St Mihiel Salient** Monsieur Norbert Kugel, President of the *Association Nationale le Saillant de St Mihiel*, ably supported by Mme Kugel and other volunteer friends like M Daniel et Mme Grandperret, guided us around the battlefields they are discovering and refurbishing and provided us with some fascinating information. The indefatigable Monsieur Michel Labriet guided us around the more inaccessible sites of **Les Eparges**. Madame Martin-Blanchet of the *Association Connaissance de la Meuse* showed us around the **Argonne** Battles and the **Kaiser Tunnel**. At the **Butte de Vauquois** the President of the *Amis de Vauquois*, Monsieur Jeannesson, gave us a fascinating and informative tour of the tunnels and opened up his interesting museum for us. In **Seringes** the Mayor Monsieur Alvoet and his wife kindly opened up the American Memorial Church for us and helped us find Oliver Ames's Memorial. Col Mery and M Baur gave us helpful information. In **Château Thierry**, Edmond Andrianavony gave us helpful information about the American Church.

Finally, our thanks to our publisher, Pen & Sword Books, for their tolerance and especially to Sylvia Menzies for achieving the impossible in the design of this book.

PICTURE CREDITS

For the picture of the authors on page 10, our thanks to *Soldier Magazine;* for the BBC Trench on page 170, to Khaki Chum Derek Pheasant; for Zouave Henri Vaumorin on page 238 to his daughter, Ghislaine Kitson; for the Bulldog drinking fountain, Belleau on page 219, the Memorial Day Decorations, Aisne-Marne US Cemetery on page 219, the USMC Ceremony in Belleau Wood on page 222 to David Atkinson, then Superintendent of the Cemetery, the US Meuse-Argonne Cemetery on page 347 to the American Battle Monuments Commission, Arlington, VA.

Western Front – North. Our apologies that our thanks to Ian McHenry for providing marvellous aerial photos of the Menin Gate and of the Kruisstraat Craters was accidentally omitted from that book.

INDEX

FORCES

These are listed in descending order of size, i.e. Armies, Corps, Divisions, Brigades, Regiments, then numerically and then alphabetically. Many more units are mentioned in the Cemetery descriptions throughout the book. 'Forces' listings include their 'Memorials'.

MEMORIALS

MUSEUMS

WAR CEMETERIES

GENERAL INDEX